Mythology in the
Middle Ages

Mythology in the Middle Ages

Heroic Tales of Monsters, Magic, and Might

Christopher R. Fee

Praeger Series on the Middle Ages
Jane Chance, Series Editor

PRAEGER

AN IMPRINT OF ABC-CLIO, LLC
Santa Barbara, California • Denver, Colorado • Oxford, England

Library of Congress Cataloging-in-Publication Data

Fee, Christopher R.
  Mythology in the Middle Ages: heroic tales of monsters, magic, and might / Christopher R. Fee.
      p. cm.—(Praeger series on the Middle Ages)
  Includes bibliographical references and index.
  ISBN 978-0-275-98406-9 (hard copy: alk. paper)—ISBN 978-0-313-02725-3 (ebook) 1. Mythology. I. Title.
  BL314.F44   2011
  398.209'02—dc22   2010040754

ISBN: 978-0-275-98406-9
EISBN: 978-0-313-02725-3

15 14 13 12 11   1 2 3 4 5

This book is also available on the World Wide Web as an eBook.
Visit www.abc-clio.com for details.

Praeger
An Imprint of ABC-CLIO, LLC

ABC-CLIO, LLC
130 Cremona Drive, P.O. Box 1911
Santa Barbara, California 93116-1911

This book is printed on acid-free paper ∞

Manufactured in the United States of America

For Emma, Chandler, and Samuel

Contents

CONTENTS

Preface

The Mosaic of the Medieval Hero: Fragments of Mythology, Legend, and Folklore

Mosaics bring together seemingly disparate pieces of material so that a discernable, coherent image emerges from a collection of castoff bits of broken glass, stone, and pottery; thus the pattern of the whole becomes much more than the sum of its fragmentary parts. Medieval heroes are generally composites of various remnants of ancient tales fashioned into new forms, and the medieval craftsman who assembled such a collection generally seems to have been unaware of or unconcerned with the original function of the fragments he used. Thus, medieval epics and heroic cycles are veritable treasure-troves of much older mythic, legendary, and folkloric elements, and the engaging and rich stories of the heroes themselves are often complemented with additional pieces of storylines drawn from ancient and sometimes forgotten traditions of gods, larger-than-life warriors, magicians, shamans, monsters, battles, magic, and marvels. In addition, many of the narrative elements of medieval heroic tales assert themselves in similar ways in very different contexts: For example, Sigurd of the far north is a classic dragon-slayer, but many of his brothers-in-arms from medieval epics also do battle with the great archetypal serpent-monster, including Basil the epic hero of Byzantine. On another front, the Welsh Culhwch beheads the Chief Giant Ysbaddaden to gain the lovely Olwen as his bride, reenacting a common folkloric motif concerning the giant's daughter, but battles with giants abound in medieval tales, including Turkish and Arabic reinterpretations of the conflict between Odysseus and Polyphemus.

Meanwhile, the Irish Cuchulainn and the Persian Rostam kill their own sons in battle, a seeming coincidence that may suggest common derivation from an ancient Indo-European theme.

Some Initial Caveats

It is vital that the reader of this text have a good working concept of the acceptable technical ways of defining *mythology, legend, folklore, hero, epic, romance*, and the like, and to be able to discern how in the context of medieval literature the lines between some of these categories may seem to blur. A salient question is why a modern reader might perceive such blurring. More provocative questions concern why and how modern scholars organize medieval texts in such ways in the first place. Certainly it is worth doing because it allows us to compare and contrast similarities and differences among many different types of tales drawn from many varied traditions. However, 21st-century students should always approach medieval texts with an awareness of how much they bring to the endeavor. It is quite certain that medieval audiences did not perceive or understand this material as we do.

Comparative analyses of mythology and folklore have long provided for us rubrics by which we might examine alongside each other commonalities amongst exceedingly disparate cultures, and the more inclusive we are, the larger the sample, and thus the richer our understanding of all of the traditions involved; on this scholarly opinion is agreed. In a similar manner, it might well be worth our while to examine how one might be more inclusive in one's use of the term "medieval," and to include in a comparative analysis the disparate contemporaneous cultures in contact and conflict with the Latin West. Part of the purpose of this volume is to attempt to outline a case for underscoring the foundational similarities—without denying the differences—among various narrative traditions included in many cultures during the several centuries we in the West usually refer to as the "Middle Ages."

Methodology and Structure

Because this is a reference book for nonspecialists, I have done away with direct citation insofar as this has been possible. It is my hope that the text thus reads much more fluidly. For each chapter I have identified roughly 10–12 major sources suitable and helpful to our target audience. The notes tend to be keyed to the rubrics, and I provide in the notes suggestions for further reading with detailed page numbers. All of the sources used in the writing of each section are those cited in that particular note. Where fuller acknowledgment seems due for concepts that I want to credit more completely to a particular author, I make it clear in the notes exactly where that author treats the related subject. In many cases, of course, any student exploring the suggested further reading would find many of the same points made in several different ways. My desire is to provide proper acknowledgment and further reading suggestions in a fair and elegant way. I have anglicized spelling wherever practical, and I have in particular dispensed with characters and diacritics not standard in English; this may well irritate my colleagues in a given field, but I am confident it will render the text more accessible to a nonspecialist audience.

Each chapter utilizes various heroic figures to examine common themes and archetypes. Thus, the whole book, while hopefully enjoyable to read simply as a collection of interesting heroic narratives and commentary thereon, and while providing a straightforward reference mechanism for finding specific figures, archetypes, and so on, also is structured to force the reader to look at connections between various traditions, some drawn from the mainstream of Western European medieval literature and some from its margins. I think that this approach makes the book an interesting anthology of and commentary upon myths as well as a primer in understanding the complexity and variety of medieval attitudes and beliefs concerning the surrounding world.

Acknowledgments

I must thank my many students, especially those in my medieval mythology, British mythology, and medieval epic courses who have read drafts of this work in progress and have made it clear what worked and what did not. Moreover, I owe special debts of gratitude to my many able student research assistants: Nuwan Jayawickreme and Kathryn Poticher helped to lay the early groundwork for the project; Maura Culkin brought her ample reference skills to bear on the person of El Cid; Eric Kozlik gets things done; Kerrin Epstein makes books appear as if by magic; Casey Chwieko possesses impressive expertise in early British mythology, which paid ample dividends in her Senior Honors Thesis and will stand her in good stead in her chosen career as a children's librarian; and Katherine Weinel embarked upon a heroic adventure that included following a quest through every word of the final draft. Many friends and colleagues have also lent a hand: Linda Miller keeps me in line; Ian Clarke and David Leeming helped me sketch the broad strokes of medieval mythology; the indefatigable Cinda Gibbon, like a battle-goddess of yore, marshaled the ensuing parade of heroes, and was ably assisted by her son, Tristan Gibbon, a hero in his own right; Bijee Burns provided vital feedback on the Byzantine chapter; and Jane Chance has been the soul of patience, perseverance, and encouragement. I also owe debts of gratitude to Heather, Elizabeth, and most especially Michael at the press. Last but hardly least, I would be remiss if I did not thank my wife, Allison Singley, who makes the impossible possible and any task a joy.

Introduction

I Need a Hero . . . The Hero as Guide in Our Quest
for Medieval Myth, Legend, and Folklore

Mythology in the Middle Ages: Heroic Tales of Monsters, Magic, and Might
will take general readers and researchers alike on a fantastic adventure on
the trail of some of the greatest heroes of medieval literature. Myths of
gods, legends of battles, and folktales of magic abound in the heroic narratives
of the Middle Ages, and we will use such stories as a framework upon
which we may organize discussions of a wide variety of fantastic episodes,
themes, and motifs. Our journey will take us across many centuries and
through the mythic, legendary, and folkloric imaginations of medieval
peoples and empires from the Atlantic and Baltic coasts of Europe; south
into the Holy Roman Empire; west through the Iberian Peninsula; across
the Straits of Gibraltar into North Africa; and thence east to Byzantium,
Russia, and even to the far reaches of Persia where we will travel to the very
border of Afghanistan.

The itinerary for these travels will include popular destinations from
the well-known European traditions to be sure, but the monsters of the
West have their counterparts in the East, and cursed treasure is not limited
to the Valley of the Rhine. Heroes, gods, quests, and monsters emerge
from the depths of time to assert themselves again and again on the human
stage, and their trappings change to conform to the audience of the moment.
This volume will chart such traditions and their relationships from various
corners of the Christendom of the Middle Ages, including some key points
of contact, conflict, and even confluence with the Islamic world.

Defining Medieval Myth,[1] Legend,[2] and Folklore[3]

Such terms as *medieval, myth, legend,* and *folklore* invite us to participate in exercises of exclusion. *Medieval* commonly refers to the Latin West of Europe from the fall of Rome to the rebirth of classical learning designated the *Renaissance.* The words myth, legend, and folktale—in the popular imagination, at least—conjure up images of otherness and falseness. Even today scholars often had best tread warily when discussing the mythologies inherent in, for example, Christian, Islamic, and Judaic religious cultures. In short, putting aside Odin and Lugh and their ilk, one is well advised to define one's terms very carefully indeed before including in a comparative analysis of mythic elements and archetypes, oh, shall we say, the flood of the Old Testament, the apocalyptic visions of the New Testament, or the lives of holy followers of the teachings of Christ, Mohammed, or the prophets of the Abrahamic tradition.

The English word *myth* is descended from the Greek term *mythos*, which may be rendered "speech" or "story." Such "stories" generally stem from traditional, oral roots, and take as their subject matter the great questions faced by all human beings: Who are we? Where do we come from? Why are things the way they are? Why do we do things as we do? In simplest terms, myths are stories that attempt to answer such questions from the perspective of the people who tell them. Myths are generally populated by the great supernatural phenomena that seem to shape the world of men, and these phenomena are often embodied as gods, demons, culture heroes, and the like, the generally superhuman yet often human-like representatives of the vast and otherwise unfathomable elemental forces of the universe around us. Myths often also explain the relationships between these forces and human beings, offer explanations concerning the origins of the rituals humans use to propitiate such gods and other powers, and indeed describe the genesis of the human race itself.

The term myth has been defined in many ways and is often used so loosely in common parlance as to render the word nearly meaningless. Indeed, many scholars would limit the category of myth strictly to narratives that evolved around material that was in its origin clearly religious in nature. Stories of divinities or superhuman protagonists descended from the gods are obvious candidates for consideration under this definition, as are the holy texts that explain the genesis of the world, the motive forces controlling the elements, the development of key cultural constructs, or the birth of such sacred rituals as might evolve around the related belief system. Thus, certain core themes common to all human beings reassert themselves again and again in mythologies across the globe; called "archetypes," these themes are a fundamental aspect of human nature, and thus it is only reasonable that stories differing in detail but similar in focus should emerge in cultures across millennia and around the globe.

In a comparative sense then, myth might be said to refer to particular cultural manifestations of the collective unconscious that explain and/or explore themes of universal significance. Myth thus may be distinguished from legend and folklore in that its primary focus concerns such archetypal universal elements rather than localized themes and details of intense import to a particular community but of less immediate applicability to outsiders. That said, medieval narratives tend to comprise a vibrant blend of the mythic, legendary, and folkloric, and it is not always easy to distinguish among these. Moreover, the medieval world also developed unique mythic structures concerned with how the institutions of men should perform in a Christian context.

Legend refers to narrative traditions transmitted as though factual. Originally oral, these tales generally have some grounding—whether real or perceived—in historical events. Although very often didactic, legends are primarily "tellings" (i.e., "stories") as the various Germanic terms for this type of narrative illustrate; indeed, the cognate Old English term, *secgan*, means "to say." On the other hand, the confusingly similar Latin word *legenda* refers to a "reading," a literary text, and this term is most notably used to refer to literary accounts of the lives of saints. Legend, in a technical sense, is a not dissimilar but entirely discrete genre with clearly oral roots. Such legends often contain supernatural elements and generally are concerned with episodes of particular significance to the community that preserves and transmits them. Legends tell stories that teach the values of a given community, preserve its sense of its own history and its place in the world, and enshrine its cultural heroes.

Legend, like folklore, takes as its subject what we might term "cultural truth." That is, legends pass along to each new generation material of weight and importance to that group. However, legends may be distinguished from folklore in that they purport to be based upon fact. Whereas legends and myths often concern themselves with specific, named, "extraordinary" heroes, folktales tend to have more generic protagonists who have an "everyman" quality that allows an audience to project themselves more readily into the narrative. Legend and folklore can be distinguished from myth in that they are usually more grounded in the specific wisdom and experience of the given community. Although all three types of narrative may be categorized comparatively, mythic archetypes speak more readily to universal concerns, whereas folklore and legend—although often developing similar or related themes of general significance—tend to be much more context specific. This specificity of local detail, including figures, locations, and actions, adds to the semblance of veracity in many legends.

Folklore refers to cultural "items" common to a particular community; such items may include stories, rituals, dances, songs, or any other aspect of life in that community that is imbued with some measure of shared experience, wisdom, or foundational belief. Moreover, folklore entails the process of the transmission of such shared community knowledge or tradition. Context is thus of paramount concern to the folklorist. Therefore, the great paradox of the study of medieval folklore is that no member of any such community remains to transmit such material. Thus, folklorists, deprived of the opportunity to directly participate in the process, must strive to reconstruct the milieu of the communities that produced the fragmentary folkloric items we may receive in some form from the Middle Ages.

Luckily, grains of knowledge concerning medieval folklore may be gleaned from various sources, including from written records describing folkloric items, from rules or diatribes condemning such items, and from literary allusions recalling folkloric themes or motifs. Moreover, scholars of folklore use a comparative approach, describing and analyzing how folkloric items from various cultures may be categorized under common rubrics. However, these traditions may or may not express aspects of what comparative mythologists might term the universal unconscious; thus, depending on context, folkloric artifacts may or may not be thought to manifest mythic archetypes. In narrative terms, folklore includes oral storytelling traditions that may be specifically attributed to particular pre- or nonliterate cultures or to nonliterate parts of literate cultures. Folktales are generally classified as oral items transmitted in varying forms by storytellers within a traditional community to amuse and to enlighten audiences; however, folktales make no pretence to historical veracity and thus may be distinguished from legends. Folklore generally, and the narrative genre of the folktale in particular, aspires to a form of cultural veracity without the modern, literate sense that historical accuracy is the *sine qua non* of discernable truth.

Sources of Medieval Myth, Legend, and Folklore

Annals and Chronicles[4]

Chronicles are quasi-historical sources that purport to record actual events over time and in chronological order. Such records also are often referred to as *annals* because events within them were generally organized according to year. Many chronicles were updated with some semblance of regularity and thus provide a glimpse into a growing medieval sense of the nature of history as well as preserving those events and accounts thereof that the chroniclers considered worthy of posterity. In point of fact, such records are as often repositories of fancy as they are sources of what we would recognize as "history," a fact that makes them valuable resources in the study of medieval myth, legend, and folklore, even if their historical veracity is not unimpeachable. For example, the *Annales Cambriae*, or "Welsh Annals," are valuable sources of early British myth and legend, just as the Kievan *Primary Chronicle* provides rich context for the Russian epic of Prince Igor.

Epics[5]

An *epic* recounts the exploits of a great hero or heroic band on a sweeping scale and in a grandiose style. Generally set in a misty, gilded past with strong heroic overtones, the epic takes as its protagonist a hero of superhuman proportions who is often the scion of the gods. The epic hero generally undergoes a significant journey upon which he fights monumental battles and achieves a fantastic quest. Sometimes manifesting overtly supernatural qualities or powers, such an epic figure is often a savior of sorts and may manifest traits of the culture hero. "Traditional" or "primary" epics are founded directly upon earlier oral models and materials and use similar techniques. The *Iliad* is an example of such an epic from the classical world, whereas *Beowulf*, which articulates a dimly remembered world of Germanic myth, legend, and folklore in the poetic idiom of Anglo-Saxon England, is a fine example of a traditional epic from the medieval world. "Secondary" or "literary" epics evoke and recast traditional themes in more sophisticated narrative terms. The *Aeneid*, which draws upon the tradition of the *Iliad*, is an example of such a secondary epic from the classical world.

Romances[6]

Originally so called because examples thereof were composed in vernacular Romance languages rather than in Latin, this widespread literary form emerged in the twelfth century or so and remained vastly popular throughout the Middle Ages. *Romances* have several points of contact with the mythic, legendary, and folkloric that make them obvious sources of material for a study of these narrative genres. First and foremost, the centrality and the treatment of the hero in most Romances provides an obvious area of resonance. The hero is the central protagonist of the Romance as a genre, and indeed, many a Romance is primarily known by the eponymous name of its leading character. In addition, such figures very often undertake adventures, quests, and battles that offer clear resemblance with those we would associate with the hero of myth and legend.

The Romance is also known, of course, for its use of the theme of courtly love, its emphasis on chivalry, and the hero's pursuit of the affection of his ladylove, often resulting in marriage. Such a focus helps to throw into stark relief the contrast between the genre of the Romance and that of the epic, which generally eschews any such concern that might detract from its central theme of the hero's martial prowess. Such "romantic" narrative patterns, although less immediately concerned with archetypal aspects of the hero, are nonetheless in fact very often embroidered with mythic, legendary, and folkloric threads, and thus the Romance regularly implicitly manifests such materials even when explicitly concerned with matters seemingly far removed from what we might on the surface consider myth or legend. In addition, Romances generally purport to recount true stories and often make references to authoritative sources, whether actual or invented. Thus the genre of the Romance has some important points of confluence with that of the legend. Likewise, the inclusion of the magical and the marvelous illustrate the resonance between these types of narratives.

Arthurian Romance[7]

It would be remiss to fail to note that many different Romances in many different languages deal with the figures, events, and adventures associated with the Knights of King Arthur; we often refer to such works under the rubric of the *Arthurian Romance*. The Arthurian landscape is vast, is populated with manifold heroes, and is rich with heroic archetypes and episodes; however, these fields have been tilled and re-tilled by many hands, and thus this volume does not include a survey of that material. The reader interested in delving deeply into the legends, myths, and folklore of Arthurian will have no difficulty in finding ample resources to guide such a search.

The Lives of the Saints[8]

Hagiography, or the narrative lives of saints, provided one of the staple literary traditions of the Middle Ages. Indeed, the fact that compilations of the lives of saints—most notably the 13th-century *Golden Legend* of Jacobus de Voragine—were amongst the most popular and widely disseminated works in medieval Europe illustrates the centrality of these traditions to the literature of the time. Although in the early Church cults tended to develop around the figures of those martyred for their faith, after Christianity became dominant throughout the Roman Empire, various types of holy protagonists began to assert themselves. Religious leaders, hermits, and sanctified virgins proved popular, as did figures associated with the conversion of pagans. In addition, sometimes Christianized pagan gods and heroes slipped into the canon.

Moreover, saints' lives are often closely tied to rituals utilized in the veneration of particular sacred figures—a relationship that underscores how crucial hagiography can be to the study of medieval folklore. More important to the study of medieval myth and legend is the standard structure of the saint's life, which is itself a typological redaction of the life of Christ with discernable resonance with various mythic archetypes of gods and heroes. Stories of saints often include elements such as unusual parentage or origin; miraculous childhood feats; preaching, healing, and related miracles; persecution and martyrdom; and posthumous wonders generally associated with the relics of the saint or the saint's place of demise or rest. The widespread appeal and persistence of hagiography is most important to this study because of the fact that secular legends—notably those of heroes of the stature of Roland, the Cid, and Prince Igor—often replicate the typological pattern of the saint's life in their narrative structure.

Medieval Heroines and Feminine Warrior Saints[9]

Although some male heroes of the Middle Ages certainly derive ultimately from all-but-forgotten gods and demi-gods, many others obviously cleave to the ancient archetypes of the hero, a figure that—although clearly more than a man—is manifestly less than a god. On the other hand, medieval heroines are often described in quite different terms, and the representation of female power can be more varied and less straightforward. Indeed, multitudes of medieval heroic narratives are driven by the adventures of "superman" protagonists, during the course of which potent and mysterious female figures obstruct or abet the hero through feminine wonders, wiles, and witchcraft. The most obvious medieval examples of heroines who exhibit what we might perceive as more masculine heroic characteristics may be found in collections of saints' lives.

The heroines in such narratives take many forms; some of them—notably well-known examples including Saint Juliana—are militaristic soldiers for the faith, the characters of whom resonate with those of the holy warriors of medieval epics. Such holy women generally are virgins who very often die protecting their chastity. However, in many other kinds of texts, perceived feminine powers associated with sexuality and fertility seem clearly derived from ancient archetypes of the goddess that are cast in medieval texts into forms ripe with sorcery, danger, and seduction. Medieval manifestations of the feminine heroic, divine, and demonic are fascinating and well worth study in their own right. Because the present volume relies on heroic epic episodes for its source materials, powerful female figures appear from time to time in various appropriate contexts but are not examined in detail upon their own impressive terms. The reader interested in pursuing an in-depth study of this field should turn to a volume dedicated to the subject such as that currently under preparation by the author.

Heroes of Medieval Myth, Legend, and Folklore[10]

The realm of medieval myth, legend, and folklore is in large measure the province of the hero. We will note and discuss several examples of archetypal figures, elements, places, objects, and creatures, to be sure, especially in the northern and western reaches represented by the Scandinavian and Celtic traditions, but again and again we will return to the adventures and archetypes of the hero, aspects of the hero's journey, and various medieval manifestations of categories concerning the hero.

Medieval heroes were developed from a variety of source materials—some mythic, others legendary or folkloric. Early pagan gods become euhemerized through a Christian lens, and in the great dragon-slayer epic the *Saga of the Volsungs*, for example, we will catch clear glimpses into the ancient pagan Germanic mythology of old. In other cases, an older epic heroic sensibility is exchanged for a Christian typological and figural representation of saints, and such Christian spiritual heroes may be recast as types of Christ; conversely, depictions of Christ and his saints may at times betray the influence of an older heroic influence.

In works such as the *Song of Roland* and the Spanish tale of El Cid, we will examine medieval concepts concerning the nature of divine will and justice and how the mandates and judgments of God might be rendered discernibly in the world of men. God sometimes participates directly in anointing temporal rulers in medieval works, and at times communicates directly with his chosen earthly representatives through the medium of dream visions, which are at times imparted by celestial messengers. More-over, in epic heroes such as the Cid, Roland, and Prince Igor, the faces of Christian martyrs are refracted through a heroic lens in the battles between these Christian standard-bearers and their opponents, who are at times explicitly demonic in nature. We will examine such heroes in terms of specific, detailed illustrative episodes drawn from the source texts, and we will note the trajectory of a given hero's archetypal journey where appropriate and helpful.

The archetypal approach—although far from perfect—does have some real advantages in any attempt to develop a comparative analysis of the functions of heroes in medieval texts. For example, a hero's conception and birth often are notable, as are his childhood deeds. Battles with the monstrous are common, of course, but so are quests for treasures and powers of value to the hero and his people. The quest trope sometimes is rendered into the archetype of the hero's journey to the Underworld, a voyage into a literal or metaphorical otherworld—sometimes depicted as a term of exile or in Purgatory—from which the hero emerges with new powers, riches, or knowledge that he generally may use or share to the benefit of his people. Rites, rituals, and the symbolism of initiation are often key elements of such heroic narratives, which sometimes culminate with the hero's death and even forms of apotheosis.

Mythologies across the globe and spanning the millennia have concerned themselves with heroes, but it is perhaps a notable characteristic of the largely monotheistic medieval West that many adventures, attributes, and characteristics we might otherwise expect to be associated with gods seem relegated to the hero. At times this is a self-conscious redaction of ancient mythologies by medieval apologists, but at other times it seems clear that the many possible manifestations of the hero of medieval mythology simply allowed for the fullest possible expression of particular traditions, hopes, aspirations, and fears within a monotheistic context.

Great historical personages and events are quite literally the material from which legend is wrought. In simplest terms, this argument asserts—given sufficient time and cultural weight—that legendary figures may begin to assume mythic proportions. We see this process developed to various degrees in such figures as Prince Igor, Roland, and El Cid, all of whom—although clearly legendary in their genesis—begin to project some aspects of the mythic archetypes of the hero as time passes and their narratives begin to become woven into a tapestry of burgeoning cultural identity.

Moreover, examining the development of several roughly contemporaneous heroes across a wide variety of cultures—some of which were often in conflict—allows an astute reader to note how the development of medieval heroes speaks to the resonance of common themes in various traditions, a commonality that provides a striking counterpoint to the dissonance between and among various peoples and belief systems. Sinbad the Sailor, to cite but one example, drapes the peregrinations of an Indo-European questing hero in the clothes of the Arab world, and he and his Turkish cousin Basat defeat the self-same man-eating monster known to their common Greek ancestor Odysseus as the Cyclops Polyphemus. In fact, the respective mythologies of the Byzantines and the Turks teach us as much about mythic confluence as the military struggles between these empires tell us about cultural dissonance.

Indeed, although the travails of Western Christendom are familiar through the epic heroes of Spain and France, less known is Basil Digenis Akritis, who hails from the border wars of Byzantium and whose enemies have their own epic heroes in the warriors mentored and valorized by the shaman and bard Dede Korkut. Further to the east, the ancient mythology of Persia is of particular import to those interested in the medieval manifestations of ancient Indo-European mythology, and the *Shahname* of medieval Persia is an epic cycle that beggars most Western counterparts in comparison. Placing heroes from this wide range of traditions shoulder to shoulder will give us the opportunity to examine what is common across a range of medieval mythic, legendary, and folkloric traditions and what seems unique in a particular instance.

Heroic narratives thus provide ideal vehicles for examinations of the foundational relationships between myth and culture, between medieval and modern, and between belief system and everyday actions. To that end, *Mythology in the Middle Ages: Heroic Tales of Monsters, Magic, and Might* will bring medieval literatures and cultures to life through the adventures of their great heroes for another generation of readers, but more than that, it promises to do so in a way that will challenge readers to think about the significance of the conflict and confluence of mythic cultures, medieval or modern.

Rubrics of Concord and Discord: Comparing Medieval Heroes

Medieval scribes divided texts into sections designated by headings written in "red" ink from which we get the Latinate term *rubric*. Our journey through the world of the medieval hero is divided into three main parts, which are organized under the rubrics "Champions of the Pagan Frontier," "Warriors for the Christian Faith," and "Heroes of the Islamic World." These divisions are designed to help us to note the similarities and differences among various medieval mythologies most heavily influenced by pagan traditions, Christian practices, and Islamic beliefs, respectively.

We begin our exploration of the landscape of medieval mythology in northwestern Europe, with traditions that clearly have grown from ancient pagan roots, and with heroes who battle monsters and magic as we are most comfortable defining these. Such supernatural "others" are of tremendous proportions and potency and represent classic bogeymen of childhood imagination, including a fire-breathing dragon, a vengeful sorceress, and a gargantuan evil tyrant. In addition, the "champions of the pagan frontier" who battle such nemeses are themselves drawn from the ranks of superhuman heroes with clear links to the otherworldly: The Norse Sigurd is advised by Odin, king of the gods; the Irish Cuchulainn is healed his father, the great god Lugh; and the Welsh Culhwch undertakes a truly Herculean set of tasks with the aid of his royal kinsman, King Arthur, who leads a band of heroes who seem little less than thinly veiled gods of yore.

From the pagan frontier, we travel to the heart of Christendom, where we meet heroes who are ostensibly overt "warriors for the Christian faith," stalwart soldiers of the Cross who battle adversaries who are often overtly satanic in nature, charting a notable progression from heroes who are Christian in name to those who genuinely seem to seek holy war with the minions of Hell. We begin with the Byzantine Basil, who is in some ways remarkably like Sigurd or Culhwch for a *Miles Christi*, or a "Soldier of Christ." The Orthodox scion of a Christian mother and a Syrian emir who converts to the faith of his bride, Basil *Digenis Akritis*, the "Twin-Blood Border-Lord," in fact battles a dragon of his own and spends much more time slaying lions and subduing brigands than fighting for his faith. The Russian Igor, whose people willingly took up the mantle of Orthodoxy from the Byzantines, battles heathen steppe raiders described in demonic terms but does so in a context rife with images from and references to ancient Slavic mythology. The Carolingian Roland fights an enemy clearly wrought into a demonic other and is himself recast into a type of Christ through his willing self-sacrifice. Roland's kinsmen and the Iberian Cid also evoke Divine Judgment through trial-by-combat sequences that clearly encapsulate and reflect ways in which a medieval mythology of holy war was enshrined in Christian practices.

The Moslem neighbors so often cast in the role of devilish enemies in European epics had heroes of their own, of course, and on the final leg of our journey we will chart points of contact, conflict, and confluence between heroes of the Islamic world and their Christian counterparts. Drawn from an ancient and vast literary tradition that marries Indo-European mythology with an Islamic sensibility, the cycle of stories concerning the Persian hero Rostam offers a glimpse into a mythic context that is paradoxically starkly alien from and distantly related to that of Christian Europe. Indeed, the central episode of Rostam's life involves the hero's slaying of his own son, Sohrab, in a tragic case of ambiguous mistaken identity clearly reminiscent of that involving the Irish Cuchulainn and his son.

Meanwhile, in the heroes of the Turkish epic cycle we will find a free-wheeling *carpe diem* spirit with only the slightest nod to Islam. To be sure, the Oghuz Turks were the enemies of Constantinople, which is referred to in these tales as *Rum*, or "Rome." We might therefore expect to see them in conflict with such Christian holy warriors as the Byzantine Basil, and we might well be tempted to identify them with the Kumans, fellow horse-warriors of the wide-open plains of Eurasia who bedeviled the Russian Igor. Although battles with Christian enemies do occur, the most striking elements of this collection include echoes of classical mythology and pre-cursors to Mediterranean and Turkish folklore. Moreover, one might posit that the Turkish heroic cycle offers a steppe-raider, horse-culture vision of a pagan warrior ethos not dissimilar from that of the Irish and Norse traditions, which cloak their own ancient substance beneath a thin veneer of Christianity. Finally, the large collection of tales offering insight into Arabian mythology and its heroes reflects many influences, from classical travel epics to Egyptian grave-robbing folklore. However, the consistent hallmark of the Arabian hero often seems to be his humble origin, a recurring theme that brings us at the end of our journey back to a discussion of the functions of the hero, his development, and his adventures, all of which speak to his abiding popularity and help us to bring together the disparate fragments that form the mosaic through which we may discern the patterns of medieval mythology.

Following in the Footsteps of Heroes: The Structure of Our Quest

We begin our discussion of "Champions of the Pagan Frontier," in the icy North: After a brief overview of the role of the Vikings in medieval Scandinavia, Chapter One describes the recurring appearance of drag-ons in medieval literature and the role of the dragon-slayer as hero.

The Norse myth of Otter's Ransom provides an introduction into the Scandinavian hero Sigurd, who is then compared with his Middle High German doppelganger Siegfried and his Anglo-Saxon cousin Beowulf, who are also dragon-slayers. We follow in the wake of Viking longships to Ireland in Chapter Two, which grounds an overview of medieval Irish literature upon a foundational understanding of ancient Celtic practices and beliefs. After a discussion of the *Tain*, the great epic of the Irish tradition, this chapter follows the development of Cuchulainn through a series of heroic archetypes. Chapter Three takes us across the Irish Sea to Wales in the southwest of the Isle of Britain and then discusses the *Mabinogion*, the great epic cycle of medieval Welsh mythology. After an overview of the elements of Welsh myth suggested by *Culhwch and Olwen*, this chapter follows the heroic Culhwch in his quest for the hand of the fair daughter of the larger-than-life king who finally yields his head to this giant-slayer hero.

Our acquaintance with "Warriors for the Christian Faith," begins on the eastern edge of the Byzantine Empire: Chapter Four opens with a discussion of the theme of "holy war" and that of the "border hero." After an introduction to Byzantium, this chapter examines the unique origin of the hero Basil, the function of coming-of-age hunting episodes and related bride-snatching sequences, and subsequently follows Basil through his battles with brigands, beasts, and amazons. Of particular note is a description of Basil's defeat of a serpent-demon that has resonance with dragon-slaying episodes. The chapter concludes with an examination of how Basil is wrought into a Christ-like symbol, representative of a lost "Golden Age." Chapter Five follows Orthodox missionaries north from Constantinople to Kiev, which converts and proclaims itself the "Third Rome." After a discussion of the Rus, their Viking roots, and their relationship with the Byzantine Empire, this chapter discusses the Kumans and the Tatars, invaders from the steppes cast by Russian authors as satanic soldiers of darkness. The chapter looks in particular at the epic *Lay of Igor's Campaign*, focusing most on Igor's capture by the demonic Kumans, his escape and flight from captivity, his subsequent apotheosis, and the clearly pagan elements of this ostensibly Christian account of holy war.

Chapter Six takes us through the narrow passes of the Pyrenees, the mountain range that divides France from Spain and traces how the story of an ambush of the rearguard of Charlemagne's army was wrought into the great epic of the Holy Roman Empire. After examining how the legend of Roland developed from the historical Battle of Roncevaux, this chapter explores how the theme of holy war is explicitly developed in the

Chanson de Roland, resulting in demonic enemies, a Christ-like hero in Roland, and a Judas-figure named Ganelon. This chapter concludes with a description of a trial-by-combat sequence intended, like the concept of holy war itself, to invite the active participation of the Divine. Chapter Seven returns us to the Iberian Peninsula, where the legend of an epic hero known as the Cid developed in the cultural hothouse of medieval Spain, where the Moorish conquest led to a vibrant mix of Christian, Islamic, and Jewish cultures unique in medieval Europe. This chapter begins with a discussion of the Moors, the significance of the Islamic conquest in the Spanish imagination, and the resulting dream of reconquest that fueled notions of holy war. This chapter then describes how the historical personage of Rodrigo Diaz de Vivar became recast as the legendary figure of the Cid and then follows this figure through several archetypal sequences, culminating in an episode of Divine Judgment that recalls that in the *Chanson de Roland.*

We first meet "Heroes of the Islamic World" on the border between Iran and Afghanistan, where ancient pagan gods are clad in Moslem garb of the Middle Ages. Chapter Eight begins with a description of how ancient Persia, more properly known as Iran, a storehouse of Indo-European mythology, provided the legacy that resulted in the medieval *Shahname,* the Iranian "Book of Kings." Having established the pedigree of the epic hero Rostam, which reaches back into the bloodlines of the gods of yore, this chapter follows the progression of that hero through several key stages, culminating in the fatal duel between this figure and his son Sohrab. Chapter Nine takes us to Anatolia or "Asia Minor," known to us today as Turkey. After introducing us to the Oghuz Turks and explaining from where they came, this chapter details how these nomadic raiders helped to change the face of the Eastern Mediterranean, cast down the Byzantines, and establish a new empire. This chapter then describes the great epic cycle of medieval Turkey and notes how this compilation provides the barest Islamic leavening for a rich mixture of classical mythology, Turkic folklore, and legendary elements. Chapter Ten invites us south into the Arabian Peninsula, where we learn about the birth of Islam and the development of the "frame tale" technique that will produce the *Thousand and One Nights.* Our travels then conclude with the close examination of three "everyman" heroes of medieval Arabian mythology—a study that helps to clarify how disparate elements of popular folklore were combined with heroic archetypes and even classical literature to produce an exciting and engaging mix. Indeed, the composite nature of these Arabian heroes and of the narrative techniques used to present them will help us to conclude our study by hearkening back to the image of the mosaic of the medieval hero.

Finding Common Ground: Recurring Patterns of Medieval Heroism

Coming-of-age archetypes are commonplace in medieval heroic tales, as evidenced by the stories of the Irish Cuchulainn, the Turkish Boghach, and the Arabic Aladdin, whereas the journey to the Underworld theme asserts itself metaphorically in such stories as that of the Russian Igor and the Iberian Cid, as well as literally in those of the Arabic Judar and the Anglo-Saxon Beowulf. At times such commonalities are the result of the transmission of tales across cultures in particular areas; for example, the popularity of the wrestling match with Death and the cave of the Cyclops themes in the Eastern Mediterranean and Near East are testaments to the abiding popularity of classical mythology throughout that region. In other instances the evidence suggests that common Indo-European ancestors gave birth to disparate but related medieval offspring in, for instance, homes as far afield as Iran and Ireland. Some texts seem to have developed along similar thematic lines, a circumstance particularly evident in the Russian and Carolingian epics, both of which quite clearly develop themes of holy war concerned with a crusading hero doing battle with a demonic enemy. Sometimes mythic archetypes and folkloric motifs assert themselves in varied texts from across a range of cultures, lending to certain of these medieval tales a timeless appeal that links them to stories and traditions from around the globe. The world of the medieval epic is in any case the world of the hero, and the visages of this hero emerge from the juxtaposition of vibrant fragments of mythology, folklore, and legend. Such heroes speak to us in a language of adventure and wonder of the fears, burdens, and challenges we all encounter, and their glorious victories and valiant defeats still offer readers today words of hope and encouragement as we embark upon our own adventures.

Notes

1. As Northrup Frye has famously noted, myths are concerned with topics of universal import rather than mere entertainment value. However, Carl Lindahl has asserted that comparative analysis of religious elements invites a certain contentiousness and thus advises a careful definition of terms rather than the exclusion of comparisons with current religions of practice. However strictly one defines the term, there are certainly as many ways to read and interpret myths

as there are definitions for the genre; of particular note in any study concerned with comparing various mythic aspects from disparate traditions are what might be termed the anthropological and psychological schools of thought. Perhaps the most well-known figure associated with the anthropological assessment of mythology is Claude Levi-Strauss, whose theory of structuralism posits that one may learn a great deal about a culture by studying its myths. The foundational beliefs inculcated in such narratives have much to teach us about the values and morals of a given society. On the other hand, Carl Jung is a key figure in the psychological analysis of myths. Rather as dreams seemed to Freud to offer a window into the unconscious of the individual, Jung saw myths more or less as the eloquent and evocative "dreams" of a culture. Jung was particularly interested in how archetypes manifested the individual's journey toward maturity, which makes it a useful approach in the study of the development of the hero across traditions. For detailed discussions of the nature and definition of "myth," see especially Baldick 143–144; Cotterell 1–6; Leeming *Voyage of the Hero* 3–8; Leeming *Oxford Companion to World Mythology* xi–xiii, 79–80; Lindahl 283–285; Puhvel 1–20; Thury and Devinney 3–22; and Trapp 605–606.

2. Scholars such as Axel Olrik, Carl Wilhem von Sydow, and Jan Vansina worked to help define how legend functions in the context of other oral traditions and how it relates to what we think of as "history." For detailed discussions of the nature and definition of "legend," see especially Baldick 121; Leeming *Oxford Companion to World Mythology* vii; Lindahl 240–243; Puhvel 2–4, 15–16, 21–22, 117–118; and Thury and Devinney 3–15.

3. Major figures associated with the development of folkloric categories include Vladimir Propp and Stith Thompson. For detailed discussions of the nature and definition of "folklore," see especially Baldick 85; Cotterell 2; Leeming *Voyage of the Hero* 4; Leeming *Oxford Companion to World Mythology* xii; Lindahl 138–148; Puhvel 18–19; and Thury and Devinney 517–537.

4. For detailed discussions of the nature and definition of an "annal" or "chronicle," see especially Baldick 36; Leeming *Oxford Companion to World Mythology* 45–46, 359; Lindahl 12–13, 31; and Puhvel 2, 125, 140, 189–190, 223–225.

5. For detailed discussions of the nature and definition of "epic," see especially Baldick 70–71; Leeming *Voyage of the Hero* 152–154; Lindahl xix; Puhvel 2, 70–71, 140; and Trapp 600.

6. For detailed discussions of the nature and definition of "Romance," see especially Baldick 191–192; Lindahl 119–120, 346–350; and Trapp 610–611.

7. The body of reference literature in this field is nothing short of overwhelming; however, the neophyte and expert alike would be well served by beginning a journey into the world of Arthur with the following two recent reference guides, each of which provides an excellent and up-to-date bibliography: Norris J. Lacy, Geoffrey Ashe, and Debra N. Mancoff offer a superb overview

of the terrain in *The Arthurian Handbook*. Garland reference library of the humanities, Vol. 1920. New York: Garland Publishers, 1997. Alan Lupack provides an excellent and in-depth starting point with *The Oxford Guide to Arthurian Literature and Legend*. Oxford, United Kingdom: Oxford University Press, 2005.

8. For detailed discussions of the nature and definition of hagiography, see especially Baldick 95; Cotterell 137–138; and Lindahl 354–357.

9. Those interested in a gaining grounding in feminist approaches to mythology might be well advised to begin with Carolyne Larrington's *The Woman's Companion to Mythology*. London: Pandora, 1997. A fundamental understanding of the narrative function of the feminine heroic in hagiography may be gleaned from Karen A. Winstead's *Virgin Martyrs: Legends of Sainthood in Late Medieval England*. Ithaca, NY: Cornell University Press, 1997. Three particularly fine examples of sanctified warrior heroines from the Anglo-Saxon tradition are the subject of Marie Nelson's *Judith, Juliana, and Elene: Three Fighting Saints*. American University studies, Vol. 135. New York: P. Lang, 1991. Gender roles in medieval Europe are explored thoroughly in Katharina M. Wilson and Nadia Margolis's *Women in the Middle Ages: An Encyclopedia*. Westport, CT: Greenwood Press, 2004.

10. Developed from Carl Jung's psychological assessment of mythology, what is commonly referred to as the monomyth of the hero—a mythic template of archetypes concerned with key transformative episodes that regularly recurs across widespread and diverse traditions—is best known to a popular audience through Joseph Campbell's *Hero with a Thousand Faces*. Campbell's work, although often enthusiastically embraced by nonspecialists, has been more severely criticized in recent years by scholars in the field. That significant caveat noted, it is only fair to acknowledge that—Campbell's work aside—such transformative episodes often do in fact provide landmarks in the geography of medieval heroic narratives. Although we must not elide "legend" and "myth" too readily, scholars of world mythology such as Arthur Cotterell suggest that the legendary may be transmuted into the mythological over time through the crucible of the potent, sometimes fervent belief systems that develop around some heroic narratives. In such cases, we do not have to look very hard to find archetypal structures asserting themselves within this material. Cotterell cites the Trojan War in this regard, noting how over oceans of time and space events from the legendary past become a structure around which mythic material might be organized. For example, the figure of Odysseus developed into an archetypal hero with clearly mythic qualities. For detailed discussions of the nature and definition of the hero, see especially Baldick 98; Cotterell 1–6; Leeming *Voyage of the Hero* 3–8; Leeming *Oxford Companion to World Mythology* xi–xiii, 79–80; Lindahl 283–285; Puhvel 1–20; and Thury and Devinney 135–142, 365–371.

Sources and Further Reading

Baldick, Chris. *The Oxford Dictionary of Literary Terms*. Oxford, United Kingdom: Oxford University Press, 2008.

Cotterell, Arthur. *A Dictionary of World Mythology*. Oxford, United Kingdom: Oxford University Press, 1991.

Leeming, David Adams. *Mythology: The Voyage of the Hero*. Oxford, United Kingdom: Oxford University Press, 1998.

Leeming, David Adams. *The Oxford Companion to World Mythology*. Oxford, United Kingdom: Oxford University Press, 2005.

Lindahl, Carl, John McNamara, and John Lindow. *Medieval Folklore: A Guide to Myths, Legends, Tales, Beliefs, and Customs*. Oxford, United Kingdom: Oxford University Press, 2002.

Montgomery, Thomas. *Medieval Spanish Epic: Mythic Roots and Ritual Language*. Penn State studies in Romance literatures. University Park: Pennsylvania State University Press, 1998.

Puhvel, Jaan. *Comparative Mythology*. Baltimore: Johns Hopkins University Press, 1989.

Thury, Eva M., and Margaret Klopfle Devinney. *Introduction to Mythology: Contemporary Approaches to Classical and World Myths*. Oxford, United Kingdom: Oxford University Press, 2009.

Trapp, J. B., Douglas Gray, and Julia Boffey. *Medieval English Literature*. The Oxford anthology of English literature. Oxford, United Kingdom: Oxford University Press, 2002.

Part I

Champions of the Pagan Frontier

The Norse Dragon-Slayer Hero

The Historical Context of Medieval Scandinavia[1]

Who Were the Vikings?

"Viking" is a term used to describe a certain class of marauding Scandinavian warrior from the 8th through the 11th century. However, when discussing the entire culture of the northern Germanic peoples of the early Middle Ages, and especially in terms of the languages and literatures of these peoples, it would be more accurate to use the term "Norse." Therefore during the Middle Ages and beyond, it therefore might be useful to speak of "German" peoples in middle Europe and of "Norse" peoples in Scandinavia and the North Atlantic. However, the mythologies of these peoples were very closely related. Indeed, as we shall see, just as the West Germanic and North Germanic languages contain many clearly identifiably related elements of their common ancestral tongue, the mythologies of the medieval Germans and Norse contain a wealth of analogous features. This is nowhere more clear than in the epic literature of both cultures, which in part relate variations of the same ancient tale of a dragon-slayer, a hero called "Sigurd" by the Norse and "Siegfried" by the Germans. The Viking world ultimately stretched in a wide arc from Constantinople in the southeast to Newfoundland in the northwest. In the Varangian Guard, the elite troops of the Byzantine emperor, eastern Vikings found honor, glory, and riches; from their island homes in the icy North Atlantic, hardy western Norse settlers pushed to Greenland and from there to coastal Canada. Mostly Swedish Vikings, called "Rus," founded trading posts and eventually cities in what would become Russia, whereas Vikings from Norway and especially Denmark conquered territory throughout Britain and Ireland, exacted tribute from the French king, and even took the English crown.

The Literary Context of Medieval Scandinavia[2]

The settlement of Iceland played a particularly crucial role in the development of Norse literature and hence with the recording of Norse versions of ancient Germanic myths and legends, as well as with the development of a uniquely Icelandic saga tradition that blends old mythic elements with medieval Icelandic concerns and sensibilities. Scandinavian settlement of Iceland began in 870; according to Icelandic accounts, this exodus was largely fueled by Norwegians chafing under the centralization of authority in their homeland by King Harald Fairhair. By 930, the collection of relatively autonomous farmers in Iceland had established the *Althing*, or national assembly, a form of representative government that provided the island's only real legislative and judicial authority until Iceland came under the direct sway of the Norwegian crown in the 1260s. The Althing embraced Christianity in 1000, but although paganism was discouraged in public, it certainly was practiced by some in private. Even well after the old beliefs were long dead, interest in Icelandic genealogy, the stories of old, and accounts of the ancient Norse heroes and gods (who were themselves often rendered as gifted humans) were extremely popular in Iceland, and because many *godar* (powerful farmers, a type of chieftain, for want of a better term) sent sons to be trained as priests, it might well seem inevitable that Icelandic scribes and their patrons would take an interest in preserving the ancient oral tales in medieval written forms.

The Sources of Norse Mythology[3]

Norse literature and the saga tradition provide us with one of the most colorful, varied, and well-documented treasure-troves of mythic material from the Middle Ages. However, it is important to note from the onset, that the written material that survived in manuscripts was recorded long after the Age of Migration and well after the conversion to Christianity. It was within the unique mythic and literary hothouse of Iceland, as unlikely as that place may seem to one unfamiliar with the Icelandic national obsession with heritage, that the Germanic myths reached their fullest flower and achieved their most lasting bloom.

Most, although not all, of the sources of Norse myth are Icelandic in origin. One of the most vital of these founts is Snorri Sturluson's *Prose*

Edda, which was written around 1220. Snorri was an extremely important politician, landholder, and poet and was the scion of a very noteworthy Icelandic family. Snorri's contributions to Iceland's literary record have guaranteed him a poet's immortality, but his more worldly concerns ended with his assassination in his own home in September of 1241. The *Prose Edda* comprises a handbook for poets, as it were, and is made up of four parts, the first of which is a prologue. The second part of the *Prose Edda* is *Gylfaginning*, or "the beguiling of Gylfi," a tale wherein Gylfi, a king from Sweden, attempts to make his way to the home of the gods to question them. Although Gylfi is fooled by the phantasm of a hall that the gods erect for his visit, the answers he gains provide a primer of sorts for a Norse poet of the Christian Age who needs details about the mythic past of his pagan ancestors. Snorri's narrative technique is more than simply a clever plot device; it effectively places the author at a significant remove from the heathen content of the work. The third part of the *Prose Edda* is *Skaldskaparmal*, a sort of handbook of poetic phrases. The fourth part of the *Prose Edda* is *Hattatal*, a list of the various forms that made up what is called "Skaldic" verse, or Norse courtly poetry.

Another of the major sources of Norse myth is the *Elder Edda*, also called the *Poetic Edda*, which includes more than 30 poems and was committed to writing around 1270, although the content obviously reflects pagan mythic material of a much earlier date. The *Poetic Edda* provides an overview of the cosmology of the Norse mythological system, complete with descriptions of the Creation, of *Yggdrasill* the World Tree, and of *Ragnarok*, the apocalyptic Norse Doom of the Gods. In between the beginning and the end of Creation are the adventures of the gods, and the poems of the *Poetic Edda* describe several of these, including battles with the giants, who, as forces representing chaos, are harbingers of the great final battle yet to come. Hero myths are represented in the *Poetic Edda* by portions of two heroic cycles: Three poems concern the hero Helgi and his wooing of the Valkyrie Sigrun, whereas several more recount episodes from the story of Sigurd the Dragon-Slayer.

Several medieval historical works are sources of Norse mythology, including Saxo Grammaticus' *Gesta Danorum*, the work of Adam of Bremen, as well as that of the Arab commentator Ibn Fadlan, and the *Landnamabok*, the Icelandic history of the settlement period. Finally, several of the Icelandic sagas, mostly from the 13th century, also provide us with gripping and fascinating mythic, legendary, and folkloric elements, many of which clearly have their roots in ancient Germanic beliefs. *Saga* (the plural is *sogur*) is a Norse word that refers to a type of prose narrative notable for its succinct, straightforward style. Sagas seem very concerned with recording every available detail of a given story and are famous for projecting an appearance of historical substance, whether or not the events of a given story can be verified; indeed, a long-standing critical debate has concerned how far sagas can be trusted as historical documents. The mythic material in sagas may include references to the Norse gods; allusions rich in heroic archetypes; and descriptions of supernatural powers, events, or creatures. There are several sagas concerned with the history of Norway and with the settlement of Iceland and beyond, as well as a set of heroic sagas that deal most explicitly with the adventures and quests of heroes.

The most famous and pertinent examples of the historical sagas include *Heimskringla*, which purports to be a history of the kings of Norway from the mists of time until 1177, as well as the *Islendinga sogur*, the "sagas of the Icelanders," a specific set of approximately 40 Icelandic prose literary works written about events in Iceland during the "Saga Age." This age is roughly concurrent with what is often termed the "Viking Age" and stretches from the time of the first Norse settlement of the island in the late ninth century AD until around the time of the conversion of Iceland to Christianity. The heroic tradition includes the *fornaldar sogur*, or the "legendary heroic sagas," as well as various heroic episodes from other sagas. Heroic sagas often reflect epic Germanic concerns with genealogy and sometimes contain references to ancient mythic traditions; the *fornaldar sogur* are distinct from the *Islendinga sogur* in that the former purport to detail characters and adventures from periods well before the settlement of Iceland. The most relevant heroic sagas discussed in this chapter include the *Saga of the Volsungs*, which contains the story of Sigurd the Dragon-Slayer, and the *Saga of King Hrolf Kraki*, which plays host to a horde of mythic elements, including a notable analogue to the Anglo-Saxon epic *Beowulf*.

Dragons in the Medieval World[4]

Magical serpents—sometimes giant, often winged, usually wily, and always powerful—inhabit mythologies as disparate and distant as the classical Chinese and the ancient Central American. Medieval Europe provided a fertile breeding ground for myths of dragons and their slayers, and the Germanic north in particular was a hotbed of such activity. Indeed, the allure of this theme was so popular that the Cappadocian Saint George was embraced as far away from his home as England on the basis of his victory over a bloodthirsty drake, shunting aside many a homegrown contender for the office of patron saint. However, Saint George's story, which evokes a Christian theme of the victory of conversion over idolatry, is best treated under the rubric of the fighting saint hero, dozens of whom were likewise associated with struggles against demonic draconic foes. Moreover, the mythology of the Middle Ages inherited a vast compendium of magical reptilian creatures of all sorts, from fabulous snakes to tremendous sea-serpents to winged flying dragons from various classical sources that ranged from outright fables to geographical treatises. Many medieval works, from travelogues to bestiaries, likewise reflected a wide assortment of such creatures.

The common image of a "typical" medieval dragon is that of a reptilian creature, usually viciously clawed and magically armored, with great bat-like wings, a formidable tail, and fiery volcanic breath. Dragons were in general emblems of voracious gluttony and avarice in the medieval world, as well as linked through Biblical allusion to Satan and to visions of fiery apocalypse. Indeed, such figurative relationships were even more widespread than a modern reader of the Bible might be prone to expect, in part because quite a number of medieval translations of Hebrew terms for Biblical monsters and creatures were rendered "dragon," which led to concrete associations of the term; for example, with the sin of pride and thus with Satan, and with desert places and thus with desolation and destruction. In addition, dragons play roles in key episodes of various medieval Welsh, English, and French texts of significant mythic importance, most notably in several Arthurian works, and the evolution of the dragons residing in these locales derives in some significant measure from Celtic folkloric traditions concurrent with and perhaps mutually influenced by their Germanic counterparts. The dragons that are denizens of Germanic mythology, then, as well as several of their various magical serpentine cousins, may have represented a particularly potent and volatile breed descended from a combination of ancient indigenous oral sources, literary materials from the classical records, Near and Middle Eastern traditions most notably transmitted through the Bible and related religious texts, and contemporary medieval learned and folkloric sources; of the last of these, various Celtic motifs might be thought to be of particular prominence.

References to dragons abound in Germanic literature and may be found therein as early as the eighth century. The traditions of the dragon and of the dragon-slayer hero were widespread throughout the northern world, and tales from these traditions abound, especially in heroic material, surviving in such primary texts as the Old English *Beowulf*, the Old Norse *Volsungasaga*, and the Middle High German *Nibelungenlied*. However, even quasi-historical accounts of dragons exist, as in the description of the year 793, in which the Vikings sacked the monastery at Lindisfarne, in the *Anglo-Saxon Chronicle*; the record attributes fiery lights in the sky as evidence of airborne dragons, which are clearly thought to be harbingers of doom and cataclysmic destruction. It has been suggested that this association of fiery devastation, dragons, and death was buttressed by ancient pagan crematory rites, which might further reinforce the relationship among dragons, death in general, and barrows in particular. These myths and legends hearken back to very ancient tales and themes, some of which may be as old as the Germanic peoples themselves; however, this is not to suggest that the medieval versions of these myths were not influenced by other traditions, and indeed, the very name "dragon," from the Latin *draco*, indicates the classical origin of the word, which, like certain medieval images of winged serpents, seems to have been influenced by Roman versions. This classical root is thought to be derived from an ancient Indo-European term having to do with vision, which might explain in part why such creatures are so often imbued with attributes such as super-acute eyesight, magical foresight, and a penchant for objects that glitter and sparkle.

Even the signature Old Norse term *dreki*, denoting the great dragon-prowed longships of the Viking Age, betrays elements of this heritage, and in the sagas the common term for flying serpents is *flugdreki*. Although *flugdreki* were fearsome and to be avoided, the figureheads of *dreki* seemed to impart a more sympathetic magic, ostensibly protecting and imparting ferocity upon those who sailed with them. Interestingly, the most usual native Germanic names for members of this family of monsters do not suggest flying creatures, and indeed more often evoke a slithering, earthbound form of great serpent-monster, commonly called *ormr* in Old Norse or *wyrm* in Old English, meaning "serpent" and cognate with the modern term "worm." These names suggest that Germanic dragons represent an extremely ancient conception of the great serpent-monster born of earth and darkness that plays a crucial and often antagonistic role in many Creation myths; indeed, the very serpent in the Garden of Eden might well have flowed from a similar mythic well-spring. The images evoked by these terms are consistent with the greatest dragons of the Germanic heroic myths. Indeed, Sigurd and Beowulf defeat enemies that crawl upon or live within the earth. Furthermore, Sigurd's very attack upon Fafnir is predicated upon the assumptions that Fafnir's heavy body will cross over the ditch wherein the hero lies in wait, and that the great weight bearing down upon the hero's sword will do much of the work for him. The compound *linnormr* in Old Norse, sometimes shortened to *linnr*, meant a marvelous, magical serpent and has survived in the Modern German *lindwurm*, meaning "dragon."

It is interesting to note that the tension in northern mythology between the dragon as protective totem and the dragon as emblem of destruction is played out in many Scandinavian stave-churches, which are ornamented with curving figures of dragons much akin to those on the *dreki* of old. Such figures also appear on various rune-stones and monumental slabs throughout the North Atlantic Viking world. Indeed, it is notable that even the most evil and ferocious of dragons could impart power to and protective charms upon those who properly harnessed their magic, as Sigurd and Siegfried found to their profit. Some Norse descriptions of dragons suggest that dragons are hatched and reared rather like fledgling birds, whereas others, notably those of Fafnir, make it clear that particularly evil, powerful, and acquisitive men may transform into such monsters, illustrating again the vast currency of shape-shifting in Norse mythology. Of course greed is the catalyst for Fafnir's transformation, and although hardly limited to Germanic dragon-lore, the themes of dragon-gold, the lust such treasure incites, and the curses associated with such hoards all hold a special place in the Norse mythic imagination. The dragon in *Beowulf* is the jealous guardian of an ancient burial mound filled with treasure, and this association seems to be more than simply literary: The great Sutton Hoo ship burial, which is often cited for the material analogues it provides to *Beowulf*'s narrative details, actually contains a shield fitting worked into the image of a dragon with huge, dagger-like teeth, folded wings swept back along its narrowing body, and a forked tail. Presumably this dragon was intended to protect the bearer of the shield on his journey to the next world, and dragons do seem to have been associated in the northern imagination with death, the afterlife, and crematory and burial rites.

In addition to Fafnir of the Sigurd cycle and the great dragon of *Beowulf*, the Germanic tradition provides several other great serpent-monsters, including Jormungandr the Midgard Serpent, which is dragon-like in many respects and that also might be termed the mother of all Germanic sea-monsters. Similar creatures also appear as *nicors*; for example, in *Beowulf*, whose cousins are called *nykrs*, or "water-trolls," in Old Norse. Many mythologies relate such creatures with miraculous fluids and with boundaries between order and chaos: Although the blood of Fafnir, to cite an obvious example, is illustrative of the former association, the Midgard Serpent is an excellent example of the frontier-genre serpent. Moreover, Germanic concepts of monstrous sea-creatures are sometimes rooted in such distant existing animals as crocodiles and hippopotami, which were legendary in the far north and thus ripe for mythical appropriation. Aside from Fafnir and Jormungandr, perhaps the most notable named dragon in the Norse tradition is Nidhoggr, the monster that gnaws upon the root of the World Tree and is associated with death, destruction, and visions of eternal punishment. If Fafnir provides the great Germanic example of how a man may be transformed by his very greed, and if the dragon in *Beowulf* helps to clarify how this greed is associated with the burial mound and hence with death, it is in the figure of Nidhoggr that these folkloric and mythic strands from epic and saga literature are woven together into the very cosmos of Norse mythology.

Grimnismal and *Gylfaginning* agree that *Nidhoggr*, "Hostile-Striker," is one, presumably the greatest, of the vile serpents that lurk in the darkness far underground and gnaw upon the root of the World Tree; it is Snorri who informs us that the messages passed between this worm and the great eagle in the canopy of the tree are insults, although we may well have assumed so. Although this role clearly identifies Nidhoggr as a destructive force that attacks the very root of all life, the seeress in *Voluspa* offers a more chilling description of this great dragon that clearly associates Nidhoggr with death, destruction, and the grave: As the doom of the world falls, Nidhoggr sucks the blood of corpses, feeding most especially upon oath-breakers, murderers, and adulterers. Then, in the very closing passage of the seeress's dark and dismal revelation of the end of the time of the gods, after the Earth has reemerged from the cataclysm of Ragnarok, after gods and men have been reborn, just as the newly reeemergent sun shines on a verdant and fertile new world, the shadow of death casts a pall over this resurgent life: Nidhoggr, his wings laden with the corpses of the dead, flies from his lair in the bowels of the Earth and shockingly reasserts the presence and the power of death even in the burgeoning moment when new life has burst forth.

The Dragon-Slayer as Mythic Hero[5]

Dragon-slayers abound in world mythology, and classical and Biblical texts bequeathed many such exemplars to the poets and scribes of the Middle Ages. The dragon-slayer is of course a subset of the hero archetype, and his conflict with the great serpent represents one facet of the hero's battle with monsters; however, this facet is often combined with a journey quest, and at times even a journey to the Underworld. Indeed, it could be argued that some heroes emerge from the dragon's lair reborn, sometimes through magical means, and thus might be said to represent the archetype of the rebirth, return, and apotheosis of the hero. The dragon-slayer generally seeks to deliver a people from the rampages of the worm, to capture the serpent's hoard, or both. In the Germanic tradition, the acquisition of glory and everlasting reputation suborns even the accumulation of treasure, and good leaders distribute their wealth with an open hand. Thus, the hero is entirely antithetical to the dragon, which embodies greed, selfishness, wanton destruction, and infamy. Although Saint George offers the most well known example of the dragon-slayer saint of the Middle Ages, he is one of literally many dozens of holy men and women said to have undergone such combat. The Anglo-Saxon hero Beowulf offers perhaps the epitome of the Germanic hero in his battle with the dragon in that he is selfless, generous, noble, and brave, and he attacks the beast out of a worthy desire to save his people and to increase his own glory.

It is perhaps most fitting that the Norse version of the great epic of the dragon-slayer of Northern Europe springs from the loins of an adventure of the gods gone awry, a tale of ill-gotten treasure and cursed gold that could only be the result of the shenanigans of the Trickster Loki. In the myth of Otter's Ransom, Loki shows his characteristic prowess in getting the gods out of a scrape of his own design. The Trickster also shows his true colors in the way that he is none too concerned with Odin's request for a dainty bit of tainted treasure. Moreover, the malediction that the dwarf Andvari pronounces over the very ring Odin desires evokes a Germanic commonplace of cursed treasure, echoed, for example, in *Beowulf*, and in the *Nibelungenlied*. Moreover, this episode also illuminates the Germanic concern with compensation, or blood money, in return for the life of a slain kinsman.

The Myth of Otter's Ransom[6]

One fine morning in early spring, the gods Odin and Hoenir went for a ramble with the Trickster Loki. The gods came upon a river and ambled along its banks until they came to a waterfall. There was a pool at the base of the falls, and, sunning itself with its eyes closed and eating a fresh-caught salmon, they saw a fat, sleek otter. Loki thought he might try his skill at slaying the otter, which he did with one cast of a stone. He was very proud to have won otter and salmon with a single throw, and the gods were delighted with their luck. They skinned the otter and continued on their way, hoping to offer a share of the food for their night's lodging. Unfortunately for the gods, the house they came upon was that of Hreidmar, a wealthy and powerful man who was the father of three sons: Fafnir, the largest, fiercest, and greediest; Otter, a shape-shifter and master angler, who kept his father well supplied with fish; and Regin, the least powerful and honored of the brothers, but a fine smith. As soon as they saw the body and hide of their kinsman, Hreidmar and his brood set upon the gods, binding them and threatening them unless they agreed to pay a blood price for Otter: The gods must cover Otter's flayed skin with gold, leaving not so much as a whisker showing. The gods sent Loki to fulfill the terms of the ransom. The Trickster first sought the watery halls of Ran and borrowed the net with which she collected the bodies of drowned men. Then Loki returned to the waterfall by which he had slain Otter and dredged the pool for Andvari the Dwarf, who hid in its deeps in the form of a pike. Loki forced Andvari to show him his gold, which the Trickster took to pay the compensation owed to Hreidmar for his son's life.

The dwarf tried to hold back a single ring—some say it would have allowed him to rebuild his fortune—but Loki spied it and forced Andvari to surrender it. However, as the dwarf disappeared back into his pool, he pronounced a curse upon the ring because of the Trickster's greed: That ring would be the death of any owner, and the curse also applied to the whole hoard. Loki returned to the house of Hreidmar well satisfied, and he covered the flayed skin of Otter with Andvari's gold; however, the ring was held back because Odin took a fancy to it and Loki let the All-Father have it. However, Hreidmar claimed the ring when he spotted a whisker poking up from the pile of gold, and thus Odin surrendered the last of Andvari's treasure. As the gods were departing, Loki pronounced the curse of Andvari upon the gold, and as it was spoken, so it came to pass: Fafnir killed his own father Hreidmar to possess that hoard, and it was murder because the body was hidden; later Fafnir transformed into the greatest and vilest of dragons and lay upon his ill-gotten treasure in the midst of the wilderness, sharing not the smallest bauble with anyone. Regin, denied his share of the compensation for Otter and unable to avenge his father, sought employment as a royal smith. Eventually Regin and Fafnir would also die under the curse. The primary sources for the myth of Otter's Ransom include *Skaldskaparmal* in the *Prose Edda*, Chapter 14 of *Volsungasaga*, and some portions of *Reginsmal* from the *Codex Regius*.

Sigurd: The Dragon-Slayer of the Norse[7]

The Norse *Saga of the Volsungs* is a veritable treasure-trove of mythic, folk-loric, and legendary materials, ranging from references to Odin's dabbling in the affairs of kings and heroes to magic rings and cursed hordes to echoes of historical struggles among the Goths, the Burgundians, and even the Huns of Attila, who himself plays a significant role in the saga. Drawing upon a wealth of Eddic material that preserved and refined the ancient oral traditions, the author of this saga brought together these various strands to weave the most popular and enduring epic of the North. Indeed, to this day scenes from the story of Sigurd hold positions of honor on many existing artworks throughout the Scandinavian lands and the islands of Britain and quite often provide a pagan counterpoint to a Christian context. Adorning stone monuments and the wooden doorways of stave-churches alike, these representations eloquently express the widespread and lasting popularity of this myth, and all the more so when one considers that it is very likely that many more such artifacts have been lost through the ravages of time, weather, fire, and war. Like the Middle High German *Nibelungenlied*, which also treats the subject of the great Germanic hero within a complex matrix of oral history, folk traditions, and sweeping archetypes, *Volsungasaga* is about much more than a simple account of dragon-slaying. Many consider Sigurd to be the "Arthur of the North," a legendary figure clothed in the trappings of myth and folklore who represents the great spirit, hope, and aspiration of the culture that spawned him. Sigurd is the last and greatest of the Volsungs, a family seemingly cursed even as it is favored by Odin.

Miraculous conception, lycanthropy, and epic proportion are staples of this family line, and Sigurd, the son of King Sigmund and his much younger second wife Hjordis, exemplifies that heroic strain. In addition to his slaughter of the great worm Fafnir, Sigurd is the only man alive who can ride through a ring of fire, break the curse of Odin, and waken and win the heart of the shield-maiden Brynhild. Possessor of a refashioned ancestral sword as outsized in its proportion as is the hero himself, Sigurd is also a shape-shifter, is gifted with foresight, and is the most powerful warrior and finest figure of a man of his age. Moreover, through his victory over the great serpent, Sigurd gains even more remarkable powers, benefiting as he does from the fabled virtues of the dragon's blood and heart—both of which he tastes. Still, these qualities avail him little in the end, and the curse of the treasure he wins from the sons of Hreidmar casts its long shadow upon Sigurd's heroic light. Indeed, Sigurd's tragic and inexorable journey toward his bloody fate recalls that of his forefathers and that of the family of Otter, as well as foreshadowing the fate of those who cause Sigurd's own death. If anything, the central lesson of this hero's journey seems to be the classic Germanic motif of unflinching heroism in the face of certain doom, a theme that Gunnar, who plotted Sigurd's death, evokes just as clearly with the music he plays with his toes upon his harp in the snake pit that claims his life as did Sigurd's own stirring assertion of his unblemished honor while his life's blood flowed from him. Furthermore, Sigurd the Dragon-Slayer wins neither deliverance for his people nor a treasure of any use to anyone; truly, Sigurd only kills the dragon as recompense to his foster-father Regin for the reforging of the sword Gram, and Regin himself has little opportunity to savor his vengeance over his monstrous sibling before he himself joins Fafnir in the eternal brotherhood of death.

Regin the smith, brother to Otter and Fafnir and son of Hreidmar, was Sigurd's foster-father, and thus was charged with educating the young hero in languages, runes, chess, hunting, and in other noble pursuits. All this Regin did, but he also tried to sow seeds of discontent in the lad and wished thereby to tempt him with the promise of Fafnir's almost immeasurable wealth. It was Regin who recounted the tale of Otter's Ransom to Sigurd, which he did to explain why we felt so strongly that Sigurd should challenge the dragon. In the end, Sigurd agreed to slay Fafnir on the condition that Regin should forge for him a marvelous sword. Regin thus crafted a blade for Sigurd, but the hero doubted its virtue and proved its flaw by shattering the sword upon Regin's anvil. Set the task of creating a better weapon, Regin grumbled at Sigurd's pickiness but promised him that the next sword would be better. However, upon testing the second blade, Sigurd found it as unsatisfactory as the first and noted that such an untrustworthy smith was cut from the same cloth as his unsavory forebears.

Sigurd then visited his mother and asked if it were true that she held for him a mighty heirloom from his father, the shards of the great sword Gram, which had been shattered against the very spear of Odin when the One-Eyed God had chosen to revoke his favor so that he might claim King Sigmund for Valhalla. The aged king thus had fallen on the field of his last battle and had thereby escaped an ignominious death in his bed. Sigurd's mother was pleased to pass the remnants of Gram on to her son, thinking that he was likely to win great honor and glory with such a weapon in his hand. Sigurd took these shards to Regin and admonished him to make from them a blade worthy of its lineage. Regin became angry at this demand, thinking as he did that Sigurd was too critical of his smithing. Nonetheless Regin refashioned the great sword Gram, and when he took it from the forge it seemed to those watching as though the flames in which it was reborn danced around its edges. The smith handed the blade to its owner, noting gruffly that if this sword were to shatter he was no smith at all. This time when Sigurd brought the weapon down upon the anvil, its blade cut through to the very ground, and the metal was so strong that no imperfection could be found in the sword. The edge of the blade was so sharp that it sliced a strand of wool in half, although it was only the force of a stream that brought the wool against the blade. Regin now demanded repayment in the form of blood vengeance against his brother Fafnir the dragon, which Sigurd promised to attempt as soon as he had avenged his own father's death.

When Sigurd had accomplished his vengeance upon the enemies of his father, Regin was quick to remind his foster-son of his oath to slay Fafnir, a quest that the hero was not loathe to attempt. Soon thereafter, Regin led Sigurd upon the Gnitaheath, the haunt of the great worm. When Sigurd saw the giant cliff from which the dragon lowered itself to drink, he knew that his foster-father had lied when he claimed that his brother took the form of an ordinary serpent. However, Regin scoffed at the young man's reservations and instructed Sigurd to dig a ditch perpendicular to the track that the serpent had worn in the ground. Lying in this ditch, Regin advised, Sigurd would be perfectly situated to thrust up into the body of the monster, killing it as it crawled forth to slake its thirst. When Sigurd asked how he would fare in that shallow trench from the shower of dragon blood he was bound to rain down upon himself as the result of executing such a strategy, Regin scoffed again, remarking that Sigurd seemed rather unlike his sires and that the timid were unlikely to prosper. At that point Sigurd rode up onto the heath to enact this plan while Regin fled into hiding. However, while Sigurd was digging the ditch, an old man appeared before him and advised the lad to show more wisdom. If he were to dig a series of branching ditches running off from the one in which he was to lie, the old man suggested, the hero might slay the dragon in safety without fear of being overcome by the worm's noxious, gushing blood. The man then disappeared, and many think him to have been Odin, he who often appeared to Sigurd and indeed all the Volsungs in critical moments.

Sigurd did as he had been advised and crawled into the central ditch before the ground quaked with the approach of Fafnir. As the monstrous serpent approached, the earth trembled and the air was filled with poison spewed forth by the hideous worm, but Sigurd lay unconcerned in his trench. However, as the dragon slithered over the hero, Sigurd thrust his blade under the left shoulder of the beast, only stopping when he had plunged it all the way up the hilt, so that his sword stung the very heart of the dragon. Feeling his death throes come upon him, Fafnir thrashed and flailed with his head and his tail, destroying everything within reach of his twisting body. Still unafraid, Sigurd pulled forth his blade and leapt lightly from the ditch, his arms bloodied all the way up to his shoulders. When Fafnir realized that he was dying and that the young man before him had dealt the blow, he questioned his killer about his identity and lineage. At first Sigurd answered obscurely, some say in the hopes of deflecting the curse that the dying may cast upon those whose names they know. When the dragon berated him for dissembling, the hero named himself and his father. Fafnir pronounced the curse of the gold upon Sigurd, but the hero's response was that, although all men must die, the brave prefer to enjoy riches in the meantime. Sigurd then tested the wisdom of the dying worm with riddles of the Norns and of Ragnarok, questions of fate and of destruction suitable for the dying day of a long-ravening monster. Fafnir lamented the treachery of his brother Regin, whom he knew to have conspired against him, but he said that he took comfort in the belief that Regin would be the death of Sigurd. The worm also bemoaned the failure of his poison and his terror-helm in the face of this foe, although always in the past these were weapons before which all men had fled. However, Sigurd remained unimpressed and repeated his intention to claim courageously and enjoy fully all of Fafnir's hoard until that day when he himself was doomed to die, and, with these words, he condemned Fafnir to the clutches of Hel.

When the worm was dead, Regin reappeared. He congratulated Sigurd on a victory worthy of song throughout all of the ages. However, the smith seemed disconsolate at the same time, and he muttered repeatedly that Sigurd had killed his brother, although he knew himself to be culpable as well. In response, Sigurd upbraided Regin for his cowardly retreat from the heath as the dragon approached, but his foster-father reminded the young hero that the great deed had been accomplished with the sword reforged by the smith. However, Sigurd was unconvinced that the credit for his deed lay in the sword that had cut the dragon to the quick rather than in the strong hand and heroic breast that had wielded that death blow. Sigurd then cut out the heart of the monster, and as the blood gushed out of the gaping wound, Regin drank his fill of Fafnir's blood. Overcome by drowsiness after slaking his thirst for the powers inherent in the dragon's blood, Regin lay down to sleep. However, first the smith asked his foster-son to roast the heart of the worm for him to eat. The hero made to do as he had been asked, but as he cooked the heart upon a spit, some juice foamed out, and Sigurd touched it with his finger to test whether it was done. Putting his hot finger into his mouth, Sigurd tasted the blood of the dragon; suddenly, the young hero realized that he could understand the speech of the birds all around him.

In particular, Sigurd comprehended the discourse of six birds that were watching him. The first exclaimed that Sigurd should roast the heart for himself; if he were to eat it, he would become the wisest of men. The second bird exclaimed that Regin, who slept nearby, intended to betray his foster-son. The third bird voiced the opinion that Sigurd should behead Regin, and then Sigurd alone would control Fafnir's vast hoard. The fourth bird concurred, remarking that the hero would be wise to follow such sage advice and adding that after he claimed the hoard Sigurd should seek the resting place of Brynhild, where he would gain true wisdom. Such a dangerous and cunning old wolf as Regin, this bird concluded, was never to be trusted. The fifth bird agreed, noting that Sigurd would not be so wise a man as one might think if he were to allow the kinsman of one he slew to live. The sixth bird summed up the advice of them all: Sigurd would be wise to slay Regin and claim Fafnir's gold for himself. Sigurd required no more counsel on the matter, and as he decided, so did he do. Decapitating the sleeping Regin, he sent one brother tumbling after the other into the frigid depths of Hel. Then the hero ate a bit of the dragon's heart and carefully preserved the rest. After he had tasted the flesh of the beast's core, Sigurd followed the worm's track back to its hiding place, a great cavernous lair with iron doors set upon iron posts set into the rock of the threshold. Within this den Sigurd found a vast hoard, including Fafnir's terror-helm, a byrnie of gilded mail, and huge quantities of gold—more, in fact, than the hero thought might be carried by several horses. However, Sigurd's noble steed, Grani, was more than up to the challenge and refused to move from the spot until laden with all of that gold packed into two mighty chests. Additionally, the horse refused to be led and insisted that Sigurd ride, sitting next to his new-won treasure.

Although the great heroic feats of this "Arthur of the North" echo throughout the medieval Germanic world, it is in the Norse version that this legendary figure is clothed most elaborately in the cloth of myth. Indeed, the central primary source for the myth of Sigurd the Dragon-Slayer is *Volsungasaga*; Regin forges Gram, Sigurd slays the dragon, Regin drinks its blood, and Sigurd slays Regin in Chapters 15, 18, 19, and 20, respectively. The marriage of Sigurd's parents and his own conception may be found in Chapters 11–13, whereas his encounters with Odin's shield-maiden, Brynhild, begin directly after his destruction of the dragon, and the repercussions of this first meeting in large measure comprise the balance of the saga. In addition to the dragon-slaying episode, the myth of

Otter's Ransom, and the numerous portentous allusions to Odin, it is perhaps in the figure of Brynhild, her relationship with Sigurd, and her role in his death and his funeral that these mythic trappings are most clearly manifested. Although she is attributed a mortal ancestry, Brynhild is clearly a Valkyrie who has fallen from Odin's favor. During the battle between two kings, Brynhild struck down he who had been promised victory by the All-Father. In revenge, Odin pierced Brynhild with a thorn, which caused her to fall into an enchanted sleep within a ring of shields. Odin also cast down his shield-maiden from her virginal post as a victory-goddess, cursing her never again to have the victory and condemning her to marriage. After his victory over the dragon, Sigurd rode to a mountain, the top of which seemed to be encircled by fire that reached to the heavens. As he drew nearer, he saw that there was a ring of shields around the peak and that a great banner flew from the top. When he passed through the wall of shields, he found what appeared to be a fully armored man asleep. The sleeper's mail-shirt was so tight that it seemed a second skin, and it was when he cut off this byrnie and removed the sleeper's helmet that Sigurd discovered that this was none other than Brynhild, whose enchanted slumber was the result of the One-Eyed God's wrath.

Brynhild had vowed never to marry any man, regardless of the All-Father's strictures, unless she found a hero incapable of fear, and in Sigurd she met her ideal match. This suitability Brynhild made clear by offering a foaming horn of beer to the conquering hero who awoke her. They talked and drank together, and the dragon-slayer, who had heard of the great beauty and secret knowledge of the sleeping shield-maiden, soon put her to the test. Sigurd asked Brynhild to share her vaunted wisdom, and in response she taught him the magic inherent in runes and offered him much valuable advice. During their time together, Sigurd gave to Brynhild the magic ring of the dwarf Andvari, which carried the curse of the dwarf and had captured the fancy of the All-Father himself. However, the happiness of the greatest of warriors and the wisest of women fell under the shadow of Odin's displeasure and the curse of Otter's gold, and although they pledged each other their troth and their love, it was not to be. Sigurd fell under the power of a magic potion brewed by the witch Queen Grimhild and forgot his vow to Brynhild until it was too late and he had married Grimhild's daughter, just as Brynhild herself foresaw and as she interpreted for Gudrun, the daughter of Grimhild, when Gudrun asked Brynhild to interpret a dream.

Furthermore, Sigurd deceived Brynhild by taking on the visage of Gunnar, Gudrun's brother, and winning the hand of Brynhild for Gunnar by doing what no other man could accomplish—entering the ring of fire and demanding that the shield-maiden fulfill her sacred vow and marry the man capable of this feat. Brynhild acquiesced, and, although they slept in one bed for three nights, Sigurd, in the form of Gunnar, placed a naked blade between them, claiming that Gunnar's marriage must be sanctified in this manner. Before he left, Brynhild gave to the man she took to be Gunnar the cursed ring of Andvari that she had received from Sigurd, and it was this wretched bauble that brought the wrath of his one true love down upon the dragon-slayer. Sigurd gave the ring to Gudrun, who showed it to Brynhild when the women quarreled over whose husband was the greater hero. When Brynhild saw this ring, she knew that she had been deceived and betrayed and that her love had bartered her to a lesser man. She then plotted Sigurd's death, vowing that she would not live with two husbands alive in one hall. However, once Sigurd was upon his funeral pyre, along with his killer and his son by the shield-maiden, Brynhild joined her lover in the eternal embrace of death, leaping through the flames to her love as Sigurd had to his.

Brynhild's vow to accept only the most fearless of men hearkens back to her identity as a Valkyrie, as does her act of serving Sigurd a flagon of ale, a traditional female role of hospitality and mark of honor in the Germanic north with literary resonance with the feasts of Hrodgar in *Beowulf* as well as mythic resonance with the nightly revels in Valhalla. Brynhild's knowledge of runes and other secret wisdom; her ability to interpret dreams; her absolute need to obtain the very best, most fearless warrior; and her towering rage and thirst for vengeance when she is deceived in this respect all mark her as Odin's own handmaid. The thorn with which Brynhild is cursed is a phallic representation of the loss of maidenhead to which the angry god has sentenced her, as is the drawn sword that Sigurd, in the guise of Gunnar, puts between them during their three nights together. Similarly, Sigurd's act of taking the betrothal ring back from Brynhild on this occasion, in addition to recalling the curse and renouncing the vows associated with that particular ring, evokes a vaginal image, as do the rings of shields and fire. Indeed, in the Thidrek version of the story, Sigurd takes these trophies after he has, with Gunnar's acquiesce, explicitly reft Brynhild of her maidenhead. Brynhild's role as shield-maiden is ended by her loss of virginity; thus, it is the reappearance of her betrothal ring on the hand of Sigurd's wife that is the proof of her humiliation that she can not tolerate. However, in the machinations that lead to Sigurd's death, we see the old power and function of the Valkyrie emerge. Brynhild chooses the greatest warrior of all, marks him out for death, and sees his body bloody and lifeless. That she then chooses to join him in the afterlife reinforces this association as much as it evokes the practice of human sacrifice sometimes associated with funeral rites.

Siegfried: The Dragon-Slayer of the Germans[8]

Composed in the early 13th century, the Middle High German epic the *Nibelungenlied* develops the ancient northern theme of the dragon-slayer hero in the context of a courtly tradition, and much of the narrative emphasis in this version shifts to Kriemhild of the Burgundians, Siegfried's wife. Kriemhild is a driving force in the plot of this iteration of the story, from her introduction as the most beautiful of maidens in the first lines of the poem to her consummation of her vengeance and her own death in the closing passage. Indeed, although Siegfried's actions are outsized and he looms, in presence and absence, over the whole of the story, in point of fact he has been slain by the midway point of the poem. Moreover, although the Norse Sigurd seems in many ways the embodiment of the epic Germanic hero, these features are mixed in the person of the Middle High German Siegfried with a healthy measure of the medieval courtier. Although the opening section of *Volsungasaga* is dedicated, as the title would suggest, to Sigurd's mythical heritage as the scion of the family of the Volsungs, the opening chapters of the *Nibelungenlied* recount the courtly credentials of the two young lovers-to-be; further, whereas Sigurd was fostered in the humble household of Regin the smith, Siegfried's coming-of-age was marked by his knighthood in a splendid and elaborate festival in the court of his parents. More to the point, the description of the dragon-slaying episode of this version of the hero is relegated to a second-hand account of Siegfried's various feats of arms. When Siegfried arrives at Worms to seek Kriemhild's hand at the very beginning of the tale, we learn that he has taken possession of the treasure of the Nibelungs and that he wields the great sword Balmung and possesses a marvelous cloak of invisibility. It is this cloak, rather than a magical shape-shifting ability, that Siegfried uses to help his brother-in-law Gunther to win and to subdue Brunhild of Iceland, although in this version Siegfried owes no vow of loyalty to Brunhild. Indeed, in true Romance fashion, Kriemhild is Siegfried's first love, and the hero sought his lady's hand on the basis of her reputation alone.

However, Siegfried is without a doubt first and foremost a dragon-slayer hero; indeed, in a significant parallel to the episode wherein Sigurd slays Fafnir, we are told that the hero of the *Nibelungenlied* bathed in the blood of a mighty dragon. In this detail, we might perceive resonance with the magical powers imparted to Sigurd through the juices of Fafnir's roasted heart and the earlier trench-digging episode in which Odin appears to warn the Norse hero to beware of being destroyed by the worm's blood. In addition, the detail of Siegfried's blood-bath is a crucial plot point in the *Nibelungenlied* because we are informed that it was through this gory baptism that the hero provided himself with his invulnerable horny hide. His secret weakness is betrayed when Kriemhild confides to her brother's confidante, Hagen, that a linden leaf covered a spot between the hero's shoulder blades and thus that the skin might be pierced in that place. Siegfried is slain almost immediately thereafter, and the bulk of the story is spent recounting how Kriemhild came to the court of Etzel (Attila the Hun), became his wife, and plotted and executed her vengeance for Siegfried upon her brother, Gunther, and his court and especially upon Hagen, who had wielded Siegfried's death blow. The secret of the treasure of the Nibelungs dies with the last of that line, and we hear echoes of Andvari's curse in the dying shrieks of Kriemhild, slain for having the temerity to have grasped her husband's sword and with it to have beheaded Hagen by her own hand. It is especially noteworthy that—as influenced by continental traditions and the genre of the Romance as the Middle High German epic may be—the essential attributes of the heroic journey of Siegfried resonate so clearly with those of Sigurd. Although the details change and the trappings reflect contemporary local cultural factors, Siegfried and Sigurd clearly hearken back to a common Germanic ancestor.

Beowulf: The Dragon-Slayer of the Anglo-Saxons[9]

The final sequence of the Old English epic *Beowulf* takes place long after Beowulf's travels to the land of the Danes and his battles with Grendel and Grendel's mother. For 50 winters Beowulf has ruled the Geats in peace and prosperity, and when his last great battle falls to his lot the hero is an old man. A servant fleeing the displeasure of his master found the entrance to an ancient barrow filled with the treasure of a long-dead people. Seeking to win the favor of his lord, this foolish thrall took from the hoard a single jewel-encrusted flagon. However, instead of gaining fortune for this audacious deed, the wretch brought upon the people of that region the fiery wrath of the dragon, which for 300 winters had claimed that barrow as its home and that treasure as its own. When the serpent discovered its loss, its rage was fearsome to behold and waxed as the day waned. When night finally fell, the beast rose into the sky, raining fire, destruction, and death upon all of the homes and farms in the vicinity. Soon the entire coastal region had fallen under a storm of flame, smoke, and ash, and nowhere in the lands of the Geats was safe. Even the mighty hall of Beowulf the king fell to a heap of smoldering embers, as did his great fortifications without number. Enraged in his turn, Beowulf considered his strategy for avenging his people upon this vile monster. Knowing well that a linden-wood shield would avail him little against such an opponent, Beowulf commanded a great target to be forged of iron. He gathered to him a select company of 11 comrades, and as a guide they added to their number the foolish thief who had pilfered the dragon's lost cup from the ancient barrow.

After recounting his past deeds and valor before his men, Beowulf determined to go into battle with the dragon alone. He commanded his thanes to wait outside of the barrow, for the glory or the doom of the serpent's wrath were his and his alone to bear. Beowulf lamented the fact that he might not wrestle the monster weaponless, as he had Grendel, but he had to acknowledge that such tactics would avail him little against the blazing breath of this adversary, and so he determined to use to his advantage his iron byrnie and buckler. Beowulf vowed that once the battle was joined he would not retreat at all, although it cost him his life. The hero then trod alone the terrifying path into the dragon's lair; he was no coward. Steams and smokes issued forth from the stone archway over the entrance to the innermost chamber, and Beowulf gave out a great war cry as he crossed that threshold. The dragon, enraged by the presence of his enemy, burst upon the ancient king. The combatants then converged, Beowulf's blade flashing in the fire of the dragon, and although shield protected him and sword smote his enemy, neither served him so well as he might have hoped. The dragon, falling back with a slight wound from his enemy, soon renewed his attacks with vigor, whereas the king, whose sword had failed him for the first time, struggled to continue the fight. The hated enemies rushed once more against one another, their struggle causing the barrow to rumble while reek and heat shot forth from the entrance.

Of all of Beowulf's picked companions, only one, Wicglaf, stood firm; the others fled into the woods to save their own lives. Remembering the king's generosity to him and to his family, Wicglaf could not hold himself back when he realized that Beowulf was perishing, broiling alive under his iron helm. The young warrior, as yet untested in battle, brandished his sword, an ancient heirloom of his family, and lifted his wooden shield, little as it might avail him against the heat of the drake. Delivering to his companions a stunning rebuke, Wicglaf reminded them of the open-handedness of their lord and of their own vows of loyalty whilst deep in their cups, goblets filled to overflowing with the drink their lord himself had so generously bestowed upon them. Seeking to save his lord or to die with him, the young thane rushed to his king's side; although his buckler was soon cinders and his armor helped him little, Wicglaf found some protection from the scorching flames of the dragon under the broad iron roof that Beowulf's shield provided for them both. Although the dragon redoubled its efforts in the rage that befell it when it discovered yet another interloper in its lair, Beowulf was himself buoyed by the words and spirit of his young retainer and thrust once more at the dragon's neck, snapping his ancient blade. The monster took this opportunity to charge for the third time, taking Beowulf's neck between its jaws so that the hero's life-blood welled up and gushed out of the grisly wounds. Desperate to protect his lord, Wicglaf thrust his sword deep into the serpent's belly so that the flames of the monster began to abate. Taking strength for a final onslaught from the inspiration of his young follower, Beowulf himself drew his short blade and thrust it into the flank of the dragon, dealing it a mortal wound. Thus, together king and thane brought down the dragon. However, the poison of the worm's bite flowed deadly in the hero's veins, and Beowulf knew that he had but a short time to live.

Beowulf as dragon-slayer is a hero who seeks to protect his people who have done nothing to incite the rage of this enemy and can do nothing to protect themselves from it. Moreover, the Anglo-Saxon epic hero is anxious for eternal fame and the glory of the battle, which will grant him an immortality denied to his line because of his childlessness; indeed, Wicglaf seems to him a son of his own heroic spirit, which is as much of an heir as Beowulf is able to claim. The dragon in *Beowulf*, like Fafnir in the *Saga of the Volsungs*, is the very emblem of greed, of a boundless avarice that might never be sated but that is, conversely, ever watchful, jealous, and likely to spark into a raging flood of anger, hatred, and retribution. Dragons signify such selfishness throughout the Middle Ages in many different contexts, of course, but here in the Anglo-Saxon epic we are presented with a clear schematic for understanding how greed, generosity, loyalty, and betrayal are seen to operate in Germanic myth and legend. The dragon, the consummation of greed who collects treasure that stagnates in its keeping, is by definition the antithesis of the good king, who is expected to be generous with the gold that flows into his coffers, directing it with justice and prudence to the worthy amongst his retainers, who then are to respond with unflinching courage and loyalty to their lord unto death. This system fails very often indeed, as the poem makes clear, but in many respects Beowulf is such a good, generous king, and Wicglaf is such a loyal, courageous thane. Thus, this dragon-slaying episode recalls and clarifies the most crucial elements of the Anglo-Saxon hero.

Notes

1. For a helpful and clear outline of the movements of the Germanic peoples through the Age of Migrations, see Jones 22–33. For the case that the Viking Age could be seen as an extension of the Age of Migration, see Jones 182. For an argument that, although the derivation of the term *vikingr* is disputed, it certainly was used in contemporary Medieval accounts to mean "raider" or "pirate," see Jones 75–77, especially 76 footnote 1, which includes a summation of the etymology of the term "Viking."

2. For an assessment of the perceptions of the saga writers regarding their ancestors' reasons for emigration to Iceland, see Byock 82–84. However, it is important to stress that Byock finds these perceptions to have been rather biased.

3. For critical commentary on and analysis of the sources of Norse mythology, see especially Branston 35–46; Crossley-Holland xxxii–xxxvi; Davidson 14–16, 23–24, 44–47; Fee 14–15; Hreinsson xxx–xxxv; Kellogg xviii–xxv; Larrington xi, xiii–xxi; Lindow 12–27; Page 10–26; and Puhvel 190–191.

4. For critical commentary concerning the mythology of dragons in the Middle Ages, see especially Branston 73, 76–79, 82, 94, 96–98, 169, and 286–290; Crossley-Holland xxii–xxiii; Davidson 159–162 and 194; Fee 112–113; Lindahl 100–103; Lindow 239; and Simek 64–65 and 231.

5. For critical commentary regarding the dragon-slayer as hero, see especially Fee 117–119, 130–133 and Lindahl 100–103.

6. For critical commentary regarding the myth of Otter's Ransom, see especially Crossley-Holland 136–142 and 222–223; Davidson 43–44; Fee 90–92; Lindow 58–59; Puhvel 217; and Simek 16. In addition, high-quality interactive images of and videos pertaining to the Otter slab at Maughold on the Isle of Man and many other related objects and sites, complete with commentary, are available via *The Medieval North Atlantic* interactive multimedia resource: http://public.gettysburg.edu/~cfee/MedievalNorthAtlantic/.

7. For critical commentary on the dragon-slayer hero in *Volsungasaga*, see especially Byock 1–29; Davidson 43–44, 49, 150–151; and Fee 119–120 and 130–131. In addition, Andersson comments on the dragon-slaying sequence of the Thidrek variation of Sigurd's tale on pages 174–177.

8. The *Nibelungenlied* is preserved in various forms in more than 30 manuscripts; two of the earliest, B and C, may come closest to the original version, but the provenance is complicated and not all scholars would agree with this assessment. For more information concerning the manuscript tradition and the dating of the poem, see especially Hatto 358–369; the present study takes

Hatto's edition as authoritative. We learn of Siegfried's slaying of the dragon through Hagen's summary of the hero's history in Chapter 3, Siegfried's vulnerability is revealed in Chapter 15, and Siegfried is slain in the next chapter. For additional critical commentary concerning the epic of the Nibelungs, see especially Andersson 105–117, Fee 120; Gentry 114–116; Haymes 101–131; and McConnell 42–66.

9. The dragon episode comprises lines 2200–2820 in *Beowulf.* For critical commentary, see especially Fee 127–128 and 132–133.

Sources and Further Reading

Andersson, Theodore Murdock. *A Preface to the Nibelungenlied.* Stanford, CA: Stanford University Press, 1987.

Branston, Brian. *Gods of the North.* New York: Thames and London, 1980.

Byock, Jesse. *The Saga of the Volsungs: The Norse Epic of Sigurd the Dragon Slayer.* New York: Penguin Classics, 1999.

Byock, Jesse. *Viking Age Iceland.* New York: Penguin, 2001.

Crossley-Holland, Kevin. *The Norse Myths.* New York: Pantheon, 1981.

Davidson, H. R. Ellis. *Norse Mythology: Gods and Myths of Northern Europe.* New York: Penguin, 1965.

DuBois, Thomas A. *Nordic Religions in the Viking Age.* Philadelphia: University of Pennsylvania Press, 1999.

Faulkes, Anthony. *Edda.* Rutland, VT: Charles E. Tuttle, 1995.

Fee, Christopher R., with David A. Leeming. *Gods, Heroes, & Kings: The Battle for Mythic Britain.* New York: Oxford University Press, 2004.

Gentry, Francis G. *The Nibelungen Tradition: An Encyclopedia.* New York: Routledge, 2002.

Hatto, A. T. *The Nibelungenlied.* London: Penguin Books, 1965.

Haymes, Edward, and Susann T. Samples. *Heroic Legends of the North: An Introduction to the Nibelung and Dietrich Cycles.* Garland Reference Library of the Humanities, Vol. 1403. New York: Garland, 1996.

Hreinsson, Viðar. *The Complete Sagas of Icelanders, Including 49 Tales.* Reykjavík: Leifur Eiríksson Press, 1997.

Jones, Gwyn. *A History of the Vikings.* Oxford, United Kingdom: Oxford University Press, 1984.

Kellogg, Robert. *The Sagas of Icelanders: A Selection.* New York: Viking, 2000.

Larrington, Carolyne. *The Poetic Edda. Oxford World's Classics.* New York: Oxford University Press, 1999.

Lindahl, Carl, John McNamara, and John Lindow. *Medieval Folklore: A Guide to Myths, Legends, Tales, Beliefs, and Customs.* Oxford: Oxford University Press, 2002.

Lindow, John. *Norse Mythology: A Guide to the Gods, Heroes, Rituals, and Beliefs.* New York: Oxford University Press, 2001.

McConnell, Winder. *A Companion to the Nibelungenlied*. Columbia, SC: Camden House, 1998.

Page, R.I. *Norse Myths*. Austin: University of Texas Press, 1990.

Puhvel, Jaan. *Comparative Mythology*. Baltimore: Johns Hopkins University Press, 1987.

Simek, Rudolf. *Dictionary of Northern Mythology*. Translated by Angela Hall. Rochester, NY: Boydell and Brewer, 1993.

The Irish Battle-Rager Hero

The Historical Context of Medieval Celtic Mythology[1]

Who Were the Celts?

As were the Germanic peoples with whom the Celts came into contact and conflict, the Celtic peoples were largely illiterate before the conversion to Christianity; thus, the vernacular written traditions that incorporate early mythic material are at one and the same time indisputably medieval and removed at quite a distance from the original pagan rites, beliefs, and vibrant oral mythological traditions. Again in a way similar to that in which we can examine the ancient Germanic pagan gods at a distance and largely through the pens of the classical neighbors and the medieval descendants of their followers, what we know of Celtic ritual and belief we glean by collating Roman contemporary accounts thereof, related archaeological evidence, and several much later medieval Irish and Welsh texts that contain echoes and reflections of pre-Christian Celtic mythic gods, goddesses, heroes, and adventures.

The Archaeological Record[2]

The main classical sources for information about Celtic mythology include works by Caesar and Diodorus Siculus in the decades preceding the Christian era, Strabo around the time of Christ, and Lucan and Dio Cassius in the first few centuries of the Christian era. The first three writers seem indebted to the now lost work of Posidinius, and all are in any case generally more concerned with the function of the druids and with religious ritual than they are with the nature of the Celtic gods per se; indeed, Caesar is in the habit of equating the Celtic deities with those Roman gods he identifies as their doppelgangers, and he offers little in the way of exploration of possible subtle differences between such pairs of gods. Moreover, Caesar, like many of his countrymen, seems most intrigued by practices the Romans found barbaric, disturbing, and therefore horrifically compelling, such as human sacrifice as an aspect of Celtic religious rites and the cultic and totemic status of the human head in Celtic society.

Where such observations may be cross-referenced with the archaeological record, these classical authors are of the most use. The material remains testify to some of the practices that seem to have held the most perverse fascination for the Romans; notable amongst these were ritual headhunting and certain sacrificial and funeral customs. However, classical literature on the whole gives relatively little voice to an archaeological record that abounds with iconography that remains, for the most part, frustratingly mute. In sum, then, the classical literary record is of certain limited use in discerning some aspects of Celtic mythology; however, the word of these contemporaries of the ancient Celts, who were often in conflict with their neighbors in Gaul, must be taken with a grain of salt. The literary record is, is any case, most helpful as a gloss on the archaeological remains. During the centuries between the time when classical authors penned their accounts describing practices of the ancient Celts and the time when medieval Christian monks put quill to parchment and absorbed and transformed the stories and beliefs of pagan Celtic culture, we have good reason to believe that the old tales were kept alive and transmitted through a rich and vibrant oral tradition.

The Literary Context of Medieval Celtic Mythology[3]

The most important medieval Irish sources containing significant mythic material include four main categories of stories surviving into the Middle Ages. The first group of narratives is usually designated the "Mythological Cycle," the main sources of which include the *Labor Gabala Erenn* or *Leabhar Gabhala*, the "Book of Invasions of Ireland," and to a much lesser extent the roughly contemporaneous *Dinnshenchas*, the "History of Places," both of which are preserved in the 12th-century *Lebor Laignech*, or "Book of Leinster." The Fenian (or Finn) Cycle, sometimes called the "Ossianic Cycle," is a collection of tales of the adventures and exploits of the hero Finn mac Cumaill and his war band, called the Fianna or Fenians. Stories of love, battle, and the hunt dominate this cycle, which is most often set in the Ireland of King Cormac mac Airt, who is purported to have ruled at Tara in the mid-third century of the Christian era. Purporting to record the history of various kings, their followers, and their battles and adventures from around the third century until the seventh or eighth century after Christ, the Old Irish Historical Cycle is often referred to as the "Cycle of the Kings." Combining records of verifiable historical events with legend, myth, and folklore, this branch of early Irish literature is sometimes neglected in the study of mythology because its content is less overtly marvelous and heroic than that of the other cycles. The Ulster Cycle, however, is the most important of the four groups of narratives for our purposes.

The Ulster Cycle[4]

The Ulster Cycle, which is also called the "Red Branch Cycle," is the primary collection of heroic narratives in Irish mythology. The Ulster Cycle is comprised in large part of the *Tain Bo Cuailnge*, the great epic account of the "Cattle Raid of Cooley." Most of the tales of the Ulster Cycle are concerned with the *Tain* itself, with its prologue, or with the fates of its great heroes, but the cycle also includes a few independent narratives. References to the pagan Irish gods, to magic, to ancient and barbaric modes of warfare and trophy-taking, and to the central preoccupation of cattle rustling abound in the Ulster Cycle. Although it may be seen as a treasure-trove containing elements of myths of the gods themselves, or at least of late Christianized reflections of such early pagan myths, the *Tain* is first and foremost the province of heroes such as Cuchulainn and Conchobar. The name "Red Branch" itself refers to a warrior band said to have been founded by Ross the Red of Ulster and led in the time of King Conchobar of Ulster by Cuchulainn, the greatest of the Irish heroes. The Red Branch warriors were the guardians of Ulster and have been compared to the Knights of the Round Table.

The extant textual sources for the Ulster Cycle include the 12th-century compilation known as the *Leabhar na hUidre*, commonly known as the "Book of the Dun Cow," and "The Book of Leinster," as well as in the late 14th century *Lebor Buide Lecain*, or "Yellow Book of Lecan." It is generally agreed that these later medieval literary versions of the cycle were based on much earlier oral forms. The oldest form of the Ulster Cycle as it is preserved is likely dated to the eighth century, and the verse passages it contains might be thought to be a century or two older; thus it might be posited that the oral tradition that transmitted these stories must have existed long before the literary one, antedating the extant texts by perhaps as much as the better part of 1,000 years.

The Irish Epic Hero: Cuchulainn, The Champion of Ulster[5]

The singular epic hero of the *Táin*, of the Ulster Cycle generally, and indeed of all medieval Irish literature is Cuchulainn, a warrior of super-human abilities and a man of prodigious appetites, a figure that, when viewed through the lens of heroic archetypes, embodies a great many of the mythic attributes that mark him as a cultural ideal. In the company of Lugh Lamfhota—named as Cuchulainn's father in the course of the *Táin* and himself usually identified as the central protagonist of tales concerning the Tuatha De Danann—as well as that of Fionn mac Cumhaill, the great hero of the Fenian Cycle, Cuchulainn is universally acknowledged as one of the three greatest figures of Irish mythology. Some argue that all three of these figures in fact emanate from a common source, a fount that has been linked by various scholars to, for example, the god equated with Mercury in the Gaul known to the classical world, the ancient Celtic deity Esus, or the ancient figure known to the Celts as Ogmios.

The Champion of Ulster displays a handful of pronounced associations with animals, most notably one with dogs; as Cuchulainn's very nick-name, which he earned early in his life, indicates, the great Irish hero displays a somewhat totemic identification with hounds. Furthermore, this connection is underscored in the hero's final, fatal conflict when he battles with his enemy Lugaid mac Con Roi, who is known as the "Son of Three Dogs." This battle proves disastrous for Cuchulainn in large measure because directly beforehand he had broken a great geis, or stricture, laid upon him that he never taste of the flesh of the hound. This hero also shows some notable relationships with ravens and other carrion birds, as well as with swans and waterfowl generally; the former association is a dark one, evoking as it does the warrior's prowess on the battlefield—through which he reaps a grim harvest upon which battle-scavengers might feed—and the hero's troubled relationship with several battle-goddesses and related shape-shifters prone to take on the forms of these birds. The latter relationship perhaps is evidenced most fully in the instance where his hunting of such prey results in his great wasting love-sickness. Moreover, like his epic Welsh counterpart Pryderi, Cuchulainn has a significant relationship with horses, and his two great battle-horses are foaled at the moment of the hero's birth.

The Genesis of the Fledgling Hound of Culann: The Irish Hero's Miraculous Conception and Superhuman Childhood Deeds

Known originally as Setanta, the great hero of medieval Irish mythology was the miraculous offspring of the great god Lugh, set apart from more ordinary heroes not merely by his divine conception but by his childhood deeds; his immense strength and prowess; his superhuman battle rage; the lust he incites in women, amazons, and goddesses alike; and the magnitude of the battles in which he fights and the tragedies that befall him. Begotten by Lugh, who, according to the version of the hero's conception recorded in the *Tain*, slipped into a sip of water consumed by Setanta's mother, Deichtine, and the boy was born prematurely when his mother became ill with shame. The god had impregnated the maiden without her knowledge, and she was too humiliated to share the bed of her betrothed, Sualtam mac Roich, while she carried in her womb the seed of another. Miraculously restored to virginity when she was delivered of her son, Deichtine went to live with her husband and Setanta went to be fostered in the royal court of Conchobar mac Nessa at Emain Macha. So great was the desire of each of the great Ulster heroes to foster the promising son of Deichtine that the lad had no fewer than seven fosterfathers, although Conchobar took primacy amongst them.

It was while he was yet within the care of Conchobar that, at the tender age of seven, Setanta earned the name by which he was evermore to be known. It happened one day that Conchobar and 50 chariots full of his heroes and champions were invited to a feast by Culann the Smith. Along the way, Conchobar stopped at the playing fields and gazed in wonder of the feats of prowess of Setanta, who competed against 150 other boys all at once and put them all to shame. Marveling at this lad's courage and fortitude, Conchobar invited him to join the guests at Culann's banquet. Setanta thanked the king kindly for this honor, but had not yet had his fill of sport, although he promised to follow Conchobar to the house of the smith just as soon as he finished. However, when Conchobar arrived at the feast, he forgot to tell Culann that the boy would arrive after him, and so the smith turned loose his huge and vicious hound, a watchdog so monstrous that it took three men holding each of three chains just to keep the beast at bay. The hound was turned loose, the gate barred, and thus Culann thought to keep his household and cattle safe for the night.

However, soon after the dog was released, the stripling lad Setanta arrived before the gates of Culann, casting and catching his hurling stick and ball in turn, and throwing his javelin well before him and racing to catch it before it touched the ground. The boy continued in this game as the hound rushed upon him, seeming to take no notice of the doom about to befall him. The revelers at Culann's feast watched in horror, sure that they could never reach the boy in time to save him. However, just as the dog leapt to destroy him, Setanta tossed aside his toys and grasped the hound with its throat in one hand and its back in the other. Most report that the lad reared up and cast the dog so hard against a standing-stone that it was killed instantly, its legs disjointed by the force of the impact. Others claim that the boy used his hurley stick to cast an iron ball into the gaping jaws of the beast so powerfully that its entrails flew out of its backside. Be that as it may, the dog was dead, and all rejoiced that the boy had saved himself, except for Culann, who mourned the loss of his hound that had faithfully and valiantly guarded the life, honor, household, and kine of his master. Grieving for the smith's loss, Setanta offered to raise with his own hands a replacement for the watchdog from a pup, and until that time vowed to serve as loyal guardian of the smith. Henceforth the young hero was called by the name Cathbad the Druid pronounced over him for his valorous deeds and noble words that day: He was known evermore as *Cuchulainn*, or the "Hound of Culann."

Cathbad's Prophesies of Cuchulainn: The Druidic Prediction of the Greatness of the Irish Hero

Cathbad was the premier druid of the court at Emain, a man of great learning from whom 100 students at a time learned druidic lore; some claim that Conchobar himself was the offspring of Cathbad. One day while Cuchulainn was yet a lad and not yet armed as a warrior, the Hound of Culann heard a student ask the great druid what wonders might befall on that given day. Cathbad answered that he who received his weapons for the first time that day would become a mighty hero indeed, his name would become the watchword for valor throughout all of Ireland, and the fame of his deeds would never die.

Cuchulainn went immediately to Conchobar and asked to be armed by him. The king asked by whose authority the young hero claimed this right, and Cuchulainn answered that he asked for his weapons in Cathbad's name. To this Conchobar assented, and he sent for 1 of the 15 sets of weapons he kept to honor new warriors or to replace worn arms. Standing in the midst of the hall, Cuchulainn received his shield and spear with such excitement and enthusiasm that he rattled them all to pieces. New weapons were brought, but each set was destroyed in turn until the king's own arms were granted to the lad. These withstood his fervor, and bedecked with these weapons Cuchulainn was well and truly accepted as a man. The hero reciprocated this honor by paying homage to his king: This he did by brandishing Conchobar's spear and pronouncing a blessing upon the subjects of such a generous ruler; he wished long life and posterity to them all.

At that moment Cathbad appeared in the hall, remarking that the lad before him seemed new to his arms. The king replied that this was indeed the case, and Cathbad bemoaned the fate of such a doomed young man. Conchobar, confused, asked if Cuchulainn had not been armed at Cathbad's own direction, and he was infuriated when the druid responded that he would never have condemned anyone to such a fate. Berated for deceiving the king, Cuchulainn recounted the prophesy he had heard uttered by the druid and stated that he claimed the right to be the greatest of Irish heroes. Cathbad acknowledged that this should be so, although at the cost of a life cut short. This was a bargain much to the hero's taste: A life of one single day would be enough and more, said Cuchulainn, to a hero whose fame would live forever.

Another time Cuchulainn overheard Cathbad speak of a similar doom: that whosoever mounted a chariot for the fist time that day would enjoy undying fame. Again the lad went to the king, asking this time for a chariot, which was granted to him. However, the first chariot broke beneath the mighty clasp of the hero's hand, as did each of 12 until Conchobar's own was placed beneath him, driven by Ibor, the king's own charioteer. The young hero performed many great deeds that day indeed, although he was still but seven years of age. By the time of the great battles of the *Tain*, Cuchulainn's favorite horse was *Liath Macha*, "Battle-Grey" or "Grey of Macha," and his chosen charioteer and loyal companion was Laeg. The weapons of his very own that Cuchulainn would carry in those latter days included his magical spear, the Gae Bolga, and his favorite sword, *Caladbolg*, "Hard-Striker," a lightning-blade carried by other Irish heroes, most notably Fergus mac Roich. Known in the Welsh tradition (perhaps most notably in *Culhwch and Olwen*) as Caledfwlch, this sword is often associated with King Arthur and is sometimes seen as the forebear of Excalibur.

The Superhuman Face of Cuchulainn: The Irish Hero's Warp Spasm and Salmon Leap

As the episode in which he gained his name indicates, although a ferocious adversary, Cuchulainn was possessed of what might be described as playful and perhaps even impish high spirits, and his looks, although always described in terms that seem somewhat awe-inspiring, never seem to have frightened women as much as they attracted them. Ordinarily Cuchulainn is described as relatively small and somewhat boyish in aspect, beardless and rather dark of complexion, with hair that grew brown out of his head, became reddish in the middle, and was blond on the ends. His appearance as well as his strength and prowess marked him as special: It is said that he had four dimples, each of a different color, on each side of his face, and that he had seven pupils in each eye, seven fingers on each hand, and seven toes on each foot. However, when he became enraged, Cuchulainn underwent a violent physical change usually termed his "warp spasm," through which his body manifested the volatile power that set him apart from lesser heroes. Moreover, the battle-howl of the Hound of Culann was so hideous and awe-inspiring that the very demons of the air would join the hero in an unearthly and horrifying chorus.

Even as a young boy, Cuchulainn was prone to become incited by his battle rage, as when he first came upon the boy troop of Conchobar as they went about their games on the great plain of Emain. This boy troop was comprised of the 150 most likely young lads in Ulster, and their games were a sight to behold: It was said that the king spent a third of each day watching the burgeoning prowess of the lads of the boy troop, a third at the royal game of fidchell, and a third enjoying his ale until sleep overtook him. On the day that Cuchulainn first came upon the boy troop, he knew nothing of the ancient rite of seeking the protection of the troop before entering the field, and so the boys turned upon him, little boy that he seemed, and their hurley sticks, iron balls, and javelins rained upon his wee wattled toy shield. However, Cuchulainn was more than a match for the boy troop, even at that tender age, catching the javelins in the sticks of his shield, dodging or batting at the passing hurley sticks, and allowing the balls to bounce off of his chest. Finally the lad got his dander up, and as the battle-rage took him, his appearance became terrifying to behold. Each hair stood on end as though it were an iron nail hammered into his head, and sparks flew from each. He squinted one orb up so small that it might be the eye of a needle, whereas the other bulged from his head like the mouth of a tankard. His lips pulled back from his teeth, and he showed his slavering jaws from ear to ear, his mouth open so wide that he exposed his gullet. Finally, a great fist of gleaming horn bulged out from his forehead. Thus horrifically transfigured, the young hero rushed upon the boy troop, routing them immediately, striking a third of them to the ground and putting the rest to flight. However, the intervention of Conchobar put an end to the conflict, and a good-natured Cuchulainn offered to the boy troop the protection he himself had failed to ask of them.

The Hound of Culann's miraculous and horrifying transformation is known as the *riastrad*, or "warp spasm," the heroic, superhuman contortions through which, not unlike a berserkr of the Norse tradition, battle rage possesses the great champion to such an extent that his body is literally reshaped in the process. In a dramatic explosion of shape-shifting that would emasculate all but the most courageous of opponents, the great Irish hero was rendered monstrous in aspect and nearly impenetrable to wounds inflicted by the hands of even the greatest of mortal warriors. This transformation culminated in a gloomy cloud of gore-mist formed from the froth of a column of blood spurting forth from the head of the hero and captured in the gleam of the *lon laith*, "heroic effulgence," the sort of fist-sized shining horn of power that jutted out of Cuchulainn's forehead; this horn denoted that the hero overflowed with battle-might and was prepared to do combat, and perhaps even evoked an ancient horn image hearkening back to the vast powers of Cernunnos himself.

If the *lon laith* might be said to mark Cuchulainn as more than mortal through its resonance with the signature attributes of the Horned God as well as with its bestial connotations of power and potency, so might the hero's mighty "salmon-leap" be said to evoke the mystical connotations and raw physical strength of the salmon, the majestic king of all fish that generally evokes an aura of magic, wisdom, and power in Irish folklore and mythology—medieval or modern. Cuchulainn's mighty salmon-leap is described in terms that suggest an acrobatic maneuver of the ancient battle field perhaps akin to the nearly incredible aerial flips and spins sometimes seen upon the modern soccer pitch: Both beggar imagination and seem at times indistinguishable from independent flight. The power and grace of the salmon-leap was such that, even in the midst of his warp spasm, Cuchulainn could spring halfway across a river to the fulcrum point of a teeter-totter trick bridge, or spring lightly into a great yew tree to place the point of his sword delicately between the breasts of an Amazon, both of which feats he performed to gain entry to the Scottish stronghold of Scathach and to force this great mistress of war craft to take him as her pupil.

The Trophies of Cuchulainn: The Irish Hero as Headhunter

The ancient Celtic practice of headhunting is well attested in the classical literary record, and medieval Irish mythology amply corroborates this evidence. Moreover, in the person of the great Irish hero Cuchulainn we are presented with a figure who represents a cultural ideal, and it is thus of particular interest to note that, amongst his very many great childhood feats and preadolescent adventures, we are informed that Cuchulainn took heads of the enemies of Ulster before his eighth birthday. After fulfilling the Prophesy of Cathbad by mounting Conchobar's chariot on an auspicious day, Cuchulainn commanded Conchobar's driver Ibor to take him in pursuit of adventure. After having greeted the boy troop of Conchobar, who paused in their sports to grant their blessing to their comrade, Cuchulainn and Ibor traveled to the very frontier of the province at Sliab Fuait, where they met Conall Cernach, the Ulsterman assigned the duty of greeting wandering poets and vanquishing possible raiders. Each man in Conchobar's war band took his turn at this duty, and so Emain was well protected from enemies and well provided with verse. Cuchulainn offered to spell the older warrior at this duty, but Conall was no shirker. It was not until the young hero shattered the wheel of Conall's chariot, seemingly in sport, that the border guard agreed to return to Emain, leaving Cuchulainn to patrol the far marches of Conchobar. The young hero spent his time there well, and from the viewpoint of *Finncarn*, the "white mound" atop Sliab Mondairn, Ibor named for him all of the ancient forts, streams, and fords in the region. They also saw from their vantage point the three sons of Nechta Scene—Fannell, Foill, and Tuchell—who had slain between them as many Ulstermen as walked the Earth in the time of Cuchulainn. These three enemies of Ulster thought to vanquish a little lad like Cuchulainn easily, but they were in error: Soon their three bodies lay lifeless gushing blood, and their three heads, trophies testifying to the valor and prowess of Cuchulainn, hung from his hand by the hair. The boy hero vowed not to set down his trophies until he reentered the court of Conchobar, although he did pause in the journey home long enough to catch eight live birds and a live wild stag to provide a fitting retinue for his triumphant return to Emain Macha. Still in the grips of his blood-lust, Cuchulainn would have wrought destruction even within the walls of Conchobar had not the queen sent forth her ladies bare-breasted to embarrass and inflame the boy in another manner. As the lad stood stock-still, covering his eyes, red-faced and confused as a result of this ploy, the king's men seized him, plunging him successively into three great vats of icy water: the first burst, the second boiled, and the third warmed. Cuchulainn thus returned to Emain Macha the seven-year-old Champion of Ulster with the heads of his enemies.

The Love-Quest of Cuchulainn: The Irish Hero Woos His Bride

It came to pass as Cuchulainn grew to manhood that the warriors of Ulster began to worry about the honor of their wives and daughters, so great was the prowess of the young hero, and so desirable did he seem to all of the womenfolk who looked upon him. It was decided that a man married to one woman would be less likely to look for opportunities to corrupt the virtue of all of the other women who desired him. Furthermore, there was the threat that Cuchulainn would die young and leave no heir, and all agreed that it would be a tragedy if the cream of Ulster manhood did not leave a son behind him. Conchobar therefore determined to seek a wife for the Hound of Culann, and to this end he sent nine men to search the length and breadth of Ireland, to comb every stronghold and settlement in every province, and to seek out the eligible daughters of every chieftain and landholder in the hopes of finding a woman suitable for Cuchulainn. A year passed in this endeavor, but in vain: No such bride was found.

Meanwhile, the great hero of Ulster went about his own business with little concern for the fears of others, and one day he sought out *Luglochta Loga*, the aptly named "Cradle (or 'Garden') of Lugh," the stronghold of Forgall *Monach*, known as the "Wily," the father of two daughters. Forgall wished to marry off the elder daughter first, but Cuchulainn favored the younger, named Emer. The girl and her friends sat outside of the fortress upon the grass, practicing their embroidery. Cuchulainn and Emer greeted each other courteously and then flirted in the form of riddles. Spying the maiden's nubile bosom beneath the yoke of her dress, the warrior let Emer know that he planned to rest his weapon in the fair and fertile country of which he had caught a glimpse. The girl answered cunningly with a series of feats of prowess a man would have to complete before he might tread those virgin fields. Cuchulainn was well pleased with her terms and reckoned it as easily said as done. The lovers parted with an understanding between them. Emer's friends, for their parts, told their fathers of this bantering talk and of its deeper meaning, and these men let Forgall know that his younger daughter had a suitor before her elder sister had a husband.

Moreover, Forgall feared the unpredictable battle rage of Cuchulainn and predicted that, should the great hero marry his daughter, he himself would meet his doom. Therefore, Emer's father decided upon an elaborate ruse: Disguised as a Gaulish emissary, Forgall arrived in the court of Conchobar where he was feted and given the honor of observing the great heroes of Ulster, whose exploits were commended to him. The visiting

Gaul allowed that the warriors were fierce and skilled, but he added that the greatest among them, Cuchulainn, would only achieve the ultimate greatness to which he seemed destined if he traveled to Scotland to study under *Domnall Mildemail*, the "Wide-Ruling Warlike One." Better yet, he should seek in that land across the sea the training camp of Scathach, the unparalleled mistress of war craft. This he suggested because such an undertaking would be so arduous that the young hero was unlikely to return to claim the hand of Emer. For his part, Cuchulainn readily agreed to seek out such training and pledged to depart at once. Well pleased with this result, Forgall departed. Cuchulainn then sought out his true love before he left for Alba. Emer informed him of her father's treachery and bid him to beware. They then pledged their troth and promised to remain chaste, and Cuchulainn departed for Scotland, where he first learned all that Domnall had to teach him and then sought the camp of Scathach.

During Cuchulainn's absence, his foster-brother Lugaid mac Nois came with 12 princes from Munster into the vicinity of Luglochta Loga seeking brides for them all. The maidens they sought had already pledged their troths to others, but, seizing this opportunity to rid himself of the worry of Cuchulainn, Forgall offered Emer to Lugaid and her 12 handmaids to his compatriots, and the Munster men were pleased to accept. However, at the wedding, Emer publicly declared her love for and betrothal to Cuchulainn and claimed the protection of the Hound of Culann. She bade Lugaid to beware of besmirching her honor and his foster-brother's, a brazen act of infamy that would assuredly lead to bloodshed. Terrified, Lugaid did not attempt to violate the maiden, and he returned to his home without a bride.

Returning to Ireland after his training in all of the arts of war, Cuchulainn wasted no time in seeking the company of his beloved. However, when he reached the stronghold of Forgall, he found his entrance barred and the way so well protected that after an entire year he still had yet to catch a glimpse of Emer. It was then that the temper of the greatest of Irish heroes began to flare, and he well and truly began his assault upon the fortress. He mounted his chariot of the dread sickle, and hundreds fell as a result of his thunder attack. A great triple salmon-leap took him into the heart of the fort, where he slew three groups of eight opponents with each stroke, sparing thereby only the three brothers of his promised bride. Meanwhile, Forgall brought his own dire prophecy to fruition, falling to an ignominious death as he fled before the wrath of the hero. Gathering to his bosom his beloved Emer and her foster-sister, as well as their combined weight in booty of gold and silver, Cuchulainn left Luglochta Loga in the manner by which he had gained entrance—using the salmon-leap as though he bore no burdens at all. Forgall's ally Scenmenn fell before the hero at the ford that now bears the doomed man's name, as did 100 more followers of Forgall at each succeeding ford. Cuchulainn slew so many of the pursuing army upon the great white plain that it became a hill of bloody sod.

Finally the hero and his companions reached Emain Macha, after Cuchulainn had performed all of the feats of courage he had pledged to Emer, as well as many more. However, a new challenge lay before the hero: It was the custom of the court that Conchobar himself should take the virginity of all of the maidens of Ulster. Cuchulainn's rage and shame at this suggestion was so great that he rushed from the hall, and all there present feared that the evening could not but end in slaughter and woe. However, Conchobar and the chief druid were equal to this dilemma. First the king sent his hero to gather the herds of wild beasts and the flocks of wild birds, and when Cuchulainn returned from this task his fury had dissipated. Next, Cathbad and Fergus slept in the same bed as Conchobar and Emer and ensured that Cuchulainn's honor was maintained. The next day all of Ulster blessed the union of their greatest hero and his bride, and Conchobar himself gave Cuchulainn Emer's bride price.

The Wasting Illness of Cuchulainn: The Irish Hero's Journey to the Otherworld

One Samain the heroes of Conchobar were gathered on the plain at the confluence of the River Boyne and the Irish Sea. A flock of beautiful birds settled upon the water nearby, and the magnificence of these fowl was so great that it soon came to pass that each aristocratic woman of Ulster desired two of the birds, one to perch on each slender shoulder. Cuchulainn set himself the task of fulfilling the desire of all of the ladies of the court, but when he had captured and distributed all of the birds he was shamed to discover that he had none left for his own wife. He promised Emer that he would make up for this oversight by gifting her with a pair of birds more charming than all those he had snared up to that point. These two were beautiful, to be sure, but they were also marvelous in two wonderful ways: A golden chain linked them, and they had the power to bring sleep with their song. As the hero hunted this quarry he managed to come close to the mark, scratching the birds slightly with his spear, but even this minor contact with the birds released a potent magic, and Cuchulainn soon fell into an enchanted slumber while leaning against a standing stone. While he slept, the hero dreamt that he was approached by two women of surpassing beauty, one robed in scarlet, and the other in emerald. These two ladies began to whip the prostrate hero, at first in seeming jest, but steadily with more vigor until at last they were scourging him mercilessly. More of the superhuman power and vigor of the Champion of Ulster was wasted from his body with each succeeding blow, until, when he awoke, he had not even the strength to stand. In this wretched state the hero was carried back to Emain, where he languished throughout the winter, spring, and summer until it was once again the season of Samain.

As the fall festival approached, a mysterious stranger sought out the invalid Cuchulainn, offering to heal the hero if he would only return to the visitor's home, where Fand, the most beautiful of women, pined for the stricken warrior. Cuchulainn had himself carried back to the standing stone where he had fallen ill, and here he was visited by the verdant woman of his vision, who claimed to seek to do him no more harm, and who indeed, made him an attractive offer: If Cuchulainn would agree to battle the enemies of the Green Lady's husband for one day, he would enjoy the favors of that lord's sister Fand, who had been released from her nuptial vows to Manannan mac Lir especially so that she might offer herself to the Hound of Culann. Because the hero was still too ill to travel, he sent the faithful Laeg in his stead, and the charioteer accompanied the Green Lady to her homeland on a brazen boat. Fand and her brother were crestfallen not to meet Cuchulainn himself, but the impression they made upon Laeg was so positive that, upon his return, he encouraged the hero to visit them himself. Meanwhile, Emer chided her husband for losing his virility through love-sickness, and called upon him to rise from his illness. Cuchulainn did so, and he found that he had regained his strength in full.

The following Samain the hero once more visited the standing stone where he had been struck down, and here again he met the Green Lady, who again invited him to visit her land. Anxious not to fall under the sway of the love-sickness of which his wife had accused him, Cuchulainn thought to reject the seductive allure of the rewards the woman offered him and again sent Laeg in his place. This time the charioteer made the journey by land, and upon his return he informed the warrior that only the most foolish of men would deny himself the pleasure of a sojourn with Fand in her brother's marvelous kingdom. The hero now agreed to make the trip with Laeg and the Green Lady, and Fand and her brother greeted him with joy and gratitude. That night the hero scouted the enemy's position, keeping solitary watch until daybreak, when he was transformed through battle rage into the form wrought by his warp spasm. His ferocity was such that he needed to be thrice dunked in a vessel of icy water. The Hound of Culann dispatched the enemies of Fand's brother, taking his reward in that lady's own amorous gratitude. For a full month Cuchulainn and Fand made love without respite.

At the end of their time of passion, as the hero took his leave from his mistress, the two lovers agreed to tryst at the foot of a certain great yew tree. Unfortunately, Emer discovered Cuchulainn's infidelity shortly before the scheduled meeting and determined to thwart the lovers' liaison and to avenge her wounded pride upon the person of her husband's paramour. Taking with her 50 women with razor-sharp knives to hack her rival into pieces, Emer's lust for vengeance came to a sudden and unlikely conclusion when all three sides of this love triangle sought to end the affair: Cuchulainn, immensely moved by his wife's lament that husbands are faithless to their wives precisely because they always seek the new and different at the cost of the known and familiar, determined to rededicate himself to his wife and be forever true to her; Fand, for her part, was touched by the deep love between Emer and her husband and decided to renounce her relationship with Cuchulainn; Emer, in turn, overcome by Fand's selfless sacrifice, offered to grant her husband his freedom so that the two lovers could be together. Just as each of the women was attempting to sacrifice her own happiness for that of the other, Fand's husband reappeared, took back his wife, and shook his cloak between the parted lovers, thus enacting a spell that guaranteed that they would never see one another again. Inconsolable, Cuchulainn wandered the wastes without food or drink until given a druidic potion that caused him to forget his loss. For her part, Emer was given the same elixir so that she might not remember her jealousy.

The concept of shape-shifters and gods taking the shape of swans and similar birds is a commonplace of medieval Irish myth; often ornaments of gold or silver, as in this case, mark these supernatural figures. Moreover, Cuchulainn's journey to and adventures in the otherworld, along with the relationships he develops with the ruler thereof and with that ruler's wife and sister, have some resonance with Pwyll's journey to and quest in Annwn in the First Branch of the Welsh *Mabinogion*. Cuchulainn, of course, consummates the relationship with the goddess he meets in the otherworld, whereas Pwyll's restraint from such intimate congress—a self-control that clearly shocks and impresses his host—has more in common with Conchobar's heavily chaperoned "first night" with Cuchulainn's betrothed Emer. Meanwhile, Fand and Cuchulainn's tryst point under the great yew tree, and the entire otherworldly lover theme it represents, as well as the emphasis on a specific time of year—Samain, a time when the portals between the mortal and magical worlds are most permeable—calls to mind similar scenarios in several medieval romances, perhaps most notably that in *Sir Orfeo*.

The Great Weapon of Cuchulainn: The Irish Hero Unleashes the Gae Bolga

The greatest skill Cuchulainn mastered under the tutelage of the great mistress of war craft was the secret use of the mysterious *Gae Bolga*, or "Spear of Lightning," a magical weapon of devastating power that he is said to have received from the hands of the great matron of warfare herself. Although a few times mentioned in the possession of other heroes, Cuchulainn is the figure most often associated with this great weapon. The curse inherent in such terrifying and unnatural potency is perhaps reflected in the fact that the two greatest battle scenes in which the Hound of Culann unleashes the hellish force of this supernatural shaft end in tragedy for the Irish hero himself, who slays, in turn, his son and his best friend. In these episodes we are informed in extensive detail how each of these victims dies an extended and horribly painful death as a result of the nature of the Gae Bolga: Entering the body in one place, like a bolt of forking lightning the head of this mystical spear would explode into thirty separate wounds within the body cavity of its victim, effectively disemboweling the opponent from within. Moreover, the weapon could only be removed by cutting each part of the head out, an incredibly painful extrication destined to drain any remaining life out of the victim of the attack. There is no recorded defense against the Gae Bolga, which seems in Cuchulainn's hands to have been a weapon of last resort. Cast from "the fork of the foot," that is to say, from between the toes, this weapon seems to have been used exclusively in fords, streams, or other bodies of water, a coincidence that may suggest a limitation of the shaft's power that could stem from the origin of the weapon, which some say was wrought from the bones of a great sea-monster, defeated in battle with a larger rival. The Gae Bolga thus evokes the powers and the terrors of sea-monsters and of thunder gods; perhaps such a combination of images might best be envisioned in the flash of many-pronged thunderbolts striking the surface of the sea in a manner that recalls the cataclysmic power of the weapon, whereas the concurrent thunderclaps might be thought to echo the clash of undersea leviathans through which the shaft came to be made.

The Tragic Pride of Cuchulainn: The Irish Hero Kills His Only Son

When Aife had announced to Cuchulainn that she had conceived the son he had demanded of her, she had vowed to send the boy in search of his father in exactly seven years and had asked the hero for a name for their child. Cuchulainn had instructed Aife to call the boy Connla and to give the lad a golden ring he pulled from his own thumb when Connla's own hand should grow large enough to wear it. Three commands Cuchulainn had laid upon his unborn son: that the lad reveal his name to none, that he make way for none, and that he refuse a fight to none. With these words Cuchulainn had left Aife for the camp of Scathach, and soon he had returned home to Ireland. Seven years to the day after Cuchulainn had pronounced these conditions, Connla followed his father's path to Ulster.

On the day that the lad was crossing over to Ireland, the men of Ulster had gathered near the shore and noted from a long way off a boy in a bronze boat with golden oars. The child had brought a pile of stones with him, and these he used to stun sea birds, which he then let escape after they regained their senses. As the birds ascended into the sky, the boy struck them down again, this time by putting his face between his hands and modulating his voice in such a way that he could immobilize or revitalize the birds at will. When Conchobar saw this he was struck with fear, because any country that produced such a lad was likely to be comprised of men of immense power; the king therefore sent Condere mac Echach to meet the boy with the command to seek his name and business and to refuse him leave to land. Condere was a man of discretion and moderate words, and he asked the visitor's identity politely; however, the boy declined, stating that he would give no man his name and declaring that even if Condere's strength should increase a hundredfold he would stand no chance of hindering the boy's approach. Condere returned to Conchobar and reported what had transpired, and the king then sent Conall Cernach to stop the lad. However, before the mighty warrior could raise his hand against the boy, the lad had stunned Conall with the thunderous blast from a stone slung high into the sky, and in a blink of an eye the hapless hero found himself hog-tied with a shield strap. Conall called to the Ulstermen to send forth another champion, but the whole army was put to shame.

At this point Cuchulainn advanced in fury, performing all manner of battle-feats as he advanced. Emer his wife discerned the truth of Connla's identity and tried, with impassioned words of reason and moderation, to dissuade Cuchulainn from killing his own son, but the Hound of Culann would give no quarter where the honor of Ulster was at risk, no matter whom he might slay; indeed, as the blood-lust overcame him, the great hero chanted a verse declaiming how his own body would be flushed with power by the destruction of such a fine young warrior as Connla had proven to be. When he came upon the boy, Cuchulainn commanded that the lad render him his name or his life, but—true to the strictures his father had laid upon him—Connla refused. Then they rushed upon each other, and Cuchulainn seemed at some disadvantage: First the boy showed his skill with a blade by shearing his father's hair with a single blow; second, they went to wrestle, and although the lad had to climb upon standing stones to be able to grasp his father to throw him, this he did three times, pushing down with such power that the stones bear his footprints to this day; and third, the pair rolled into the sea to drown one another, and the lad ducked his father twice in a row. Finally, Cuchulainn thought to put an end to this upstart, and he cast the Gae Bolga deep into the boy's guts so that the bowels poured out and piled around his feet.

As Connla writhed in his death throes, Cuchulainn carried him up to the Ulstermen and presented the lad to them as his son. Connla then spoke the prophesy that, had he been given five years to reach his full growth amongst the heroes of Ulster, no warrior might have withstood his attack, and Conchobar would have ruled even so far as Rome. However, with death upon him, the lad asked for the embrace of each famous warrior in the company and died as he bid his famous father farewell. The people of Ulster mourned his death with a loud keening, and after a stone had been set above his tomb no calf was allowed to suckle upon its mother for three full days and nights, such was the grief of Conchobar's warriors. The horrible tragedy of a heroic young son's death at his father's hands, the conditions of single combat, the issues of honor and restrictions of behavior, and the concept of enforced anonymity all link this episode with that of Rostam and Sohrab, a father and son who duel to the death in the great medieval Persian mythic cycle known as the *Shahname*.

The Divine Father of Cuchulainn: The Great God Lugh Heals the Irish Hero

In the midst of the struggles of the *Tain Bo Cuailnge*, at a site hard by the grave mound at Lerga, Cuchulainn's wounds were grievous and his heart was heavy. However, just as his spirits dipped to their lowest point, Laeg called out to the Hound of Culann that he was gifted with the most wondrous vision: Out of the northeast a lone man approached, clad in a cloak of green clasped in silver and girt in red silk embroidered with gold. In his hands he held a forked javelin and a spear with a head of five points. His shield was black with a gold boss, and he performed fearsome feats as he came, although none of those within sight of his route paid him any heed at all. Cuchulainn realized that the warrior must be invisible to everyone else and therefore was likely to be a sympathetic member of the race of the Sidhe, come to offer the great warrior aid in his hour of need. These words turned out to be prophetic, because the mysterious stranger, after exchanging greetings with Cuchulainn, identified himself as the hero's father, Lugh mac Ethnenn, a lord of the Sidhe. He commanded the lad to sleep for three days and nights, assuring him that he himself would face all enemies in Cuchulainn's stead until the hero awoke refreshed and healed of his wounds. Lugh then sang a magic chant over his son, put him into a charmed slumber, and cleaned and healed all of the hero's wounds with an infusion of grasses and herbs. The Hound of Culann then slept deeply and rested well after his many hurts and unceasing labor; indeed, it was hardly surprising if the warrior were weary because the hero had hardly closed his eyes from Samain until Imbolc. When he woke he was refreshed, invigorated, and prepared to do battle, but he was shamed and grieved to learn that, during his stupor, the boy troop of Conchobar had marched from Emain to lend aid to the Hound of Culann, only to be slaughtered one and all. Cuchulainn wasted no time on tears but called for his chariot, anxious to reenter the fray, enraged by the loss of his friends but revitalized through the ministrations of his divine father.

Medb Brings Sorrow to Cuchulainn: The Irish Hero Slays His Sworn Blood-Brother

The entire cataclysmic conflict of the *Tain Bo Cuailnge* might well be said to have been the result of the pride and willfulness of Medb. However, just as she caused dissension on a great scale that rocked all of Ireland, such were the wiles of Ailill's wife, and so great her love of brewing trouble among men that she was able to sow strife even between the closest of friends. Indeed, the Queen of Connacht managed to pit her chief nemesis Cuchulainn himself against his own beloved blood-brother *Fer Diad Conganchness*, the "Horn-Skinned Man of Smoke." The horn-skinned hero and the Hound of Culann had perfected their arts under the tutelage of Scathach, and they had vowed eternal friendship and brotherhood. The two were in fact nearly evenly matched in skills and strength, although Ferdiad had not the secret of the Gae Bolga. When the men of Ireland arrayed against the Hound of Culann sought another champion to stand against the great hero of Ulster, they chose Cuchulainn's blood-brother, the only warrior in that entire island well matched against Conchobar's favorite. That this Ferdiad was lacking in the skills of the Gae Bolga was, so they thought, counterbalanced by the nearly impenetrable armor of his horny hide.

When Medb first sent messengers to seek the aid of the horn-skinned hero he shunned her advances and refused to accompany these ambassadors back to the court of their queen. However, not to be out-foxed, Medb changed her tact and sent forth minstrels, poets, and bards to shame and humiliate Ferdiad, lamenting the cowardice and lack of manly virtue that caused him, so they implied, to fear and avoid conflict with the more virile Cuchulainn. Few could assess the vanity and weakness of a man more ably than she of the friendly thighs, and this stratagem soon bore fruit: The man of smoke sought the tent of Medb and Ailill, and the fair daughter of Medb herself, *Finnabair*, the "Fair-Browed One," served him with her own hands, filling his cup with drink, his mouth with kisses, and his ears with tender words of love; a true daughter of her mother, Finnabair—whose name is cognate with that of the seductive Guinevere of the Arthurian tradition as well as with those of that queen's Welsh and Cornish counterparts—went so far as to tempt the horny-skinned one with fair and succulent apples that she offered to him suggestively, from the gaping neckline of her dress.

When Ferdiad was thus well plied, Medb came to the point, offering in exchange for Cuchulainn's head slaves, land, war gear and a chariot, treasure and freedom forever from taxes or tribute, all with Finnabair for a wife and even—should the hero require it—Medb's own sexual favors in addition to everything else. However, when Ferdiad still refused, Medb once more pressed her advantage in his weak spot, implying that the Hound of Culann himself had boasted that defeating his blood-brother would be a matter of little consequence or honor. Again, the horn-skinned one's armor proved no match for a skillful attack upon his reputation, and they soon came to terms: Ferdiad demanded all that Mebd had offered, witnessed and bonded by six great champions against whom would be pitted whichever of the two parties dared to renege on the agreement. So did the horn-skinned hero determine to seek his own sworn brother's head.

Fergus mac Roich, hearing of Ferdiad's decision, rode to Cuchulainn to tell him to expect his blood brother in all his wrath the next day. All who loved those two grieved that one or both would surely die in the conflict. The Hound of Culann and the horned-skinned warrior met at the ford the next day, where they broke off their friendship. Thus began a three-day battle in which each fought the other to a stand-still, wounding one another in equal measure and embracing every nightfall and sharing equally the food and medicine sent to each. Finally, Ferdiad agreed to fight in the water of the ford, although he knew that this played to his opponent's strength. However, the horned-skinned one fought like a demon, and the Hound of Culann was saved only by the timely insults of his loyal charioteer Laeg, which cunningly caused the Warped One to rise up in his battle rage. In the end, Cuchulainn called for the Gae Bolga, and although Ferdiad tried desperately to defend himself, it was a lost cause: No man was safe from that dread weapon, even behind a skin of horn. Thus Cuchulainn was forced, through the malice and treachery of Medb, to slay Ferdiad, his own sworn blood-brother, whose death the hero mourned deeply.

The Heroic Demise of Cuchulainn: The Irish Hero Dies Standing

Cuchulainn's death is recounted in different ways in various sources, but two of the most famous strands of the story share in common the theme that the hero took great pains to ensure that he would die standing up. In one version of the story of the end of the Hound of Culann, Medb seeks to avenge the dishonor and insults heaped upon her by the hero in the course of the *Tain*. The great warrior is lured through various wiles arranged by Medb to a hopeless battle wherein his mount and companions are slain and he himself is mortally wounded. Seeking an honorable death on his feet, Cuchulainn ties himself to a standing stone, and his enemies fear to approach even the corpse of such a champion until they are assured that he is well and truly dead. This assurance is provided by a great black carrion bird, which mounts the body, some say to drink deeply the fluid of his eyes. Others suggest that this bird is the Morrigan, come to savor the dying breaths of the great hero who mortally insulted her. Some claim the goddess watched in ecstasy as an otter drank the dying hero's life-blood.

According to some sources, Medb accomplishes her vengeance through the agency of the children of Cuchulainn's old enemy, the monstrous sorcerer Cailitin. This wizard wrought havoc through a corporate warrior "body" made up of himself and his 27 deformed and diabolical offspring who never missed with their devilishly accurate and deadly toxic javelins. Known collectively as the Clan Cailitin, this war band was completely wiped out by Cuchulainn, although they quite nearly killed him first.

However, soon after the death of Cailitin and his brood, the wizard's widow whelped six more of his demon seed, and these monstrous children are those who were trained in black magic by Medb as they grew to maturity and bided their time until an opportunity arose to put to death the slayer of their father and older siblings. When this occasion came about, the children of Cailitin used their powers as shape-shifters to dupe and endanger Cuchulainn. Foremost amongst this group was Badb, who according to some readings of the death of the hero took upon herself the iconic form of the crow as she alit upon the shoulder of the dying hero.

In another iteration of the tale of the demise of the great Irish hero, the version that is perhaps the most famous, drawn from the text commonly known in English as "The Death of Cuchulainn," his death comes about when Cuchulainn breaks the geis—or stricture laid upon him—that he never eat the flesh of a dog. In this tale, the Hound of Culann tastes the forbidden flesh of a roasted dog, which is offered to him by three hideous hags. Cuchulainn, having supped upon the food forbidden to him, is confronted by his old nemesis Lugaid mac Con Roi, who is also known as *mac Tri Con*, or "Son of Three Dogs." The three hounds in question are usually identified as the Hound of Culann, Conall Cernach (who is known as "Wolf-Strong"), and Cu Roi. Lugaid desires to put an end to Cuchulainn throughout the *Tain*, although he is not able to enact his vengeance upon the Champion of Ulster until after the events of that great cattle raid are played out. It is generally believed that this animosity was a result of Cuchulainn's adultery with Lugaid's mother, who conspired with the Hound of Culann in her husband's death. In their final battle Lugaid disembowels the great Irish hero with his spear, although he allows his old enemy the dignity of tying himself upright to a standing stone before he dies. Lugaid then moves in and takes the hero's head, a trophy that avails him little because Conall Cernach soon returns the favor.

The term *geis* generally refers to a sacred prohibition or requirement, often associated with a druidic prophecy; in some cases such gessa take forms akin to curses or other magical words of power. The flouting of a geis most often results in instant death, destruction, or great sorrow of the hero himself or that of his people. Gessa are generally associated with the greatest kings and heroes of the Irish tradition, and the sanctions upon rulers, in particular, may suggest that the geis traces its origins to rites and requirements of sacral kingship; indeed, the Sovranty figure is regularly associated with gessa, often in her trademark disguise of a wizened crone. In such cases the old woman generally plays a guessing game with the hapless hero, who, when he loses, is set a seemingly unattainable quest as a geis. This trope traveled from the Celtic fringe into the heart of medieval European literature through the medium of the Romance; perhaps the best-known challenge of this type is set to the young knight in Chaucer's *Wife of Bath's Tale*.

In sum, then, nearly all commentators seem to agree that the Hound of Culann had earned Medb's undying enmity through his humiliation of her during the course of the *Tain*, and it is likewise commonly accepted that the Morrigan, enraged by Cuchulainn's rejection of her sexual advances and subsequent harsh treatment of her in that same text, also finds special savor in the hero's demise. Moreover, it is often suggested that it is this self-same spurned battle-goddess in her characteristic form of a raven, who marks the advent of the hero's death at the moment when she could safely perch upon him. However, sometimes this winged specter is said to be the Morrigan's doppelganger Badb, avenging her father and brothers, who died at the great hero's hand. Moreover, in some sources such a black-feathered harbinger of death adds insult to injury by pecking the fluid from the dead warrior's eyes. However, although the details vary somewhat from source to source, in most of these cases it is apparent that the Hound of Culann, the hero formerly known as Setanta, died as he had lived, heroically and stoically facing down his enemies alone and on his own two feet.

Notes

1. For critical commentary on and analysis of the sources of Celtic mythology, see especially Ellis, *Celtic*, 3–12; Ellis, *Irish*, 6–11; Fee 63–64; Gantz 1–25; Green, *Gods*, 7–17; Green, *Myths*, 7–14; Green, *World*, 465–488; Jones ix–xxix; Kinsella ix; Lindahl 63–66, 212–217, 369–375, 429–432; MacKillop xvi–xix, 109, 125, 185–187, 259–262, 301, 372–374; Maier 204–205; and Smyth 11–14.

2. For critical commentary on and analysis of the Celtic archaeological record, see especially Green, *Gods*, 7–14, 17–22; and Green, *World*, 465–472, 473–481.

3. For critical commentary on and analysis of the Mythological Cycle, see especially Ellis, *Celtic*, 81, 129; Ellis, *Irish*, 87, 144; Fee 169; Green, *Gods*, 16; Green, *Myths*, 9; Green, *World*, 481; Jones ix–xxix; Kinsella ix–xvi; Lindahl 63–66, 212–217, 369–375, 429–432; MacKillop xvi–xix, 43–44, 109, 125, 185–187, 259–262, 301, 372–374; Maier 94–95, 168; and Smyth 11–14. For critical commentary on and analysis of the Fenian Cycle, see especially Ellis, *Celtic*, 96; Ellis, *Irish*, 116; Fee 175–176; Green, *Gods*, 16; Green, *Myths*, 10, 20; Lindahl 131–133; MacKillop 1–2, 185–187, 317; Maier 118, 218–219; and

Smyth 11–14. For critical commentary on and analysis of the Historical Cycle (also known as the Cycle of the Kings) as well as concerning the Dalcassian Cycle, see especially Fee 177–181; Lindahl 215–216; MacKillop 50–51, 81, 109, 113, 119, 251; Maier 148–149; and Smyth 11–14.

4. For critical commentary on and analysis of the Ulster (or Red Branch) Cycle, see especially Ellis, *Celtic*, 185; Ellis, *Irish*, 199; Fee 170–175; Gantz 24–25; Green, *Gods*, 15–16; Green, *Myths*, 9–10, 21; Green, *World*, 481–482; Kinsella ix–xvi; Lindahl 418–419; MacKillop 372–374, 380; Maier 276; and Smyth 11–14.

5. For critical commentary on and analysis of the great epic hero of the Irish tradition, see especially Ellis, *Celtic*, 70–71; Ellis, *Irish*, 71–73; Fee 119, 170–175; Green, *Gods*, 31, 101, 120, 187, 188; Green, *Myths*, 17, 23–28, 59, 61, 71; Green, *World*, 426, 783; MacKillop 61, 64–65, 91, 102–104, 129–130, 160–161, 188–189, 200–201, 213, 217, 221, 239, 268, 273, 275, 329, 333, 338–339, 370; Maier 85–86, 115, 124, 247; and Smyth 41–46.

Sources and Further Reading

Ellis, Peter Berresford. *Dictionary of Celtic Mythology*. New York: Oxford University Press, 1994.

Ellis, Peter Berresford. *A Dictionary of Irish Mythology*. Oxford reference. Oxford: Oxford University Press, 1991.

Fee, Christopher R., with David A. Leeming. *Gods, Heroes, & Kings: The Battle for Mythic Britain*. New York: Oxford University Press, 2004.

Gantz, Jeffrey. *The Mabinogion*. New York: Barnes & Noble, 1996.

Green, Miranda J. *The Celtic World*. London: Routledge, 1995.

Green, Miranda J. *The Gods of the Celts*. Stroud, United Kingdom: Sutton, 1996.

Green, Miranda J. *Celtic Myths. The Legendary Past*. Austin: University of Texas Press, 1993.

Jones, Gwyn, and Thomas Jones. *The Mabinogion*. New York: Knopf, 2001.

Kinsella, Thomas, and Louis Le Brocquy. *The Taâin*. Oxford, United Kingdom: Oxford University Press, 2002.

Lindahl, Carl, John McNamara, and John Lindow. *Medieval Folklore: A Guide to Myths, Legends, Tales, Beliefs, and Customs*. Oxford, United Kingdom: Oxford University Press, 2002.

MacKillop, James. *Dictionary of Celtic Mythology*. Oxford, United Kingdom: Oxford University Press, 1998.

Maier, Bernhard. *Dictionary of Celtic Religion and Culture*. Woodbridge, Suffolk, United Kingdom: Boydell Press, 1997.

Smyth, Daragh. *A Guide to Irish Mythology*. Dublin, Ireland: Irish Academic Press, 1996.

The Welsh Giant-Slayer Hero

The Historical Context of Medieval Welsh Mythology[1]

Who Were the Welsh?

Welsh history has long been seen as a somewhat marginalized field within the broader study of the Isle of Britain, just as the Welsh generally have seen themselves as a breed apart, distinct from and often misunderstood by their English neighbors. This is not an entirely baseless assumption; the very word *Welsh* is of Old English derivation, a term used by the Saxon invaders to denote the "foreign" British of Celtic stock to the west with whom, over the centuries, they fell into an uneasy and often disrupted truce of sorts. That these foreigners were "others" to be conquered or at the very least kept at bay was reinforced by the building of Offa's Dyke, an earthwork named for the Mercian king who constructed this rudimentary defensive system at the end of the eighth century. This structure has in some measure helped to define the border between these countries ever since. Paradoxically, the modern Welsh name for the country, *Cymru*, means something more akin to the "land of countrymen," denoting a sense of Welsh unity rather than of otherness.

When the Roman legions departed Britain for good in the fifth century, they left a power vacuum that was filled in the next century or so by Anglo-Saxon invaders, usurpers who quickly claimed most of what we now know as *England*, or "land of the Angles." The Roman influence was most lasting in the southeastern part of Wales, and the trading practices and culture of this region remained discernibly distinct from those of the rest of the country almost until the time of the Normans. The Norman conquest of England also had lasting repercussions for Wales: The fragile détente between the Welsh and their English rivals, which had long been punctuated by border raiding and shifting alliances that led to no long-term threat to Welsh autonomy, was about to collapse.

By 1070, the Normans had begun a wholesale attack on Wales, and within 20 years they seemed poised to control the bulk of the country. However, a successful counteroffensive in northern Wales in 1094 effectively staved off the complete conquest of Wales for nearly two centuries. Although certain areas of the country continued to be under Norman control—including the Welsh/English border region, traditionally called the *Marches*, and most of the south, apart from some regions in the west— the north of Wales remained independent until the death of Llywelyn ap Gruffydd in 1282. Llywelyn had attempted to unite an independent Wales under his authority, which was based in his ancestral seat in Gwynedd in the north. The mounting of Llywelyn's head upon a gibbet at the Tower of London was a macabre and an eloquent sign of the subjugation of Wales under English rule. Therefore, the Welsh world that gave birth to the heroes of the *Mabinogion* was a world in flux and a world that looked back to halcyon days of yore in which mighty Welshmen such as Culhwch the Giant-Slayer and even Arthur himself kept monsters and foreign invaders at bay.

The Literary Context of Medieval Welsh Mythology

The Mabinogion, the Great Welsh Epic Cycle[2]

The great repository of medieval Welsh myth is known to us as the *Mabinogion*, a collection of texts comprising four main branches of the collection proper, each of which is most correctly known by the name of its central protagonist, Pwyll, Branwen, Manawydan, and Math, respectively. In addition, the umbrella title *Mabinogion* also covers four independent Welsh tales and three later Arthurian Romances. Although the two codices—the *White Book of Rhydderch* and the *Red Book of Hergest*—that serve as our main sources for this material may themselves be dated, respectively, to the early 14th century in one case and roughly a century later in the second case, the narrative traditions themselves may date back as early as the 11th century, and those pertaining to *Culhwch and Olwen*, the first great tale concerning the Court of King Arthur in Welsh, might be as much as 100 years older still; indeed, as in the case of the medieval Irish tradition, some fundamental narrative concepts might represent early Iron Age traditions, and the faces of ancient Celtic gods may be discerned time and again by those who examine the tales carefully.

The title *Mabinogion*, like so many names applied by later scholars to medieval texts, is evocative and intriguing at the same time that it is misleading and perhaps even entirely inappropriate. Unlike so many other such titles, we can attribute this one to a particular person— Lady Charlotte Guest—who applied this name to her translations of the tales in the 19th century. Her use of this title as a rubric under which all of these tales might be gathered is misleading in that, even as she understood the word, it would properly apply only to the four main branches of the collection: The title may be a complete misnomer in that it represents what might represent a misreading of a term, *mabynogyon*, which occurs but a single time in the sources and that could have been a scribal error in the first place. These significant caveats aside, the title has become useful as the standard collective term for the texts that make up the great medieval Welsh epic cycle; however, more than that, the very term *mabon* is evocative in that it encourages the reader to seek organizing principles for the collection in the archetypes of the "young man," or the developing hero, in general, and to trace the possible relationships between the parallel adventures of the medieval Welsh Mabon and his mother Modron, their ancient forebears Maponos and Matrona, and their contemporary counterparts Pryderi and Rhiannon.

Culhwch and Olwen: The Welsh Arthurian Hero Wins the Giant's Daughter[3]

Culhwch and Olwen, the great Welsh Arthurian contribution to the folkloric tradition known as the motif of the "Giant's Daughter," is preserved in the two great compendia of the *Mabinogion*, which both date from the 14th century. However, some of the material within the text points to a much earlier date of composition, and most scholars concur that the narrative had reached something like the form in which it comes down to us by 1100 or so. Some of the tropes and details may be far earlier and may be thought to illustrate links between early Welsh and early Irish traditions stemming back into antiquity. *Culhwch and Olwen* is of particular interest to the student of Arthuriana because it reflects a native Welsh tradition untouched at the time of its composition by the continental conventions of the Arthurian Romance. Furthermore, it is of particular significance that this independent Celtic material resonates at some points with these very same Romance motifs, which it predates and in some measure prefigures.

Such resonance, although hardly evidence of a direct relationship between the traditions, strongly suggests earlier sources common to both.

The Unusual Origin of the Great Welsh Hero: Greatness Born in a Pig Run

The hero of *Culhwch and Olwen*, the Culhwch of the title, is—like Arthur himself—born under unusual circumstances, and he earns his name (according to folk etymology, in any case) and inherits the legacy of his quest for the hand of the lovely Olwen, daughter of Chief Giant Ysbaddaden, as a result of his unique origin. The story goes that Cilydd, son of Cyleddon Wledig, sought a wife as nobly born as he himself. As a result of his desire for such a bride, he eventually married Goeleuddydd, daughter of Anlawdd Wledig, and soon thereafter she grew great with child. However, with her pregnancy came madness, and Goeleuddydd wandered in the wilderness until she came within sight of a swineherd and his charges, at which point she went into labor because of her fear of the pigs. That very swineherd then fostered her infant son until the lad was of age to come to court, and they baptized him *Culhwch* because he was born in a "pig run."

Soon thereafter Goeleuddydd became mortally ill, and—fearing the influence of a stepmother upon her son—she called her husband to her deathbed, making him promise not to remarry until a two-headed briar should grow upon her grave. Having received such an assurance from Cilydd, Goeleuddydd then called her caretaker to her in secret and bade that he should ever keep her grave free of growth of any kind. In this endeavor her servant was diligent for seven years, but with the passing of time he grew careless. Soon thereafter, her husband the king was hunting near her resting place, and when he examined the grave he found just such a briar as she had described. Cilydd then determined to remarry, if only he could find another wife worthy of him. Such a woman was found, although she was already married to the King of Doged. Applying a quick remedy to this minor dilemma, Cilydd slew his unfortunate rival and took possession of that lord's domain and of his lady.

Not long after her arrival in the court of the man who had murdered her first husband simply to obtain her hand, the new queen learned from a toothless old hag that her present lord already had a son, and so Culhwch's stepmother asked that the boy be presented to her at court. However, when this was done in good faith, she cursed the lad with the pronouncement that his thigh might never strike against that of a woman until he had won the hand of Olwen, daughter of Chief Giant Ysbaddaden, to be his bride. The young man, although not yet of age to take a wife, was nonetheless immediately flushed with the desire to possess this maiden, although he had never seen her.

Meanwhile, Cilydd, far from perplexed at this turn of events, thought such an adventurous endeavor to be eminently achievable by a kinsman of King Arthur, and soon thereafter Culhwch began his quest. This entire sequence of episodes, in addition to providing the background for the main events of the narrative, crucially underscores the heroic identity of the young Culhwch: The unusual birth of this hero, the fanciful etymology of his name, the fosterage of such a cousin of the great King Arthur under the tutelage of a common man in the wastes, the folktale concerning the father's vow not to remarry except under special circumstances, the stepmother's curse, and Culhwch's resultant quest all mark the protagonist as unique and as a hero with a date with destiny.

Eager to embrace this destiny and outfitted with the accoutrements appropriate to his station—described with a brief yet loving attention to detail that offers a tiny foretaste of the lingering descriptions of arms and armor common to later Arthurian Romance—the young hero proceeded from the hall of Cilydd to the court of Arthur to seek the aid necessary to complete the quest that his stepmother's curse required of him. The hero was set on his way to complete this adventure by his father, who instructed him to seek the aid of his kinsman Arthur, whose help was to be ritually sought through the agency of a hair-cutting coming-of-age ceremony. However, when he reached the gate of Arthur's court, Culhwch was denied entry on the basis of the tradition that none might enter the king's company once meat was served and ale was poured except for the son of a true king or an artisan practicing his craft; such a tardy visitor as Culhwch would be treated with all due courtesy in the traveler's hostel but might not enter the hall of the king until the gates were opened again the next day. Bristling at such a delay, Culhwch threatened the porter with ill-report and Arthur himself with ill-fame; moreover, the young hero vowed to raise three shouts that would be heard throughout Britain and Ireland and that would cause miscarriage and barrenness amongst the women of the court.

In response to these words, Glewlwyd Gafaelfawr, the porter at the gate of the court of Arthur, rushed to the side of his lord to report that, throughout the many years and adventures of his life, he had never seen a handsomer and nobler youth. Arthur immediately granted dispensation to allow the young hero to enter, and so—over the protestations of Cei, who did not wish the laws of the king flouted for one man's sake—Culhwch came into the presence of his cousin the king. This description of the Welsh Culhwch's arrival at the court of King Arthur is highly reminiscent of that concerning the Irish Lugh Lamfhota's entrance to the company of the Tuatha De Danann in the *Cath Maige Tuired*; indeed, in the terse reception of the young hero by the porter guarding the gate of Arthur's stronghold—as well as in Cei's stubborn adherence to custom—those with ears to listen might well hear a faint Welsh echo of the ancient Irish tradition of Lugh standing at the threshold of Tara, recounting skill after skill until finally the company grudgingly accepted him on the basis of his combination of talents. Moreover, in the context of the Welsh Chief Giant Ysbaddaden's resonance with the monstrously huge Irish Balor this echo is greatly amplified, especially considering the role each young hero plays in blinding his nemesis with a spear and overthrowing his rule of terror.

In a bold departure from the custom most familiar to readers of medieval English Arthurian Romance through the very similar entry of the Greene Knight into Arthur's Christmas feast, Culhwch refused to dismount before riding his steed directly into the hall of the king. Once in Arthur's presence, the young hero politely addressed the lord and all his vassals. Although courteously greeted in return by Arthur even in the face of his unorthodox entry to the court, Culhwch rejected the king's offers of food, cheer, gifts and deference, asking only that King Arthur grant him the boon he had come to seek or else let him be on his way. Graciously offering the young lad whatever his heart might desire—except for his ship, cloak, spear, shield, dagger, and queen—the king quickly assented to Culhwch's request to have his hair trimmed, handling the golden comb and shears himself.

Considering the importance of precise wording in the granting of boons in the *Mabinogion*—a precision that Pwyll, Head of Annwvn, famously flouts at his peril in the First Branch—a careful reader will take heed of those items Arthur exempts from the general largess he offers Culhwch. The most important of those exemptions apply to Caledfwlch, his sword, and Gwenhwyfar, his wife. Moreover, it is of even greater significance that the main action of this quest is framed by a set of ritual grooming episodes: Culhwch enters manhood and evokes the right to solicit the aid of his kinsman King Arthur through such a ceremony, and the various Herculean tasks set for the suitor of Olwen by Ysbaddaden her father act as a prelude to—and, indeed, necessarily culminate in—the ritual shaving of the chief giant himself, a glorified mutilation ritual masquerading as a grooming ceremony that ends with the decapitation of the father of Olwen and his replacement by Culhwch as the primary man in her life.

As he trimmed the lad's hair, Arthur felt his affection for Culhwch increase as he came to the conclusion that the boy must be his kinsman. Queried on this point, the young hero gave his lineage and thus acknowledged that he and Arthur were first cousins. Upon this disclosure Arthur reiterated his offer to grant whatever his kinsman might desire, this time without reservation. Culhwch then declared that he had come to Arthur to seek the king's aid in obtaining the hand of Olwen, daughter of Chief Giant Ysbaddaden, in marriage, and he that did so in the name of all of the champions of Arthur's court, whom he went on to list in great number and detail.

The Earliest Knights of Arthur: The Welsh Hero in the First Court of the Once and Future King

Although undeniably extremely long and at times seemingly impenetrable to a modern reader, the roll-call of Arthur's retainers in *Culhwch and Olwen* is of special significance to one interested in medieval Arthurian mythology; this introduction is crucial perhaps especially because this gathering of warriors often bears more resemblance to the war band of a Celtic chieftain of yore—populated by superhuman heroes of the ilk of Cuchulainn of the Irish tradition—than it does to the chivalrous court of Arthur we think of as the home to the Knights of the Round Table. However, present in this assembly are several figures recognizable to any student of King Arthur: Cei, Bedwyr, and Gwalchmei, in particular, correspond to the Kay, Bedevere, and Gawain more commonly known by modern readers. More to the point, these friends familiar from medieval Arthurian Romance are joined at the ancient Welsh court of *Culhwch's* Arthur by various colorful native characters, scores of which are listed by Culhwch as he ritually evokes his right to ask for the aid of Arthur his kinsman.

Some of the notables amongst this brood of heroes and henchmen include Glewlwyd *Gafaelfawr*, "Mighty-Grip," the curmudgeonly porter to the court of Arthur; Osla Big Knife, whose eponymous weapon—the gigantic dagger called *Bronllafn*, "Hillside Blade"—might serve a company as great as all of the hosts of the British Isles as a bridge across a raging river, even were they burdened with booty; *Drem*, son of *Dremidydd*, "Sight" son of "Seer," whose vision was so keen he might view all of the landscape from Cornwall to the land of the Picts; Sgilti Lightfoot, who sprinted along the canopy of the forest and atop the tips of the reeds on the mountainside, never so much as bending a branch or breaking a stalk in the process; Gwrhyr the Linguist, who could interpret all tongues; and *Sugyn*, son of

Sugnedydd, "Suck," son of "Sucker," whose fevered breast caused him an unquenchable thirst that could drain the sea itself.

In addition to heroes such as these, some of whom clearly smack of folkloric influences, the court of Arthur visited by Culhwch boasts such important representatives of the Welsh pagan past as Gwyn ap Nudd, known in earlier texts as the Lord of Annwfn and the demonic master of the wild hunt led by that pack of hell hounds known as the cwn annwfn; indeed, Gwyn is a key mythic figure in this text. For example, his ancient identity as an otherworldly huntsman may well explain his role in Culhwch's hunt for the great boar Twrch Trwyth. Moreover, that he was a son of Nudd is in itself significant given that Nudd is the Welsh equivalent of the Irish Nuadu, both of which figures were descended from the ancient Celtic god Nodons. Most notably, Gwyn's feud with Gwythyr fab Greidawl over the possession of the maiden Creiddylad in *Culhwch and Olwen* may well provide a medieval Welsh echo of an ancient elemental struggle between the forces of life and of death most commonly known to us through the classical myth of Persephone. In addition, Nudd's other son Edern—an important figure in many early Welsh tales who rose to the level of a saint, however uncanonical, in Brittany—likewise joins Arthur's company in welcoming Culhwch, and even the great bard Taliesin himself is in attendance.

The new religion and its mythological sphere are also represented in this court in the notable form of Saint Gildas and his kin. Thus, ancient figures from the misty mythic past rub elbows in this court with their more up-to-date Christian counterparts, and heroes representing mythic archetypes are cheek by jowl with figures of folkloric significance. Some of the seemingly innumerable members of Arthur's court clearly represent embodiments of particular physical attributes of prowess, whereas others possess mighty weapons or magical talismans; the aggregate effect is a cavalcade of superhuman traits and abilities of truly mythic proportions. Some such figures hearken back to the demigods and euhemerized heroes of Celtic antiquity, even as some amongst them look forward to the more human chivalric heroes of the Knights of the Round Table. *Culhwch and Olwen* thus serves as a bridge text of sorts, linking—rather in the manner of the blade of Osla Big Knife—the hosts of ancient mythic figures of the Arthurian canon with the armies of Romance heroes who will succeed them.

Moreover, it is well worth the effort required to note the similarities and contrasts between different faces of the same recognizable figures that loom large in the early Welsh and later medieval Romance Arthurian traditions. For example, in *Culhwch and Olwen*, the first mention of Cei ap Cynyr occurs when Glewlwyd the porter reports to Arthur of a noble young man at the gate who threatens that court with infamy and infertility if the rules regarding latecomers are enforced upon him. In the context of such threats, Cei's response—that he himself would not relax the law of the court for such a traveler—might seem moderate; however, Arthur's mild rebuke—that the greater his largesse and hospitableness the greater his nobility and reputation—implies that Cei's adherence to the letter of the law, although unimpeachable on its face, betokens in some measure a smallness of mind and meanness of spirit unbefitting a truly noble lord. This subtle prompt alerts us to a duality of the Welsh Cei's character: Although at some points—and most especially in the early texts—a great and courageous warrior, Cei is in other instances—and seemingly ever more so as the tradition evolves—a petty and spiteful steward and on occasion even a bit of a clown.

However, this suggestion of some blemish in Cei's character is at this point quite minor, and indeed his primacy of status in the court of Arthur is underscored shortly thereafter when his is the very first name that Culhwch invokes in his appeal for his kinsman's aid in his quest. Moreover, later in that same listing of the heroes of Arthur's court and their attributes we learn that Cynyr, Cei's father, prophesied to his wife that a son he begot upon her would have many special traits, including stubbornness but also great strength and the power to endure fire and water like no other. Other superhuman attributes of Cei reported in *Culhwch and Olwen* include the ability to hold his breath for nine days and nights, the capacity to go without sleep for the same space of time, the power to transform himself into a giant as tall as the tallest tree, and the possession of a radiant heat emanating from his body that evaporated the rain a handsbreadth on either side of his fist, which would keep whatever he held in his hand dry. Indeed, his heat was so great that his companions could—in bitter cold—kindle a fire from it.

Further, Cei had in his keeping a marvelous sword the wounds of which might not be healed even by the most talented physician. Moreover, Cei proves himself courageous time and again during Culhwch's adventures and is also on occasion quick thinking. However, he is short-tempered and quick to take offense; indeed, he refused to help his lord ever again, even in the direst of need, after Arthur composed a mocking verse about Cei's adventure securing the facial hair of Dillus the Bearded. In sum, then, the Cei of *Culhwch and Olwen* is a superhuman hero in many respects and most notably is the great champion of Arthur's band, a role often relinquished to Lancelot in the French tradition and to Gawain in the English. However, this great champion also displays a contrasting smallness of spirit, especially as exemplified in the episode concerning Culhwch's first appearance at the court of Arthur and that regarding his king's jesting poem. It is in large measure this obstinate and obstreperous nature that is reflected most clearly through the mists of time in the recognizably similar attributes of the Sir Kay of later medieval Romance.

According to *Culhwch and Olwen*, second only to Cei in the court of Arthur is *Bedwyr*, the "Birchwood Hero," who is reflected in the later Romance tradition by Bedivere—also known by such names as Beduers—and perhaps by such figures as Pellinor and Bellinor. The third handsomest man in all of Britain, Bedwyr is also one-armed but is nevertheless unequaled in his skill with a spear; indeed, in the heat of the fray he could wound his opponents three times faster than any other warrior. It is, as a matter of fact, none other than Bedwyr who catches in flight the first of Ysbaddaden's poisoned stone spears meant for Culhwch, returning it neatly into its owner's knee, so that the chief giant was lamed ever after. Bedwyr's own spear, too, was marvelous, at least in his hand: For every thrust it made it gave nine counterthrusts. Moreover, Bedwyr is Cei's almost constant companion and will never shirk from any adventure in which this companion takes part.

Together these two heroes are vital to the rescue of Mabon, son of Modron, one of the chain of feats vital to the success of Culhwch's quest for Olwen's hand. Moreover, the adventure concerning Mabon is another key mythological episode in *Culhwch and Olwen*: In addition to containing several key folkloric aspects—notably a series of ancient talking animals culminating in the Great Salmon of Llyn Llyw, a classic manifestation of the Celtic motif of the Salmon of Wisdom, on whose very shoulders Bedwyr rides with Cei to the place of Mabon's imprisonment—this sequence evokes an extremely ancient Celtic tradition concerning the theft of the child of the Great Goddess. *Mabon*, "Youth," represents the embodiment of the powers of life and fertility resident in *Modron*, "Mother," and the theft and imprisonment of this embodiment symbolizes an ancient mythological trope of the constant elemental and cyclical struggle between the forces of life and death, light and dark, summer and winter. Bedwyr aids in the rescue of Mabon, which represents a significant if impermanent victory in the cycle of this eternal conflict. After this adventure, Bedwyr again accompanied his steadfast companion to seek the beard of Dillus, and after Cei's estrangement from Arthur, the Birchwood Hero played an active role in such adventures as the quest for the cauldron of Diwrnach the Irishman and the hunt for the great boar Twrch Trwyth.

Gwalchmei, "Hawk of May," son of Gwyar, is the early Welsh version of the Knight of the Round Table we recognize as Gawain. We learn in *Culhwch and Olwen* that Gwalchmei was the greatest of all walkers, the ablest of all riders, and was an ideal participant in any quest because he never came home without having achieved his objective. We are also informed that Gwalchmei was Arthur's sister's son, and thus his nephew, as well as his first cousin. We know from the Welsh Triads that this early figure was credited with being one of the most fearless and most courteous men in Britain, attributes that—along with his reputation for the successful completion of quests—are echoed in most Romance interpretations of Gawain. Gwalchmei's courtesy, in particular, is often cited in contrast to Cei's churlishness. It is perhaps of some note that, although his reputation for achieving objectives is specifically cited when Gwalchmei is chosen as one of Culhwch's companions, the May-Hawk hero plays little of an active role in this particular adventure.

The Great Welsh Hero's Love-Quest: Culhwch Seeks His Bride in the Court of the Chief Giant

Arthur, having heard from his kinsman's own lips of his desire to wed the daughter of Chief Giant Ysbaddaden, was obliged to admit that he knew nothing of that lord or of his daughter. Impressing upon Culhwch to remain at his court while the maiden was found, Arthur sent messengers to seek out Olwen and her father. However, when a year had passed in this endeavor and still Culhwch's bride had not been located, Arthur's young cousin declared his intention to leave the king's court, taking its honor with him. However, Cei would not hear of such a thing, and he vowed—if the lad would but accompany him—to search for Olwen until she was found or Culhwch was satisfied that she did not exist. Thus, Arthur gathered a band of heroes from his court to seek out Culhwch's heart's desire; therefore, the young hero was accompanied on his quest by several of Arthur's champions, including Cei, Bedwyr, and Gwalchmei.

These luminaries were joined by three additional figures of considerable folkloric significance. Acting as the scout and pathfinder for the party was Cynddelig *Cyfarwydd*, whose second name is actually a term denoting a category of "storyteller;" moreover, this term also connotes a kind of a "wise one" who might offer his companions aid in the form of guidance, information, or even magic. Indeed, Cynddelig was a guide so accomplished that he was no less adept at finding his way in a foreign land than he was in his own country. The interpreter for the party was Gwrhyr

Gwalstad Ieithoedd, who spoke all tongues of men and—in a folkloric touch that smacks of the shaman guide—could even communicate with beasts. The magical protector of the party was Menw fab Teirgwaedd, the sorcerer, who played even more clearly the role of a shaman guide and who certainly is evocative—in his desire to help the hero achieve his quest to procure his mate—of Merlin. It was a notable skill of Menw that he might conjure a spell of invisibility so that his companions might see all without being themselves seen, and his ability to transform himself into a bird—which he does in the course of *Culhwch and Olwen* to seek out the treasures between the two ears of the great boar Twrch Trwyth—is further evidence of Menw's shamanistic qualities.

In the course of their journey, the travelers spied from afar a great fort, the greatest—as it turned out—of all forts in all the world. It was in the midst of a mighty plain, and although they seemed close enough to come to it on the first day they spied it, they were deceived. It was so vast a structure that it appeared to them much closer than it really was, and it was only after three full days of travel that they came into the neighborhood of the stronghold. However, as they finally approached it they noticed a giant shepherd atop a mighty mound keeping watch over a vast flock of sheep in the fields there around. With this shepherd was a mastiff of vast proportions, a beast more like a full-grown horse in size than it was a dog. This herdsman was called Custennin, and he had never lost a lamb or a sheep. Moreover, this shepherd never let any party go by him unscathed; indeed, his very breath scorched the trees and shrubs around him, burning them to cinders on the charred earth.

When Gwrhyr the interpreter hesitated to approach this intimidating figure on his own, Cei offered to accompany him, and Menw charmed the giant mastiff so that it might not harry them. Custennin, although gruff, received the party more peaceably than might have been expected, informing them that they indeed stood at the very threshold of the caer of Ysbaddaden, who had in fact tormented the shepherd himself miserably on account of Custennin's wife. Moreover, when he learned of their quest he advised them to forsake it because no suitor had ever left the court of the chief giant alive. As the shepherd stood to leave, Culhwch made him a present of a gold ring. Although the ring was too small to fit around his massive finger, he put it in his glove for safekeeping. When the shepherd's wife discovered the ring he told her who had come into their domain and why, and she was overjoyed by the thought of a visit from Culhwch, whom—giant that she was—she would have crushed to death in her loving embrace had not a fast-thinking Cei cast a log between her hands to take the place of the hero's neck.

However, this joy was understandable because Custennin was Culhwch's uncle by marriage. The husbandman's wife was none other than the sister of Goeleuddydd, the mother of the hero. After offering her visitors a hospitable welcome, Custennin's wife released from a cupboard her last surviving son, a promising lad with golden curls who in due course would come to be known as Goreu, an epithet he would be given because of his prowess on the battlefield. The lad's parents had kept him hidden, it seems, because the chief giant was wont to slay their offspring—so he had done three and twenty times before, and so, the lad's poor mother concluded, would he do again. However, Cei swore that the boy and he would both survive, or else die together, and for the rest of Culhwch's quest the lad who would one day earn the name Goreu fought as one of the company of Arthur's warriors.

In general, this "hidden lad" is an example of the theme of the hero's sidekick, a role often reserved for a youthful companion who is portrayed as bumbling, unpromising, or at least—as in the present case—legitimately under threat; this figure often emerges as a champion in his own right through the ministrations of the hero. More specifically, this particular storyline concerning poor cottager parents who fear for the life of their only remaining son, a lad who later goes on—in the company of a great hero—to become a mighty warrior himself, reminds one of the Norse saga concerning the humble Hottr, who is transformed under the tutelage of Bodvar Bjarki into Hjalti, one of the great champions at the court of King Hrolf.

Discussing Culhwch's quest, Custennin and his wife expressed their horror at the prospect of their nephew's visit to the hall of the chief giant to seek the hand of Olwen because they had never heard of any suitor escaping alive from the clutches of Ysbaddaden. However, despite their protests, they agreed to arrange for the hero to cross paths with *Olwen*, the "Flowery Trail" maiden, whom the lad found receptive to his suit. The love of Culhwch's life earned her name, our author tells us, because snowy clover blossoms bloomed in her wake. However, Olwen was adamant that she would not agree to go with the young hero until he achieved the Herculean set of tasks demanded by her father. She revealed to Culhwch that she had vowed never to marry until her father gave his blessing because he was doomed to die when she left his house. This detail is notable in that it evokes a common folkloric motif and mythological device concerning the marriage of daughters and the replacement of their fathers as the primary male figures in their lives. Culhwch thus determined boldly to enter the stronghold of Olwen's father and therein to announce his suit, and so the company from Arthur's court did, slaying nine guards and nine mighty mastiffs at nine gates in the process.

Reaching the hall of the chief giant, Culhwch and his comrades offered their host courteous greeting and gave voice to Culhwch's determination to have Olwen for his bride. Feigning courtesy, Ysbaddaden called for his servants to put to use the massive forks needed to lift the giant's drooping eyelids so that he might see for himself what sort of son-in-law his visitor might be. The giant then called Culhwch closer so that he might examine the lad more closely and give some answer to this suit. As the hero moved toward the duplicitous chief giant, this answer came in the form of the first of three poisoned stone spears that Ysbaddaden kept ever close to hand. However, as this missile streaked toward Culhwch, Bedwyr caught it in mid-flight and cast it back from whence it came, sending it through the joint of the giant's knee. Ysbaddaden howled in pain and rage at this turn of events, cursing the savagery of such a son-in-law as well as the smith and anvil that fashioned the weapon. The giant lamented that ever more he would limp up any slope, stung as he was by the poisoned tip of the weapon that pained him like a horsefly.

Leaving the court then, Culhwch and his cohorts returned to the house of Custennin, where they spent the night. The second day the course of events was much the same, although the tone of Culhwch's suit was more demanding and threatening. Claiming he needed to take counsel with Olwen's grandparents, Ysbaddaden again cast a spear at the suitor, and this time Menw returned the favor, sending this spear right through the giant's chest. Again yelping curses, the chief giant mourned that he would ever after suffer heartburn as he walked uphill and would lose his taste for food; the pain of the spear he likened this time to the bite of a huge leech. The visitors then went to their meal.

The third day Culhwch and his party called for the giant to cease his attacks, and Ysbaddaden again called for his servants to hoist up his eyelids so that he might better see the youth who wished to become his son-in-law. As the hero stood, the chief giant took this opportunity to cast his third spear. This time Culhwch himself intercepted the flight of the javelin, casting it right through the eye of his nemesis so that it came out the back of the giant's neck. Cursing his son-in-law's barbarous ways once more, Ysbaddaden remarked that he would never again be clear-eyed and free from headache, and he compared the pain of the spear to the bite of a mad dog. Then the party of the suitor again departed to take their food. The fourth day Culhwch returned and repeated his suit, threatening Ysbaddaden with death if he were to refuse it. This time calling the suitor to sit before him face to face, the chief giant exchanged vows and sureties with the young hero: Culhwch would have Olwen when he had completed all of the tasks demanded by Ysbaddaden, and not before. The parties agreed, and then Olwen's father recounted his conditions.

Ysbaddaden Bencawr, "Hawthorn Chief Giant," is the Welsh equivalent of the Irish mythic giant Balor of the Evil Eye, King of the Fomorians. Like Ysbaddaden, Balor's gargantuan eyelid might only be opened through the agency of several servants. Moreover, the relationship between these giants is most overtly manifested by means of the spear each monstrous king receives through his orb from the hand of a hero. It has been suggested that Balor reflects vestiges of a Celtic sun deity of old, an identity most clearly illuminated in the light of his single powerful eye. A similar line of thought might suggest that Ysbaddaden represents an echo of an ancient Celtic sky or thunder god. It is certainly the case that, in the impact of his three poisoned stone spears, we might well discern the rumble of the characteristic thunderbolts of a god of sky and storm from long ago.

Moreover, in the number of those weapons we see replicated the ancient Celtic trope of triplism. In addition, just as Culhwch has a curse laid upon him concerning the possibility of his marriage—what in the Irish tradition might be termed a *geis*—so, too, are Ysbaddaden and his Irish counterpart bound to specific dooms: Balor was destined to die at the hands of his grandson, whereas Ysbaddaden might live only so long as his daughter remained unmarried. It is not difficult to see the relationship between these two prophesies that ultimately link the death of the father with his daughter's sexual coming of age. To try to stave off inexorable fate, both giants go to extraordinary lengths to avoid the fulfillment of the prophetic terms of death. In Balor's case, the giant tried to ensure that his daughter Eithne would never be seduced, an attempt that was confounded by Lugh's father. Ysbaddaden, for his part, having obtained Olwen's vow that she would not marry without his consent, destroyed any suitor for her hand at the earliest opportunity, presumably by using his poisoned stone spears. However, when that tried and true method failed, the chief giant imposed a seemingly impossible combination of conditions upon the hero seeking to marry his daughter. Indeed, even the chief giant's personal name, "Hawthorn," might—in its imagery of a series of short but thick trees locked together by their branches into a single, impregnable hedge of sharp and merciless thorns—evoke the concept of an insurmountable barrier, the sum of which is even greater than its already nearly impenetrable component parts.

The Great Welsh Hero Comes of Age: The Herculean
Tasks Set for Culhwch

Most of the tasks imposed by Ysbaddaden upon Culhwch to win Olwen's hand might be roughly grouped into a handful of categories, the most important of which seem to relate to the coming of age of a young hero or to the qualities associated with effective kingship in the Celtic world. In addition, many of the tasks—across various categories—on the surface are concerned with preparations for the wedding and for the ritual grooming of the father of the bride. One set of these tasks relates to agriculture, and thus might be said to be primarily concerned with the Celtic king's traditional role in ensuring fecundity. This set includes the clearing and sowing of a given field to produce the food and drink for the wedding feast.

Tellingly, the chief giant demands that the field be plowed and prepared by none other than Amaethon, son of Don, and that Gofannon, son of Don, be the one who sets the plow irons. The fact that these two tasks stipulate the participation of the children of Don—herself the Welsh descendant of the ancient Celtic Mother Goddess, and thus equivalent to the Irish figure Ana—is of particular significance because it overtly draws ancient fertility myths into an Arthurian context. Moreover, such mention also explicitly links this medieval Welsh text to the Irish traditions concerning the Tuatha De Danann—the Tribe of the Goddess Ana—which comprises the Hibernian manifestation of a sizable portion of the ancient Celtic pantheon.

Another set of tasks assigned to the young suitor by the chief giant concerns the coming-of-age trope of the hunt. The slaying of the Chief Boar Ysgithrwyn and of his great counterpart Twrch Trwyth each represent the hero's maturity in facing ferocity and in mastering the forces of fecundity, twin measures—in the ancient to the Celtic mind—of a great hero and king. Both of these hunt episodes also include elements of an archetypal heroic quest. In each of these cases this quest is manifested in the search for items necessary for the preparation of Ysbaddaden himself for the sacrificial feast. For example, the tusk with which the giant may be shaved hangs from the jaw of the chief boar, which is the object of the first hunt quest. On the other hand, the comb and shears needed to groom the chief giant's unruly hair reside between the ears of another great boar that is the object of the second hunt quest.

In addition, the quest archetype is extended in several other tasks that include several battles with men and monsters, including the procurement of the blood of the Black Witch, which is necessary to serve as the lotion with which to prepare the chief giant's wiry beard for its ceremonial shave.

Moreover, Culhwch is required to obtain the cauldron of Diwrnach Wyddel, the vessel that is required to provide the meat for the wedding feast. This feat again resonates with the ancient Celtic king's association with abundance, this time in the powerfully charged culturally specific context of the theme of the Cauldron of Plenty. The final condition Ysbaddaden demands is the capture of the sword of Wrnach the Giant, a task that represents a mythic quest for the ultimate symbol of manhood, the status of a warrior, and the power of a king.

Diwrnach *Wyddel,* an "Irish" man, sometimes called a giant, was the steward of the Irish King Odgar fab Aedd and owned a fabulous cauldron that—amongst its other marvelous properties—would not produce food for a coward. Arthur intercedes with Odgar to attempt to peacefully gain the cauldron for Culhwch, but when this fails Arthur seizes the vessel and brings it back to Britain overflowing with the spoils of war. The vessel of Diwrnach Wyddel is clearly evocative of the ancient Celtic theme of the Cauldron of Plenty, which is associated—to cite the most obvious example—with the Irish god the Dagda, amongst many other figures; indeed, this cauldron itself appears in the Second Branch of the *Mabinogion* and in *Preiddiau Annwfn,* the "Spoils of Annwfn."

Of course, such a cauldron reflects the cornucopia theme, a symbol in many traditions of agricultural fertility and plenty often associated, in Celtic mythology, with the rule of a rightful king. Moreover, in the Celtic tradition such cauldrons are also evocative of veritable powers over life and death, including the ability to resurrect slain warriors; indeed, the medieval Irish and Welsh mythological traditions include overt examples of this concept. Thus, the successful completion of this task plays the practical function of ensuring that the wedding feast will be bountiful and serves the emblematic function of illustrating that Ysbaddaden's replacement will provide for his people in terms of agricultural bounty and military protec-tion. Indeed, the twin theme of the Cauldron of Plenty evoked in this tale in the context of the slaying of the chief giant and his replacement by his son-in-law, Culhwch, in Olwen's life and his killer Goreu on his throne suggests that the death of Ysbaddaden reflects the ceremonial slaying of the Corn King, the ritual sacrifice of a real or symbolic ruler to ensure successful harvests, peace, prosperity, and protection for his people.

The last task listed by Chief Giant Ysbaddaden is the first completed by Culhwch's companions: The slaying of Wrnach the Giant by his own sword—which is the only weapon that might slay the great boar Twrch Trwyth—and the capture thereby of that wondrous blade. Because only a master craftsman might enter the court of Wrnach—a revisitation once again of a recurrent theme most famously illustrated by the story of Lugh Lamfhota attempting to gain entry at the gates of Tara—Cei claims to be a sword smith come to refurbish the giant's weapon. Once handling the blade freely with the permission of Wrnach, it is relative child's play for Cei to take the giant's head and thus to win the sword for Culhwch. Bedwyr and the son of Custennin also play supporting roles in this episode, and it is notable that the latter earns his nickname *Goreu*, "Best," through his prowess slaughtering the henchmen of Wrnach.

More to the point, it is significant that Ysbaddaden would require Culhwch to win a sword—an obvious coming-of-age ritual for a warrior, and still more so for a prince who would be a king—and it is of particular note that this task culminates in the beheading of Wrnach, an act that prefigures the ritual decapitation of the chief giant himself. This episode is well worth close examination, especially considering *Culhwch and Olwen's* highly charged context of themes of burgeoning manhood, the attainment or loss of virility, the coming of age of the son-in-law versus the displacement of the bride's father, and a final act of ritual decapitation that precedes the sexual consummation of the replacement of the father in the daughter's life.

In addition, the ancient Celtic reverence of that fierce and fecund beast the boar—along with the equally venerable and closely allied theme of the boar hunt as a measure of manhood—is twice evoked in *Culhwch and Olwen*. In the first instance, Ysbaddaden demanded that the tusk of *Ysgithrwyn Pen Beidd*, "White Tusk Chief Boar," be drawn from the head of the king of the most ferocious of beasts so that the chief giant might be able to shave himself to prepare for his daughter's wedding. Ysbaddaden made it clear that the tusk would be useless to him unless the razor tooth in question were taken fresh from the warm, still-slavering jaws of the beast, underscoring how such a tusk is emblematic of the vitality and power associated in Celtic mythology with the wild boar. The chief giant named Odgar fab Aedd was the only man who might pull the tusk of the chief boar, and *Cadw*, "Keeper," the Pict was the only one worthy of trust to take that valuable artifact into his possession. In fact, in the event it was Cadw the Pict, mounted upon Arthur's very own mare, who brought Ysgithrwyn to bay, boldly dismounting and attacking the chief boar with nothing but a hand-axe and then cleaving the beast's head, taking the sacred tusk thereby. Arthur's own hound Cafal, we are told, was the dog that felled the mighty Ysgithrwyn.

Cafal also played a role in the hunt for *Twrch Trwyth*, "Potion Boar". According to Arthur himself, Twrch Trwyth was once a mortal king who—as his name implies—had been magically transformed into a giant beast as penance for his sins. The enchanted boar that is the object of this hunt episode clearly resonates with any number of magical and divine wild pigs drawn from ancient mythologies from across Northern Europe. In addition, the trope of the sinner transformed into a pig recalls the second year of the penance of Gwydion and his brother Gilfaethwy for the rape of Goewin in the Fourth Branch of the *Mabinogion*.

In the present tale, Ysbaddaden demanded that Culhwch procure the comb and shears stowed between the ears of Twrch Trwyth, which were the only tools in the entire world capable of taming the wild and stiff hair of the chief giant in preparation for Olwen's wedding. In addition, Ysbaddaden noted a litany of related tasks that had to be completed in succession to make it possible to hunt this great boar successfully. For example, the hunt might only proceed led by the great hound *Drudwyn*, "Starling," the whelp of Greid son of Eri; Drudwyn might only be held by the collar of Canhastyr Hundred Hands connected to the leash of Cors Hundred Claws and the chain of Cilydd Hundred Holds; and Drudwyn might only be led by a Mabon son of Modron as houndsman.

Once the hunt was under way, the battle between Arthur and his champions on the one side and Twrch Trwyth and his magical piglets on the other ranged across the countryside of Ireland and Britain, and the slaughter on both sides was great. Furthermore, the story is illuminated by marvelous folkloric and mythic details, such as a conversation between Gwrhyr the Interpreter and Grugyn Silver Bristle, one of the offspring of the great boar whose eponymous metallic hair lit up the forest as he passed. This fearsome beast, one of the last two of Twrch Trwyth's piglets to fall, calls to mind *Gullinborsti*, "Golden Bristle," the magical boar from the Norse tradition that could illuminate the night as he ferried his master Freyr across the sky. At long last, the treasures held by Twrch Trwyth were won, although only at great cost, and then the magical pig disappeared into the sea, pursued by Aned and Aethlem, mythic huntsmen who had never theretofore lost any quarry they sought, and neither the boar nor his pursuers were ever seen again. Thus closes an episode that combines a classic Herculean laundry list of tasks with a totemic animal theme plumbed from the depths of Northern European mythology and that is embroidered with nearly countless mythic, legendary, and folkloric details drawn from the ancient Celtic, early Welsh, and medieval Arthurian traditions.

Taking the Giant's Head: The Ancient Celtic Decapitation Theme in the Hands of the Great Welsh Giant Slayer

When the chief giant's terms and conditions had been met, the hero arranged for the grooming of his father-in-law. Cadw of Prydain sheared the giant, shaving not just the beard of his face, but also slicing the flesh off of Ysbaddaden's visage right down to the very bone and taking both ears as trophies. After Culhwch had then forced Olwen's father to announce publicly that the terms of the marriage contract had been fulfilled and his daughter belonged by rights to her suitor, Goreu, son of Custennin, took the giant by the hair of his head. Rather than merely cutting Ysbaddaden's locks, Goreu pulled the giant's neck taut so that he might take Olwen's father's head, thereby gaining vengeance for the humiliation of his father and the slaughter of his brothers—previously slain at the hand of the chief giant—and taking for himself Ysbaddaden's caer and kingdom into the bargain.

The decapitation theme is prevalent throughout medieval Welsh and Irish literature, clearly resonating with—and perhaps even deriving in some measure from—practices of headhunting and human sacrifice among the ancient Celts. Moreover, the ritualized mutilation and subsequent decapitation of Chief Giant Ysbaddaden, the twin episodes with which the present narrative concludes—and that clearly echo Culhwch's own formalized grooming ceremony at the court of Arthur—evoke a thematic relationship between ritual decapitation and symbolic castration; after all, the hero's purpose has been to replace the giant father in Olwen's life, and the culmination of this suitor's quest is the consummation of his own marriage bed.

Indeed, it has been suggested that the two ritual grooming sequences of *Culhwch and Olwen*—marking the arrival of the virility of manhood in Culhwch's case and its departure in Ysbaddaden's—in fact represent a folkloric echo of ancient rites regarding manhood as well as the relationship between a potential husband and his putative father-in-law. Indeed, it is not a huge leap from such an assertion to see in the ritual shearing of Culhwch's hair a celebration of burgeoning manhood that some cultures might associate with a ritual circumcision, whereas the unmanning of his father-in-law, culminating in a ritual beheading, might be seen to reflect a form of castration anxiety. After all, Culhwch does take Ysbaddaden's life and power as well as his daughter. From ancient times, mythic and folkloric episodes have dealt with the father's fear of being supplanted—on at least some level—by his daughter's husband.

It should perhaps come as no surprise then that immediately after the description of the chief giant's decapitation we are informed that Culhwch took Olwen to his bed and made her his wife. Although it is not Culhwch himself who performs the mutilation of Ysbaddaden through the ritual shave or enacts the decapitation of the giant and the appropriation of his stronghold and territories, these acts may be performed only through the agency of such a suitor as Culhwch, and Chief Giant Ysbaddaden cannot be forced to relinquish his daughter—and, concurrently and as a result, his life and his lands—until such a suitor and his allies have successfully performed the set of tasks determined by Ysbaddaden himself.

Notes

1. For critical commentary on and analysis of the history of Medieval Wales, see especially Carr 1–7, 8–82, 133–134; Davies 1–3, 194–218; Jack 15–46; Jones ix–xxix; Lindahl 429–432; MacKillop 427–428.

2. For critical commentary on and analysis of the great epic cycle of Medieval Welsh mythology, see especially Ellis, *Celtic*, 149–150; Fee 69, 80, 100, 181–185, 198, 220; Gantz 9–34; Green, *Gods*, 16, 73, 101, 147, 187; Green, *Myths*, 29–35; Green, *World*, 785–791; Jones ix–xxix; Lindahl 431–432; MacKillop 276–280; and Maier 180–181.

3. For critical commentary on and analysis of elements of Welsh myth suggested by *Culhwch and Olwen,* see especially Alcock 316; Barron 4–5, 6, 7, 206; Castleden 110, 168, 183, 214, 241; Ellis, *Celtic*, 71; Fee 181, 186, 187; Gantz 134–135; Green, *Gods*, 16, 180; Green, *Myths*, 35–36; Green, *World*, 786, 787, 788; Higham 8, 88, 90, 129, 219; Lacy and Ashe 25–26, 286, 301, 308–309, 320, 325–326, 341, 354; Lupack 16–17, 435, 445–446, 453–454, 473; MacKillop 34, 74, 105–106, 108, 109, 127, 134, 152–153, 225–226, 229, 231, 232, 233, 271, 290, 308, 314, 368, 382; Maier 86; Snyder, *Britons* 264–265; Snyder, *World* 24, 78, 93–97, 105, 113; and White 7–12.

Sources and Further Reading

Alcock, Leslie. *Arthur's Britain: History and Archaeology, AD 367–634*. Classic history. London: Penguin Books, 2001.

Barron, W. R. J. *The Arthur of the English: The Arthurian Legend in Medieval English Life and Literature*. Arthurian literature in the Middle Ages, 2. Cardiff: University of Wales Press, 2001.

Carr, A. D. *Medieval Wales*. British history in perspective. Houndmills, Basingstoke, Hampshire: Macmillan Press, 1995.

Castleden, Rodney. *King Arthur: The Truth Behind the Legend*. London: Routledge, 2000.

Davies, Wendy. *Wales in the Early Middle Ages*. Studies in the early history of Britain. Leicester, United Kingdom: Leicester University Press, 1982.

Ellis, Peter Berresford. *A Dictionary of Irish Mythology*. Oxford reference. Oxford, United Kingdom: Oxford University Press, 1991.

Ellis, Peter Berresford. *Dictionary of Celtic Mythology*. New York: Oxford University Press, 1994.

Fee, Christopher R., with David A. Leeming. *Gods, Heroes, & Kings: The Battle for Mythic Britain*. New York: Oxford University Press, 2004.

Finke, Laurie, and Martin B. Shichtman. *King Arthur and the Myth of History*. Gainesville: University Press of Florida, 2004.

Gantz, Jeffrey. *The Mabinogion*. New York: Barnes & Noble, 1996.

Goodrich, Norma Lorre. *King Arthur*. New York: F. Watts, 1986.

Green, Miranda J. *The Celtic World*. London: Routledge, 1995.

Green, Miranda J. *The Gods of the Celts*. Stroud, United Kingdom: Sutton, 1996.

Green, Miranda J. *Celtic Myths. The Legendary Past*. Austin: University of Texas Press, 1993.

Higham, N. J. *King Arthur: Myth-Making and History*. London: Routledge, 2002.

Jack, R. I. *Medieval Wales*. London: Hodder and Stoughton for the Sources of History, Ltd., 1972.

Jones, Gwyn, and Thomas Jones. *The Mabinogion*. New York: Knopf, 2001.

Lacy, Norris J., Geoffrey Ashe, and Debra N. Mancoff. *The Arthurian Handbook*. Garland reference library of the humanities, Vol. 1920. New York: Garland Publishing, 1997.

Lindahl, Carl, John McNamara, and John Lindow. *Medieval Folklore: A Guide to Myths, Legends, Tales, Beliefs, and Customs*. Oxford, United Kingdom: Oxford University Press, 2002.

Lupack, Alan. *The Oxford Guide to Arthurian Literature and Legend*. Oxford, United Kingdom: Oxford University Press, 2005.

MacKillop, James. *Dictionary of Celtic Mythology*. Oxford, United Kingdom: Oxford University Press, 1998.

Maier, Bernhard. *Dictionary of Celtic Religion and Culture*. Woodbridge, Suffolk, United Kingdom: Boydell Press, 1997.

Snyder, Christopher A. *The Britons*. The peoples of Europe. Malden, MA: Blackwell Publishers, 2003.

Snyder, Christopher A. *The World of King Arthur*. New York: Thames & Hudson, 2000.

White, Richard. *King Arthur in Legend and History*. New York: Routledge, 1998.

PART II

WARRIORS FOR THE CHRISTIAN FAITH

4

The Byzantine
Two-Blooded Hero

The Historical Context of the Byzantine Epic[1]

Who Were the Byzantines?

Byzantine is a term used to describe the residents, customs, and culture of *Byzantium*, which is to say the Eastern Roman Empire. The emperor Constantine the Great founded the capital of this region of the empire in 324 AD. After his great victory over Maxentius at the Battle of the Milvian Bridge in 312, Constantine consolidated his control over the western half of the Roman Empire. It was on the eve of this conflict that Constantine was said to have received a vision of the Cross and to have heard the words, "by this sign ye shall conquer." Medieval tradition held that this experience was the turning point in Constantine's personal spiritual life and in that of his empire, and such accounts mark the conversion of the Roman Empire to Christianity from this moment, which also was to provide the archetype of the dream vision throughout the Middle Ages.

Following his victory at the Milvian Bridge with one at Chrysoupolis on the shore of the Bosphorus twelve years later, Constantine became sole ruler over all of the widespread holdings of Rome. The emperor chose for the site of his new administrative center for the eastern portion of the Empire *Byzantion*, a Greek city dating from some seven centuries before Christ. Byzantion was located on the southern side of the Bosphorus, a waterway with a strategic location on the Black Sea. The emperor named his new capital after himself, calling it *Constantinople*, or the "City of

Constantine." Constantine divided the Roman Empire into two sections for administrative purposes. This division was to prove auspicious: Although the city of Rome was to be sacked within a century, and the last puppet emperor of the Western Empire deposed in 476 AD, the Eastern Empire ruled from Constantinople was to stand for nearly one-thousand years after the fall of its western counterpart.

Although the denizens of the Arabian Peninsula had always posed a threat to the Byzantine heartland, it was with the rise of Islam in the seventh century that Arabic onslaughts began to make substantial inroads into Anatolia, the peninsula we now know as Turkey. However, although the great Byzantine epic purports to record the exploits of the border warriors who held the frontier against raiding Arabs, in fact there was much cultural and commercial intercourse between the Byzantine and Arabic worlds. However, as the Arab threat paled in the 11th century, the specter of a new, Turkic threat began to raise its profile, and although it would prove the process of centuries, it would be to Turks that the walls of Constantinople eventually would fall.

Byzantium was of immense cultural importance in Eastern Europe and Western Asia throughout the Middle Ages, serving as the model for the fledgling Russian state, acting as the seat of the Eastern Orthodox Church, and providing the great rival to the Persians and then later to the Ottoman Turks, to whom Constantinople fell in 1453. However, this great capital on the Bosphorus rose again in a new guise and became known as Istanbul, the seat of a great new empire that did not fall from grace until the close of the World War I. In common usage, *Byzantine* has come to connote a sophisticated and cynical labyrinthine bureaucracy steeped in conspiracy and intrigue, a meaning suggestive of the political structures and realities of the Eastern Roman Empire at the height of its civilization.

The Concept of "Holy War" in the Byzantine Epic

The phrase "holy war" evokes an image of a cataclysmic struggle between the forces of good and evil, a temporal battle resulting from and resonating with a cosmic conflict between the heavenly powers of light and the hellish forces of darkness. Thus, because the very term itself offers mythic ramifications of mighty proportions, it comes as no surprise that medieval epic accounts regarding the trope of holy war often offer treasure-troves of mythic archetypes and legendary details. Sometimes these elements concern the sanctified battle against the demonic other seemingly defined by the essence of the concept of holy war itself, whereas at other times they concern the development of the medieval epic hero, a figure similar to but distinct from the culture hero of more ancient mythologies. More surprising is the fact that these epics and their heroes are at times more nuanced in their treatment of their religious enemies than one might expect. Furthermore, the texts sometimes seem far less concerned with a universal struggle of good versus evil than with the details of the particular hero's own life and death. The Byzantine epic *Digenis Akritis*, to cite what might be the most extreme example of these two deviations from the expected pattern, is at points considerably sophisticated and even sympathetic toward the Arab enemies of the empire, and the poem, in any event, primarily focuses upon the hero Basil Digenis Akritis himself.

The Theme of the Border Hero[2]

The epic heroes of medieval mythology who defend homeland and faith differ from the culture heroes of more distant ancient mythologies in several ways. Roland, El Cid, Igor, and Basil all are situated in specific historical contexts, limiting boundaries that rather precisely prescribe their ranges of activities. It is noteworthy that the period we term the Middle Ages saw the rise of a series of mighty conflicts between great monotheistic traditions that each incorporated earlier mythic traditions in its own ways; these conflicts obviously extend with significant repercussions into the present day. Moreover, it is no surprise that the infidel, the "monstrous other," displaces to some extent in these traditions the giants, dragons, and other nonhuman and demonic enemies with which we may be more familiar and more used to construe as "mythic." All of these heroes are concerned ostensibly with battling the demonic other, although this combat is often sublimated within a context of archetypes concerning the epic heroes themselves. Moreover, frontier areas are naturally unstable and thus foster insecurity. As a result of such instability, loyalties may ebb and flow according to changing conditions, and those who inhabit border regions may find more common ground with neighboring enemies than with distant kin. Love matches and sexual liaisons with rival groups add to this volatile mix, as do the renegades and outlaws who tend to populate the frontier. Such is the context that produced the hero Basil Digenis Akritis.

Historical and Social Realities Reflected or Distorted in *Digenis Akritis*[3]

The mixed blood of Basil, the heroic border lord of *Digenis Akritis*, illustrates on some level the reality of the vibrant mixed cultures to be found on the borders—and in some measure even in the capital—of the Byzantine Empire. Scholarship concerning the epic has often focused on the relationship between the text (its settings, characters, descriptions of social structures, and manifestations of cultural concepts) and the realities of the Byzantine life at the time described by *Digenis Akritis*. In brief, this relationship is extremely irregular and full of surprises. Although some of the references in *Digenis Akritis* to the practices associated with Islam and the customs and natures of Arab peoples are obviously stock descriptions of savage, inhuman enemies, many of the details regarding Islam and Arabs in the poem in fact betray a nuanced and at times sympathetic view of these enemies of Byzantium.

The Literary Context of *Digenis Akritis*[4]

Although there is general agreement that the earliest forms of this poem were originally recited orally, textual versions of the Byzantine epic *Digenis Akritis* are preserved in six main manuscripts, of which two, the Grottaferrata (G) and the Escorial (E), generally are considered to reflect most clearly the spirit of the oral narrative that preceded the recording of the epic in written form. The exact relationship between the two earliest sources is still the subject of some lively debate, but it is without a doubt most helpful, whenever possible, to compare the parallel episodes from these two versions. In any case, although these two manuscripts are dated to the early 14th and late 15th centuries, respectively, they are thought to reflect much earlier oral narratives.

The stories that came to form *Digenis Akritis* may have traveled to Constantinople from the frontier along the Euphrates. It has been suggested that the oral traditions comprising the *Digenis Akritis* cycle of stories may have migrated to the capital along with refugees from the aftermath of the Battle of Manzikert in 1071. It is thought that about a century after this migration an attempt was made to organize disparate elements of these traditions into a coherent narrative sequence, perhaps influenced by the contemporary genre of the Romance flowering at that time in Western Europe and brought to Constantinople by Latin Crusaders. Other textual sources may have included historical records and devotional works. It is likely that during the next century or so, something like the narratives preserved in the manuscript records took shape.

In Greek-language folklore surviving into the modern world, especially in the eastern dialects, the hero of *Digenis Akritis* has assumed the mantle of a sort of everyman in a valiant but doomed attempt to wrestle the figure of Death. A great segment of the scholarship on the epic has been concerned with its relationship to later folksongs, but as seductive as such lines of inquiry are, it has been forcefully asserted that one must take special care in ascribing relationships between an epic text from the Byzantine Age and folk texts from much later periods. Although the literary narrative undoubtedly reflects debts to folksongs and stories that preceded it, we cannot expect that these traditions have remained as static as the manuscript texts have, although some recent scholarship has attempted to reaffirm the relationship with recent folksongs. In any case, one should be wary of expecting too much continuity from a living, changing folk tradition.

The Epic of *Digenis Akritis*, The "Two-Blooded Border-Lord"

Digenis Akritis is the story of the unique heritage of a Byzantine aristocrat and military official named Basil, of his precocious development as a hunter and warrior, of his heroic exploits and sexual dalliances, and of his marriage and early death at his post on the Euphrates at the very edge of the Empire. Basil's father, generally referred to in the poem as "the Emir," was an Arab who captured Basil's mother in a raid, eventually forsaking his god, land, and family for the sake of the love of his beautiful Byzantine captive. The opening portion of the narrative is dedicated to recounting Basil's parentage, and the balance of the poem tends to focus on Basil's personal heroic endeavors rather than on his role as a Byzantine army commander. Indeed, the ease with which a reading of the text may be organized around major episodes concerning the life of Basil lends it to a discussion of mythic archetypes of the hero.

Heroic Archetypes in *Digenis Akritis*

The Birth of Basil: The Unique Twin-Heritage of the Hero of Digenis Akritis[5]

The unusual origin of Basil, including the difficulties confronted by his parents, marks him as special. The story begins with a description of the man who would become the father of the Byzantine border-lord, an Emir of Syria who regularly raided Byzantine territory, destroying property and taking many captives. On one such raid that took him into Cappadocia, the Emir came upon the house of a Byzantine general and took, along with a great deal of booty, the virgin daughter of the general, who was himself in exile. The general's wife managed to escape and to write to her five sons, who were posted along the borders. The mother pleaded for her sons to rescue their sister and pronounced her curse upon them should they fail to do so. The brothers, shedding tears at this catastrophe and at their sister's likely fate, made their way to the camp of the Emir, of whom they asked their sister's release.

The Arab lord admired their loyalty and pluck and offered to meet one of them in single combat—winner take all: If the brother were victorious he would redeem his sister and the siblings all could go free; however, if the Emir were to prevail, the brothers would join their sister in bondage. Pleased by this chance to gain their sister's freedom, the brothers drew lots to determine which would face the Emir, and fate determined that their champion should be the youngest brother, Constantine, he who was a twin to their stolen sister. Crossing himself, the young Byzantine lord rode forth to meet the Emir, and although some thought to mock at Constantine's youthful boldness, one Saracen advised the Emir to take care against an opponent who handled his arms and his mount so well. After a mighty clash and much blood-letting it became apparent to all that Constantine might well kill the Emir, who was therefore advised to withdraw and to grant his opponent the victory. This the Arab lord did, making the customary sign of submission with his fingers and granting the brothers the right to search his encampment for their sister.

However, in this endeavor they were deceived, because they met a Saracen in the camp who told them that they might find the bodies of many slaughtered virgins in a nearby ditch. This they did indeed, but the hacked heads and limbs, stabbed and mutilated corpses, and bloody gore were so disfigured and confused that the brothers could not hope to identify their sister among the dead. Their only consolation was that their sister appeared to have been slain for preserving her virginity. Weeping, sprinkling their heads with dust, and evoking the Sun in their grief, the brothers piled the corpses in a common grave and returned to the Emir, demanding the return of their sister or the oblivion of death. Again moved by the dedication and courage of the girl's brothers, the Emir asked for their lineage, which was of the utmost nobility, although their father had fallen from favor and had been exiled. The Emir responded with his own family history, which was every bit as worthy as that of the girl and her brothers.

After having determined the courage, commitment, and noble blood of the family of his captured maiden, the Emir revealed that he had been testing her brothers. Struck immediately by her beauty and captivated by her grace, the Emir had protected the girl during her captivity so she had not been despoiled nor had she suffered the fate of the murdered maidens that the brothers found in the ditch. She had asked for her brothers continually throughout her captivity, and having tested those brothers the Emir determined to return the girl to her family and to forsake his own family, religion, and station and return with his love to her home, if the girl's brothers would accept the Emir as their brother-in-law. To this request the brothers assented immediately, and after a tearful reunion with her brothers, the girl and her future husband returned to Byzantium, where they were to make their home. All who witnessed or heard of these events were astounded that through her beauty this one girl had bested the mighty army of the Syrians and brought its greatest general home a prisoner to her love.

It is noteworthy that the mother of Basil the Border-Lord, like his wife, is not identified by name and is generally referred to as the "girl," or in terms of family or marital relationships. She seems not to have been consulted concerning her marriage, but her position as a potential bride, which very likely could have been ruined by her capture and by the actual or assumed loss of honor associated with such kidnapping, seems to have been redeemed by a speedy and honorable marriage to a man of high rank. His role as a bride-snatcher seems to represent in this poem an honorable heroic pursuit, rather akin to a rarefied form of hunting, and his son likewise will prove his mettle through similar exploits.

For his own part, in addition to a beautiful bride and the fulfillment of the love he claims to bear for her, the Emir gains a powerful, worthy, and influential family of in-laws through his marriage. Indeed, in the terms of mythic archetypes, an important aspect of the "Lay of the Emir," as this first section of the narrative is often called, is the establishment of the person of Basil Digenis Akritis as the product of a union between two of the most noble and favored members of two competing rival empires. Thus, the story of the marriage of Basil's mother and father, in addition to providing a suitably unusual and impressive origin of the hero in terms of the battles and adventures involved, also illustrates that Basil is particularly special, noble, and heroic by virtue of his pedigree as the son of the noblest houses of Byzantium and Syria.

Several other mythic elements contained in this episode also bear examination. Constantine, the uncle of Basil, appears to go into battle brandishing a stick or cudgel, which is in the G version the signature weapon of the border-lord. This weapon is reminiscent of that of several gods, demi-gods, and heroes in the Indo-European tradition, perhaps in the Eastern Mediterranean resonating most closely with the club of the classical Hercules and with Gurz, the ox-head cudgel of the Persian Feridun. Further, the ritual of lament manifested by the brothers that evokes the Sun and the soil is also thought to be of great antiquity.

A considerable portion of *Digenis Akritis* is dedicated to recounting the history of the hero's parents, their marriage, and the obstacles facing their union. The birth of the hero Basil Digenis Akritis himself is mentioned almost as an afterthought in this section, and the narrative does not take up the threads of Basil's story until approximately one third of the way through the poem. The two parts of the narrative are woven together in several ways, not least by the practice of bride-snatching and perhaps most notably in the Emir's direct reference to his prowess fighting bandits and overcoming fierce wild animals. The Emir alludes to this prowess in his speech to the brothers of his abducted bride in which he pronounces his willingness to convert to Christianity, defect to Byzantium, and marry their sister. This reference underscores the Emir's son's future destiny as a hero who primarily subdues brigands and beasts through single combat, rather than as his official function might be thought to require (i.e., as a true imperial border-lord who mainly gains military glory by leading engagements against Arab armies, as the Byzantine term *akritis* suggests).

The twin origin of the hero of *Digenis Akritis*, made clear through the story of his parentage and by his name, is further illuminated by the double plotline of the narrative, which shifts from an account of the Arab emir to one of his Byzantine son the border-lord; moreover, the shifting perspective of the poem, which moves between that of the Arab world of Basil's father and that of the Byzantine world of Basil's mother, further emphasizes this double provenance. In addition, *Digenis Akritis* is sometimes referred to as a double genre "epic Romance"; those who favor this view see more epic themes developed in the earlier section and suggest that the second part illustrates more Romance motifs. Such an emphasis on the duality of a hero wrought from a forbidden love that transcends and to some extent binds two separate worlds resonates with the echoes of ancient heroes born through the confluence of divine and mortal bloodlines, confluence which brings two worlds together in the flesh of one person. Such heroes are common enough in the classical world that gave birth to Byzantium (Hercules and Perseus leap to mind).

Perhaps more to the point, the parentage of Christ was held by the Eastern Orthodox Church to bring together the flesh of Man and the spirit of God in just such a birth through Mary Theotokos (i.e., "Mother of God"); indeed, the bitter theological disputes concerning the dual nature of Christ comprise a vital chapter of Byzantine history. It would overstate the matter to suggest that Basil's origin was necessarily perceived by a Byzantine audience to reflect the duality of the Godhead made flesh, but, in the intellectually sophisticated and theologically concerned Byzantine culture that produced the literary versions of the epic, it would perhaps be a safe assumption that a heroic dual nature might well resonate with several important religious and literary themes. Thus, in the way that the hero of *Digenis Akritis* illustrates duality on a mortal scale, the birth of Basil as scion to two competing traditions from two disparate worlds indeed might profitably be categorized under the mythic archetype of the miraculous or unusual conception of the hero.

Basil and the Beasts: The Coming-of-Age Hunt in Digenis Akritis[6]

Testing one's mettle is a central concern of heroic narratives, and *Digenis Akritis* is no exception: Indeed, the poem reflects a consciousness of this aspect of heroism, as when Basil implores his father to allow him to test himself by means of the hunt. Rites of passage comprise the bulk of the early part of the portion of the narrative dedicated to Basil himself, and the first such childhood feat that marks the youth as a hero is his prowess battling ferocious beasts. After only three years of education at the charge of a teacher assigned by his father, Basil moves on to horsemanship and the hunt, and at the age of twelve he wishes to prove his manhood through exploits becoming of a hero. He entreats the Emir to be allowed to hunt dangerous game. Although extremely pleased by his son's precocious valor, Basil's father informs his son that these tasks are far too daunting for one so young and that Basil should wait until he is fit to prove his mettle in this way. The son laments to his father that such caution is for the commonplace and hardly stands to the benefit of the glory of a true hero. Basil perseveres in his entreaty, the Emir ultimately relents, and Basil accompanies a hunting party including his father and his uncle Constantine.

The party comes upon a family of bears and, at the behest of his uncle, Basil does battle with the beasts unarmed. The female bear the young hero encircled with his mighty arms and squeezed her guts out through her mouth. When the male fled, Basil rushed him until the bear turned and charged, opening its fearsome jaws to bite off the boy's head. Undeterred, Basil grabbed the beast's jaw and flung it to the ground, twisting its neck and breaking its back. The tumult of this battle was such that a deer was flushed from hiding and sprang away; at a word from his father, Basil took chase afoot, and with the fleetness of a great hunting cat he caught it by the hindquarters and ripped the deer in half. The Emir and Constantine were immensely gratified by Basil's superior abilities and cried out that God had sent him as a model for bold-hearted heroes. As the young man came forth from the grove in which he had struggled with the beasts, he had the bears in the grip of his right hand and the deer in the left. At that moment, a gigantic lion rushed toward the hero, so the boy dropped his trophies and charged it, only taking his sword at the express command of his uncle. With a mighty blow Basil clove the lion's head in twain to the shoulders, joyfully declaiming to his uncle that he had enacted the work of God. After these feats Basil's father led him to a nearby spring, where he washed his son's feet with his own hands while others laved the boy's hands and feet. All drank of the water that ran off of the hero to share in a measure of his courage.

Basil's empty-handed battle with the bears illustrates the archetypal hero's superhuman strength and courage in general and resonates specifically with such unarmed combat as Beowulf's hand-to-hand struggle with Grendel, to cite but one well-known example. However, given the emphasis of this hunt as a coming-of-age episode, perhaps the myth of the infant Hercules strangling the serpents in his crib provides a closer parallel. The fleetness of foot that Basil demonstrates in running down the deer likewise exemplifies a heroic commonplace, although it is particularly noteworthy that in the Byzantine tradition the emperor Basil the First was reported to have caught and killed a deer in the manner described in this passage. The ritual washing scene seems to enact a sort of baptismal rite of some sort that marks the boy's passage into manhood at the same time that it evokes a folkloric attempt to distill the essence of heroism in the young man's bathwater. However, the hunting of ferocious beasts is hardly the ultimate test of Basil's mettle, and in his attainment of a bride the young hero reflects the actions of his father the Emir and he passes fully into the rights and responsibilities of manhood.

Basil Takes a Wife: Bride-Snatching as the Ultimate Hunt in Digenis Akritis[7]

Returning victorious from his hunt for ferocious beasts, Basil and his party passed the dwelling of a famous general whose house was within sight of the road. Drawn to the sound of the youth's voice, the maiden daughter of the general peered out from her chamber, and, enchanted by his noble and lovely features, the girl was struck at once with love for the young man. Noting the grand and fearsome exterior of the house, Basil inquired of his father whether this might be the home of the well-known commander and his lovely daughter. The Emir answered that it was, and noted that the renowned beauty of that daughter had incited many a would-be lover to try to gain her hand, but all to no avail: The general learned in turn of each plot to steal his daughter, and his cruel response to each such attempt was to trap each suitor and kill or maim him—some he decapitated and some he blinded, but none won the general's daughter.

Basil responded to the Emir in this instance with the same confidence with which he had dismissed the dangers of the hunt and asked only that his father seek the girl's hand for him. However, the general had already rebuffed the Emir in such an entreaty, and so Basil's only hope of winning the girl as his bride was to steal her away. At this point the young hero saw the maiden gazing at him through her window, and his heart was struck with love for her, just as hers had been for him. Basil called out to the virgin that he would seek her hand if she offered no refusal, and the girl sent her maid to answer that the youth had won her heart, although she knew him not, and to inquire as to whether this young man were indeed Basil Digenis Akritis, the rich and aristocratic young man descended, as the girl herself was, from the noble Doukas family. She warned him of her father's cruel answer to suitors but did not dissuade him from an attempt to take her, and the boy left with the girl's agreement to meet him the next day.

Basil went home and prepared for the abduction of his bride, returning as night was about to turn to day, and the waiting girl had finally fallen into slumber. Wakened by the strains of Basil's stringed instrument, the girl called out to her lover, who reproached her for her sleepiness. She in turn found fault with the lad's tardiness and begged him to cease playing music, which might soon bring her father's wrath upon the young suitor. Terrified for his sake because of the general's cruelty, the girl attempted once more to persuade Basil to forsake the dangerous task he had set himself; however, the young man would under no circumstances leave without the girl. And so, giving herself up to shamelessness and to the dictates of her heart, the girl who had remained cloistered, unseen, and unheard by her many other suitors, forsook her family, wealth, and position and stole away with her lover Basil, giving herself over to his command in everything and admonishing him at the same time not to forget his love of and commitment to her, who had sacrificed so much to be with him.

Calling out for the general's blessing and thus announcing the girl's departure from her father's house as a stolen bride, Basil and the girl rode off with the followers of the general in hot pursuit. When he reached a spot he thought suitable, Basil put the girl in a safe place and, assenting to her wish that he avoid harming her brothers, he promptly dispatched many of the general's troops. When the father of his bride arrived with his immediate bodyguard, Basil decimated them also, although he took great care to cast the girl's brothers off of their horses without doing his brothers-in-law any damage he could avoid. At this point Basil showed proper respect and courtesy to the general, offering the father of his bride his service to prove what a fine son-in-law he was. The general then thanked God that he had been granted such a hero as Basil to be the husband for his daughter, acknowledging that such a man as Basil was peerless and exactly what he had wished for his daughter.

The virgin in the citadel and the slain suitors are familiar motifs in mythology generally and in the genre of the medieval Romance specifically. The fact that Basil's lady love is the sole daughter in a family of five brothers reflects his own mother's situation when the Emir took her, of course, providing yet another link between the two sections of the narrative. Further, this domestic structure may reflect something of a Byzantine ideal, as does the fact that Basil's lady seems entirely sequestered from the outside world, a description that resonates with Islamic practices but that may well have been less true in the reality of Byzantine life than in an idealized vision thereof. The girl's account of her family's relationship to Basil, like the Emir's conversation with the brothers of his captive bride, underscores the nobility of the possible match; further, it reflects the reality of 12th-century Byzantine aristocratic attitudes that favored the nobility of a potential marriage partner over the Church's concerns regarding consanguinity and degrees of incest.

Basil's wounding by the beauty of the object of his love is another motif common to myth and to Romance, but it is noteworthy that the Amazon Maximou, who cannot best Basil with lance or sword, deals him a stunning blow in the same manner as Basil's bride to be does. On the other hand, the erotic desire manifested by the girl in her initial decision to elope with Basil, articulated most clearly in her words to him upon his return after he has conquered her doubts concerning his own safety, seem more appropriate to an ardent male lover of the Byzantine tradition than they do to the virgin object of his desire, and it has been suggested that these sentiments reflect a uniquely 12th-century view of sexuality in counterpoint to the strictures of Byzantine morality.

The girl's passion-driven decision to renounce her family and position reflects the Emir's defection to Byzantium for the love of his stolen bride, of course, but moreover, Basil's theft of his own bride provides a telling inversion of his father's act. The distinction between the two acts of bride-snatching is vital: Whereas the Emir abducted a defenseless bride against her will and then announced his desire to wed her upon his defeat in single combat by her brother, Basil convinced his beloved to elope with him of her own volition, and then used the occasion of the ensuing pursuit and combat for her hand to win her, to prove his mettle, and to establish his credentials as the greatest of heroes. When the young man addressed him in the aftermath of this conflict, the general immediately validated Basil's pursuit for the girl's hand and his identity as the peerless suitor by acknowledging the youth as a hero without equal and therefore accepting him as his son-in-law there and then, before entering into negotiations concerning dowry or the wedding itself.

Consensual elopement, we infer from the sources, might lead to legal marriage, whereas forcible abduction, we are led to believe, generally would result in legal proceedings; the special exception of the Emir notwithstanding, Basil's act of bride-snatching clearly falls into the former category. It is also noteworthy that the general quickly articulates a desire to ratify the union with a laudable dowry that would win general acclamation and fame to eliminate the possibility of accusations of "match-stealing," charges that would demean all parties involved because this practice was associated with those too impoverished to negotiate a reasonable bride price and thus was held in contempt by the aristocracy.

The consensual nature of the elopement and the desire of the parties to enter into lawful matrimony are underscored by the fact that Basil announces his intention to depart with the girl and asks for the general's blessing before riding off with his new bride. This announcement, which emphasizes that flight under cover of darkness is unacceptable to Basil, suggests elopement rather than kidnapping and adds to the heroic nature of the act because it ensures that the general's troops will be hot on the trail of the fleeing couple. Thus, Basil virtually guarantees that he will have to engage in combat against overwhelming odds to secure his bride. The general's words to Basil after the pursuers have been subdued imply that the successful theft of the girl and the defense of that theft were the objects of the jealous watch that the father had kept over his daughter: This test was designed to ensure that only the greatest of heroes might win and keep the daughter of the general.

Indeed, as Basil himself said to his groom and then to his mother concerning his coming adventure to win his love, bride-snatching may be described as the most dangerous and glorious form of hunting in the narrative traditions associated with *Digenis Akritis*, and contemporary scholarship has illustrated how this motif continues into the modern period in, for example, certain types of Cypriot folksongs concerning heroes.

The greatness of the strongest and bravest hero is thus manifested through his abduction of the most beautiful and noble bride and/or through his successful protection of his bride from such attempts of abduction. Moreover, some recent criticism has suggested that the language of abduction concerning Basil's bride, as well as her ceremonial induction into his family, is reflective of ritualized aspects of bride-theft associated with wedding ceremonies. In *Digenis Akritis*, bride-snatching is without doubt an important archetypal adventure of the hero passing from a precocious boyhood into a fully realized heroic manhood.

Basil's Proving Ground: Battles with Monsters, Brigands, and an Amazon in Digenis Akritis[8]

The Emperor Basil's visit to Basil's domain on the Euphrates, culminating in the hero's wrestling of a wild stallion and slaying of a lion that terrifies even the sovereign, in large measure duplicates and serves to underscore the importance of the earlier coming-of-age hunt scenes involving the deer and the lion. The grounds for Basil's reputation for heroism are thereby manifested before the person of the emperor, and thus the hero validates in feats of valor the imperial favor he has been granted in terms of the title of *patrikios*, the restoration of his ancestral estates, the appropriate imperial robes, and the ratifying documentation in the form of an imperial *chrysobull*. The fact that the honors bestowed upon Basil Digenis Akritis appear to reflect with some degree of accuracy those that might be granted to a general or governor of the 8th to 10th centuries lends a veneer of veracity to the episode. Most vitally, the poet takes this opportunity to reemphasize Basil's identity as a hero of epic proportions by observing that those who witnessed Basil's acts were amazed and terrified by his superhuman strength, and by having the emperor himself give voice to the fact that Basil's strength exceeds that of all other men.

Some time after the visit of the emperor, in the most sweet month of May, Basil and his bride settled in a beautiful garden filled with lovely flowers and trees, inhabited by peacocks, parrots, and swans. An icy spring bubbled up in the center of the grove, the many delights of which yet paled in comparison with the lovely young girl at Basil's side. One day at noon Basil lay down on his couch within his tent, surrounded by pungent burning spices, sprinkled with rose water by his ladylove, and lulled into slumber by the song of nightingales. The girl, thirsting for a drink, made her way to the spring at the center of the garden, where she bathed her feet in the cool water and otherwise refreshed herself. As she lounged by the spring, the girl was approached by a hideous serpent-demon, which had taken upon itself the semblance of a beautiful young man. In this guise the monster attempted to seduce the girl, who refused its advances, recognizing it for the demon that it was. Spurned in its seduction of the object of its desire, the demon attempted to violate the girl by force, but she called out to her husband Basil the Border-Lord, who ran to her rescue.

As the hero rushed to attack it, the demon transformed before his very eyes into a great, three-headed serpent. From each head emitted great flames like lightning flashes, and as the serpent shifted on its coils the earth and all the trees shook and the monster emitted a sound like a thunderclap. Some say that one head had the semblance of a young lad, one looked like an old man, and one revealed the demon's true nature, embodying the head of the Serpent of Gehenna. The body thickened and the tail thinned and sharpened as the demon sprang from its coils and struck at the hero, but Basil was the faster and struck off its three heads all at once. As the body of the serpent-demon twitched in its death-spasms, the hero cleaned his blade, called his servants to remove the noisome corpse, and returned to his couch to complete his slumber, with which he was not yet sated.

Laughing long and loud in her joy at the destruction of the serpent, the girl wandered over to a tree so that she might calm herself and so that her laughter might not wake her lover. Suddenly a huge lion, drawn by the sounds of the serpent's demise and by the music of the girl's mirth, charged from a thicket and made as though to devour the girl. Hearing his wife shriek with terror, Basil leapt up from his couch, snatched up his club, and rushed toward the menacing lion, which he dispatched with a single blow to the head. After the lion's body was taken away, the girl asked her husband to play for her upon the same instrument with which he had enchanted her before their elopement; she hoped thus to beguile her soul and to forget the horror of the beasts.

As Basil played for her, his young wife sang a song of joy for having been matched with such a wonderful husband. Drawn by the melodious sound of her voice, a band of brigands caught sight of the girl and, wounded by her beauty, they thought to steal her for themselves. Before joining combat, they called out to Basil that he might save himself if he were to abandon his bride. Overcome by terror and sorrow, the bride thought never to see her husband again; however, citing the Gospel of Matthew, Basil soothed his wife's fear of their separation by the brigands: What God has brought together, he assured her, men will not put apart. Taking up his stick and shield, Basil put all of the brigands to death.

Filthy and covered with blood, the young hero went to bathe while his bride fetched him clean clothes. Basil rested under a tree while he waited for her, and soon three riders came toward him. They were handsomely armed and dressed, and some say that one was a beardless youth, one a fully bearded warrior in his prime, and one a gray-bearded veteran. The riders asked the young hero if he had seen a group of brigands pass by, and Basil answered stoutly that he had indeed seen just such a party, all of whom had desired to abduct his wife; he had paid them out without mounting his horse, Basil added, moreover, offering to give the same attentions to these three riders. These three brigands discerned that only Basil Digenis Akritis might have performed such a heroic feat of arms, and they determined to test him.

Pretending to scoff, the eldest, who was the spokesman, asked how they could believe that an unarmed man afoot could defeat such a band of seasoned fighters; thus, he offered the young man the opportunity to prove his claim by choosing one of the present three to engage in single combat. Basil responded with a smile that, if they wished to learn his identity for sure, they might as well rush him, all three at once, and that they need not dismount if they felt no shame at enjoying such uneven odds. At these words the border-lord took up his stick and shield and moved toward the riders. The old brigand claimed that such a dishonorable attack would shame them all, dismounted, and rushed at Basil, shivering the young hero's shield with one blow from his sword; only the grip was left in the borderer's hand. However, as his comrades were urging the old man to finish his opponent, Basil brought his club down upon the head of the old Brigand with such force that, had the man's shield not softened the blow, his skull would have been shattered. Even as it was, the old man was knocked completely senseless, his body wracked by spasms as he lowed like an ox.

Dispensing with their erstwhile pretensions of honor, the two other Brigands, still mounted, charged Basil in tandem. Seizing the old brigand's shield, the young border-lord ran to attack his opponents, who attempted to outflank him, but although they were both battle-hardened and skilled at combat, neither could get the better of Basil, and each time he brandished his bludgeon they flew from him like sheep from the lion. So the brigands circled the young warrior until the girl, coming to watch the battle, stood in Basil's line of sight and he gained a second wind. Then Basil shattered the sword-arm of his second foe, who fell from his horse, and broke the back of the mount of his third opponent, who was pinned beneath the body of his horse, trembling with terror that the border-lord would finish him off.

However, Basil reassured the wretch that he would never hit a man while he was down and offered to let the brigand regain his feet and finish the combat in an honorable fashion. The old man, having regained his senses, sued Basil for peace and submitted to his will: He offered his services and those of all of the brigands, who would be overjoyed to follow a warrior and leader such as Basil Digenis Akritis. The young hero spurned this offer, noting that he, like the only child he was, did not wish to rule or command but wanted only to roam the frontier alone with his bride, whereas the likes of the brigands were destined to give or receive orders, to fight battles, and to raid the borders. Basil set the brigands free with the invitation to return and try their luck again with a fresh army of brigands, and so, the three riders departed, happy to escape with their lives.

The three brigands traveled some distance away and then sat down to regroup and to take counsel together. First they lamented their lost honor, hard-won through many victories over mighty opponents and great armies. Then the younger warriors began to speculate that a single man, unarmored and carrying only a stick, could not hope to match fully armed, strong, and experienced fighters such as themselves. He who defeated them so soundly must have been more than a man; he must have been a spirit of the locale, or perhaps a monster of some other sort. As further evidence for this idea they noted that the girl of the garden appeared herself to be more than human; her beauty seemed to them supernatural—that of one of the ancient statues brought to life. However, the old man cut short these excuses, stating without doubt that he had been defeated by the greatest of men and that his young comrades were comforting themselves with mere fantasy.

However, even granting that Basil was the mightiest of warriors, the ancient brigand still doubted that the greatest soldier in the world could have killed all of their comrades, and so he advised that the signal fires be lit to muster their remaining fellows so that they might plan and execute a surprise attack upon the young border-lord. This was done, and the night was lit with the fire of the beacon, while its smoke marked the day. However, as time passed it became clear that Basil had offered no vain boast, and thus that no one was left to answer the call of the beacon. Every member of the brigand band was dead. The younger brigands then upbraided the old one for making them work for no reason because any warrior who could defeat them as Basil had might indeed have destroyed the rest of their forces. Therefore, they counseled the old man to seek out their kinswoman Maximou, who kept a great band of warriors, but they advised him to speak to her with cunning because she might not send a whole army for the purpose of fighting one man.

Maximou was of the race of Amazons, those fierce women who had been brought back by Alexander from the land of the Brahmans. Like her mothers before her, she took her delight in battle. Upon his arrival before Maximou, the old brigand related to the Amazon a fabricated tale of how he had happened upon the most beautiful girl in the world, one of noble birth, that he intended to bestow upon his son. The only obstacle to this union was the man who had found this vision of loveliness first, and it was in the matter of disposing of this stumbling block that the brigand had called upon his kinswoman. Quickly won over to such a scheme, Maximou called forth her lieutenant to gather and sift their band of warriors so that they might set forth with a chosen party to claim this girl, whom the Amazon thought to be the most valuable of quarries.

The younger two brigands rejoined their comrade and Maximou's company along the way, and as they drew near to Basil's outpost, the ancient one advised that they divide their force, sending scouts out first, so that they might find their enemy and the girl without flushing their prey. To this the Amazon agreed, and so the old brigand and a few others, including Maximou's lieutenant, moved ahead of the main party and soon found the border-lord. At this point the old brigand would have returned for reinforcements, but the Amazon's lieutenant thought this shameful, and he charged Basil. However, the young hero soon paid this fool for his vanity, knocking the man senseless to the ground. Meanwhile, while Basil's attention was on this foe, the crafty old brigand wounded the hero's horse and rode quickly away, not willing to suffer again at the club of Basil.

The border-lord took advantage of this respite to hide his beloved in a secret vantage point from where she might watch the battle, although he cautioned her not to call out from there. He also changed his horse and armed himself. Basil then returned to where he could see the gathering host of his enemy and where he might admire their leader Maximou, the person and mount of which were bedecked with the finest accoutrements. When the Amazon perceived that her opponent was only one man, she was furious with the old brigand, and she questioned his manhood. Then she determined to meet Basil in single combat, to take his head as a trophy, and to bring back the young girl herself. However, as she spurred forward to cross the river, the border-lord called out to her to wait because it would be more seemly for a man to cross to meet a woman.

Maximou tried to make the most of Basil's disadvantage in the crossing, but to no avail; he knocked aside her lance with little effort and slew her horse, although he spared the Amazon herself. Basil then slaughtered or drove off Maximou's followers, many of who fled like cowards before him.

Although he knew that it was shameful to fight with a woman, Basil was still willing to spar with Maximou because of her reputation as a warrior, and he agreed to meet her in single combat again the next day. However, the end result was the same: Basil with ease parried the blows of the Amazon and slew her mount from under her, and yet again he spared Maximou's life. This time the Amazon offered herself to her conqueror, body and soul.

Basil's battle with the serpent-demon manifests the dragon-slaying motif common to many mythologies, and the setting for that conflict evokes the Garden of Eden described in *Genesis*. Although *drakon* might be read "ogre" here, and certainly is related to the *drakos*, or "ogre," of Greek folklore of the Modern Age, this monster clearly is parallel to the serpent in the Garden of Eden in several ways. Certainly the demon's attempt at seduction resonates with sexual wantonness associated with the serpent, and its three heads may echo a classical motif of a tripartite representation of Eros. Moreover, local folklore makes reference to several three-headed dragons, and a reading of the monster as a serpent is further implied by the setting of the garden itself. A serpent coupled with the description of that blossoming oasis in the verdant month of May together emphasize an association between Basil's personal paradise and the Garden of Eden. The hour of Basil's nap also seems significant because noon is a dangerous hour, from the era of the Psalmist, who mentions "the destruction that wasteth at noonday" (Psalm 91:6).

The fact that Basil's bride seeks refuge near a tree seems noteworthy. This is the third tree in this poem to offer sanctuary to a girl. In a grove that recalls the Garden of Eden, trees potentially are fraught with symbolism, of course, and in this text a series of trees seems related to safety: A tree offers safe haven to his stolen bride when Basil the borderer pauses to battle her father's pursuing army, and another tree is the place where an abandoned bride whom Basil ultimately rescues from the wilderness hides from those who would harm her until Basil ultimately rescues her from the wilderness. Of course in a Christian context, a tree offering sanctuary resonates with the Cross, especially in a setting that recalls the scene of the Fall of Man, undone by the fruit of one tree and reclaimed by the sacrifice of the Son of God upon another.

The three brigands, young, mature, and old, represent the three ages of Man and recall to some extent the three heads of the serpent, altogether perhaps suggesting some inversion of the Trinity. The passage describing Basil's battle with the three brigands speaks to a crux of the poem in that the three brigands seem to represent border-raiders of a sort known to the

Romans as *miles limitaneus*, which is to say the very Byzantine akritic class to which Basil, according to his surname, his imperial chrysobull, and the theoretical theme of his eponymous epic, rightfully belongs. In his speech to the defeated brigands, the two-blooded Basil emphasizes his role as an only child: He is alone, he is without peer, and he is uninterested in dispensing or following commands. Here Basil overtly articulates his desire for solitude, his preference for heroic single combat, and his role outside of established society in terms of his geographical position on the frontier and of his autonomous position outside of the institutional hierarchy.

It is doubly significant that, at the same time that he denies the political and military roles officially designated to him, he ascribes similar functions to the brigands one assumes an akritis might fight as a part of those roles. In this speech Basil makes crystalline his identity as the timeless epic hero who stands alone for the benefit of his greater glory, rather than as the Byzantine border-lord who polices the frontier to ensure the security of the empire. One might almost surmise from this speech that, rather than the representative of centralized authority he is purported to be, Basil, like the Icelandic Grettir Asmundarson, is the heroic brigand who survives outside of the law by dint of his superior ability, wit, and fortitude. The figure of Maximou evokes the legendary stories of Alexander, the greatest general of all time, and the archetype of the warrior maiden, the martial prowess of which is manifested as the Amazon in classical mythology. Basil's defeat of Maximou and her army thus emphasizes his prowess as the greatest of champions, but his subsequent treatment of this vanquished foe also underscores some of the more troubling aspects of the poem and of the nature of its hero.

Basil's Losing Battle: Lust as the Hero's Downfall in Digenis Akritis[9]

The role of women in *Digenis Akritis* and the protagonist Basil's relationships with women are, to say the least, problematic from a modern vantage point. Bride-snatching is a central heroic concern of the narrative and its chief figures, and Basil's mother and his wife represent trophies of this practice, which is portrayed as a stylized and rarefied form of hunting. However, not all criticism of the treatment of women in this text is anachronistic, and at times even the hero castigates himself in the first person for some actions. For example, in an episode prefaced with an admonishment to guard against licentiousness, Basil rescues a damsel in distress and forces her abductor to restore her honor, although he himself has taken advantage of her in the meantime. Basil saves from death and brigands an abandoned young bride only to rape her himself, finally restoring her to the rogue who had abandoned her and forcing him to marry the girl, thereby legitimizing their original elopement.

Basil's treatment of the Amazon Maximou is similarly morally reprehensible by Byzantine and modern standards. When Maximou the Amazon is defeated, she reverts from her role as a warrior attempting to defeat an opponent through a dominating masculine force of arms to that of a temptress attempting to seduce a lover through submissive feminine wiles and charms, thus shifting her position in her gendered encounter with Basil. In fact, Maximou first offers herself as a virgin wife to Basil, acknowledging her function as the spoils of combat and thereby alluding to the Romance motif of a heroic knight claiming the hand of a damsel as an appropriate reward for his deeds of valor. Although Basil makes clear to her that he is already married, he does not cut off her advances, and thus she defeats him through his lust rather than through her own strength. As she removes her armor the Amazon enemy is miraculously transformed into the seductive lover: Although unable to wound Basil's body to the quick with the weapons of war, Maximou's beauty, we are told, deeply wounds Basil's soul, especially the high breasts visible through the "gossamer-thin" shift Maximou revealed when she cast off her mail-coat. This sequence has a parallel in classical literature and in Byzantine imitations thereof, which were contemporaneous with the development of the epic poem.

Prompted by the jealousy of his wife, a jealousy that Basil assuages with lies, Basil's feelings of guilt over his unlawful union with Maximou prompts him in the G text to return to his lover and kill her. The murder of Maximou has never been satisfactorily explained, especially because, his protestations regarding her role as adulteress to one side, according to Byzantine law it would be Basil who would be guilty of adultery and of despoiling a virgin, however willing and seductive that virgin might be. Her cross-dressing certainly aggravates her appropriation of a masculine martial role, both of which practices might be implicitly condemned, especially by some Byzantine religious writers, but it is not in the least clear that Maximou has done anything at all serious enough to warrant death.

On the other hand, in the E version, Maximou is allowed to live but is demoted, in word and deed, from the position of a Valkyrie-like virgin shield-maiden to the role of a prostitute. It is hard to say which narrative tradition portrays Basil in the more negative light. In the G version, Basil treats Maximou with dignity and even affection until his guilt prompts him to kill her, and even then he rationalizes his murderous act, albeit unconvincingly, by alluding to Maximou's role as an adulteress. On the other hand, in the E version, Basil seems eager and even pleased to take advantage of the opportunity to defile Maximou's virginity, all the while scornfully degrading her with humiliating epithets. Maximou also exhibits a more crude sensibility in E, perhaps befitting an Amazon, a warrior, and an estimable battle leader; however, her coarse language and her war-like demeanor and actions perhaps reflect a transgressive appropriation of male gender roles that explains her treatment by the poet.

Nowhere is this more true than when she realizes that the old brigand has tricked her into marching an entire army against one man. She accuses her ancient kinsman of possessing a shriveled penis and offers in almost the next breath to take Basil's head and steal the girl on her own, without help from the likes of the brigands. Thus Maximou directly demeans the masculinity of one male warrior and then indirectly alludes to her appro-priation of the manhood of another, through her proposal to decapitate Basil and to claim his wife, thus taking two trophies that represent life, power, and virility in a warrior ethos. Perhaps the ancient archetype of the virgin warrior that is manifested in the figure of Maximou seemed transgressive enough, by the time the epic took written form, that it required censure by the Byzantine hands that recorded it in the E text; in other words, Basil's battle with Maximou might have seemed to be a hero's proper struggle with a monstrous perversion of femininity.

In any case, Maximou certainly represents the Amazon archetype (i.e., the virgin warrior who resonates with various Valkyrie-like demi-goddesses and warrior-queens from the Indo-European tradition), and it seems likely that this legacy of an earlier mythic tradition did not fit smoothly into the context of *Digenis Akritis*. Thus, the violence done to Maximou may represent in a sense the violence done to the text and to the archetype by their forced marriage. What begins as a violent conflict of arms continues as a sexual confluence of bodies and ultimately ends with Basil's cold-blooded killing of his Amazon lover in the G text, providing a microcosm for the reality of the eponymous border conflict of *Digenis Akritis*, which often comprises confluence and commerce punctuated with sporadic violent conflict. The hero's sexual liaison with Maximou, especially as this liaison is the result of an initial conflict between opposing forces, in any case in a way also reflects Basil's own genesis and his role on the frontier.

Basil's Meets His End: The Death of the Hero in Digenis Akritis[10]

After a brief Golden Age in which all who lived under his protection enjoyed unblemished peace and prosperity, Basil died young, succumbing at the height of his powers to a fever caught while bathing. As a ruler over a peaceable kingdom Basil resonates with many mythic figures, of course, but in a reference to the Trinity, which closes the account of this Golden Age, Basil all but achieves apotheosis as a Christ figure. However, in his manner of demise he reverts to heroic mode in that Basil's death echoes that recounted in the legends of Alexander the Great. As he struggles with mortal weakness for the first time, Basil wrestles with Charon, a doomed contest that is to become the primary subject of the folk traditions concerned with *Digenis Akritis*; moreover, the hero's strength ebbs and his courage fails for the first time in the face of the descending fiery Angel of Death. Basil's wife is overcome by grief as she watches him die. She has never before experienced anguish, and thus she collapses and dies at the same moment that he does, as though by a pact between the lovers. Her demise on her husband's deathbed evokes a common literary and mythic motif that also has resonance with ritual sacrifice in, to cite just one example perhaps familiar to the Byzantines, the pagan Rus tradition.

The death of Basil and his wife is followed by ritual lamentation and the invocation of universal mourning, another familiar motif. Later, at Basil's funeral, the mourners evoke the *ubi sunt* theme, asking what has become of the courage, strength, and heroism that shook the foundations of Basil's world and instilled terror in the hearts of the hero's human enemies and ferocious beasts alike. The answer is that all of Basil's courage and glory molder with him in the grave. Death, Charon, and Hades then are evoked as the tripartite destroyer of life, and thus as a pitiless inversion of the Trinity, granted dominion over man through Original Sin. The story of the hero Basil Digenis Akritis closes with a prayer that evokes the promise of the redemption of Basil and his wife at the Judgment, a promise extended to all who wish to live eternally with God. Thus, the border hero crosses the limits of his domain for the final time, blazing a path for the faithful to follow.

Notes

1. Partner succinctly examines the theme of holy war; see especially page xvi. Concerning the shortcomings of the "clash of cultures" model, see Bulliet, especially 15–30. See Geanakoplos's discussion on 155–156 of the Byzantine appropriation of Arab cultural aspects as such is manifested in *Digenis Akritis: Medieval Western Civilization*; see especially his note on the lack of potential for Byzantine racial animosity on 155.

2. See Papadopoullos, 131–138, for a thorough definition of the akritic hero that clearly distinguishes ancient cosmological heroes from their medieval epic counterparts. See Hook, 73–85, for an analysis of the resonance between the

Byzantine epic and its Old Spanish counterparts; he opens his discussion with reference to the "Wild West" frontier motif that has been noted in *Digenis Akritis*. See Partner, 53–56, for a brief comparison of the Byzantine *akritai* and the Muslim *ghazi*, both classes of border warriors that spawned heroic literary traditions.

3. See especially Bryer, 93–102; Geanakoplos *Byzantium,* 334–345; Geanakoplos *Medieval Western Civilization,* 155–156; Jeffreys, xvi–xvii, xxx–xli, and the notes on ll. 97–98 and 101–103 on 9; Magdalino, 1–14 (most especially 5–7 and 9–10); Partner, 48–50; and Rautman, 15–18.

4. The primary sources of *Digenis Akritis* include those versions found in the so-called Grottaferrata, Escorial (E), Trebizond (T), Andros (A), Paschalis (P), and Oxford (O) manuscripts, but the last four are now thought to have been derived from a late compilation created in reference to the Escorial and another, now lost version, which resembled in some facets the Grottaferrata; thus, the Grottaferrata (G) and the E are for present purposes the most authoritative manuscript sources of the epic. The most comprehensive and up-to-date edition of the G and the E texts is by Jeffreys, although the Mavrogordato edition of G—supplemented at a few points with material from T and A—is very good if a bit dated, the Ricks version of E is excellent, and Hull provides a useful, readable student edition of G; all four provide good introductory and ancillary materials. For contemporary critical commentary upon the text, see especially Alexiou, 15–25; Baldwin, 213–217; Beaton, 55–72; Galatariotou, 38–54; Geanakoplos *Byzantium*, 418–420; Hull, xv–xlvii; Jeffreys, xiii–xxx and xli–lxii; Jeffreys, 26–37 in Beaton and Ricks; Littlewood, 51 and 82–89; Magdalino, 1–14; Mavrogordato, xi–lxxxiv; Ricks, 1–17; and Ricks, 161–170 in Beaton and Ricks.

5. The primary sources for the unique provenance of the hero Basil and the problems associated with the unusual marriage of his parents include most of G Books I–III and E ll. 1–609, comprising the so-called "Lay of the Emir," which is the first of the two major parts of the narrative. See also the commentary of Ricks on 17–19.

6. The primary sources for the coming-of-age hunting episode include G Book IV ll. 66–212 and E ll. 739–791; see especially G Book IV l. 74, in which Basil uses the form *dokimasai* to describe his desire to examine his abilities; in addition, the verb *dokimago* is used in this sense throughout the E text. On 75, Jeffreys relates in a note on ll. 140–145 regarding the similar feat of deer-slaying ascribed to Basil the First (who ruled 867–886). On 75–76, Mavrogordato makes reference in a note on l. 159 that the comment of the onlookers regarding how Basil serves as a model to "the brave" relates to a developing Greek concept of the courageous as a category of national heroes. On 78, Mavrogordato remarks in a note to ll. 217–218 that what he terms this "curious piece of magic—drinking the hero's bathwater" is purported to be reflected in an as yet undiscovered Russian ballad; meanwhile, Jeffreys simply notes on 79 that no parallels to this bathwater episode are known to exist.

7. The primary sources for the episode wherein Basil steals away his bride include G Book IV ll. 254–855 and E ll. 792–1068. Previous to the account of

Basil's hunt in E is his interaction with the brigand chief Philopappous, which also treats the theme of bride-snatching; see E ll. 622–701. This passage is absent from G and is not crucial to the present discussion, but because it reinforces some of the themes related to the heroic archetypes manifested in *Digenis Akritis*, I refer to it where appropriate. For an in-depth discussion of the heroic implications of acts of bride-snatching, see especially Mackridge, 150–160; see also Jeffreys's note to l. 408 on 177, that to l. 665 on 289, that to l. 803 on 301, and that to l. 1383 on 341.

8. The primary source for the emperor's visit is G Book IV ll. 971–1086; in a note to ll. 973–974 on 133, Mavrogordato identifies this fictional imperial figure with the historical Emperor Basil II, known as *Bulgaroktonos*, "Bulgar-Slayer," whose rule Mavrogordato dates to 960–1025. Mavrogordato notes on lxxxii the difficulties with ascribing an actual historical emperor to this episode. On 389, Jeffreys emends the dates of Basil the Second's reign to 976–1025, noting that the death of this emperor might be associated with the demise of "Byzantine glory;" see also Jeffreys's note to ll. 971–1086 on 125. The primary sources for the battle episodes in *Digenis Akritis* include G Book VI ll. 1–766 and E ll. 1097–1561; these episodes are recounted in these sources in the first person, as are the events of G Book V. Note also the commentary of Ricks concerning the adventures of the hero on 19–22. On 155, Jeffreys details in a note on l. 47 that "serpent" is the traditional reading of the term *drakon* in this context. Moreover, for further evidence that Basil's battle with the serpent-demon has resonance with dragon-slaying myths, note that Ricks asserts in his note to ll. 1100–1101 on 115–116 that tripartite dragons (or ogres) were endemic in local folklore and bear mention in the *Strategikon* of Kekaumenos. In support of a reading of the serpent-demon as emblematic of lust, see Jeffreys's discussion in her note on l. 1109 on 323 of the three-headed allegorical figure of Eros and the classical provenance thereof. The citation of Matthew 19:6 in the G and E texts helps to date the poem because this motif is indicative of the Byzantine 12th-century Renaissance of narrative fiction: See Jeffreys xliv; see also her note to l. 143 on 161, as well as that to l. 1170 on 327. In addition, in her note to l. 163 on 163, Jeffreys recaps the argument that the girl seems to be the only person who doubts Basil's powers.

9. Concerning the role of women in *Digenis Akritis*, see especially Mackridge, 150–160; Jeffreys xvii and 201; and Littlewood 7. The episode of the abandoned young bride makes up G Book V ll. 1–289 but is not recorded in E.

10. The main source for the "golden age" of *Digenis Akritis* is G Book VII; see especially the closing passage of that book on ll. 221–229. In Jeffreys's note to l. 229 on 215, she asserts that Basil has "become a Christ-like symbol of peace and unity." The primary sources for the death of the hero Basil include the bulk of G Book VIII, especially ll. 31–313, and E ll. 1695–1867. See especially the commentary of Ricks regarding the retirement and death of the hero on 22–25; the treatment Ricks offers of the theme of the relationship between this episode and later Greek folk traditions is of special interest.

Sources and Further Reading

Alexiou, Stylianos. "*Digenes Akrites:* Escorial or Grottaferrata? An Overview." *Digenes Akrites: New Approaches to Byzantine Heroic Poetry.* Brookfield, VT: Variorum, 1993, 15–25.

Baldwin, Barry. *An Anthology of Byzantine Poetry.* London studies in classical philology, Vol. 14. Amsterdam: J. C. Gieben, 1985.

Beaton, Roderick, and David Ricks. *Digenes Akrites: New Approaches to Byzantine Heroic Poetry.* Brookfield, VT: Variorum, 1993.

Bulliet, Richard W. *The Case for Islamo-Christian Civilization.* New York: Columbia University Press, 2004.

Cheynet, Jean-Claude. *The Byzantine Aristocracy and Its Military Function.* Aldershot, Hampshire, United Kingdom: Ashgate Publishers, 2006.

Galatariotou, Catia. "The Primacy of the Escorial *Digenes Akrites:* An Open and Shut Case?" *Digenes Akrites: New Approaches to Byzantine Heroic Poetry.* Brookfield, VT: Variorum, 1993, 38–54.

Geanakoplos, Deno John. *Byzantium: Church, Society, and Civilization Seen through Contemporary Eyes.* Chicago: University of Chicago Press, 1984.

Geanakoplos, Deno John. *Medieval Western Civilization and the Byzantine and Islamic Worlds: Interaction of Three Cultures.* Lexington, MA: D. C. Heath, 1979.

Hook, David. "*Digenes Akrites* and The Old Spanish Epics." *Digenes Akrites: New Approaches to Byzantine Heroic Poetry.* Brookfield, VT: Variorum, 1993, 73–85.

Hull, Denison Bingham. *Digenis Akritas, the Two-Blood Border Lord: The Grottaferrata Version.* Athens: Ohio University Press, 1985.

Hussey, J. M. *The Orthodox Church in the Byzantine Empire.* Oxford history of the Christian Church. Oxford, United Kingdom: Clarendon Press, 1991.

Jeffreys, Elizabeth. *Digenis Akritis: The Grottaferrata and Escorial Versions.* Cambridge medieval classics, Vol. 7. Cambridge, United Kingdom: Cambridge University Press, 1998.

Jeffreys, Elizabeth. "The Grottaferrata Version of *Digenes Akrites:* A Reassessment." *Digenes Akrites: New Approaches to Byzantine Heroic Poetry.* Brookfield, VT: Variorum, 1993, 26–37.

Littlewood, Antony Robert. *Originality in Byzantine Literature, Art, and Music: A Collection of Essays.* Oxbow monograph, 50. Oxford, United Kingdom: Oxbow Books, 1995.

Mackridge, Peter. "'None but the Brave Deserve the Fair:' Abduction, Elopement, Seduction, and Marriage in the Escorial *Digenes Akrites* and Modern Greek Heroic Songs." *Digenes Akrites: New Approaches to Byzantine Heroic Poetry.* Brookfield, VT: Variorum, 1993, 150–160.

Magdalino, Paul. "*Digenes Akrites* and Byzantine Literature: The Twelfth-Century Background to the Grottaferrata Version." *Digenes Akrites: New Approaches to Byzantine Heroic Poetry.* Brookfield, VT: Variorum, 1993, 1–14.

Mango, Cyril A. *The Oxford History of Byzantium*. Oxford, United Kingdom: Oxford University Press, 2002.

Mavrogordato, John. *Digenes Akrites*. Oxford, United Kingdom: Clarendon Press, 1999.

Papadopoullos, Theodore. "The Akritic Hero: Socio-Cultural Status in the Light of Comparative Data." *Digenes Akrites: New Approaches to Byzantine Heroic Poetry*. Brookfield, VT: Variorum, 1993, 131–138.

Partner, Peter. *God of Battles: Holy Wars of Christianity and Islam*. Princeton, NJ: Princeton University Press, 1998.

Rautman, Marcus Louis. *Daily Life in the Byzantine Empire*. The Greenwood Press "Daily life through history" series. Westport, CT: Greenwood Press, 2006.

Ricks, David. *Byzantine Heroic Poetry*. Bristol, CT: Bristol Classical Press, 1990.

Ricks, David. "*Digenes Akrites* as Literature." *Digenes Akrites: New Approaches to Byzantine Heroic Poetry*. Brookfield, VT: Variorum, 1993, 161–170.

5

The Russian Holy-Warrior Hero

The Historical Context of Medieval Russia[1]

Who Were the Rus?

The "Rus" were largely comprised of the descendants of Vikings, mainly from Eastern Scandinavian stock, many of whom had plied the trade routes to Constantinople or had even served in the Varangian Guard, the personal bodyguard of the Byzantine emperor himself. After their conversion to Orthodox Christianity, the Rus of Kiev and its early pale of influence saw themselves as the standard-bearers of the One True Faith, Eastern Orthodoxy, a belief that gave birth to a concept of "Holy Russia." An understanding of this concept informs any discussion of Russian epic accounts of holy war.

Byzantine Missionaries to the Rus

The Byzantine Empire had intimate contact not just with Arab neighbors, but also with many pagan groups, and the tales of Byzantine missions amongst the principalities of the people known as the Rus can be particularly compelling in a discussion of the mythologies of holy war. It is logical to move from a discussion of the Byzantine epic hero to his Russian counterpart for several reasons, not the least of which is the fact that the Russians saw themselves as the "Third Rome"; in other words, as the guardians of the political and—most importantly—religious legacies of Byzantium.

The Historical Context of the Great Medieval Russian Epic[2]

Who Were the Kumans and What Was the "Tatar Yoke"?

The Kumans were Turkic nomads of the steppes with whom the Kievan Rus came into constant contact and conflict. However, these raiders from beyond the River Don represent but one link in a long chain of such marauding tribes, the apex of which would sweep across the steppes in the form of the Golden Horde of the Mongols who, not long after the time of Prince Igor, would dominate all of Russia for centuries. The "Tartar Yoke" is the evocative title given to the period of Russian subjugation under the Mongols, a conquest affected by the devastating military machine developed by Genghis Khan. Charting the major medieval Russian epics in retrospect, it is difficult not to see in Prince Igor's defeat and imprisonment by the Kumans a harbinger of the Tatar Yoke that will all too soon—within a mere generation or so—utterly enslave the Russian people, a subjugation that will not end until the Russian princes—divided amongst themselves in *Igor's Campaign*—unite to defeat the overbearing Mongols as they do in *Zadonshchina*, "Events beyond the River Don," an epic account of the great Russian victory that served notice that the days of Mongol domination of the steppes had come to an end.

The Literary Context of Medieval Russia: The Lay of Igor's Campaign[3]

Slovo o polku Igoreve, or the "Lay of Igor's Campaign," is an epic account of several historical events surrounding a battle fought in 1185 between Russian forces led by Prince Igor of Novgorod-Seversk and the Kuman raiders he sought to pacify, Turkic tribesmen more accurately known today as Polovtsians, successors to the feared Pechenegs. The Kumans ranged across the steppes north of the Black Sea for a period of some two centuries or so beginning in the 1100s. This campaign proved disastrous, and his enemies took prisoner Igor himself; indeed, the evocative conclusion to the poem concerns Igor's flight from captivity and return to his people.

In its purported general theme of a Christian people fighting against the incursions of infidel enemies, the *Lay* could be said to bear some resemblance to the French *Chanson de Roland*—especially in the defeat of the protagonists at the hands of their overtly devilish opponents—and in point of fact many scholars have drawn precisely such a comparison. However, the poet's overt criticism of the squabbling amongst the Russian princes that contributes to their defeat might be thought to resonate more closely with some of the subtext of *Cantar del mio Cid*, in which the nobility of the title character is in sharp contrast to the cowardly duplicitness of the Infantes.

Preserved in a single somewhat defective manuscript from the late Middle Ages, which was itself lost in the great Moscow fire of 1812, the *Lay* is presumed to have been misplaced for centuries before its rediscovery in the 18th century; an edition was not printed until just twelve years before the destruction of the manuscript, and that edition was unfortunately indicative of the amateur antiquarian nature of the scholarship of the Middle Ages of that era. Because there is no extant version of the manuscript containing the *Lay*, it is perhaps inevitable that some would doubt its authenticity.

It would be fair to say that a good amount of ink has been spilled quite recently regarding this very matter; however, it would also be fair to add that there is certainly no scholarly consensus agreeing with the theory that the *Lay* is a forgery, and that—moreover—many senior scholars in the field are firmly entrenched against just such a position. Furthermore, the seemingly self-conscious appropriation and adaptation of many of the patterns, themes, and indeed at times even the phraseology of the *Lay* in the later *Zadonshchina*—the epic account of the late 14th-century Russian victory over the Mongols that is itself preserved in several extant medieval manuscripts—offers eloquent testimony that some version of the *Lay* most likely predated the *Zadonshchina*.

Mythic Archetypes in the *Lay of Igor's Campaign*[4]

The Great Russian Epic Hero's Dual Heritage: Igor as Inheritor of the Mantle of Guardian of the Faith and the Shield of the Russians

As the kinsman and godson of Sviatoslav III, the mighty Charlemagne figure of Kievan Russia, Prince Igor is clearly associated with the forces of light that are meant to keep at bay the infidel raiders on the edges of Christian Russia, enemies descended—according to the poet—from the Devil himself and therefore clearly evil-doers who represent the forces of darkness. Igor is in contrast clearly identified in the *Lay* as one of "Four Suns" of the Russian firmament, dazzling beacons of heroism and leadership that reflect the effulgence of Prince Vladimir, the original "Brilliant Sun" who brought the Russians from the darkness of pagan idolatry to the light of Christian faith. Igor's campaign against the demonic Kumans, then, however successful or otherwise, is explicitly represented by the author of the *Lay* as an attempt by an army carrying the standard of Christ to destroy the forces of Satan.

Moreover, in the context of Sviatoslav's role as the protector of the Orthodox Faith, Igor's attack of the Kumans may be interpreted as in ill-fated attempt to take up the role of the champion of Holy Russia, an office to which Prince Igor clearly has some claim by his blood kinship and spiritual relationship with Sviatoslav. However, Igor's heritage is more complex and problematic than his ties with Sviatoslav might imply, and the poet exploits to ironic advantage the fact that the failure of Igor's attempt to assume the mantle of Guardian of the Faith and Shield of the Russians may be linked explicitly in some measure with internal squabbling amongst the Kievan princes that originally was engendered by an ancestor of Prince Igor himself.

The Great Russian Epic Hero's Dual Heritage: Igor as Scion of the House That Sowed the Seeds of Russian Discord

Although—unlike the "Two-Blooded" Byzantine Hero Basil Digenis Akritis—Igor did not share part of his heritage with his borderland foes, he did in fact spring from the loins of a family involved in the very rivalry and feuding that ultimately resulted in his own defeat at the hands of his enemies. Although Igor's line is not accused by the poet of ever having come to concord with the Kumans, it is clear that it was this same hero's grandfather who began the process of civil strife between the Russian royal houses that ultimately resulted in some princes coming to just such unholy alliances with the outside infidel enemy, thus securing a temporary advantage against some petty rival within the ranks of the Christian princes of the Rus.

In point of fact, Igor was the grandson of Prince Oleg, son of Sviatoslav, who engendered the internecine slaughter amongst the rulers of Russia. In the end, this feuding led some Christian Russian princes to make wicked pacts with the forces of darkness through alliances with the infidel Kumans against their own cousins and co-religionists. Prince Boris, the son of Vyacheslav, was the first to debase himself in this manner, a practice that—as the poet's contrast between the Christian Russians and pagan Kumans and his emphasis on the sinful and foolish nature of the strife between the Russian rulers makes crystal clear—might well be perceived as tantamount to selling one's soul to the Devil.

The theme of the sinful bane of Russian discord as the fatal flaw that opened the way into Holy Russia for the satanic forces of darkness represented by the Kumans is again clearly emphasized in the *Lay* by the poet's careful framing of the description of the final defeat of Igor's armies: Just as the historical recounting of the feuding of the Russian princes leads into that description of the prince's defeat, so does the author's lamentation concerning this humiliation dovetail immediately into an account of the additional civil unrest resulting from the Kuman victory. After the destruction of Igor's host, kinsman made claims against kinsman, and childish disagreements earned the name of mighty matters. As this shadow fell across the Russian soul, infidels gathered like scavengers to feast upon the spoils of that domestic squabble.

The Troubled Sleep of Sviatoslav: A Mythic Dream Vision in the Great Russian Epic

Close on the heels of the *Lay's* description of the internal dissension related to Igor's fall comes a description of the glories of Prince Sviatoslav, besides whose effulgence Igor's descent into the dim Underworld of captivity is pointedly contrasted. Immediately thereafter, the great Sviatoslav is once more called to center stage in the *Lay* as the oracular voice whose powerful Dream Vision foretells the defeat of Prince Igor. The Dream Vision was a popular genre of medieval literature, and such narratives and the dreams they described took many forms. Among the most popular of these texts were those concerned with the prophetic insight that might be imparted to sleeping mortals from supernatural sources. Medieval belief in the visionary power of dreams had many sources—some drawn from the classical traditions, some from regional folklore. However, a potent validation for the efficacy and acceptability of such supernatural insight in the Christian world was the Bible itself, which contains many examples of prophetic dreams, perhaps most notably those interpreted by the prophet Daniel, who, we are told in Daniel 2:17, was uniquely talented in this capacity. Indeed, the role of the boyars in the episode at hand seems grounded in the example of that Old Testament prophet, who clarified for Nebuchadnezzar the impending doom expressed by that king's disturbing nightmares.

Vseslav the Werewolf: The Sorcerer of the Great Russian Epic [5]

Prince Vseslav of Polotsk, who died in 1101, is evoked by the poet of the *Lay* as one of the shining Russian princes of the previous century whose descendants are not worthy of comparison with him, fools whose civil conflict opened the door for the Kumans to enter Russia. Although the *Lay* is quite explicit and pointed in its criticism of the lesser sons of Yaroslav and grandsons of Vseslav who have tarnished the glory of their forebears, the figure of Vseslav himself is presented as morally ambivalent, at best, a valiant and cunning warrior, to be sure, but also a sorcerer and a werewolf whose victory was balanced by defeat and whose glory was tempered by the knowledge of inevitable and inescapable Divine Judgment for his sins, which seem to be manifested by his association with magic and most especially with the bestial transformation that affords a window into his tortured soul.

Although there is no direct evidence to support this assertion, the historical figure of the 11th-century Prince Vseslav of Polotsk is often assumed to be the legendary kernel within the folkloric and mythic trappings of Volkh Vseslavyevich, one of the three great *Starsie Bogatyri*, or "Elder Warriors," of the byliny tradition. However, Vseslav's identity as a sorcerer and a shape-shifter certainly offers some indirect support for such a belief, and the two figures in any case bear remarkable similarities and likely common origin in pagan Slavic and ancient Indo-European chaotic and volatile battle gods. Indeed, volatility and sorcery might even be said to mark such deities as somewhat demonic, as is the case with the Norse Odin, a shape-shifting sorcerer of a war god himself, who is likewise closely associated with the wolf.

Igor Makes War on the Kumans: The Great Russian Epic Hero Battles the Forces of Darkness

The poet of the *Lay* begins his account with an allusion to the great bard Boyan, a figure thought to refer to a historical 11th-century poet who composed heroic odes to the mighty princes of the Rus. The tale of Prince Igor is thus provided foreground by a context of the deeds of great heroic leaders that clarifies for the modern reader Igor's impetus to mount a preemptive raid upon the infidel Kumans, an act that otherwise might seem precipitous and inexplicable. The young prince, we are told, was determined to slake his thirst for adventure and glory by tasting the water of the mighty flood of the great River Don, on the Kuman frontier, from the vessel of his own helmet; the proud prince offered his own head as surety in this attempt. Igor hoped to shatter his trusty lance upon the bodies of the infidels, thus sating his thirst for blood. He challenged his peers and vassals to join him in his attack upon the Kumans, arguing that it would be better to be slain in combat than to be enslaved by enemies.

Prince Igor was joined with enthusiasm by his brother Vsevolod, the Great Battle Ox, Prince of Trubchevsk and Kursk, who called Igor his solitary shining beacon and offered his own well-prepared warriors in support. Blinded by his desire for glory to the host of ill omens and portents from the birds in the trees, the winds and the earth, and even the Sun itself, Prince Igor put his foot in his golden stirrup and at the head of his army began the long ride to the land of the great River Don. Meanwhile, the Kumans, hearing upon the wind and in the tremors of the Earth the rumor of the great Russian prince's advance toward their territory, made their own trek along pathless ways to the Don. The stillness of the prairie night was reft by the squeaking of their approaching carts. The Russian homeland was far, far behind Igor.

Finally, the last night of that long journey melted into dawn, and the harbingers of battle rose up their song. The lilting notes of the nightingale were replaced by the harsh cries of the jackdaw. The two armies came together. The proud Russian warriors formed a wall of scarlet shields to block the way of the Kuman advance. Early that Friday morning the Russians routed their enemies, shooting across the open prairies like arrows into the heart of the Kuman encampment, taking beautiful maidens, rich clothes, and golden treasure. They forded streams and crossed swamps as they progressed, scattering across the prairie, which provided their bed for that night. This early victory, apparently despite the warning of the omens, seems—at least according to the account offered by the author of the *Lay*—to have dispersed the Russian forces somewhat and to have given them a sense of confidence that proved, in the end, to have been false.

Igor, as described by the poet in the opening sequence of the *Lay*, thus appears—like many a mighty but arrogant and precipitous hero before him—to have been led by pride and the desire for glory to ignore signs that portend the doom of his venture. Pride is the fatal flaw of some of the most notable heroes, and such heroes also are subject to the decrees of fate and the will of the gods, regardless of their faith in their own abilities. Prince Igor's willful disregard for the manifold omens declaring the impending destruction of his army thus seems to evoke the theme of the prideful hero and the motif of the hero who unrepentantly acts in defiance of divine will.

However, there is an implicit tension inherent in this poet's portrayal of Igor, a tension that is intensified by the rhetoric of that same poet regarding Igor as the clever and courageous captive hero who escapes to rise once more as the beacon of the True Faith in the Orthodox sky at the conclusion of the *Lay*: Indeed, although in retrospect Igor seems to have been willfully blind to manifestly obvious warning signs, in the context of the poet's clear description of the Kumans as satanic agents of darkness and the four Russian princes as the "bright suns" who lead the armies of Christ in righteous battle, it seems clear that Igor's impulse is meant to be lauded, even if his discernment of the signs was faulty. This tension is resolved to at least some extent by the author's appeals to the Russian princes for unity and his laments of the internal discord that allowed external threats such as the Kumans to grow into the threat to Russian security that caused Igor to feel the need to confront them.

Moreover, the greatest of the warning omens described in the epic, the dimming of the Sun, is not merely a literary device or mythic element evoked by the author of the *Lay*: An eclipse actually occurred on the first of May in the year 1185. This fact not only provides a compelling natural phenomenon that would be remembered in the folk memory of Igor's contemporaries and the next few generations that followed them; more than that, the very real fear and confusion caused by an eclipse would have provided an almost visceral reminder of the stakes involved in the battle between the forces of Orthodox Russia and those of the infidel Kumans, pawns of the unholy one who are explicitly described by the author of the *Lay* as the scions of Satan. The ultimate defeat of the Russians, then, would represent the victory of the forces of darkness, the minions of the demonic; such a loss represents not just the slaughter of regiments or the enslavement of a people, but the destruction of the very souls of those who fall into the clutches of the Devil. The Russian offensive is representative, in such a context, of nothing less than the battle of the forces of Heaven and Hell for dominion over the soul of every believer.

The Captivity of Igor: The Great Russian Epic Hero Journeys to the Underworld[6]

The racket of the daws and ravens—a macabre choir singing for a grisly supper of corpses—is mentioned by the author of the *Lay* at a portentous moment immediately preceding the description of the final Russian defeat. This strident cawing embodies the popular trope of the music of the scavenger, a bestial accompanist to the slaughter of the battlefield that so often is described—in traditions from across Northern Europe as widespread as the Slavic, Baltic, Norse, and Celtic—as keeping time during the symphony of battle. Wolves and ravens are very often depicted in such roles, and the dark, croaking heralds of battle especially beloved to and identified with deities of destruction as diverse as the Scandinavian Odin and the Irish Badb play a significant role in providing the background to battle descriptions in the *Lay*.

Prince Igor was descended from Prince Oleg, who taught the Russians to war amongst themselves. The ravens and jackdaws sang often in delight at the feast of blood and bone offered to them through this wanton discord, although the peasants spoke but little in such sorrowful times. So it had been in former days, when there were many battles, but none so mighty as that fought between Igor's Russians and the Kuman infidels on that final, fateful day. From dawn to dusk to dawn again the battle raged, swords, arrows, and lances falling down in a rain of death upon the black soil of the Kuman steppes, a prairie sown with the grisly seeds of broken bones watered in a torrent of flowing blood. The Russian land was utterly bereaved.

What grating sound, the poet asks, disrupts the stillness of the early morning so harshly? He answers that it is the clanking of the harness of Igor's horse as the prince turns his troops, struck with sorrow at the fate of his brother Vsevolod. After fighting for three days, the tide of the first day's battle has turned completely, and the force of the waves of Kumans overruns the Russians. On that fateful third day, the bright banners of Igor's hosts fell. By the swift streams of the River Kaiala the kinsmen were divided, the bitter, bloody cup of battle having been drained to its very dregs. However, the armies of Igor had shared this cruel chalice fully with their guests as they lay down their lives for the land of the Russians, a sacrifice reflected by the mourning of that land itself for the fall of its heroes. The grass of the steppes shrank into itself, and the very trees of the forest bowed down in sorrow.

The agricultural metaphor hinted at by the poet in his description of the final day of the conflict—and the poet does, in fact, express himself in a way that might be interpreted as a rain of swords upon helmets in a field of dark, fertile earth soaked with blood and covered with bones—speaks eloquently to the archetype of the dying god, which is thematically linked with that of the hero's descent into the Underworld. The dying god is himself often represented explicitly as a gruesome seed planted into the soil of the grave from which new life might miraculously spring. Having prefaced this passage of doom and defeat with reference to the cawing of the scavengers drawn to the field of battle, the poet notes the turn in the tide of this battle by focusing attention upon another discordant sound: this time the clanking of the metal of Igor's mount's tackle, a seemingly disruptive element until one considers how such a noise echoes the clinking of the chains of a prisoner such as the prince is about to become. Meanwhile, the author's shift to the metaphor of the bloody feast, at which the Russians and their guests drank in common from the chalice of death, clearly evokes an inversion of the Last Supper and thus explicitly strengthens Igor's association with Christ, the sacrificial dying God of the Orthodox Russians, whose sojourn in the Underworld brings hope of new life for his followers and for whose true faith the armies of Igor ostensibly have fought and died.

This mythically charged, somber, and graphically described passage concerning Igor's capture and imprisonment by the Kumans clearly resonates with the dark descent into death or a death-like state that presages the archetypal hero's journey to the Underworld, and the discordant song of the feathered chorus of death and destruction provided by the ravens and daws emphasizes the theme of Igor's passage between the plane of light and life to that of a dark and dismal living death. The mighty Prince Igor of Novgorod-Seversk, we may well believe, made a poor trade, losing his gilded saddle and bridle for the tackle of a slave. All of the joy of the Russian cities evaporated like the ephemeral morning mist.

Igor's Escape from the Kumans: The Great Russian Epic Hero Returns from the Underworld [7]

As if in direct response to the mournful song of Yaroslavna, Igor's wife, who lamented her husband's fate from the walls of the city of Putivl and who decried the role of the powers of the winds, waters, and Sun in his tragic ill fortune, the prince's escape from his enslavement in the Kuman camp occurred under the mantle of darkness within a cloaking veil of tumult and tempest. In the midst of storms at sea and whirlwinds on the Earth that raged through the nighttime fog, Igor awakened to the warning whistle of his loyal retainer Ovlur. The very ground shook with the forces of earthquake and the blades of grass tore against each other in tempestuous waves in the gusting winds as the prince made his escape, right before the Kumans arose in the darkness just before the dawn. Described by the poet in the terms of various animals and birds, Igor fled to the cover of the reeds, from whence he leapt to his horse's back and rode for freedom. We are told his flight took him toward the great sickle-shaped bow of the River Donets, the bulge of Russian territory on the Kuman frontier.

Calling to mind and yet contrary in import to the elemental voices that warned of Igor's impending doom earlier in the *Lay*, the natural forces that rose in uproar in this episode betokened the reversal of Igor's fortune and indeed seem to harbor and hide Igor just as Yaroslavna would have desired. In this context, the natural forces that aided and abetted Igor's escape seemed to have been summoned by Yaroslavna's prayer, a possibility that reemphasizes the subtext of her prayer as an echo of the role of proprietary pagan rites hidden within this Christian poem.

The poet specifically describes Igor's thoughts as flying across the steppes from the channel of the great River Don, in the heart of the Kuman Pale, to the smaller River Donets, which marks the frontier of the sphere of Russian influence. This characterization clearly marks the waterway of the Donets as a liminal signpost, a borderland of sorts through which one may travel between the world of the Christian Russians and the otherworld of the demonic Kumans. As he reaches the haven of the River Donets, that tributary of the Don that marks his escape from the clutches of his enemies, the Donets itself heralds Igor's escape and arrival in the embrace of a friendly river god.

At the conclusion of Igor's discourse with the River Donets, the discussion of the pursuing Kuman Khans Gza and Konchak is described in comparison to the hoarse cries of magpies; meanwhile, however, we are told that the chorus of the crows and jackdaws—a highly symbolic part of the cacophony of battle emphasized just before the defeat of the Russians and the capture of their prince—has fallen silent, a peacefulness in the realm of nature that indicates that the emancipation of Igor is at hand. Although the elemental forces, the birds and beasts, and even the mythical Div itself had trumpeted a discordant tune of doom that heralded the defeat and capture of the Russian princes, the winged harbingers of war—the black birds so closely linked with battles, death, and war deities in the Northlands—seem to have fallen silent as Igor slipped the bonds of his captivity.

Whereas the classic hero's trip to an otherworldly plane often has shamanistic qualities, and such heroes generally return with great gifts of hidden knowledge to share with their community, Igor returns to lead his people once more and to provide the head and reason that will—so the poet seems to hope—govern the body politic and control the passionate dissention amongst the Russian princes that allowed the nomadic raiders to make such in-roads into the spheres of Russian power and influence in the first place. However, the prince's dialogue with the great river god of the Donets evokes the hero's crossing of the border with the otherworld—so often delineated by a river or other body of water—and at the same time utilizes the ancient pagan Slavic practice of anthropomorphizing and venerating the forces of the natural world, most especially those that might be appeased or propitiated so that they would grant their favor.

The comparison drawn between the friendly and helpful River Donets and the treacherous and deadly River Stugna makes it clear just how real and vital such favor might well seem to the traveler faced with a perilous river crossing. Moreover, the natural and animal imagery utilized in Igor's dialogue with the river god and in the discussion of the two pursuing khans helps to underscore the manifold ways in which nature manifests the fate and character of and the conflict between the Russians and the Kumans in the *Lay*. Such conceits are literary devices, to be sure, but they also evoke and articulate ancient Slavic mythic and folkloric concepts of the numinous qualities of the natural world.

The Sun Returns to the Russian Sky: The Apotheosis of Igor [8]

In the concluding passage of the *Lay*, the poet once more evokes the great bard Boyan, who acts in this text as something of a prophetic seer and oracle, the dispenser of the insight and wisdom necessary to provide context for and to interpret the significance of the most vital events of the *Lay*. Just as the head cannot survive without the shoulders, we are told that the wise one remarked, so the body fails without its head. Here the bard echoes the apostle Paul, who asserted that Christ provided the head to the body of the Church; this ruler we are thus to understand as the head of his nation, a head the return of which is the cause of great joy throughout all the members of that body. The Sun, the poet says, has returned to the Russian sky in a passage that directly recalls the dawning of the bright day of the ascent of Vladimir, the Brilliant Sun of the Russian tradition, who poured the light of God into every corner of Russia to lift the darkness of pagan idolatry. In the closing lines of the *Lay*, the author makes clear that this new day is one in which the forces of light fight the satanic darkness of the infidels of the steppes, a new shadow that threatens to dim the shining beacon of the Orthodox faith. The *Lay* closes with praise for the Russian princes who keep this darkness at bay.

The ironic epilogue to this conclusion, of course—an afterword that could not be known in Igor's time—was that soon enough the Mongols would sweep across the steppes, a horrible reality in the depths of the darkness of which the fading nightmare of Igor's defeat and capture seems at most a vestige of a dire prophetic dream, a harsh vision like that of Prince Sviatoslav of Kiev, which foretells the disaster, sorrow, and tragedy of the Tartar Yoke to come. However, unlike the dream of Sviatoslav, Igor's escape and reunion with his people offers a glimmer of hope at the conclusion of this vision, a portent that perhaps, many years hence, a new day might dawn with a new Russian hero to throw off the shackles of oppression fixed on a subjugated people by nomadic overlords. That hope would be fulfilled in the events recorded in *Zadonshchina*, in which Dmitry, the Great Prince of Moscow, would ascend as the new sun in the Russian sky that would betoken that the vast darkness of the black night of Tartar dominion would soon be at an end.

Slavic Gods, Pagan Folklore, and Didactic Legends in the Christian *Lay of Igor's Campaign*[9]

Several ancient Slavic pagan deities warrant explicit mention in this medieval Russian Christian epic, a somewhat ironic situation in a text largely concerned, at least ostensibly, with the conflict between true believers and their infidel enemies. However, these references to the gods of old are generally oblique and thus seem to be suggestive of a unifying Slavic identity in keeping with the poet's general theme of the dangers of civil discord amongst the Russian princes rather than any indication of a throwback to pagan belief systems.

The Div[10]

The figure of the Div is referenced early in the *Lay*, toward the beginning of the passage relating the various natural signs portending the coming disaster for the Russians. We are told that this being rose to the level of the tree-tops, screaming its dire warning in a fell voice that echoed across all the lands of the Russians, from the banks of the Volga to the shores of the Azov, from the tributaries of the Dnieper to the cities of the Crimea, its vestiges reaching even to the ears of the idols of the Kumans in their homelands. Often described as a bird-like spirit of omen, the name *Div* seems clearly derived from a Slavic term for "demon," denoting a potent and possibly malicious spirit; this word in turn seems related to Persian equivalents.

Volos[11]

Although Volos is unmentioned in the major chronicle account of the Slavic pantheon enshrined by Vladimir shortly before the Kievan conversion to Christianity, we know from other sources that this deity, also referred to as *Veles* or *Velesu*, was, along with Perun, one of the two most important gods of the Eastern Slavic pantheon. This figure, designated *Volosu* in the *Primary Chronicle*, appears to have been an ancient god of troth, and as such was evoked—along with Perun—in several treaties between the Rus and the Byzantines. The Orthodox Byzantines concluded each compact by kissing the Cross, whereas the Rus swore their oaths upon their weapons, evoking the names of Volos and Perun.

Fundamentally a cattle god in the bulk of the extant overt references to this pagan deity, Volos seems to have survived in the Russian Orthodox Christian tradition as Saint Vlasii, the patron of livestock. Saint Vlasii commonly appeared on icons with attendant cows and sheep, and his image often adorned mangers and preceded the animals into the fields upon their return to pasturage in the thaw of spring. Saint Vlasii was called upon to heal sick animals and was venerated with a feast upon his day in parts of Russia. The priest ensured the health of the livestock at this ceremony by offering his blessing over bread that was then fed to the animals.

Dazhbog [12]

Dazhbog was, according to the *Primary Chronicle*, one of the fundamental gods of the Slavic pantheon embraced by Vladimir before he rejected them in favor of the Christian God. The *Lay* poet even describes the Russians themselves as the grandsons of this god Dazhbog, a figure often thought to represent an ancient Slavic sun god associated with elements of fire worship. Dazhbog is the progeny of the earlier god Svarog, traditionally asserted—on little hard evidence, it is to be emphasized—to be the Slavic sky god and progenitor and ruler of the other gods of the pantheon. About Dazhbog we have a bit more evidence: An entry dated 1114 in the *Primary Chronicle* explicitly indicates that Dazhbog was the Ruler of the Sun, equivalent with the Greek Helios. The god's name is generally thought to be a compound of a term suggestive of "giving" and that for "god." In addition, some scholars have pointed to a relationship between the Russian Dazhbog and the Serbian figure Dabog.

Stribog [13]

The author of the *Lay* calls the winds the grandsons of the god Stribog; these scions of the deity are said to blast a storm of arrows against the hosts of Prince Igor. Indeed, the name *Stribog* commonly has been assumed to have been derived from a Slavic root for "wind" combined with the common term for "god," and general consensus associates Stribog with the trappings of a wind god; the relevant passage in the *Lay* certainly augments and helps to validate this identity. Some have questioned why the forces of nature associated with the Slavic god of the wind might be said in the *Lay* to pummel the Russian forces in the manner described by the poet, but in the context of an epic rife with natural omens foretelling the impending defeat of Prince Igor, this circumstance is perhaps not so confusing.

Khors[14]

Khors is generally taken to have derived from some ancient sun deity, in large measure because of the single reference to this figure in the *Lay*; the poet evokes Khors—who, interestingly, he clearly acknowledges to be a mighty deity—in the context of his description of Prince Vseslav's nocturnal prowling in the guise of a werewolf. Neatly sandwiched between references to the cock crow and the ringing of the bells for matins—two clear references to impending dawn—the path of Khors is used as another nod to the coming day that marks the border between Vseslav's supernatural existence and his more ordinary life in the world and affairs of men. Moreover, it has been posited that the name *Khors* itself, sometimes rendered *Hors* or *Khursu*, may be derived from the Persian *Xorsid*, denoting "sun;" however, other scholars have suggested that this figure was originally adopted from Turkic neighbors.

The River Gods in the *Lay of Igor's Campaign*[15]

As he fled to freedom from the captivity of the Kumans, Igor was addressed by the River Donets, which acclaimed his escape and glory and proclaimed the joy of the Russians and the distress of the Kumans at this turn of events. Igor paused in his flight to honor the great river god for his aid and succor in this escape, acknowledging that no small part of the glory must be offered to the river that caressed the prince with its gentle waves and offered him the soft footing of the grass on its gleaming riverbanks as well as the concealing shadow of its bordering trees and its moist fogs, which dampened the track and threw off the scent of the chase. Indeed, Igor continued, the very ducks and gulls that abided along the stream had served as guardians watching over the prince's progress.

How different in character was the River Stugna, the poet notes, which was shallow and choked with mud and had overrun its banks to swallow up the surrounding tributaries in a watery embrace, a death grip that likewise swallowed poor Prince Rostislav, who drowned in its murky waters in 1093. The land itself was so sodden that trees tumbled and blossoms rotted, as if in sympathy with that luckless prince's bereaved mother. Such personifications of features of the natural world hearken back to the pagan Slavic mythological subtext of the *Lay*: What has become a seemingly unimportant folkloric detail in point of fact evokes the ancient gods of the natural world who once were believed to inhabit the landscape; in such a context, Igor's courteous speech to the River Donets takes on the character of a pre-Christian ritual invocation to a river god seeking safe passage across his stream. On the other hand, the much more sinister characterization of the Stugna illustrates the dangers of such a landscape and thus illustrates the need, to the pagan mind, for appropriate offerings to the ancient gods.

Animal Imagery in the *Lay of Igor's Campaign*[16]

From its earliest lines, the *Lay* exhibits a rich and repetitive use of animal imagery. Such representations are especially noteworthy in the context of a tradition in which elemental forces clearly are to be associated with divine powers and portents, in which lycanthropy and shape-shifting are folkloric commonplaces, and in which bestial images often are easily recognizable signifiers: Wolves and ravens in the *Lay* clearly act as harbingers of battle, whereas seagulls and swan-maidens embody sorrow and mourning. The magical powers and properties of the werewolf are of course extensively developed in reference to Prince Vseslav.

In the opening invocation of the poem, the great bard Boyan is said to have flown on the wings of his mind high over the Tree of Wisdom. A few passages later in the *Lay* this concept is repeated and refined in that in those lines Boyan is said to have floated into the heights above that mythical tree in the form of the nightingale poet of old, the bird-bard who sang the song of Russian victories. The reference to the bard of yore soaring bird-like over the Tree of Wisdom thus links the lays of the elder days of Vladimir the Brilliant Sun with the latter day tribulations of Prince Igor, whose travails, the author of the *Lay* assures us, will be less cleverly composed than those of Boyan, who is also compared in the invocation to a wolf loping across the steppes or to a great eagle soaring beneath the canopy of the clouds. Perhaps most evocatively, the 10 fingers of the legendary bard are likened to 10 swift falcons set upon a bevy of swans, which in turn are meant to represent the strings of Boyan's instrument.

Igor himself is described in terms of beasts as diverse as an ermine, a duck, and a wolf. Perhaps most evocatively, during his dash for freedom Prince Igor is compared to the noble falcon, winging its way to the safety of the great bend of the River Donets, which marked the beginning of Russian territory. It is noteworthy in the context of this allusion that this episode is introduced with a passage comparing Khan Gza and Khan Konchak to noisy, ridiculous chatterers rather than to the noble prince of birds or to the grisly harbingers of battle. It is not the caw of the crow or jackdaw that interrupted the song of the nightingale floating through the dawn mist the morning after Igor's escape; no, interspersed with the drumming of the woodpecker in the river bottoms was the fractious gibbering of the two khans, which the poet likens to the screeching of magpies. It is perhaps no coincidence that the only other creatures in evidence are snakes, crawling on their bellies along the ground.

If falcons are the princes of birds and crows and daws the avian heralds of battles and of slaughter, in Russian lore the seagull and the swan each represent embodiments of sorrow and of mourning in the *Lay*. Yaroslavna herself, Prince Igor's wife, is described and refers to herself as a seagull, a traditional symbol of grief in Russian folklore. The author of the *Lay* tells us that the princess, like an anonymous gull, sings a song of mourning from the walls of the city of Putivl. In this song she cries out that she will come to her beloved in the form of a seagull, catching the water of the River Kaiala in the furred cuff of her sleeve to wash the wounds of her prince.

A similar folkloric theme is developed in the author's treatment of the Swan Maiden of Sorrow; in the passage immediately after that detailing the final victory of the Kumans on the third day of battle, the author of the *Lay* offers an image of the entry of the figure of sorrow and despair into the land of the Russians: Despair held sway over the army of the offspring of the deity Dazhbog, winging into that domain in the shape of the Swan Maiden, dipping the tips of her feathers into the great River Don, scattering that blue water—tearlike drops of sorrow—across the land of the Russian and thus dampening joy and luck for all.

During the section of the poem detailing Igor's incitement of the Russians to join him upon his campaign, his most fiery supporter was his brother Vsevolod, Prince of Trubchevsk and Kursk, who promised Prince Igor the support of his own warriors, an army said to have been nurtured since infanthood upon the arts and weapons of war. To describe the bestial ferocity of Vsevolod himself, the poet designated him as a great beast generally given as an *aurochs*, which is to say a particularly fierce but now extinct species of "wild ox" known from Caesar as the *urus*; interestingly, the Latin and Greek forms of this term seem to be loans from an Old Teutonic name.

Not to be confused with the still extant European bison with which it is now too readily conflated, the *aurochs*—which might best be rendered in this context as "battle ox"—is a creature representing battle frenzy of mythical proportions in the *Lay*. Rather like the implicit reference to animalistic savagery—with undertones of lycanthropy—attributed to the "bear-shirted" and "wolf-skinned" Odinic warriors of Scandinavia, such references to the aurochs serve in the *Lay* as a kind of shorthand for connoting a host of characteristics associated with this beast that, although grounded in beliefs concerning an actual animal, ultimately transform our understanding of the warriors designated by that epithet. Vsevolod, the mighty battle ox of Igor, and—in this holy war—the battle-maddened war beast of Christ, is several times denoted an aurochs in the *Lay*.

Perhaps most evocatively, in the closing passage of the *Lay*—which offers a benediction of sorts for the glorious princes of Russia who continue to fight to protect their motherland from the encroaching infidel hordes—the poet again mentions Vsevolod, and significantly, although the other two princes named in that closing passage (Igor and his son Vladimir) are identified in relation to their fathers, Vsevolod is once again evocatively compellingly designated simply as the ferocious aurochs, the mighty battle ox of the *Lay of Igor's Campaign*.

Yaroslavna, Igor's Wife, and the "Seagull of Despair," Chastises and Cajoles the Capricious Spirits of Wind, Water, and Sun[17]

Suggesting a notable literary theme with obvious folkloric significance, that of the lament for the husband, Yaroslavna's pensive and emotional appeal upon the walls of the city of Putivl combines the heart-rending desire of a wife for her husband's safe return with a significant example of folkloric animal imagery as well as with an explicit supplication to the spirits of the natural world which seem to her to hinder—although they well could help—her husband. Yaroslavna's lament begins with a dual identification, first by the narrator and then by the speaker herself, of Igor's wife as a seagull, which is to say the harbinger of sorrow and despair. However, Yaroslavna transforms this image into one of hope and declares her intent to fly to her beloved and cleanse him with the soothing waters of the Kaiala.

The princess then evokes each of three nature spirits in turn, beginning with the wind. Elsewhere in the *Lay* the winds are identified with spirits descended from Stribog, the wind god, a reference Yaroslavna may well conjure when she mentions that this spirit has—through his turbulent and heartless facilitation of the attack of the Kumans by breathing force behind their arrows—dispersed her joy, a phrase that evokes a possible etymology of the name of the deity of the winds as one who "scatters wealth." Yaroslavna then beseeches the spirit of the River Dnieper to bring her love home upon its sweet and gentle waters so that she might not be forced to seek her beloved only through the coursing of her bitter tears that run into the saltwater of the sea. Finally, Yaroslavna upbraids the sun, burning and thrice bright, a giver of warmth and life for most people everywhere, which has nevertheless through rays of too much intensity sealed the quivers and dried the bows of Igor's forces. Although this final passage is perfectly intelligible on a literal surface level, one might be forgiven for straying into related agricultural and even sexual metaphors.

However that may be, it is certain that the trope of the personification of and supplication to the forces of nature is a staple of later Russian folklore: Rivers and other bodies of water are commonly anthropomorphized, and the winds, in particular, are singled out for attention, having as they do the capacity to augment or reduce the effects of the Sun, rain, and frost. In their characteristic attribute of carrying blessings and curses huge distances along upon their vast peregrinations, the winds are identified time and again with the "scattering" motif so eloquently evoked by Yaroslavna upon the walls of the city of Putivl. However, this theme is more often than not articulated in negative terms, and the magical ability to harness the awesome powers of the grandsons of Stribog is often depicted as a terrifying tool of evil in various sources, as notably in the bylina concerning Ilya of Murom, who battles a demonic enemy with just such skills. Moreover, in an interesting clash of elemental powers, Ilya himself is perhaps a heroic euhemerization of the thunder god Perun.

Omens Foretell Igor's Travails[18]

Omens and portents are a commonplace of Russian mythology and folklore, and the *Lay* offers a wealth of significant examples of such signifiers of otherworldly foresight concerning the fates of mortals. Indeed, several rather dramatic signs are said to have warned the Russians of their impending destruction at the swords of the Kumans. As Prince Igor led his hosts out into the steppes, the very fire of the sun seemed to be quenched, a ghastly omen soon echoed by similarly dire warnings, the report of which resounded across the Russian landscape. As this unnatural nightfall fell at the height of day, a great storm rose and raged across the prairie, shocking the birds to wakefulness with its tumult and evoking cries of terror in the throats of animals.

The very Div itself, that mythical harbinger of catastrophe, flew to the level of the highest branches in the trees to proclaim its portentous song of doom across the whole of the Russian land. Echoes of its lamentations reached even so far as Tmutorokan, home of the idol of the devilish god of the Kumans themselves. Moreover, such portents of disaster continued to dog the Russian armies as they made their way toward the great River Don: The oaken forests were filled with the screeching of the birds that flew about the hosts; the gullies overflowed with a storm of noise wrought by the howling of the wolves; the eagles of the sky summoned the scavengers, heralding with their cries the grisly banquet of battle that would soon glut their belies with bones; and the foxes yapped at the blood-red shields of the Russians as they passed.

Clearly the *Lay* makes extensive use of elemental and bestial portents of doom, obvious omens that are all the more poignant for Igor's seeming inability to read them. Specific mention of the response of the eagles and the wolves to the Russian advance deserves particular attention, especially in the context of the clearly stated role of the former as heralds of the imminent feast of the scavengers; meanwhile, the latter beasts—ever associated with deprivation, danger, and death in Russian lore generally and with battle in northern epic descriptions specifically—impart an almost Odinic prescience of conflict and destruction in the relevant passage. The mention of the Div is one of several overt references to pre-Christian mythology in the *Lay*, describing as it does the specific way in which this supernatural, bird-like creature enacts its role as an oracle of doom.

Perhaps of most interest, the poet makes mention of an eclipse of the Sun in two critical passages, a pair of references that neatly frame the brief section in which Igor's ill-fated decision to mount an offensive against the Kumans is detailed: The shadow of an eclipse falls over the Russian hosts just before Igor rallied his troops with the suggestion that it would be better to die in battle against the Kumans than to be enslaved by them; then, in the very next section—which describes the entire array of omens of the natural world presaging the disaster about to befall the Russian armies—we are told that Igor's very progress was blocked briefly by the darkness that suddenly obscured and obstructed the path of the Russian army, an impediment the description of which suggests a black night at noontide with the force of a physical obstacle, almost as if comprising a shadowy divine hand meant to warn the prince of the folly of his rash decision. A similar portent is described at the beginning of the second day of battle, upon which the tide turns in favor of the Kumans: Blood-red fingers of dawn illuminated the inky clouds that threatened that morning to smother the brightness of the Four Suns of the Russian firmament, Igor, Vsevolod, Oleg, and Sviatoslav, the noble leaders of the Russian hosts.

In the first instance Igor had just looked up into the Sun in the sky when the eclipse is mentioned; in the second darkness falls immediately after the prince had put his foot into a golden stirrup and ridden into the steppes. Although certainly tackle appropriate for a prince, this detail concerning Igor's stirrup also evokes the gleaming brightness of the Sun, especially in the context of a poem in which Vladimir, the great Christianizer of the Russians, is referred to as the "Brilliant Sun" and in which the set of princes who led the armies of the Russians against the Kumans are called the "Four Suns." In the *Lay* the Russian princes are clearly the forces of God, goodness, and light in battle with Kumans, who represent Satan, evil, and darkness. Moreover, the Russian leaders are referred to elsewhere—albeit in a formulaic manner, it must be emphasized—in the *Lay* as the descendants of the Slavic sun god Dazhbog, a slight but suggestive reference that may add an ancient pagan element that resonates with the clearly Christian association between the Russian princes and the light of the Sun, literal giver of temporal abundance and metaphorical representative of the immortal light of the Word of God, Jesus Christ, the Light of the World that offers eternal life.

Finally, the image of impending engulfing darkness poised to swallow whole the bright light of Igor, the princely sun, serves to set the stage for the forthcoming eclipse of that brilliance, the darkness brought on by the defeat of the Russian forces and Igor's capture and imprisonment, his symbolic death that manifests the mythic archetype of the hero's journey to the Underworld as well as evoking, if somewhat obliquely, the experience of the dying god, whose life-giving light is extinguished briefly so that it may burn all the more brightly once he ascends once more from the darkness of the grave. Given the obvious identification of the Russian princes as the standard-bearers of Christ, the recurring trope of omens of darkness and eclipse seems to function on several mythic levels as well as simply foreshadowing the doom of the Russian expedition.

Nature's Response to Igor's Travails[19]

Given the emphasis in ancient Slavic mythology and medieval Russian folklore on elemental forces and the supernatural powers they exert over human beings, it is hardly surprising that the author of the *Lay* frames the defeat of the forces of Prince Igor with references to a kind of cosmic grief manifested by signs in the natural world; although the signs before that defeat might be identified as oracular, they are very nearly anthro-pomorphized in the way that they are described. The very ground moans, while the riverbed and the surface of the steppe seem to cover their faces with swirling mud and dust. Although those signs might be classified with the omens of catastrophe with which the author embellishes the *Lay*, the passage immediately after the Russian defeat—and immediately preced-ing the sequence concerning the entry of the Swan Maiden of Sorrow—clearly describes how the natural world shares the despair of the forces of goodness and light: The author informs us that the identifying vegetable life of the forest and the steppe respectively illustrated this despair; the trees bent down in grief and the grass dried and shrank in distress at the defeat of the Russians.

Thus, the very elements themselves seem despondent at the falling of Igor's standard; this sequence resonates that in laisse 111 of *La Chanson de Roland*, in which a great storm and mighty earthquake mourn the passing of Roland, whose death throes were obscured by a blanketing dimness at noon. Both of these sequences may be surmised to derive ultimately from the references in the Synoptic Gospels to the veiling darkness that fell from the sixth to the ninth hour on the day of Christ's crucifixion; more-over, the Gospel of Matthew adds elemental responses including tremors, splitting rocks, and related signs of cataclysm that provide the basis for the *Lay's* account of nature's response to Igor's defeat.

Death and Funeral Imagery in the *Lay of Igor's Campaign*[20]

Given the subject matter of the *Lay*, it is perhaps no surprise that this work is a veritable treasure-trove of images of slaughter and destruction, as well as of references to mythic, legendary, and folkloric traditions concerning death and funeral rituals. Moreover, given the Russian fascination with death and the otherworld, or *Tot Svet*, it is probably fair to assert that a study of medieval Russian mythology would be incomplete without at least a passing exami-nation of some of the major motifs concerned with these common themes. Medieval Russian conceptions about death and the otherworld represent a unique and vibrant combination of ancient pagan Slavic myths, Orthodox Christian theology, and abiding folk practices and beliefs. Indeed, it might well be said that death has for time immemorial been a central facet of Russian life; more to the point, the fact that many pre-Christian elements of folk beliefs perhaps ultimately derived from death-cult agricultural practices remained for so long a part of Russian consciousness may help to make sense of one or two of the more grisly and otherwise inexplicable images in the *Lay*.

The *legendy*, or "holy legends," the popular didactic religious tales that artfully contextualize Christian beliefs within a framework of ancient mythology and oral folk traditions, are particularly rich in visionary visits to the realms of the dead, especially in the company of Saint Nikolai, who often takes on the role of the gatekeeper to Heaven, a sort of Orthodox expression of one aspect often assigned to Saint Peter in Roman Catholic traditions. Sleepers and the unconscious are often depicted as particularly receptive to such out-of-body experiences, which also occur in the byliny. The Russian *skazki*, or "folktales" proper, are themselves rife with stories concerning manifold aspects of death in which the border between the worlds of the living and the dead is permeable and in which death itself may be at times impermanent; inconsolable grief and even tears themselves may serve to wake the dead, although seldom to lasting advantage.

In addition to those who may completely reenter the living world without lasting ill-effects through a miraculous cure of sorts, the skazki record many tales of *mertvyaki*, "ghouls," and *zalozhnye*, "covered ones," those who—unlike the *roditeli*, the "ancestors," the properly restful dead—died in an untimely manner because of murder, suicide, or disease. Special torments await and particular terror accrues to wizards and other egregious sinners, who may at times be reanimated as revenants or zombies, corporeal ghosts not unlike those of Scandinavian lore; such undead visitors often have, in the skazki, a disturbing appetite for human flesh and in some cases a thirst for blood. However, Russian folklore is replete in a commensurate manner with methods for avoiding such visitants, including ritual practices such as the removal of certain roof rafters, a practice that may have an echo in the *Lay*.

The *Lay* is a tale of a military defeat replete with images of death and destruction, and so it is hardly surprising that it includes ample details concerned with ceremonial aspects regarding the treatment of the dead. In fact, some such descriptions of death motifs and funeral rituals offered in the *Lay* appear on their surface to be somewhat pragmatic, almost utilitarian, related in a straightforward manner to historically attested practices. More than merely concerned with the fate of particular princes and champions, however, the *Lay* simultaneously provides an account on a larger scale of a catastrophic Russian defeat at the hands of the Kuman enemies; the details of the fate of individual warriors in this context, then, reflect the larger realities of the Russian people as a whole. Thus, even a subtly evocative reference alluding to, for example, the slaying of the father of Sviatopolk more than a century before Igor's debacle serves to reinforce the *Lay*'s theme of the relationship between the death of the individual and the dire blow dealt to the nation.

Just as Sviatopolk commanded that his father—slain as a result of the civil warfare between the Russian princes—be carried to Kiev in the traditional manner, slung in a carpet between two horses, so all Russia reeled under the blows of the Kumans upon the forces of Igor, whose loss is likewise ascribed to the same internal strife. Moreover, the funeral journey of Sviatopolk's father from the shores of the Kaiala to holy Kiev precedes and prefigures Igor's own journey from the same riverbanks to the Underworld of Kuman captivity; ultimately, of course, Igor returns from the dead, as it were, arriving, after his flight from the Kumans, back home in land of the Russians, where he sought the shelter of the Church of the Holy Virgin of Pirogoshch in Borichev, in the environs of Kiev. However, in the context of the earlier pilgrimage of death, the songs of joy celebrating Igor's return, which reverberate from the Danube to Kiev, might be thought to ring a little hollow because the *Lay* as a whole seems to sound a darker tone of warning of further sorrow to come as a result of the discordant princes of the Russians; in such doleful notes one might hear the echo of the lamentations of the dirge for Sviatopolk's father.

Some other funeral rites described in the *Lay* have, in addition to their likely provenance in actual practice, additional folkloric significance derived from cultural hopes, fears, anxieties, and expectations concerning the behavior of the dead and the nature of the otherworld. The dream vision of Prince Sviatoslav of Kiev, to cite a particularly fecund passage, contains several references to rather evocative images that may illuminate Russian folkloric practices and beliefs. At the beginning of his vision, the prince notes that he was robed in a shroud and given a cup of a dark draft of the vintage of grief. At that point, giant pearls, representative in folk tradition of the onset of tears, fell like a rain of sorrow into his lap. In tandem with the common Russian association of pearls with tears is the folk belief that an abundance of tears may in fact wake the dead for whom one is mourning. Although the disturbing of the slumber of the dead is generally to be avoided in Russian folklore, in the case of Igor's defeat and symbolic death we might see such an association as indicative of the silver lining of Igor's return, which is hidden during this vision behind the veil of the darkness of his fall.

As the prince's recounting of his dream continued, he noted that the girding had been removed from the beams of his palace; such a detail resonates with an actual folk practice of unfastening such structures from the porch of a house before a body was taken from that home to be buried. One can thus account for this detail as another strand in an increasingly elaborate pattern of funereal references woven into the fabric of Sviatoslav's dream vision: Clearly the author of the *Lay* utilized this tapestry of folk practice and ritual to emphasize the sense of despair associated with the immediately preceding passage, which detailed the catastrophic defeat of the Russians and the capture and entry into the Underworld and bondage of Igor, their shining prince. Such a reading is more troubling when we recall that folk practices concerning the removal of certain rafters before a funeral were enacted in part to ensure that the dead would not return from the grave. However, in the present case it may well be that the sense of foreboding associated with the underlying fear that was the impetus for the ritual practice in the first place might be unconsciously evoked to underscore the dread associated with the crushing Russian defeat.

The concluding funeral image in the dream vision of Sviatoslav concerns the appearance of an ominous sledge in the hills around the Galician city of Plesensk, a sledge that raced from the mountains surrounding that fortress-town all of the way to the blue waters of the sea. Sledges were the conveyance upon which the bodies of the dead were traditionally carried in Russian funerals, and thus the appearance of such a vehicle clearly serves as a harbinger of death and doom. Moreover, given the fact that Prince Igor's wife Yaroslavna was the daughter of a Galician prince, it might well be asserted that this sledge represents specifically the funerals for all of the Galician warriors slain on Igor's campaign while also evoking the grand scale of the tragedy of the loss of Russian life in the conflict in general.

Finally, some developments of death motifs and images of mourning seem to have deep-seated mythological resonance. Perhaps the most graphic and evocative of these concern what might be termed the "harvest of death" motif; a stunning example of this genre is contained in the section of the *Lay* concerning Prince Vseslav the Werewolf Wizard, in which we are told that in a battle along the banks of the River Nemiga—soil stained scarlet with the blood of the Russian dead and scattered with their bones—veritable haystacks of heads were heaped up, while tormented bodies were violently reft of souls on the pitiless threshing floor of the battlefield, struck time and again with iron blows until the last seed of life was dislodged, like grain shorn from stems beneath the threshing rod. This passage, explicit in its agricultural metaphor, may in some measure evoke and help to explicate an earlier image in the *Lay*, one concerning dark fields of blood sown with bone and flooded with torrents of weapons on the last day of the battle. Such references to violent slaughter couched within the terms of reaping the bounty of the fruits of the field may well echo ancient Slavic rituals of blood sacrifice concerned with ensuring the harvest and may in this text resonate with Igor's manifestation of the dying god archetype, in which the entry of the sun figure into the grave from which he will emerge bursting with new life parallels the seeming death of the seed in its miniature grave. In Russian folklore, in any case, the cult of the dead has long been associated with agricultural fertility rituals.

A final image of mourning in the *Lay* concerns what might be termed the "flaming horn of grief," which the author evokes during his lament just after his account of the final Russian defeat on the third day of the battle. Noting that mourning and despair have spread across the Russian land the doleful message of Igor's cataclysmic loss, the poet notes that this message is accompanied by a dirge of grief sung by the widows of Russia, who simultaneously shake the burning cinders from the horn of grief. This may by a generic reference to sorrow, of course, and it may also evoke a mourning ritual of some kind. Moreover, in the context of the relationship between the founders of the Rus states and their Scandinavian neighbors, it is probably also worthwhile to mention the possible resonance between this "flaming horn of grief" and the Gjallarhorn, the great trumpet of doom with which Heimdalr announces the onset of Ragnarok, the fiery apocalypse of the Norse gods.

Notes

1. For the early history of the Rus and in particular their contact with Byzantium, see especially Martin 1–23 and Milner-Gulland 38–42. For examinations of the conversion of the Rus to Orthodox Christianity, see especially Geanakoplos *Byzantium*, 346–355; Mango, 230–247; Martin 6–12; and Milner-Gulland 42–44.

2. For critical commentary on and analysis of elements of the "Tatar Yoke" and in particular its implications upon a study of the mythological theme of holy war, see especially Lindahl 387–388; Milner-Gulland 42, 50–56; and Zenkovsky 17–21, 19.

3. For critical commentary on and analysis of elements of the *Lay of Igor's Campaign* and in particular its implications upon a study of the mythological theme of holy war, see especially Lindahl 388; Martin 102; Milner-Gulland 39, 40, 42, 45, 57; and Zenkovsky 15–17; 167–169.

4. For critical commentary on and analysis of mythic archetypes manifested in the *Lay of Igor's Campaign*, see especially Warner 13 and Zenkovsky 167–169.

5. Concerning Vseslav the Werewolf, see especially Warner 65–66; see also Zenkovsky 185–186.

6. Concerning Igor's captivity, see especially Zenkovsky 179–187.

7. Concerning Igor's escape and flight from captivity, see especially Zenkovsky 187–189.

8. Concerning Igor's apotheosis, see especially Zenkovsky 189–190.

9. For critical commentary on and analysis of elements of the pagan elements in the *Lay of Igor's Campaign*, see especially Warner 7–22 and Zenkovsky 175.

10. Concerning the Div, see especially Puhvel 232–232 and Zenkovsky 172.

11. Concerning Volos, see especially Lindahl 934; Puhvel (*Velesu*) 227–228, 233, 234; Warner 14–15, 20; and Zenkovsky 53, 171.

12. Concerning Dazhbog, see especially Puhvel (*Dazibogu*) 233–234; Warner 15–16, 18; and Zenkovsky 176.

13. Concerning Stribog, see especially Puhvel (*Stribogu*) 233–234; Warner 15–16; and Zenkovsky 174.

14. Concerning Khors, see especially Puhvel (*Khursu*) 233, 234; Warner 15–16; and Zenkovsky 185.

15. For critical commentary on and analysis of the river gods in the *Lay of Igor's Campaign*, see especially Warner 13 and Zenkovsky 188.

16. For critical commentary on and analysis of animal imagery in the *Lay of Igor's Campaign*, see especially Warner 13 and Zenkovsky 171, 174, 176, 182, 183, 186–187, 189, 190.

17. For critical commentary on and analysis of Yaroslavna's "lament for the husband" in the *Lay of Igor's Campaign*, see especially Warner 13, 24, 31 and Zenkovsky 186–187.

18. For critical commentary on and analysis of the function of omens in the *Lay of Igor's Campaign*, see especially Warner 13 and Zenkovsky 170, 172–174.

19. For critical commentary on and analysis of the response of nature to the defeat of the Russians in the *Lay of Igor's Campaign*, see especially Warner 13 and Zenkovsky 174, 176.

20. For critical commentary on and analysis of death and funeral imagery in the *Lay of Igor's Campaign*, see especially Warner 45–55 and Zenkovsky 175–176, 178–179, 185.

Sources and Further Reading

Balzer, Marjorie Mandelstam. *Russian Traditional Culture: Religion, Gender, and Customary Law*. Armonk, NY: M. E. Sharpe, 1992.

Birnbaum, Henrik, Michael S. Flier, and Daniel B. Rowland. *Medieval Russian Culture*. Berkeley: University of California Press, 1984.

Hubbs, Joanna. *Mother Russia: The Feminine Myth in Russian Culture*. Bloomington: Indiana University Press, 1993.

Levin, Eve. *Sex and Society in the World of the Orthodox Slavs, 900–1700*. Ithaca, NY: Cornell University Press, 1995.

Lindahl, Carl, John McNamara, and John Lindow. *Medieval Folklore: A Guide to Myths, Legends, Tales, Beliefs, and Customs*. Oxford, United Kingdom: Oxford University Press, 2002.

Martin, Janet. *Medieval Russia: 980–1584*. Cambridge medieval textbooks. Cambridge, United Kingdom: Cambridge University Press, 2007.

Milner-Gulland, R. R., and Nikolai J. Dejevsky. *Cultural Atlas of Russia and the Former Soviet Union*. New York: Checkmark Books, 1998.

Puhvel, Jaan. *Comparative Mythology*. Baltimore: Johns Hopkins University Press, 1987.

Váňa, Zdeněk, Pavel Vácha, and Pavel Major. *The World of the Ancient Slavs*. Detroit: Wayne State University Press, 1983.

Warner, Elizabeth. *Russian Myths*. The legendary past. Austin: University of Texas Press, 2002.

Zenkovsky, Serge A. *Medieval Russia's Epics, Chronicles, and Tales*. New York: Penguin, 1974.

The Carolingian Sacrificial-Lamb Hero

The Historical Context of the Holy Roman Empire

Who Were the Carolingians?

Carolingian refers to the line of Frankish kings founded by *Charlemagne*, or "Charles the Great." Charlemagne's dynasty supplanted that of the Merovingians, the Frankish royal house that ruled from the time of Clovis in the late fifth and early sixth centuries until the mid-eighth century. On Christmas day in the year 800, Charlemagne consolidated his power and asserted his legacy when he had himself crowned Emperor of the Holy Roman Empire. Leaving aside old jokes that the realm over which Charles the Great ruled was not holy, nor Roman, nor an empire, it is without doubt true that the structure of modern Europe owes great debts to Charlemagne's seemingly indefatigable efforts to recapture and reassert the lost glory, majesty, and power of Rome.

Just as Byzantium wore the mantle of the Roman Empire in the East, and as the Kievan Rus saw themselves as heirs to that tradition and as the guardians of the One True Faith, the legends and myths of Carolingians assert this dynasty as the successor of Rome in the West and as the buttress of Christendom against pagans, heretics, and—most especially—against the growing infidel onslaught of Islam. The Moslem threat was most obvious on the Iberian Peninsula, where Moorish armies largely had subdued Christian Spanish lords. In this context, the sacrificial figure of Roland looms large, and the occasion of his death became the seed of the great medieval French myth of the holy warrior.

The Historical Battle of Roncevaux[1]

In the *Chanson de Roland,* what the Carolingian chroniclers perceived as a deceitful and dishonorable ambush by Christian Basque bandits is recast as a cosmic battle between the forces of good and evil. In the summer of 778, Charlemagne himself raised the standard of holy war when he sought and received a papal blessing for a campaign against an Iberian Moorish overlord on the grounds that his was a preemptive strike against a coming infidel invasion. In the context of the fact that he was entering the Spanish peninsula at the behest of less powerful Moslem rulers of a largely Christian region, this pretext seems disingenuous at best.

Charlemagne abandoned this unsuccessful campaign to quell a rebellion in Saxony. On August 15, 778, as the Frankish rearguard made its way through the narrow defiles of the territory of the Basques, a contingent of Charlemagne's army was cut off and destroyed in detail. This is the historical germ that was to blossom into the legend of Roland's Last Stand, a legend that was itself to take on mythic resonance as it became more fully conflated with the trope of holy war. By transforming opportunistic Christian Basques into demonic infidel Saracens, the poet elevates this borderland skirmish, which ended in a humiliating military defeat, into a clearly rendered portrayal of sacred conflict ending with the martyrdom and apotheosis of the Christ-like Count Roland.

The Literary Context of the *Chanson De Roland:* Sources and Manuscripts[2]

The story of Roland's last stand seems to have been a popular one in medieval French literature; indeed, this interest appears to have been widespread and abiding because versions of this tale also appear in Middle English, Dutch, Old Norse, Middle High German, and Welsh. Several 13th and 14th century versions of the *Chanson de Roland* survive in French, including three in French libraries and two in the Library of Saint Mark in Venice. A 15th century version resides in the library of Trinity College, Cambridge, and numerous fragments are also extant.

The oldest existing manuscript containing a full version of the poem is from the mid-12th century and is preserved in the Bodleian Library in Oxford. Known as Digby 23, this manuscript contains a version of the poem in an Anglo-Norman dialect of French and appears to be a copy of a copy of an original, a fact that is underscored by the many dozens of errors corrected by a hand from the late 12th century. Despite such shortcomings, the Digby 23 text of the *Chanson de Roland* displays considerable literary sophistication and is the primary source of modern translations of the great epic French poem recounting the fate of the hero Roland.

Various scholars have posited several possible dates concerning the original composition of the manifestation of the poem preserved in the Digby 23 text; that seminal source must have preceded the compilation of the manuscript by at least a few years, it seems, and perhaps by a good deal more. Estimates concerning the date of this *ur*-text range from the mid-11th to the late 12th century. However, the general consensus, which more or less splits the difference, suggests that the poem as we know it from Digby 23 probably originated around the year 1100. Several possible historical references, some of them more obscure than others, have been used as evidence to establish this likely date of composition.

Although some such pieces of evidence may seem more compelling than others, in the aggregate it seems safe to suggest that the ethos of the poem as it is preserved in the Digby 23 manuscript seems to resonate with the spirit of the First Crusade, a cumulative impression that may support the contention that the *Chanson de Roland* was first composed around the close of the 11th century. The closing line of the poem in Digby 23 names one Turoldus, who may have been the author, copyist, or corrector of the text. Although it is impossible to be sure of his role in preserving the *Chanson de Roland*, a great deal of energy has been expended trying to determine who he may have been. Two Norman notables from the generation after William the Conqueror have been suggested as likely candidates—an evocative possibility, especially given the poet Wace's claim that the story of Roland was recited before the Normans by a bard named Taillefer on the very eve of the Battle of Hastings.

The Battle Between Heaven and Hell: Cosmic Combat in the Chanson de Roland[3]

The military campaign that provides the central narrative structure around which the episodes of the *Chanson de Roland* are organized is clearly cast as a reflection of the cosmic struggle between the forces of Heaven and those of Hell: Charlemagne himself leads the armies of righteousness as a surrogate of God the Father, whereas his enemies are described in terms that often identify them as the minions of the Devil, if not incarnations of the Devil himself. Both of Charlemagne's primary adversaries, first the Saracen King Marsile of Spain and later Emir Baligant of Babylon, provide obviously infidel foils for the ruler of Christendom, a noteworthy emendation of the historical record by an author who was appropriating for his own purposes—and thereby ennobling—the dramatic story of a haunting Frankish defeat that had no bearing upon religious strife and that occurred some three centuries before he composed this narrative extolling its heroes. However, after the complete rout of Marsile's forces, described in laisse 180 in which the infidel hosts were driven into the River Ebro to drown, the Saracen king was forced in his despair, we are informed in laisse 189, to call upon Emir Baligant for aid. If such assistance were not forthcoming, the narrator continues, Marsile was prepared to accept Christianity and to make peace with Charlemagne.

Indeed, Baligant does bring the forces of darkness to bear upon those of light led by Charlemagne, and thus Marsile remains a pawn of the Devil, only to die in despair in laisse 270 for his defeats while the darkness of Hell swallows his soul; forsaken by his false god and *pecchet l'encumbret*, "encumbered by sin," his soul, we are assured, is forfeit to horrible demons. However, the author provides thematic balance by placing the conversion of Marsile's queen, Bramimonde, in laisse 297 at the very end of the narrative, thus offering a glimpse of the new beginning promised by salvation through Christ in the figure of the newly converted Queen Juliana of Spain.

Although the aside in which Marsile calls upon Baligant for help may seem tangential, it marks an important plot point in the narrative and a thematic shift in the author's shaping of the holy war trope in the *Chanson de Roland*: Many scholars have noted that the entire Baligant episode is less artistically wrought than that concerning Charlemagne's conflict with Marsile, and it is arguable that the poem as a whole would be more coherent without it; however, it must be emphasized that the Baligant episode may in fact help to render into sharper focus the battle between good and evil into which the author has sought to reshape this story.

The Saracen followers of Mohammed, our narrator explicitly tells us in laisse 270, are beguiled by a *false lei*, an "untrue faith." The religion protected by Charlemagne, in stark contrast, is that of the *lei de salvetet*, the "faith of salvation," as even the treacherous emissaries of King Marsile themselves allow as they deliver their deceitful message to the King of the Franks in laisse 9; the implication of this passage is that in their description of the promise of salvation offered by Christianity these false ambassadors told the truth, although they only meant to honey their lies and thus to make them palatable to their Christian enemies. As Charlemagne makes clear in an angry exchange with Baligant in laisse 266, the Franks consider their faith to be a gift of grace, *nos apresentet*, "revealed unto us," by God.

As the Franks declare in laisse 248, overcome with blood-lust in the heat of battle as they avenge their comrades slaughtered at Roncevaux upon the bodies of their infidel enemies, they believe that *Carls ad dreit*, "Charles is in the right," as God himself has placed the Franks on the side of *verai juise*, "true justice." This sentiment is echoed by the mighty King of the Franks himself when he encourages his assembled hosts in laisse 252 with the assurance that they themselves are witnesses to the fact that he is in this struggle *cuntre paiens*, "against the pagans," and he is *ai dreit*, "in the right." Indeed, the miracles of the Christian God stand in sharp contrast with the powerlessness of the figures venerated by the infidels. For example, in laisse 180 the author declares that *[p]ur Karlemagne fist Deus vertuz mult granz*, "for Charlemagne God wrought a mighty miracle" by causing the Sun to stop in the sky overhead, which allows the Franks the time to destroy their enemies in detail by virtue of a celestial manifestation of Divine Will familiar from the Bible.

The poet's description of the false faith of the infidel enemy is rendered in such a way as to emphasize those elements that contrast it most sharply with the true faith of the Christian Franks, and to achieve this end the author seems to display at one and the same time some knowledge of Islam and an utter disregard for some of the most basic tenets of that religion. In simplest terms, the *Chanson de Roland* is concerned with developing the theme of holy war as fully as possible, the realities of Islam—like the historical events of the Battle of Roncevaux—notwithstanding. For instance, the infidels are often portrayed as polytheistic pagans, as when "Jupiter" is evoked in the episode describing the sorcerer Siglorel, or when the Saracens, after their defeat on the banks of the Ebro in laisse 180, take out their rage upon their unholy trinity of false gods in laisse 187.

Having heaped manifold but impotent curses upon their Frankish enemies and most especially Charlemagne himself, the Saracens seemed to need to give vent to their anger by attacking the symbols of the false faith into which they had put their trust: Rushing en masse into the vault in which their idols were worshipped, they reviled the figure of Apollo as a *malvais deus*, an "evil god," blaming it for their humiliation and for the emasculation of their king. Not satisfied to limit their repudiation of this idol to words alone, they took from it its crown and scepter, pulled it from its perch, tied it to a column, and shattered it with mighty cudgels. Then they tore the jewel from the statue of Tervagant and cast down the idol of Mohammed. It should be noted that the followers of Baligant worship this same unholy trinity and march to battle in laisse 241 preceded by an idol of Apollo and banners bearing the images of Tervagant and

Mohammed. Moreover, at the very front of the host flies the dragon standard, an emblem that evokes the imagery of Satan himself.

Furthermore, it is clear from the phrasing of the "destruction of the idols" passage in laisse 187 that each of the gods in question is, in fact, represented in the infidel shrine by a statue, a physical manifestation of each deity that the despairing Saracens despoil in their rage. Moreover, the most violent and contemptuous act of vandalism is reserved for the idol representing the Prophet Mohammed himself, which is cast into a ditch, where it may be defiled by *porc e chen*, "pigs and dogs," two animals considered amongst the most unclean by any Moslem. This detail seems calculated to be particularly insulting to Islam and thus betrays at least a rudimentary sense of some of its basic precepts. On the other hand, somewhat paradoxically, even a cursory knowledge of that rigidly monotheistic faith is enough to know that it has no such "unholy trinity," and that, moreover, no graven image or idol of any kind is permissible in the worship of Allah. However, the author seems little interested in such details of the faith of those he considers heathens and heretics and is in fact much more invested in creating a satisfying sequence of events that underscores the distinctions between the True God of the Christian Franks and the false idols he attributes to their infidel Saracen enemies.

The Demonic Enemy: Infidels as Devils in the Chanson de Roland

Sometimes the demonic identity of the Saracens is articulated quite explicitly, as in laisse 108, wherein we learn that Archbishop Turpin slew one Siglorel, a mighty sorcerer amongst the Saracens who had been granted by Jupiter a glimpse of Hell itself because of his mastery of the infernal arts. Turpin also matches himself against Abisme, a great champion of the forces of Marsile. Our narrator informs us in laisse 114 that this Saracen was as inky as melted pitch, the greatest of criminals, a repudiator of the One True God born of the Virgin Mary who was instead a lover of evil and treason, a sinner who prefers such calumnies to all of the gold of Galicia. To the archbishop, Abisme is more than just another infidel; indeed, this foe seems to Turpin a *mult herite*, a "great heretic," a designation that implies that—no mere sinner—he in fact leads other souls down the same sinful path that he himself has trodden.

Indeed, Abisme is something of a standard-bearer for Satan himself, inasmuch as he carries a dragon emblem, a sign of his worship of that great dragon that consumes the souls of men. Moreover, Abisme carries, we learn in laisse 115, a jewel-encrusted shield that was a gift from an actual devil, granted to him in Val Metas, a present that was transmitted to Abisme through the agency of Emir Galafe. Val Metas provides another thinly veiled reference to the nether regions wherein such demons make their homes, as does the very name of the miscreant *Abisme*, which might well be read as a play on "Abyss." It seems significant that Siglorel and Abisme, two great leaders of the followers of the false god and his black arts, are laid low by none other than Archbishop Turpin, the ecclesiastical representative of the forces of God on earth. The Franks allude to Turpin's role as their spiritual leader when they reference his crozier, an ensign of the true God in direct opposition to the dragon-banner and devil-shield of Abisme; indeed, laisse 115 closes with a wry comment upon Turpin's quick destruction of that shield and concurrent dispatching of that evil-doer that makes specific reference to the symbol of his episcopal office: *Est ben la croce salve*, "the crozier is very safe," they laugh, in the Archbishop's hands.

Wizards and warriors who have visited and received gifts from the rulers of Hell suggest a clear association between the Saracens and the satanic; moreover, at least one infidel soldier is described in terms that suggest that he may in fact be a devil incarnate. In laisse 78, Chernubles of Munigre is said to have hair that reaches down to the very ground and to be imbued with such inhuman strength that he lifts for amusement as much as four fully laden beasts of burden might carry on their backs. Still more evocatively, Chernubles is identified as a native of a desert waste where the Sun never shines, grain cannot grow, no rain falls, and no dew collects. Most tellingly, the color imagery of the Underworld is manifested in the fact that, in the barren homeland of Chernubles, *piere n'i ad que tute ne seit neire*, "not a stone was not completely black."

This otherworldly realm seems to be nothing other than Hell itself; indeed, with characteristic understatement, our narrator informs us that *dient alquanz que diables i meignent*, "some say that devils abide there." Chernubles's wish to act as the champion of evil underscores Roland's role as a Christ figure in this passage: The demonic warrior claims that he will slay Roland if he meets him, that his satanic blade will conquer Durendal, and that the French will be therefore bereft of hope of life; all France will become a wasteland like unto the hell-hole that spawned Chernubles himself—*France en ert deserte*, "France will be deserted." Chernubles's perception of how the people of France might be overcome through the slaughter of the messianic Roland echoes Satan's blunder in assuming that Christ's death would definitively secure—rather than ultimately thwart—his own infernal desire to ensnare and to destroy the souls of God's faithful.

Many of the infidel warriors are identified with valleys, a recurring theme that serves to suggest the infernal associations of the pagans, the fact that some of these names may reference actual sites notwithstanding. The descriptions of the armies of darkness that march forth from such hellish homelands also give overt cues concerning the demonic nature of their denizens. Although Siglorel, Abisme, and Chernubles provide detailed portraits of satanic figures within the ranks of Charlemagne's enemies, they are by no means the only such examples; indeed, the forces of darkness that blacken the pages of the *Chanson de Roland* are replete with demonic infidels, many of which are described collectively, providing a veritable rogues' gallery drawn from the depths of Hell.

Demonic identity and hellish origins are also denoted by color imagery in the *Chanson de Roland*; pitch-black in particular, the signature hue of the hellish home of Chernubles, also is used in this poem to describe the physical appearance of many of the infidels. Although it is entirely logical that these passages might first and foremost evoke for a modern reader thoughts of racist ideology, the use of color is charged with spiritual significance in this context of holy war. Indeed, the primary function of such imagery in the *Chanson de Roland* may well to be to associate the Saracen forces with Satan and his abode within the black pit of Hell. Thus the author's details concerning the skin color and facial features of Saracens from North Africa seem designed to emphasize the relationship between these infidels and their demonic overlord; hence, that between their homeland and Hell itself.

Roland Recast as Christ: Echoes of the Crucifixion in the Chanson de Roland

In laisse 111 we are offered a description of storm and cataclysm that implicitly associates the doomed Roland with the crucified Christ. This apocalyptic vision is recounted directly after a passage in which it is made clear that, despite the heroic efforts of Roland and his companions, who have slaughtered the infidels a *millers e a cent*, "in the thousands and in the hundreds," the Franks themselves are losing their best warriors, are doomed, and *[n]e reverrunt lor peres ne lor parenz*, "shall not see their fathers nor kinsman again." At this very moment back in France a storm of monumental proportions lays waste to the kingdom, which is showered with rain, hail, high winds, and lightning strikes. Moreover, there is a mighty *terremoete*, an "earthquake,"and walls the length and breadth of the land are cast down. Finally, "at noon all the heavens were obscured, and no light shone except that which rent the sky with lightning": *Cuntre midi tenebres i ad granz, n'i ad clartet, se li ceils nen i fent.* All of this, our narrator explains, is nature's response to the impending tragedy about to devastate the Franks: *Co est li granz dulors por la mort de Rollant,* "this is the great sorrow occasioned by the death of Roland."

This tempest, which the poet explicitly declares presages the death of Roland, recalls the storm that marked the defeat of Prince Igor in the Russian *Lay,* of course, and both texts ultimately derived this motif from the description of Christ's crucifixion in the Synoptic Gospels. The Gospels of Matthew, Mark, and Luke all agree that the Sun was darkened at the moment of Christ's death, and that this darkness lasted from the sixth until the ninth hour, which is generally understood as from noon until three o'clock. Furthermore, Matthew's account, which is included in Chapter 27 of his gospel, adds several details that serve to emphasize the earth-shattering cosmic response to the crucifixion, including in verse 51 a description of the terrifying tremors and resultant destruction wrought by the despair at Christ's death manifested by elemental forces: *[e]t terra mota est et petrae scissae sunt,* "and the earth moved and the rocks were rent." Indeed, it is as a result of the catastrophic cosmic grief made clear by the turbulence of the natural world that, in verse 54, the on-looking centurion and his companions so famously uttered the words *vere Dei Filius erat iste,* "verily, this was the Son of God."

Roland Ascends to Heaven: The Apotheosis of the Hero in the Chanson de Roland

The *apotheosis* of the hero (i.e., to render the Greek roots rather literally, his "complete deification") is the culmination of the journey of a hero; indeed, not every heroic figure undergoes such a mythic transformation. In this process of ultimate refinement, a hero from the ranks of the ordinary humans, from whom he so often is drawn and whom he generally represents and protects, steps up into the company of the gods, representing the most compelling aspirations of his people. Although the process of apotheosis may seem, to many modern readers, matter more suitable to polytheistic traditions wherein the frontier between the worlds of men and gods may seem more permeable, it is vital to recall that the most foundational beliefs of Christianity presuppose that the Divine may be rendered into flesh; furthermore, the Cult of the Saints, which provided such a vibrant aspect of medieval Christianity, took as a core tenet that the souls of the Holy might commune with the Divine shortly after death and before the Final Judgment.

Having propped himself beneath a tree and placed beneath his body the two totemic objects most closely associated with him (i.e., his mighty sword Durendal and the cloven horn Oliphant), in laisse 174 Roland turned his face toward his enemies and prepared himself for death. Although he allowed himself to remember briefly his many temporal victories in laisse 175, Roland was most focused on celestial matters, confessing his sins and asking forgiveness of God again and again in laisses 174, 175, and 176. Most significantly, Roland thrice offered his gauntlet to God, in token of his penance for his sins and his desire steadfastly to serve his eternal Lord. This tripled ritual act offers a progression through Roland's death scene leading from the hero's initial act of contrite confession through his ascension into Heaven with an angelic escort.

Moreover, the heroic figure of Roland specifically—sketched as he is with a sharp eye for drawing connections with Jesus Christ, the ultimate hero of medieval Christianity—is provided not just with Christ's model regarding how heroic death might provide a bridge to life everlasting, but also with Christ's Ascension into Heaven, which is generally described as having taken place on the 40th day after his Resurrection. The Ascension is described in several scriptural passages, although those in Acts 1:9 and the Gospel of Mark 16:19 might be amongst the most illuminating for the present purposes. In the Acts account, Christ *elevatus est*, "is elevated" in the sight of his disciples until *nubes suscepit*, "the clouds took" him and he disappeared from earthly sight. The Gospel of Mark, while developing the narrative also found in the Gospel of Luke, specifically mentions that, having been *assumptus est in cælum*, "assumed into the sky," Christ *sedet a dextris Dei*, "sits at the right side of God." In this context, the detail that Roland offered his right glove to God might be said to evoke a feudal practice concerning the manifestation of subservience to one's lord and to resonate with Christ's position at the right hand of the Father.

Although the scriptural basis for them are less clear, narratives concerned with the Assumption of the Virgin Mary provide descriptions of heavenly escorts similar to that which accompanies the soul of Roland to Heaven, as do the many saints' lives modeled on those accounts. In addition, there is, for example, the Old Testament figure of Enoch about whom, we are told in Genesis 5:24, *Ambulavitque cum Deo, et non apparuit: quia tulit eum Deus*; "And he walked with God, and he was seen no more, for God took him." The suggestion of the text seems to be that Enoch was translated directly into the heavenly sphere without having to undergo the pain of death. In any case, it is clear that the mythic archetype of apotheosis is well represented in Judeo-Christian scripture, and that the *Chanson de Roland* uses to good advantage this archetype in the death scene of Roland.

Ganelon Provides a Judas: The Typology of Treason in the Chanson de Roland[4]

At one and the same time more chilling and more intriguing than the flat demonic caricatures that so often represent the forces of darkness in narratives of holy war, the Judas figure, a sort of "Great Traitor" archetype sometimes augmented with elements drawn from the story of the Fallen Angel Lucifer, provides a deeper, at times more distressing, and arguably somewhat more nuanced portrait of the nature of evil. The treacherous Devil within is always far more dangerous and consequently much more reprehensible than the demonic enemy without, with whom one knows oneself to be at war. Some have suggested that Ganelon is perhaps based on the historical personage Wanilo, the Archbishop of Sens from 837; in 859 Wanilo betrayed Charles the Bald, who had been his patron. In the *Chanson de Roland*, any such fabric of historical fact has been ornately embroidered with the threads of myth, legend, and folklore, transforming the figure of Ganelon into a veritable emblem of betrayal. At some times manifesting a traceable lineage from the biblical Judas Iscariot, at others displaying more general characteristics associated with medieval conceptions of Satan and of the tradition known as the "comedy of evil," the Ganelon of the *Chanson de Roland* is at all times a striking, memorable figure that adds up to more than the sum of its parts.

Ganelon's identity as a "type," or allegorical reflection, of Judas Iscariot is emphasized in our very first introduction to this figure: In laisse 12, the emperor calls his council to him in the shade of a pine tree so that they may discuss the merits of the offer of homage and tribute that Charlemagne has received from Marsile. Although he mentions in the antepenultimate line of the passage that *[d]es Francs de France en i ad plus de mil*, "of Franks from France there were more than a thousand," the poet specifically names twelve barons who were in attendance upon their king; what is more, he does so in a way that specifically mirrors the language of Matthew 10:4, a formula that is replicated in Mark 3:19 and Luke 6:16. In each of these cases, the twelve apostles are listed, with some variation in the format and extra information given for some apostles; furthermore, in each case Judas is mentioned last, and in every case his treachery to come is foreshadowed by some words to that effect. For example, in the Matthew version, verse 4 closes with the line *Iudas Scariotes, qui et tradidit eum*, "Judas Iscariot, who betrayed him." Just so, the prelude to the description of the Council of Charlemagne comprises a list of the barons involved, which included Duke Ogier, Archbishop Turpin, Richard the Old, his nephew Henry, Count Acelin of Gascony, Tedbald of Reims, his cousin Milon, Gerier, Gerin, Roland, Oliver, and Ganelon. Moreover, the mention of Roland's stepfather and betrayer parallels precisely that of Judas in the gospels: *Guenes i vint, ki la traisun fist*; "Ganelon came as well, he who committed the act of treason."

When Roland argues rationally in laisse 14 for the rejection of the most recent offer made by Marsiles—a known perjurer who took the heads of Count Basan and Count Basile, who had served as the Frankish emissaries—Ganelon responds in the next laisse very angrily, stating baldly that Charlemagne should ignore the advice of such a *bricun*, or "fool"; the king should not heed such *cunseill d'orguill*, "prideful advice," as Roland offers, Ganelon suggests, imploring his sovereign to turn away from *fols*, "fools," and heed instead the words of *sages*, the "wise." Thus, in this passage the Judas of the Court of Charlemagne not only condemns his own stepson for speaking like a fool, but also juxtaposes this characterization with an implicit comparison to his own level-headed wisdom. The paradox of a claim to wisdom by one counseling craven foolishness underscores Ganleon's incipient resonance with Satan himself, an identification compounded by his accusation of Roland's "arrogant" advice, a description that emphasizes the Fallen Angel's own greatest sin.

The other Franks apparently see some merit in Ganelon's position concerning the likelihood of the Saracens to keep the peace they are offering. Duke Naimes, speaking in laisse 16, acknowledges that Ganelon's speech may be worth considering, noting that there is *[s]aveir i ad*, "wisdom therein indeed." We know that this phrase reflects the thoughts of many of the assembled barons because, in response to the speech of Naimes, *[d]ient Franceis: 'Ben ad parlet li dux,'* "the French say: 'The Duke has spoken well.'" However, it rapidly becomes apparent how little faith Ganelon himself has in the course of action he has suggested when Roland suggests that Ganelon is the obvious candidate for the Frankish embassy to King Marsile; his stepfather's reaction is nothing short of explosive. As he hears Roland suggest him as the messenger in laisse 20, his reaction is first one of visible anguish and then one of massive rage: *E li quens Guenes en fut mult anguisables*, "but Count Ganelon was exceedingly tormented." Moreover, in laisse 21, Ganelon overtly threatens to avenge himself upon

Roland, proclaiming that as soon as he has performed the task upon which his lord is sending him, *jo n'esclair ceste meie grant ire*, "I [will] assuage my great anger." Roland laughs at this assertion, thereby increasing his stepfather's wrath. In addition to the obvious hypocrisy of Ganelon's reluctance to serve in the capacity of the ambassador charged with the embassy for which he had argued so forcibly—a paradox that clearly highlights his duplicity—there seems also to be some discernable taint of cowardice in this count. This suspicion is most notably manifested by the king himself, who, in laisse 23, suggests that Ganelon has a *tender coer*, a "soft heart." In addition to cowardice, an evil disposition is also suspected in Roland's stepfather in the very next laisse, wherein Charlemagne notes that his messenger is *maltalant*, "ill-tempered."

Moreover, Ganelon's immoderate response to what any objective observer might perceive as the reasonable suggestion that he should put his money where his mouth is sets into motion and foreshadows the betrayal to come. Indeed, in his wrath Ganelon disowns his stepson in laisse 24, publicly proclaiming that *[n]e l'amerai a trestut mun vivant*, "I shall not love him for the remainder of my lifetime." Moreover, his rage is such that Ganelon goes even further, castigating not only Roland but also his companion Oliver and his cohorts the Twelve Peers, all of whom he perceives as accomplices in the treachery he ascribes to his stepson. Unable to contain his bile, Ganelon takes the unusual step of calling upon the king to act as a witness to his defiant challenge to all of these he sees as his enemies at the court of Charlemagne: *Desfi les ci, sire, vostre veiant*, "I challenge them here, my lord, in your sight."

Ganelon's noble qualities and polished exterior contrast sharply with such moral flaws and inner turmoil; indeed, this combination of features again begs a comparison with Satan himself, whose original princely mien may yet beguile the unwary through a noble countenance that disguises his wicked intent. The duality of the Great Deceiver thus provides a model through which we may understand the mixed attributes of the Frankish traitor. First introduced as an aristocratic figure, strikingly handsome and fashionably attired, Ganelon is pleasant and fearsome to behold: Bedecked in *pels de martre*, rare "marten furs," as well as a *blialt de palie*, a costly "silken tunic," the visage of Roland's stepfather becomes nearly incandescent in his rage at his stepson's suggestion that he should be the one to attempt the embassy to Marsile, an assignment Ganelon clearly perceives as tantamount to a suicide mission: *Vairs out les oilz e mult fier lu visage*, "His eyes flashed and his countenance was fearsome." However, as terrifying as he might be in his wrath, the poet is careful to point out how princely Ganelon was in form and how notably broad through the chest; in short, we are assured, in the midst of such a passionate outburst "all those around him gazed wonderingly at his handsome features": *Tant par fut bels tuit si per l'en esguardent.*

In addition to a noble bearing and handsome face, Ganelon is possessed of an artful and cunning mind and tongue, attributes that are characteristic of deceivers in the mold of Satan. Indeed, when Roland suggests his stepfather for the vital assignment of acting as Charlemagne's representative in the Court of Marsile in laisse 20, it is precisely, the stepson ingenuously states, because this assignment will require a *saives hom,* "a wise man." Indeed, the Franks all approve of this choice for the same reason, noting that *n'i trametrez plus saive,* "one will find no wiser man." Paradoxically, it is his very powers of reason, wit, and guile that stand him in good stead in his dealings with the Saracens; indeed, in addition to the implicit structure of Ganelon's interactions with Blancandrin and Marsile, which emphasizes the ambassador's innate cunning, our author several times specifically extols the count's superlative intellectual and rhetorical abilities. The most striking example of such commentary is found in laisse 33, which begins with the assurance that *[m]ais li quens Guenes se fut ben purpenset,* "Count Ganelon had considered everything carefully;" he addressed the Saracen king with *grant saver,* "great cunning," in these extremely treacherous circumstances, in which his life clearly hung by the merest thread. However, Ganelon was more than equal to the challenge; as the poet makes clear, he spoke *[c]ume celui ki ben faire le set,* "as one quite practiced in such interactions." Ganelon's thematic descent from the Great Deceiver is emphasized by the fact that he is more than able to work his wiles upon the Saracen lords, figures who are themselves clearly associated in this text with demons.

The reticence of Ganelon to undertake this embassy for Charlemagne is manifested in his reluctance in laisse 25 to accept the emperor's right glove, the symbol of this charge, a reluctance that results in a sign interpreted by the Franks as an ominous one. Ganelon, our narrator informs us with a characteristic hint of understatement, *iloec ne volsist ester,* "had no desire to be there," and—presumably as a direct result of this lack of enthusiasm—the count dropped the gage of commission as his lord offered it to him. This clumsiness was taken as an ill omen by the Franks, who as a body declared that *[d]e cest message nos avendrat grant perte,* "we will suffer greatly as a result of this sign."

Ganelon has a rendezvous with the Saracen ambassadors in laisse 28, in which they are said to have gathered beneath a tall olive tree. Moreover, the poet emphasizes that Roland's betrayer meets with one with whom he can do business in Blancandrin, *ki envers lu s'atarget*, "who tarries behind," so that they might speak privately with each other. The affinity between these two dark spirits is suggested by the fact that, we are told, they spoke to one another *[p]ar grant saveir*, "with great guile." Clearly the Judas of the *Chanson de Roland* has met a kindred spirit. These two conspirators soon come to terms, and Ganelon offers Roland to Blancandrin as a sacrificial lamb in laisse 29: When the Saracen emissary remarks upon the general nobility of the Franks and suggests that these fine vassals do their lord an injustice when they counsel him ever to sow the seeds of discord and war, Ganelon replies that he would bring this charge to bear against none of the Franks, with the lone exception of *Rollant, ki uncore en avrat hunte*, "Roland, who will be humiliated for it someday." Coming quickly to the substance of his plot against the life of Roland, Ganelon concludes his speech in that laisse by claiming that peace for all might be purchased with the blood of Charlemagne's nephew, who is in fact innocent of any such charge and who in reality is his lord's truest vassal. The words of the traitor reveal his true diabolical nature as truly as they seal his own fate and that of his stepson: *Seit ki l'ociet, tute pais puis avriumes*, "if one were to kill him, all would have peace."

Binding themselves together through the instrument of this wicked bargain, Ganelon and Blancandrin compact their conspiracy to bring about the death of Roland in laisse 31, in which they pledge one another their troth *[que] il querreient que Rollant fust ocis*, "that they would seek out a way to have Roland killed." This passage also reiterates Ganelon's role as a Judas figure. Indeed, the very words of his agreement with Blancandrin provide a distant echo of the agreement between Judas and the chief priests: After receiving his blood money, Matthew tells us in Chapter 26 Verse 16, *exinde quærebat opportunitatem ut eum traderet*, "from thenceforth he sought opportunity to betray him."

Brought by his co-conspirator Blancandrin into the presence of the Saracen king, through his cunning Ganleon first enrages Marsile through an arrogant statement of Charlemagne's terms in laisse 33, which he concludes by warning the pagan sovereign in no uncertain terms that to defy the will of the Frankish ruler would inevitably result in ignominious death, stating baldly that *murrez vus a hunte e a viltet*, "you will die shamefully and disgracefully." Once Marsile is suitably terrified of what he may expect from Charlemagne—*mult esfreed*, "very frightened," to use the poet's phrase—Ganelon seals the deal when, in laisse 36, he skillfully introduces the idea that Marsile will be forced into a partnership with an insufferable

Roland: Marsile will hold half of Spain in fief from Charlemagne, whereas the other half will be under the jurisdiction of Roland, whom Ganelon describes—as if in an aside—as *mult orguillos*, "extremely haughty." When Marsile has been perfectly played out, a hair's-breadth from striking down Ganelon on the spot for his impertinence, Blancandrin steps in in laisse 38, assures the Saracens that Ganelon has agreed to act *[d]e nostre prod*, "to our advantage," and brings the parties together in *la traisun seinz dreit*, a "betrayal without justice." In laisses 40 and 41, Ganelon emphasizes Charlemagne's warlike nature and disinclination to live peacefully, artfully begging the question that Marsile is, at length, impelled to pose: Would the King of the Franks ever settle into a peaceful life? *Co n'iert, dist Guenes, tant cum vivet sis nies*: "That may not be, Ganelon replies, so long as his nephew remains alive."

In laisses 43–45 Ganelon unfolds his plot: Marsile is to pay Charlemagne the tribute demanded of him and to agree to all of the terms required to compact a peace; then, as Charlemagne takes his armies back into France, the Saracens will have their opportunity to destroy Roland, and—so Ganelon claims—with this one victory extinguish forever the martial spirit of the King of the Franks. The death of Roland, the traitor assures his paymasters, *[d]unc perdreit Carles le destre braz del cors*, "would bring about the loss of Charles's right arm from his body," and peace, he claimed would be ensured. The Great Traitor's prediction is reflected in detail in laisse 56, in which Ganelon himself figures in the prophetic dream of Charlemagne, which clearly foretells the doom of Roland: In this vision it is none other than Ganelon himself who snatches and shatters the lance from the hand of his lord, and in this vision Charlemagne also foresees what Ganelon had predicted to the Saracens; *[e]l destre braz li morst uns uers si mals*, "a fearsome bear ravaged his right arm." The King of the Franks, like his traitorous ambassador, identifies Roland in this dream with his own right arm. Furthermore, Ganelon clearly is to be associated with the rampaging beast attacking Charlemagne.

In laisses 46 and 47 the conspirators compacted their unholy bargain: First Ganelon foreswore his loyalty to his king and his stepson; *[l]a traisun jurat*, "he took the oath of treason," we are told, *[s]ur les reliques de s'espee Murgleis*, "upon the relics of his sword Murgleis." Then Marsile took a similarly villainous oath upon the false *lei i fut Mahum e Tervagan*, "the scriptures of Mohammed and Tervagant." Having agreed to betray Roland, Ganelon accepts the diversionary tribute of the Saracens intended to deceive and placate the unsuspecting Franks and departs for Charlemagne in laisse 52, in which Marsile cautions him to remember their compact and to avoid a change of heart.

This Judas receives his metaphorical 30 pieces of silver in laisses 48–50; to ensure against any wavering in the traitor's resolution, in his parting words the Saracen king indicates a rich annual reward Ganelon can expect for successfully enacting his treachery. In addition, Ganelon receives rich gifts from three named individuals, gifts that act as contractual bonuses over and above the blood money offered by Marsile as annual tribute. Indeed, the elaborate gestures concerning friendship vows, and especially the kissing between Ganelon and the two Saracen knights, might also serve to echo Judas's betrayal of Christ with a kiss. Moreover, it seems noteworthy that each of the first two sequences are described in parallel terms that help to clarify and to refine the Saracen desire not just to destroy Roland, but to render ridiculous the martial nobility in the service of his rightful lord for which he stands; this episode thus evokes the diabolical desire not just to kill Christ but to humiliate him.

First, *uns paiens*, "a pagan," named Valdabron came forward, giddy with the knowledge that through these acts they were sealing Roland's doom: *Cler en riant*, "Loudly with laughter," he addressed the traitor, presenting Ganelon with his sword as a token of friendship, so that the Saracens through Ganelon's intercession might find Roland amongst the rearguard. To this the traitor answered *[b]en serat fait*, "so will it be done," and the conspirators sealed their bargain affectionately: *[S]e baiserent es vis e es mentuns*, "they kissed one another about the face and chin." Next, another Saracen explicitly identified as "a pagan" stepped up to the traitor, this one called Climborin. Also speaking mirthfully through bellowing laughter, this knight gifted Ganelon with his helmet, in earnest of aid in the desire of the Saracens to make Roland himself, and by extension his lord, laughable: *Par quel mesure le poussum hunir*, "So that we may humiliate him greatly." Again Ganelon responded that "it will be done so," and again these words were sealed with a kiss.

Finally, in an ironic twist, the laughter of the Saracens falls quiet, and even as Ganelon acts the buffoon, he is, paradoxically, taken seriously: Queen Bramimonde, we are told, offered Ganelon *dous nusches*, "two brooches," for his wife. The detail that these gifts—*valent mielz que tut l'aveir de Rume*, "more valuable than the treasures of Rome," and finer than any such treasure in the possession of Charlemagne—should be ignominiously "thrust into his boot" by the traitor, *en sa hoese les butet*, like ill-gotten gains hastily secreted by a bandit, seems designed to add a bit of low comedy to the scene, providing a slapstick routine that plays off the earlier immoderate laughter of the Saracen warriors and serves to underscore the bathos of Ganelon's treasonous act. The point of these three scenes is that it is the traitor himself who—like the prototypical turncoat Judas, or even the *ur*-betrayer Satan himself—behaves foolishly, turning his back on his rightful lord. The Saracens, like the priests of the temple who paid for the treason of Judas, or even akin to the devils who flocked to Satan's banner, act as keystone cops in this comedy of evil, blindly and blithely plotting the downfall of powers of which they cannot properly conceive and in so doing ultimately sealing their own doom.

So blinded by his hatred of his stepson that he is hell-bent on ensuring that the Saracens have the time to complete their rout of the Frankish rearguard, Ganelon foolishly unmasks himself as Roland's betrayer in laisses 133 and 134, in each of which Charlemagne expresses dismay at the hearing the distant call of Roland's mighty horn. However, in each instance Ganelon contradicts his lord, claiming that the sounding of the Oliphant, so disturbing to the Franks who hear it, is not in fact a hero's last desperate effort to summon aid, but rather is merely the arrogant preening of a reckless youth. However, the third time the Franks hear the sounding of the Oliphant, Duke Naimes gives voice to the suspicions of the court.

Finally identified as the Judas of the Court of Charlemagne, Ganelon's humiliation seems complete when he is bound over in shame as a common criminal to—of all people—the court cooks in laisse 137; turning to Besgon, the chief cook, Charlemagne orders him to take charge of this traitor, whom he deems a "felon" finally articulating the truth about Ganelon. The once great count, now an object of scorn and ridicule, is treated no better than a captive beast, and we are explicitly told that he is chained *cum un urs*, "like a bear," perhaps a reference to the traitor's role in the vision of Charlemagne. However, although Roland himself exits the epic that bears his name just over halfway through the narrative, the traitor Ganelon abides to reemerge to play a key role in the closing passages of the poem, in which Divine Judgment is made manifest and fitting retribution is meted out in the ancient ritual of trial by combat, a form of jurisprudence that comprises almost an entire medieval mythology unto itself.

The Dreams of Charlemagne: Prophetic Visions in the Chanson de Roland

In laisses 56 and 57, Charlemagne—like many other figures of note, includ-ing the Kievan Sviatoslav III, often called the "Russian Charlemagne"—passes an uneasy night, envisioning a series of troubling images. In laisse 67, Charlemagne himself interprets this dream, lamenting the treason of Ganelon. In laisses 185 and 186, Charlemagne receives another set of visions; however, this time we are specifically informed that these portents are delivered through the agency of a celestial messenger. Saint Gabriel, the poet claims, was sent by God *a guarder*, "to keep watch over" Charlemagne; the angel, we are told, spent the entire night *a sun chef*, "by his head," and from this position *[p]ar avisiun li ad anunciet*, "announced to him by means of a vision" the battle to come. Gabriel commonly plays the role of the herald of such portents in medieval dream visions and performs a similar function in *Poema de Mio Cid*, although in that text he imparts a much more joyful message to the Campeador.

Sacred Duel as Holy War: The Judgment of God in the Trial by Combat Sequence of the Chanson de Roland[5]

The mythic theme of the battle between the forces of good and the champions of evil is rendered in microcosm in the trial-by-combat sequence in which Ganelon's guilt and fate are finally decided. Trial by combat was a popular means of judicial redress amongst the Norman French, and in Anglo-Norman England it largely supplanted the widespread practice of trial by ordeal popular amongst the Anglo-Saxons. Indeed, it comes as a surprise to many modern readers that the introduction of trial by jury met with considerable resistance because the shortsighted and self-serving assessment of one's peers seemed infinitely inferior to and more threatening than the omniscient and impartial verdict of God Almighty.

This unease with human arbitration is highlighted in laisses 282 and 283, in which the Frankish jury advises the acquittal of Ganelon, who does not even deign to deny the charges brought against him; on the other hand, in laisse 289, no less a personage than Charlemagne himself calls upon the agency of God to make manifest his Divine Justice. Indeed, trial by ordeal and trial by combat are rituals predicated upon the foundational faith that the Divine Will may be evoked as the final arbiter in human disputes, a concept that is similar to the belief that God will take an active hand in ensuring the victory of the righteous and faithful over the sinful adherents to false faiths, which belief is a cornerstone of the trope of holy war in general and is specifically referenced explicitly time and again in the *Chanson de Roland*.

When Ganelon is brought before the council of the Franks to face the charge of treason, it at first appears as though he is likely to be exonerated and to walk free. Given a chance to speak in his own behalf in laisse 279, Ganelon does not deny the charges but rather falls back on a two-fold argument: First, that he had ever been a loyal and courageous vassal to Charlemagne; second, that, as he had publicly challenged Roland, Oliver, and the Twelve Peers, he was guilty of no treason at all but had merely escaped from a suicidal embassy and wreaked his vengeance for having been sent thereon through the agency of his own quick wits. Moreover, this favorable turn of events to Ganelon's favor is largely due to the intercession on his behalf, in laisse 280, of Pinabel, from Castel de Sorence, reputed to be skilled as an advocate at a trial by jury and as a champion upon the judicial field of combat. Indeed, in laisse 281 Pinabel makes it clear how a keen blade may outweigh a sharp wit in a Frankish court of justice when he assures Ganelon that the count will be saved from the condemnation of any Frank *sempres*, "at once," because Pinabel proposes to dispose of any accuser by *desmente*, "contradicting" the case against Ganelon with his *brant d'acer*, "sword of steel."

The Franks seem nearly united in their inclination to set Ganelon free in laisse 282; all but Thierry agree that Roland is dead and that nothing can bring him back. Any person who would risk his life in the attempt to punish Ganelon would be, according to this craven counsel, nothing but a great fool. Charlemagne remarks on the injustice of this assessment in laisse 283, in which he refers to the jurors as accessories in Ganelon's crime, crying out passionately that *[v]os estes mi felun*, "You all are guilty of this crime against me!" The King of the Franks clearly perceives that such a judgment is cowardly and dishonorable and repudiates it, but he seems impotent to force a just verdict and thus to enact a more righteous sentence. At this dramatic juncture, Thierry offers himself as something of an underdog champion; in fact, he is described explicitly in laisse 284 as *[h]eingre out le cors e graisle e eschewid*, "slender of body and lean and shapely," and thus consequently smaller and less imposing than his opponent, of whom it is said, when he responds to Thierry's accusation in laisse 285, that he *[g]ranz est e forz e vassals e isnel*, or "is large and strong and brave and fast." This contrast of course helps to emphasize the fact that God takes a hand in Thierry's ultimate victory.

Thierry clearly and succinctly articulates the treasonous nature of Ganelon's actions in laisse 284: No matter how valid Ganelon's grievances against Roland may have been, at the time of the betrayal Roland was serving in his capacity as Charlemagne's vassal; indeed, he was the right arm of the emperor's dream, and thus, as Thierry puts it to his king, *[v] ostre servise l'en doust bien guarir*, "service to you should have been ample protection." Therefore, in Thierry's view Ganelon is *fels*, "guilty," because he has *parjurez*, "foresworn" himself, disregarding his oath of fealty to his lord. For such a monstrous crime Ganelon should, according to Thierry, suffer a painful and humiliating public execution, *[s]i cume fel ki felonie fist*, "like a common criminal who has committed a wicked deed." If Ganelon's case should be championed by any *parent*, "kinsman," who would like *desmentir*, "to contradict" the accuser, Thierry states that he is ready *guarantir*, "to warrant" this *jugement*, "sentence," *a ceste espee*, "with this sword."

The terminology Thierry uses in this laisse, like that his rival Pinabel uses in the related passages, is often explicitly legal, although the subtext is one of violent combat. Indeed, this sequence is notable precisely because it conflates a judicial proceeding with a martial challenge: Following Germanic legal practice of ancient provenance, Thierry has brought case, judgment, and sentence against the accused; it falls to Ganelon, then, to find an advocate who will present the case for the defense in exactly the same terms. What often seems, at least of on the surface, a bald challenge to a duel is a much more complex process than it appears to most modern readers and draws upon ancient mythological conceptions of the role of the Divine in the disputes of men. Both Thierry, who is prosecuting this case, and Pinabel, who is defending against it, are in actuality evoking the Judgment of the Almighty, and all of the witnesses to the proceedings understand that the verdict of God will be written upon the flesh of the advocate who falls under the sword of his rival.

According to this ancient judicial ritual, Thierry is in point of fact declaring that Ganelon is guilty and that his sentence should be death. Therefore, the advocate for the accused is in his answer not disputing the charges per se but rather is rejecting the judgment handed down by Thierry, who as the accuser in such a case is taking upon himself the roles of judge, jury, and de facto executioner. Pinabel's words in laisse 285, in which he declares his intention to overturn Thierry's assertions with the point of his sword, underscore this distinction. Moreover, Pinabel emphasizes that he has chosen to utilize trial by combat as the court of last resort.

The resultant ritual duel proceeds in several steps, beginning with a ceremonial exchange of gauntlets that signifies the offer and acceptance of the challenge. The king for his part demands that the accused be redeemed through the persons of a given number of kinsmen who pledge themselves in surety for his bond; only after 30 kinsmen have offered themselves as surety does the king assent to the procedure Pinabel has requested.

Here Charlemagne clearly represents the personification of the apparatus of the temporal judicial system and the embodiment of the representative of the Divine in the affairs of men; thus he acts as the impartial vessel through which the challenge is delivered and accepted and in the capacity of the bailiff of the Divine Court: Ganelon is released into the custody of his advocate in much the same way that a modern defendant might be granted liberty in exchange for posting a given bail bond, a cash sum that is returned to the accused if he does not flee justice. Although the modern bail bond is only forfeit if the defendant flees, the kinsmen who redeem Ganelon place their very futures in jeopardy in the belief that the accused will be exonerated. They are, in fact, staking their lives and honor on this proceeding; more than mere hostages who have exchanged their liberty for that of Ganelon, their vows on his behalf act in a legal sense as a framework that echoes and bolsters the assertion of innocence Pinabel has made on Ganelon's behalf. The fact that so many kinsmen support this case emphasizes the accused's social status and kin network. Moreover, under traditional Germanic law, the defendant's case was materially strengthened by large numbers of such supporters.

Indeed, functioning as far more than the mere character witnesses they may appear to modern readers, the ritual hostages demanded by this literary Charlemagne in fact evoke an actual legal tradition known as compurgation, a system that relied on a mythology of personal honor that resonates harmoniously with the system of Divine Justice with which it came to be used in concert. In the Anglo-Norman England that produced the Oxford manuscript of the *Chanson de Roland*, the ancient Germanic rite of compurgation enshrined in Anglo-Saxon law was still in force and indeed was an extremely popular method of jurisprudence. Under this system, several "oath-helpers" (i.e., those who would swear to the veracity of the accused and to the value of his own oath) would "purge" or clear the charge against the accused through their sworn testament. Known as *apfultum* in Old English, or *consacramentales* in Latin, these oath-helpers were a key component to the process of compurgation, which comes from the Latin term for the process in Church Law; this *purgatio canonica*, or "sworn vindication," came to be used in tandem with the *purgatio vulgaris* (i.e., vindication through the ordeal proper), and this system reached its apex in the century that produced the Oxford manuscript. Such judicial processes—including trial by ordeal, trial by combat, and ritual compurgation, which relied explicitly upon overt manifestations of the agency of Divine Will to determine innocence or guilt, became known collectively as the *Judicium Dei*, (i.e., the "Judgment of God").

Once the challenge has been issued and accepted and the terms of the trial by combat have been arranged—in short, to use the poet's phrase, once the *bataille justez*, the "duel has been arranged"—Thierry and Pinabel undergo ritual cleansing ceremonies in laisse 287 that reflect actual practices associated with the practice of trial by combat. We are told that the combatants *sunt cunfes*, "were shriven," and *asols e seignez*, were "absolved and blessed with the sign of the cross," that they *[o]ent lur messes*, "went to mass," and *sunt acuminiez*, "took communion," and that they both *[m]ult granz offrendes metent par cez musters*, "endowed well the monasteries." Having thus been purged of sin and blessed in preparation for the coming conflict, and having made ritual offerings before the altar of God, whose judgment in this travail each seeks on his own behalf, each combatant is now prepared to duel to the death to prove his case, and thus they appear before the emperor prepared to do battle. The rites of sanctification associated with actual ordeal rituals were similar to those described in the *Chanson de Roland*. Indeed, although such ordeals were explicitly disavowed by the Church and ecclesiastical participation was officially forbidden, it was in fact commonplace for priests to give such blessings to these practices. As a result, the mythic subtext of the *Judicium Dei* was tacitly condoned by a church enriched by the practices associated with the rituals surrounding such ordeals. Over time these practices became commonly accepted as canonical, the protestations of learned theologians notwithstanding.

The trial by combat sequence itself is perhaps most notable for the mutual respect articulated by the combatants, each of whom makes an overture of reconciliation toward the other, on the single condition that the opponent recant his position. Each refuses the other's offer with repugnance, and the poet sets up the climax of the sequence by noting that this struggle will only end with the death of one of the two duelists. The tension builds as the poet describes the violence of the combat and the horror of the onlookers, until finally, in laisse 292, Pinabel strikes such a blow upon the helm of Thierry that the wounded knight's face is covered with blood and his mail-coat is rent to his waist; it is only the protection of God, we are told, that guards Ganelon's accuser: *Deus le guartit, que mort ne l'acraventet*, "God protected him from being struck dead." Divine Judgment alone, we are to understand, acted as Thierry's shield before a blow that should have killed him.

The function of the trial-by-combat sequence as a court that reveals Divine Judgment is clarified in the way the poet structures the description of Thierry's victory over Pinabel: In rapid succession in laisse 293 the poet describes the blow that concluded the combat, the onlookers assessment of God's hand in the battle, and the condemnation of Ganelon. First, the fatal blow is described in graphic detail that emphasizes the final and indisputable outcome of this duel: Striking Pinabel through the helmet, Thierry splits his opponent's head right down to the nose, so that the brains erupt from the force of the blow. Immediately thereafter, the reaction of the Franks makes it clear that they believe that Thierry might only have overcome Pinabel through an act of Divine Intercession, an act through which the hand of God writes Ganelon's guilt upon Pinabel's ruptured and gory head. Finally, the poet closes this passage with a comment upon the righteousness of the condemnation of Ganelon that must follow this violent verdict.

It is no coincidence that laisse 293, which takes as its focus Thierry's miraculous victory over Pinabel, whose very brains are dashed from his skull in evidence of Ganelon's guilt, concludes with the notation that he will die in the company of his kinsmen *ki plaidet unt pur lui*, "who supported his case." Ganelon's execution is in fact preceded and prefigured by that of his compurgators in laisse 295 in a sequence that emphasizes for the reader the sacred nature of ritual compurgation: Not only one's honor, but one's very life could be staked upon such oath-helping. When the emperor calls upon his Franks to decide the fate of the compurgators, they call with one voice for blood vengeance to purge the false oaths given in support of the traitorous Ganleon. Moreover, the poet emphasizes that it is Ganelon himself, and not the Provost Basbrun, who is acting as Charlemagne's executioner, who is responsible for the death of his kinsmen. Given the understanding that the practices involved in assessing the *Judicium Dei* were in fact founded upon a belief that the hand of the Divine would manifest itself in the course of the proceedings, the severity of such condemnation by association perhaps makes more sense.

Charlemagne most fully explicitly articulates the mythic subtext of the *Judicium Dei* when, in laisse 289, he calls directly upon the Divine to render a judgment made manifest in a manner that will illuminate the moral vision of mortal men. *E! Deus*, "Oh! God," the mortal king responsible for earthly justice implores his celestial sovereign, the fount of eternal judgment, *le dreit en esclargiez*, "let justice shine brightly!" The *Judicium Dei* is, in this context, clearly envisioned as a brilliant beam of the pure light of God that will elucidate the truth of the case being decided by the combat of Pinabel and Thierry; the sin of Ganelon will stand out like a dark blot in stark contrast to the effulgence pouring forth from this beacon. Indeed, once this guilt has been revealed through the fatal flow of Pinabel's blood upon the field of combat, Ganelon's sin may no longer remain hidden, revealed as it is by the bright light of God's justice. The blood of the recalcitrant sinner, which pours forth at the last in laisse 296 to stain the green grass of the meadow of judgment, reflects this concept: Just as the traitor's gore stands out in sharp contrast against the verdant field beneath the brilliant light of day, just so was the dark blot wrought upon his soul by his sin clearly illuminated by the blazing brightness of the *Judicium Dei*.

The Mythic Wheel Turns: Vengeance, Spiritual Rebirth, and a Renewed Call to Arms in the Conclusion of the Chanson de Roland

Justice is vengeance in the *Chanson de Roland*, a fact that is perhaps not to be wondered at in a stirring paean to the trope of holy war. The poet explicitly links Charlemagne's desire for justice with his personal anger and with his attempt to sate his own lust to avenge the death of his nephew and right hand. Indeed, the emperor has the Saracen Queen Bramimonde baptized in laisse 290 only after he has done so; then and only then, *esclargiez est la sue grant ire*, "his mighty wrath has been appeased." At that moment when the *Chanson de Roland* is about to end, day is drawing to a close and Charlemagne may finally lay his hoary head down to rest. He is summoned from his slumber by another celestial vision, this one drawn directly from the tradition of the Roman emperor Constantine the Great, who was reputedly converted to Christianity because of a heavenly voice saying of the sign of the Cross glowing in the sky "by this sign shall ye conquer."

Clearly in the *Chanson de Roland* this is a more doleful message for a warrior of the faith who can find no respite from the constant struggle of holy war on his Heavenly Lord's behalf. Indeed, when Saint Gabriel appears before Charlemagne with a message of the dire need of the Christians besieged at Imphe, the emperor's words are striking for their very lack of martial spirit and willingness to fight the good fight. Indeed, we are told in no uncertain terms that he laments his fate, crying out to his God in despair. The poet then closes the tale of Roland's fate with the dry comment that thus the tale Turoldus told ends. Although the *Chanson de Roland* offers a clearly articulated vision of a mythic battle between the forces of good and evil as this struggle is manifested in the temporal world, the treason of Ganelon, the loss of Roland himself, and the final despair of Charlemagne all underscore the ambiguities and the costs of such a battle, even when the demonic enemy himself is identified.

Notes

1. For critical commentary on and analysis of elements of the historical Battle of Roncevaux and in particular its implications upon a study of the mythological theme of holy war as it is manifested in the *Chanson de Roland*, see especially Barbero 58–59; Becher 63–64, 138–139; Brault xiii–xv; Burgess 9–10; Butt 50–51; Collins 67–68; Gaunt 26; Merwin vii–xv; Morrissey 53, 56, 80, 87, 90; Uitti 65–66; and Vance 8–9.

2. For critical commentary on and analysis of elements of the manuscript record of the *Chanson de Roland*, see especially Brault xxix–xxx; Burgess 7–9, 14; Cook xvii–xix; Duggan 1–6; Gaunt 18, 25–26, 118–126, 155; Merwin xiii–xv; Morrissey 288; Uitti 65; and Vance 101.

3. For critical commentary on and analysis of the mythological theme of holy war as it is explicitly manifested in the military campaigns described in the *Chanson de Roland*, see especially Brault xxiv; Burgess 19–21; Cook 207–222; Gaunt 26–37; Kelly 207; and Vance 21–38, 64–71.

4. For critical commentary on and analysis of the transformation of Ganelon into a Judas figure and in particular the implications of this transformation upon a study of the mythological theme of holy war as it is manifested in the *Chanson de Roland*, see especially Brault xvi–xviii, xix–xxix; Burgess 23–24; Cook 13–17, 27–41; Gaunt 120–121, 126; Morrissey 38, 47–49, 56; Uitti 102–108; and Vance 8–20.

5. For critical commentary on and analysis of the concept of trial by combat and especially the related sequence in the *Chanson de Roland*, see especially Barbero 202–204; Brault xvii–xviii; Burgess 13; Cook 120; Morrissey 47–49; and Vance 7, 81–93. Moreover, it is important to note that the concept of the frailty of human judgment was a commonplace of medieval literature; for example, see the discussion of "immanent justice" in Maddox, 51 and 141.

Sources and Further Reading

Barbero, Alessandro. *Charlemagne: Father of a Continent*. Berkeley: University of California Press, 2004.

Becher, Matthias. *Charlemagne*. New Haven, CT: Yale University Press, 2003.

Brault, Gerard J. *La Chanson De Roland: Oxford Text and English Translation*. University Park: Pennsylvania State University Press, 1984.

Burgess, Glyn S. *The Song of Roland*. London: Penguin Books, 1990.

Butt, John J. *Daily Life in the Age of Charlemagne*. The Greenwood Press "Daily life through history" series. Westport, CT: Greenwood Press, 2002.

Collins, Roger. *Charlemagne*. Toronto: University of Toronto Press, 1998.

Cook, Robert Francis. *The Sense of the Song of Roland*. Ithaca, NY: Cornell University Press, 1987.

Duggan, Joseph J. *The Song of Roland: Formulaic Style and Poetic Craft*. Berkeley: University of California Press, 1973.

Gaunt, Simon. *Retelling the Tale: An Introduction to Medieval French Literature*. London: Duckworth Academic, 2001.

Hodges, Richard, and David Whitehouse. *Mohammed, Charlemagne & the Origins of Europe: Archaeology and the Pirenne Thesis*. Ithaca, NY: Cornell University Press, 1983.

Kelly, Douglas. *The Art of Medieval French Romance*. Madison: University of Wisconsin Press, 1992.

Maddox, Donald. *Fictions of Identity in Medieval France*. Cambridge studies in medieval literature, Vol. 43. New York: Cambridge University Press, 2000.

Merwin, W.S. *The Song of Roland*. New York: Modern Library, 2001.

Morrissey, Robert John. *Charlemagne & France: A Thousand Years of Mythology*. The Laura Shannon series in French medieval studies. Notre Dame, IN: University of Notre Dame Press, 2003.

Uitti, Karl D. *Story, Myth, and Celebration in Old French Narrative Poetry, 1050–1200*. Princeton, NJ: Princeton University Press, 1973.

Vance, Eugene. *Reading the Song of Roland*. Englewood Cliffs, NJ: Prentice-Hall, 1970.

The Iberian
Unjustly-Accused Hero

The Historical Context of the *Cantar De Mio Cid:* The Conquest of Spain By the Moors and the *Reconquista* for Christ[1]

Who Were the Moors?

The term *Moor* commonly designates North African Moslems who conquered the Christian states in what is now Spain and Portugal. Beginning in the early eighth century with an incursion of Arabs and Berbers from across the Strait of Gibraltar, the Islamic presence in the Iberian Peninsula lasted nearly eight hundred years, ending only in 1492, at the dawn of the great age of Spain as an international power. Sweeping into Spain and quickly asserting political dominance—if not outright rulership—across the entire peninsula, the invaders set up their power base in Cordoba, a convenient location relative to North Africa, but undeniably remote from most of northern Spain, in the mountainous regions where resistance to Islamic supremacy fomented.

Unable ever to complete the conquest of the most far-flung areas of Iberia, the Moslem forces contented themselves with seasonal campaigns that raided the territory of the independent city-states beyond the pale of Cordoban influence. Spanish dreams of throwing off the shackles of their Islamic overlords might have seemed beyond hope of fruition until the fall of the Umayyad Caliphate in Cordoba in 1031. However, successive waves of new Moslem invaders stymied the movement of the Spanish Christians to reclaim their lost territory. First, the Almoravids pressed into

Iberia from Morocco to fill the vacuum left by the Umayyads. The Almohads followed in the mid-12th century, extending the Islamic presence in Spain by hundreds of years.

What Was the Reconquista?

During the time in which the Cid lived and campaigned, the dream of the "Reconquest" or *Reconquista*, of Spain from the Islamic invaders was an active part of the Christian Spanish consciousness. Although this political and military concept has been challenged on occasion in recent years as an anachronistic perception of modern historians, the trend of contemporary scholarship is to acknowledge that the basic desire underlying such a concept was born shortly after the initial North African invasions in 711 and developed into a precept of mythic proportions by the end of the ninth century. More than simply a series of military campaigns or the reflection of the desire of individual leaders to control more territory, the *Reconquista* was an outgrowth of a belief commonly held by Iberian Christians that the Islamic population among and often above them had no legitimate right to the territory they had appropriated.

The Literary Context of the *Cantar De Mio Cid:* Sources, Manuscript, and Structure[2]

Comprised of 3730 lines grouped into 152 verse paragraphs or laisses (sometimes called by the Spanish term *tiradas*) of irregular length, the *Cantar de Mio Cid*—also known as the *Poema de Mio Cid*—survives in a single manuscript in very poor condition. The date of the composition of the epic itself has been much debated, with a traditional argument based on archaic language positing the mid-12th century as the era of origin; however, most scholars now concur that the evidence suggests a date of composition in the first decade of the 13th century. Although the extant manuscript itself comes from the 14th century, it contains a notation dating an earlier copy to 1207, which is now generally taken as the latest possible year for the completion of the poem as it comes down to us. The treatment presented here follows the Hamilton and Perry edition; laisse numbers and direct citations in Spanish follow Hamilton and Perry, whereas translations are the author's.

From Legendary Soldier to Mythic Hero: The Historical Rodrigo Diaz de Vivar[3]

A warrior of the class known as the *infazon*, which is to say a member of the minor Spanish nobility who held a hereditary knighthood, Rodrigo Diaz de Vivar earned the epithet *El Cid* from his conquered Islamic opponents, who referred to him as *Sayyid*, "Lord"; his Spanish title *Campeador* comes from the Latin *Campidoctor*, meaning "Master of the Battlefield." The Cid rose to such prominent heights as a result of his strategic acumen and resultant military victories that he was named *alferez* by Sancho II of Castile; from the Arabic term *al-faris*, meaning a "knight," the title *alferez* was the equivalent of the Latin name *signifer*, which refers to the post occupied by the aristocratic marshal who served as the king's "standard-bearer" and who directed the forces in the field in the monarch's absence.

Rodrigo obviously stood high in the favor of Sancho II, but the Cid's fortunes fell with the death of that king in 1072. Sancho was succeeded by his brother—and enemy—Alfonso VI of Leon, who unified the kingdoms of Castile and Leon under one crown. Suspicious of the great military leader who had been a favorite of his brother, Alfonso banished Rodrigo twice, first from 1081 to 1087, and then again from 1089 to 1092. The poem's representation of the Cid's exile seems to draw upon the traditional understanding of the circumstances of his first exile and primary substance developed from events associated with his second exile. The Cid spent most of his first banishment in the service of the Moorish Emir of Saragossa, who employed Rodrigo to combat for him several enemies, including the emir's own brother, lord of Lerida, as well as Berenguer Ramon II, the Count of Barcelona. During his second exile the Cid enriched himself by continuing some of these endeavors, notably capturing the Count of Barcelona for a second time in 1090. However, most notably the Cid's second term of banishment included his great siege of Valencia, which began in 1092. He finally wrested the city from the Moors in 1094, having successfully defended his forces against the relief efforts of the Almoravids. Poetic license aside, then, it is clear that the poet drew upon the second exile of the Cid to develop a large part of the narrative of the *Poema de Mio Cid*.

However, the reader searching for the historical Cid in the laisses of the *Poema de Mio Cid* must proceed with caution: Many of the seemingly historical details offered by the poet—elements that in parts lend to this epic a sense of verisimilitude often at odds with the genre as a whole—are, upon closer examination, out of context or markedly divergent from the facts. For example, the poetic figures of Alvar Fanez and Bishop Jeronimo, although undoubtedly based on historical personages, are given roles in the entourage of the Cid that they simply did not play in real life. In addition, the poet conflates the two historical exiles of the Cid into one, presumably to balance the exile theme with that concerning the Cid's vengeance against the Infantes of Carrion. He also changes the names of the daughters of the Cid and the details of their marriages. Most striking in an examination of the theme of holy war is the poetic license taken with the historical Cid's ambivalent relationships with the Moors: Rodrigo Diaz de Vivar not only consistently won victories of the battlefield, but successfully played various factions—Christian and Islamic—against one another, and profited handsomely for his efforts in pecuniary gain and personal glory, in addition to the spiritual benefits promised to the champions of the faith.

After the death of the Cid in 1099, his wife Jimena Munoz attempted and failed to maintain autonomy; when she left Valencia, Jimena protected the honor and mythic status of her husband when she took the embalmed body of the Cid with her, saving it from desecration and thus in a sense granting his memory a measure of immortality. Jimena had the body interred at the monastery of San Pedro de Cardena, which was near Burgos, and therefore close to the small village of Vivar, which saw the birth of Rodrigo Diaz a little more than a half century before. Her generous gifts to that monastery combined with the presence of the relics of the great Campeador further enhanced the Cid's reputation after his death; indeed, various legends and cultic rituals developed around the Cid's grave. Valencia fell under the control of Alfonso VI in 1102, but he was unable to hold back the tide of the Moors, who took the city after Alfonso abandoned it after a short sojourn, taking the Christians with him and setting the city to the torch. The fact that the city he had taken so famously and held so steadfastly fell so quickly after his own demise helped to increase the Cid's standing still further.

Heroic Archetypes Transformed by Christian Typology in the *Cantar De Mio Cid*[4]

The Iberian Epic Hero's Journey to the Underworld: El Cid in Exile

Hero myths often contain journeys or quests, and sometimes these travels require the hero to descend into the Underworld, leaving the light, life, and the existence of the ordinary world behind him. Sometimes the hero's descent into the Underworld entails a literal sojourn in the realm of the dead, whereas sometimes the pilgrimage is more metaphorical, involving the hero's exclusion from the comforts, conveniences, and community of home. In most cases, what marks the hero's travels in a shadowy otherworld as different from the workaday experiences of ordinary life and as a significant aspect of that figure's heroic identity is what the hero gains through making that journey: Whether it be secret knowledge, hidden treasure, or magic powers, the hero empowers his people with the gifts he gains through his period in perdition.

The protagonist of the *Poema de Mio Cid* embarks on such a journey into the Purgatory of exile when he is cast out of the domain of King Alfonso at the instigation of his enemies for a crime he did not commit. As a result, the Cid is banished from the court of his king, from his own home, and from all of the lands under the sway of his sovereign; what is more—as we learn from the lips of a nine-year-old girl in laisse 4—all of the subjects of that land have been warned not to aid the Cid in any way whatsoever lest they risk the loss of their property, the sight of their eyes, and even the salvation of their very souls. Although the legal realities of such edicts were in general far less severe than is depicted in this sequence, the poet is emphasizing that the Cid is cut off from the life and community he has known, poetic license that serves to emphasize the theme of the hero's exile as his descent into the Underworld.

The theme of banishment as a form of Purgatory—here not a painful reconstitution of the spirit, but rather a more temporal journey through the nether regions in an attempt to find the way to gain the victories, booty, and power to be received back into the "land of the living" (i.e., the court of the king)—is emphasized by the Cid's vision of his erstwhile home through the veil of tears wetting his cheeks. He witnessed a scene of the desolation of a house bereft of its occupants, much like the body bereft of its soul: *[V]io puertas abiertas e ucos sin canados, alcandaras vazias, sin pielles e sin mantos, e sin falcones e sin adtores mudados*; "He saw doors hanging open and gates unlatched, racks and perches without furs and without mantles, and without falcons and without moulted hawks." All signs of life had gone, and the Cid mourned the memory of the life that had so recently abounded in that now empty shell of a dwelling.

Clearly the vacant home the Cid leaves behind may represent the corpse of the soul sent forth into Purgatory; moreover, the lands into which the Cid enters as he embarks upon his banishment are explicitly described in terms that evoke a medieval and indeed even Biblical understanding of a soul cast out into the wilderness. In laisse 22, to cite the first great example of such imagery in the *Poema de Mio Cid*, the Cid pauses on the evening of the day after a dream vision has encouraged him to take heart; gazing across the range of peaks that mark the frontier between the life he has known within the realm of his king and his new marginal existence beyond that pale, the Cid remarks on the wild and untrammeled wasteland that lies before him: *Passaremos la sierra que fiera es a grand, la tierra del rrey Alfonso esta noch la podemos quitar*, "Tonight we will pass over the untamed and mighty mountain and leave the land of King Alfonso." This phrasing is somewhat conventional and clearly reflects a common medieval literary conception of the wilderness as a terrifying otherworld.

In addition, the supernatural and otherworldly aspects of the hero's journey into exile are marked by the poet by an ominous portent, the appearance of a crow, the black bird that so often acts as a mythic and folkloric harbinger of battle, death, and disaster. In a text that—unlike many other epics—keeps supernatural phenomena to a minimum, it is in general noteworthy that the Cid's term in exile is prefaced by a reference to omens; further, it is of specific interest that the Cid's departure into the Underworld of his banishment is marked by the appearance of a crow, which also represents a recurrent theme and folkloric motif in the text, that of the perception and interpretation of such signs.

Several passages in the *Poema de Mio Cid* make specific reference to supernatural omens, and the historical record suggests the Rodrigo himself was, in fact, an astute observer of such phenomena. The first example of such a portent occurs at the very opening of the poem, in laisse 2, as the Cid departs his hometown on his way into an uncertain future in exile. In this passage the poet weaves together in a veritable handful of lines two related but distinct mentions of the folkloric symbol of the crow with a subtle classical reference. First, as the Cid and his companions depart from Vivar, *ovieron la corneja diestra*, "a crow flew on the right." This event is generally thought to symbolize the successful tenor of the Cid's endeavors throughout the term of his banishment. However, as the travelers enter Burgos they are witnesses to a darker portent when *ovieronla siniestra*, "it flew on the left;" this latter sign portends the dismal reception the exiles may expect within the town, the dwellers within which having been threatened with blinding, dispossession, and excommunication if they should provide succor to the outlaws.

Seeing and immediately comprehending this unfortunate sign, the Cid does not rail against what is to be; indeed, *mecio . . . los ombros e engrameo la tiesta*, "shrugging the shoulders and nodding the head," the Cid encourages a companion with the admonition *[a]lbricia*, "Good news!" Some have suggested that this stoic acceptance of the signs of immutable fate draw upon the tradition of Aeneas, who, in Book V, lines 530–531 of the account of his own wanderings in exile from his homeland, embraced the sign of the flaming arrow of Acetes with equanimity whereas others cringed in fear: *[N]ec maximus omen abnuit*, "nor did great [Aeneas] deny the portent." Further mention of omens appear in laisse 46—in which the Cid encountered *buenas aves*, "birds of good omen," on his journey from Alcocer—and in laisse 125—in which the Cid *[v]iolo en los avueros*, "perceived in the omens," that the marriages between his daughters and the Infantes of Carrion would end badly.

The Iberian Epic Hero Short-Changes the Moneylenders: El Cid as a Trickster Figure

The trickster archetype as commonly understood involves a figure firmly rooted in bestial appetites and scatological functions, a shape-shifter with often insatiable sexual drives that generally lead to comical escapades; clearly the Cid is not a figure we would categorize in this way. But the trickster is more than this: He is cunning, he is inventive, and he does what needs to be done at the cost of polite propriety. The trickster uses these gifts to his own advantage, to be sure, but he also acts to secure gifts for his people necessary for their survival. Some have suggested that in this face of the trickster we may, in fact, discern some attributes of the savior figure. In the episode with the moneylenders described in laisses 6–11, the Cid manifests all of these latter attributes.

As the Cid departed into exile, he realized that he had depleted all of his gold and silver; he would need money, he remarked, to wage *toda mi compana*, "my entire campaign." Enlisting Martin Antolinez to act on his behalf, the Cid conceived of a plan to dupe Rachel and Vidas, two money-lenders of Burgos. Filling two very large, ornately worked, and copiously studded chests with sand, Martin was to approach the moneylenders with the offer to leave the trunks as security on a loan paid immediately in ready cash. Claiming that the treasure within the chests was made up of the profit from the alleged embezzlement for which the Cid was being banished, Martin told the moneylenders that the chests were too burden-some to take on campaign. By extracting a promise in laisse 9 from the moneylenders to reveal this secret neither *a moros* "to Moors," nor *a cristianos*, "to Christians," the Cid's middleman incites the greed of Rachel and Vidas and implicitly convinces them that they may make a tidy profit at little risk. Falling prey to the Cid's ruse, the moneylenders agree to advance a sum of 600 marks against the collateral of the chests, which—as an added precaution—the Cid had them swear not to open or examine for a period of one year upon penalty of losing the interest they would gain on the loan. The Cid's scheme is a perfect scam: The Cid receives an unsecured loan to finance his campaign, his dupes are sworn to silence, and—best of all—if the moneylenders should discover the Cid's duplicity by examining the worthless contents of the chests they have accepted as collateral, they would lose any profit they might stand to gain on the venture.

Moreover, although he repeatedly asserts his reluctance to pursue this course of action in laisses 6 and 7, and however much his very words in those passages make it clear that he does not approve of his own actions in this instance, the Cid clearly sees this ruse as necessary for his own survival and for that of his followers joining him in exile. Indeed, in this instance the Cid is responding to one of his primary responsibilities as a leader; the poet makes reference in several places to the perception that a good lord was understood to be one who enriched his followers in substantive ways. The description of the Cid's sale of Alcocer in laisses 44 and 45 provides a clearly articulated case in point: The language is effusive in laisse 45 concerning *que bien pago*, "how well he paid" his many followers; not a man remained poor among all that assembly, from the most humble infantryman to the noblest knight. Tellingly, the laisse concludes with a shift from the specific description of the division of booty in this case to a general assessment of the fortunes of those who serve a beneficent lord: *[Q]ui a buen senor sirve siempre bive en delicio*, "Those who serve a good lord always live in delight."

In addition to emphasizing how the Cid's ruse in the pawn fraud episode is a necessary response to Rodrigo's duties to his followers, the poet also evokes medieval stereotypes of Jewish moneylenders to mitigate his audience's sympathy for the victims of this ruse, as when he has them articulate their greed in laisse 9, when they say they are entitled *ganar algo*, "to make a little something," in all of their transactions. Further, the subsequent actions of the moneylenders further emphasize the suggestion that they get what they deserve, and that the Cid was clever to promote his own well being through his witty manipulation of their greed. In fact, the Cid's obvious relish in concocting and executing this deception is additional persuasive evidence of his role as a trickster, a figure that asserts itself in traditions across the centuries and continents to revel in just such elaborate displays of crafty guile.

The Iberian Epic Hero's Dream Vision: An Angelic Messenger Heralds the Victories of El Cid

With the exception of a handful of examples of the Cid's historically attested predilection for crediting and interpreting omens, a practice steeped in folklore and legend as well as some trappings of myth, the single great supernatural episode in *Poema de Mio Cid* concerns the Campeador's dream vision, which is related in laisse 19. The dream vision was a popular literary genre throughout the Middle Ages and is well represented in the epics of holy war, appearing as an important plot device in the *Lay of Igor's Campaign* and the *Chanson de Roland*; it is noteworthy that the dream vision of Charlemagne in laisse 185 of the latter text is likewise imparted by the angel Gabriel, who is often the celestial herald in such episodes of medieval mythology. Whereas in each of those two works the portent involved is a harbinger of loss and grief, in the *Poema de Mio Cid* it is a herald of victory and joy, a characteristic that links it with its *ur*-source in medieval literature and mythology: Indeed, although dreams and dream interpretation certainly were fields replete in the Middle Ages—as they can be to this day—with folkloric and legendary elements, rituals, and significance, the Cid's dream primarily draws upon one of the great well-springs of medieval Christian mythology, the dream vision of the emperor Constantine.

After a good meal, the poet tells us, the Cid fell into a deep sleep, wherein the angel Gabriel *a el vino en sueno*, "came to him in a dream;" very much as the heavenly voice advised Constantine that "by this sign ye shall conquer," so Gabriel informed the Cid that the Campeador will be successful in all of his endeavors throughout his career. The angel also comments on the auspiciousness of the present moment for beginning any such endeavor, remarking that no man had ever set forth at such a *buen punto*, "fortuitous point in time"; the trope of the fortunate moment is a commonplace of the *Poema* that is a literary device and speaks eloquently to the Cid's known concern with omens and their augury. It is not without significance then, that, immediately upon waking, the Cid himself makes the sign of the victory promised to his spiritual forbear Constantine: *[L]a cara se sanctigo, sinava la cara*, "[H]e sanctified his face, he made the sign of the cross upon his face." It is also hardly a surprise that, having given thanks to God, the Cid was very well pleased with the vision granted to him.

Fighting the Good Fight? Multivalent Moors in El Cid's Holy War[5]

The 12th-century *Historia Roderici*, or "History of Rodrigo," which details the many victories of El Cid over Moslem forces, does so with none of the strident condemnation of the Moors as the "Demonic Enemy" so prevalent in Spanish sources, and so familiar from the *Chanson de Roland* and the *Lay of Igor*. No aspect of the *Poema* elucidates such unexpected ambiguity concerning the Islamic enemy more clearly than the figure of King Abengalbon of Molina, who serves as the exception that proves the rule, as it were, personifying the Cid's loyal and steadfast friend amongst the Moors.

In the *Poema de Mio Cid*, Abengalbon provides a figure that represents a paragon of virtue—not simply in the context of a stereotypical understanding of Moorish enemies as demonic, as is the case in the *Chanson de Roland*—but in contrast to the craven and cowardly Infantes. These dastardly figures may be of noble blood (in contrast to the Cid, whose parentage is explicitly impugned in laisse 148), but they are of vile character and thus they provide the perfect foil for the "good Moor," who is noble, dependable, and true, and—although a Moor and an infidel—is the model for all that a good knight, vassal, and friend should be. The poet is deliberate in developing the comparison between Abengalbon and the Infantes, a technique that provides the stark contrast through which we may begin to understand the mythic function of the Infantes as "anti-heroes," figures that fail the various tests of manhood that larger-than-life personages such as the Cid pass as a major part of their initiation into manhood and thus achieve their status as warriors and heroes. The episode in laisses 126–128, wherein the Infantes meet and decide to betray Abengalbon, provides the perfect opportunity to sketch the contrast between these mythic figures in broad strokes; it also provides the prologue to the abuse and abandonment of the daughters of the Cid in the Forest of Corpes, the seminal event that eliminates any remaining vestiges of doubt concerning the character of these despicable figures and their paucity of potential for redemption and development.

In laisse 126 the Cid sends his daughters and their husbands to Carrion in the company of Felez Munoz. The Cid commands Munoz to travel via Molina, where he requests that his ally—whom he identifies as *mio amigo el moro Avengalvon*, "my friend the Moor Abengalbon"—should give them the most gracious welcome possible. After a painful parting between the Cid and his daughters, the Infantes and their party went on their way, spending one night on the road before arriving in the domain of Abengalbon, who was delighted to receive them, offering them every possibly courtesy with joy and in good faith. The King of Molina gave the daughters of his ally rich gifts and their husbands fine horses. However, when the Infantes saw *la rriqueza*, "the wealth," of the Moor, between themselves they *consejaron traction*, "plotted treachery," an objective—for this duo, who are as inept as they are cowardly and duplicitous—as unattainable as it is repugnant. This very ludicrous nature of this conspiracy serves to emphasize the immaturity and naïveté of the Infantes, who represented the mirror image of the hero prepared and able to undergo the rites of initiation into manhood. In this passage the Infantes also give voice to their plot to humiliate and abandon their wives in an illogical and ill-advised attempt to avenge themselves on the Cid for their own embarrassment concerning their cowardly response to the lion. However, a bilingual retainer of Abengalbon heard the plot of the Infantes on his lord's life, and thus the scene is set for a confrontation between the good Moorish king and the faithless Christian princes.

Abengalbon confronts the Infantes in laisse 127, and his own words sum up the contrast between these treacherous and cowardly Christian princes—who ill serve the Cid as warriors or as husbands for his daughters—and himself, a steadfast and courageous Moorish ally who always attempts to serve his friend and overlord well. Noting that he has done nothing to earn their enmity, Abengalbon implicitly contrasts his nature as a heroic and noble warrior with that of the craven and duplicitous Infantes when he notes that *[y]o sirviendovos sin art e vos, pora mi, muert consejastes*, "I was of service to you without artifice, and you conspired in plotting my death." Stating that he held his hand back only out of respect for the Cid, the King of Molina makes explicit that he would much rather free the wives of the Infantes from such ill-advised marriages by widowing them and returning them to their father. If he were free to act upon his instincts, Abengalbon concludes the laisse, the Infantes would never return to Carrion.

Having made exactly clear in the previous laisse how he would have avenged himself upon the Infantes for their treachery were it not for his duty to the Cid, to whose daughters they are married, in laisse 128 Abengalbon takes leave of the Infantes with contempt and disdain, underscoring with his words our sense of their base nature, an understanding that has comic roots in the lion episode, which is more fully formed in the plot against the good Moor and that will reach its low point of infamy in the Forest of Corpes. In his dismissal of the Infantes, Abengalbon emphasizes the evil and duplicitous nature of the Cid's sons-in-law: *Aquim parto de vos como de malos e de traidores*, "Here I part from you, who are evil ones and traitors." It is fitting that this assessment closes the episode of contrast between the vile Infantes and the noble Moor.

To be sure, this noble Moor throws the flaws of the Infantes into sharp relief; however, more than that, he also underscores the complexity of the Cid's relationship with Moslems. Not all Christian figures in this poem help to highlight such ambiguities. Indeed, it is notable in this context of a sanctified battle of Christian versus Moslem that the *Poema de Mio Cid* and the *Chanson de Roland* share the characteristic of using archetypal militant ecclesiastical leaders who look with relish upon the opportunity to slaughter unbelievers. Bishop Jeronimo is certainly much akin to Archbishop Turpin in this regard, and both exemplify a common theme of the cleric knight and holy warrior who battle the forces of the infidels, not simply out of need or duty, but with an infectious enthusiasm that serves to emphasize the message that to die in such a battle is to win life everlasting. Indeed, Jeronimo says as much when he notes in laisse 78 that he wants nothing more than to follow the Cid's lead into the fray, and that, should he fall in the heat of such sacred combat, *non le llorassen cristianos*, "Christians need not cry for him." Moreover, the Cid was so pleased with this prelate's attitude that he named *este buen cristiano*, "this good Christian," the Bishop of Valencia, reinstating the bishopric of that city; this investure won the acclaim of *todo cristianismo*, "all Christians everywhere," we are told in laisse 79.

The phraseology concerning "good Christians" is to a certain extent, formulaic. We may well expect accounts of holy war to valorize and sanctify the combat against a satanic enemy, and so this attitude seems, in a figure such as Bishop Jeronimo or Archbishop Turpin, a logical extension of the demonization of the Saracens. Although a relatively straightforward subtext in the *Chanson de Roland*, this stereotype is more evocative in the somewhat more ambiguous context of the *Poema de Mio Cid*. Moreover, considering the similarities between these two figures, it is intriguing to wonder if it is more than a coincidence that Bishop Jeronimo, who is so warlike and so determined to eradicate the Moors by force of arms, is—like his counterpart Archbishop Turpin—in fact French. Some scholars have in fact suggested that French clerics were famous for such martial attitudes.

The Envious Enemy Within: The Insidious Infantes [6]

During the period of his exile, the Cid regularly won great victories and subsequently attempted to reconcile himself with King Alfonso by means of glorifying his name and sending to him shares of the plunder as appropriate tribute from a vassal. The king's displeasure was eventually mitigated through the Campeador's consistent attempts to regain his favor, and the effect of the Cid's successes was no less marked within the royal court, although such effect took different forms: In laisse 99 we are told that those nobles who were inclined to support the Cid were pleased by his successes, whereas others—notably Rodrigo's *enemigo malo*, "bitter enemy," Count Garcia Ordonez—were incensed not just because the Cid was coming back into favor, but more pointedly because his own magnificent glory eclipsed entirely their own steadfast mediocrity. In the count's own words, *[e]n la ondra que el ha nos seremos abiltados*, "by the honor that he gains we will be humiliated."

Others, specifically Diego and Fernando, the Infantes of Carrion, saw in the Cid's re-ascendance into royal good will an opportunity to advance their own positions at court, a plan the two princes discuss amongst themselves in laisse 101 and put to the king in laisse 102. Although King Alfonso himself voices doubt that the Cid will be enamored of this match after his harsh treatment at the royal hands, and although the Cid articulates his own reservations in the same laisse, the Campeador agrees to enter into marriage negotiations, and the lavish wedding ceremonies are themselves described in some detail in laisse 111, which concludes the Second Cantar. The Infantes *[m]ucho eran alegres*, "were very happy," with every aspect of the procccdings, and, when the wedding guests withdrew, Diego and Fernando remained for two years at Valencia with their father-in-law. Much was made of the Infantes within the household of the Cid, a fact that, we are informed, *[a]legre era el Cid e todos sus vassallos*, "delighted the Cid and all of his vassals." Although the passage concludes with a prayer that asks that these unions might be blessed, we are given little indication of how quickly they will in fact erode and how soon the character flaws of the Infantes will be manifested when they are put to the test.

The Cowardly Infantes Flee the Lion

The Third Cantar begins with an episode that brings this honeymoon period to a close. Although up to this point Diego and Fernando seem to have been accepted as full members of the Cid's retinue, through their own cowardice in an escapade with a beast on the loose the Infantes are humiliated, and consequently their resentment toward their father-in-law begins to fester and grow. Laisse 112 concerns the escape of the Cid's pet lion, a wild animal that is injected into the poem at this point as a plot device but that might find some precedent in the menageries sometimes kept by medieval nobles. One afternoon while the Campeador slept, his lion slipped its collar and terrified the Cid's followers. Whereas his retainers wrapped their cloaks about their arms and gathered around their lord to protect him, the Infantes fled in abject terror: Fernando scrambled under the couch, and Diego, sobbing *[n]on vere Carrion*, "I shall not see Carrion again," climbed between the winepress and the wall, staining his clothing. Awaking at the ruckus, El Cid met the lion with a steady gaze and felt no need to display alarm, to protect himself in any way, nor even to touch the beast: Indeed, the lion dropped its eyes and behaved submissively at the moment *quando lo vio*, "when it saw him." The Infantes were at first nowhere to be found, and when they were finally discovered, they were so terrified that they were *sin color*, "without color," so pale with terror that they became the laughingstocks of Valencia. Although the Cid forbade jokes at their expense, the damage was done, and the Infantes felt deeply the shame of their cowardly flight and resented this humiliation.

It is not simply the Cid's personal example that places this episode in proper context; other heroes—Basil Digenis Akritis leaps to mind—successfully defeat wild beasts and also properly protect their wives from peril rather than abuse them. These are the two tests of manhood that the Infantes fail so miserably, a fact that underscores their low character, failed initiation into manhood, and status as anti-heroes of noble birth, all of which provide the counterpart for the Cid's own hero-hood, despite the possibility of his humble origins. It has also been suggested that the Cid's nap helps to contextualize this episode as a rite-of-passage myth, albeit one in which the details are somewhat skewed: The careful reader will remember that Basil Digenis Akritis woke from a nap to protect his lovely bride from a lion, and some have noted that the Irish hero Cuchulainn likewise rose from slumber to prove himself. In this case, this particular hero has long since proven himself, to be sure, but the fact that he arises from sleep in a way evocative of the initiation motif underscores the failure of his sons-in-law to react appropriately in this episode.

The Dastardly Infantes Abuse the Daughters of El Cid

Shortly after the episode with the lion, the Infantes were offered another opportunity to distinguish themselves as men and as warriors when a vast army of Moors under the command of King Bucar besieged the city of Valencia. When, in laisse 114, Diego and Fernando looked out upon the vast sea of Moorish tents surrounding the city, they found this sight *non avien sabor*, "not to their taste." When the brothers discussed together their terror of the impeding battle, they were overheard by Muno Gustioz, who reported the substance of this conversation to the Cid. Confident in his own abilities without such aid as they could offer—and indulgent of the new husbands of his daughters—the Campeador offered to allow Diego and Fernando to remain in Valencia during the battle.

The poet's account of the events immediately after this passage are unclear because of a missing folio that leaves a lacuna of approximately 50 lines in the poem; consequently, laisse 115 begins in mid-sentence, but it seems that Fernando may have made some arrangement with Don Pedro because a reference to doubled repayment is followed immediately with the information that Fernando's bragging was corroborated by Pedro. However, the terror of the Infantes in the face of the Moorish drums soon put the lie to any such boasting, and although the Cid remains vocal in his belief in the character of his sons-in-law throughout this episode, laisse 115 closes with his request to his nephew Pedro Bermudez that he *[c]uriesme a don Diego e curiesme a don Fernando*, "watch over Diego and Fernando." This request and—more explicitly— Pedro Bermudez's curt refusal thereof in the opening lines of the next laisse make abundantly clear the fact that the Infantes, far from being accepted as brave warriors and mature men amongst the retinue of the Cid, are in fact generally considered to be cowardly, immature, and entirely unable to fend for themselves.

After a detailed description of the martial spirit and prowess at arms of Bishop Jeronimo in laisses 116 and 117, we are informed of the utter rout of the Moors at the hands of the Cid's forces, culminating in an account of the Campeador's personal valor in laisse 118, in which he rode down and dispatched King Bucar himself. To be sure, the details of these descriptions enliven the passages, but they also echo loudly in the damning silence surrounding the courageous deeds of the Infantes, which in fact appear to have been nonexistent. Throughout the next few laisses the Cid continues to praise his sons-in-law, and they appear to have taken great pleasure in spending their allotted portion of the plunder. However, rifts in the relationship between Diego and Fernando and their father-in-law became pronounced in laisse 119, in which the Cid attempted to praise them, noting that whatever they had accomplished thus far was merely a precursor of better things to come. The Infantes took offense at this remark; our poet tells us that his sons-in-law—presumably because of their insecurity of their status as warriors and with full knowledge of their own cowardice—heard mockery where their father-in-law meant only praise: *Por bien dixo el Cid, mas ellos lo tovieron a mal*, "Although the Cid spoke in good faith, they took it ill."

In laisse 123 it becomes evident just how little stock the vassals of the Cid put in his sons-in-law: The warriors of the Campeador smiled at the vanity of the Infantes, and when they recalled the heat of the battle and the thrill of the chase, they noted how little they had seen of Fernando and Diego. Such minor jokes became daily mockery until finally the Infantes plotted to teach the Cid and his vassals a lesson. They think that they may dispense with their relationship with the Campeador because of their belief that they have gained such enormous wealth through their association with him that, however long they should live, *despender no lo podremos*, "we would not be able to part with" it all. The Infantes clearly see the daughters of the Cid as well beneath them in the social hierarchy; thus, having gained the material wealth they may have sought, and being mocked in comparison to rather than esteemed through association with their father-in-law, they determine in laisse 124 to abandon their wives to seek better ones. With their new wealth the Infantes believe that *podremos casar con fijas de rreyes o de enperadores*, "we will be able to marry the daughters of kings or emperors." However, their plot is not limited to exchanging low-born for high-born wives: Sick to death of the humiliation born of the escapade with the lion, it is their intention that *escarniremos a las fijas del Campeador*, "we will humiliate the daughters of the Campeador." Having failed in the tests of manhood provided to them, Fernando and Diego think to assuage their wounded pride by substituting the daughters of the Cid for the lion and the Moors and to transfer their own humiliation for their inadequacies onto the Cid by the ill treatment and abandonment of their wives.

Another aspect of this conspiracy that illuminates the fact that the Infantes have not developed fully nor appropriately as heroic figures, warriors, or indeed even as men is the duplicity of their interactions with the Cid, which foreshadow their abusive treatment of their wives, which—as the *Poema* makes clear in numerous instances, not least those detailing the chivalric behavior of the Moorish Abengalbon and the celibate Bishop Jeronimo—is exactly the opposite of the expected role of the male warrior and husband in a heroic context. To enact their feeble and wrong-headed "vengeance," the Infantes realize that they must deceive the Cid, whom they could never hope to defeat in combat, and to strip, beat, and humiliate the Campeador's daughters in his stead. The poet therefore makes it clear that the Cid consistently was straightforward and un-ironic in his speech with the Infantes, and that the Campeador—who does not dissemble to Diego and Fernando—absolutely does not suspect such a conspiracy. Although the Cid certainly felt unease at certain omens before the marriage, in laisse 124 it is explicitly stated that he had no inkling of the treachery to come.

When the Infantes approached him in the same laisse for permission to depart to their homes in Carrion with their wives, the Cid not only granted them leave but settled upon them a substantial dowry of 3,000 marks and several gifts. The most notable of these gifts were the Cid's own swords, Tizon and Colada. The Campeador commended his daughters into the hands of their husbands, assuring the Infantes that, if they cared well for their wives, *yo vos rrendre buen galardon*, "I will grant you both great rewards." Although the Infantes and their wives traveled in the company of numerous retainers, notably Felez Munoz, and although they sojourned with the Cid's Moorish ally Abengalbon, in laisse 128 the Infantes created an opportunity to execute their plot in the Forest of Corpes.

Having spent the night by a spring in a grassy clearing showing their wives loving affection, Fernando and Diego sent all of the rest of the party ahead. Completely alone at last with Dona Elvira and Dona Sol, the Infantes were free to humiliate their ladies in this desolate wilderness. They stripped their brides of their rich garments and then—despite the protests of Dona Sol, who begged that *cortandos las cabecas, martires seremos nos*, "cut off our heads, so that we might be martyrs" with Tizon and Colada—they whipped the defenseless women with their spur straps until their wives' flesh was rent and their shifts soaked with blood. More than simply administering a physical beating, the Infantes were successful in their goal of humiliating the daughters of the Cid: *Ya lo sienten ellas en los sos coracones*, "The women were shamed in the depths of their hearts." The two Infantes continued to rain blows upon their wives until the men were too weary to continue, each challenging the other to hit harder, until, finally, the daughters of the Cid *por muertas las dexaron en el rrobredo de Corpes*, "were left for dead in the Forest of Corpes."

Dona Sol's admonition that this shameful act will earn the Infantes the condemnation of *moros e cristianos*, "Moors and Christians," alike proves prophetic of course, but moreover, it draws upon the context of the trope of holy war itself to underscore just how horrific such an act of cowardice would appear, even in the eyes of the enemy infidels. The pathetic undercurrent of this episode is emphasized by the fact that the two Infantes completely exhausted themselves in their cruel endeavor, literally competing with one another to see who might deal the most violent blows; thus, instead of expending their energies and competitive spirits in truly heroic efforts, we are given to understand, Fernando and Diego commit themselves to a twisted and even macabre perversion of a traditional understanding of heroic violence.

Felez Munoz was uncomfortable leaving the ladies behind, and so he disobeyed the order of the Infantes and returned into the heart of the forest, secreting himself from Fernando and Diego as they passed, and thus overhearing their boasting concerning their grievous crime. While Felez Munoz led the battered women to the safety of the domain of a vassal of Alvar Fanez, the Infantes, as they continued to their home, *[a]labandos seian*, "were bragging" of their terrible crimes. Word of these misdeeds reached the ears of King Alfonso himself, who was sorely saddened. Discovered by their cousin in laisse 131, Dona Sol and Dona Elvira were reunited with their father the Cid in the next laisse, which concludes with the Campeador's private decision to submit the matter to the king.

Object Myths in the *Cantar De Mio Cid:* The Symbolic Roles of Tizon and Colada

As does the *Chanson de Roland*, the *Cantar de Mio Cid* provides some clear examples of mythic objects, notably the two great swords of the Cid, Tizon and Colada. *Tizon*, generally rendered something like "firebrand" or "flaming torch," is a name that evokes common names and metaphors for blades in several traditions; *brand* or *brandr* are terms denoting torches in Old English and Old Norse that are also used to describe swords and that are cognate with the French *brant*. On the other hand, *Colada* denotes something along the lines of "purely forged," which might put one in mind of one of the alternative etymologies for Excaliber, which suggests descent from a term for "steel." Tizon and Colada have survived to the present day in the Spanish mythic imagination because both swords are believed by some to have survived into modern times; indeed, there are those who think them to be two well-known objects of veneration preserved in museums in Burgos and Madrid, respectively.

In the context of the *Cantar de Mio Cid*, Tizon and Colada play a special function relative to the mythic coming-of-age rituals concerned with the Infantes. In laisse 124, after Fernando and Diego have asked the Cid leave to return to their homes in Carrion with their wives, the Campeador bestows his favor upon his sons-in-law in several significant ways, perhaps most notably by bestowing upon them his prize possessions, the two swords which represent his martial prowess, his status as a hero, and his maturity as a man—the three rites of passage that the Infantes have most notably failed to navigate. In fact, it is this gift that most persuasively argues that the Cid is utterly un-ironic in his assessment of the qualities of his sons-in-law. Further, it is notable that the Cid demands the return of these gifts after the abuse and abandonment of his daughters by their husbands and that each blade plays a crucial role in the ritual duels that follow. Finally, the phallic symbolism associated with a psychoanalytical understanding of these swords—which represent the mature virility of the Cid and play key roles in the public manifestation of the unmanning of the Infantes—should be mentioned in passing, if not dwelt upon.

Trial by Combat: El Cid is Vindicated Once More

Just as El Cid was vindicated time and again through the force of his arms on campaign, so is his family's honor restored and rightful place reasserted through a trail-by-combat sequence that makes manifest the justice of Divine Judgment. The poem closes with the assurance that the daughters of El Cid became queens of Navarre and Aragon, and that the Kings of Spain ever after have been related to El Cid and have gained honor through his memory. The poet completes his tale of El Cid Campeador by noting that Rodrigo departed this life upon the day of Pentecost, when the Holy Spirit ascended into Heaven, a detail that serves to suggest a spiritual apotheosis of the hero to match the political ascendancy of his lineage.

El Cid writes to King Alfonso in Castile asking for redress in laisse 133, pointing out that it was not in fact the Cid, but rather the king himself, who gave Dona Sol and Dona Elvira in marriage to the Infantes of Carrion; thus, as the Campeador cleverly points out to his sovereign, the *grant desonor*, "great insult," is not just a blot upon the honor of the father of the brides but upon that of the king himself. The Cid therefore asks of his lord a court or judicial assembly that will give him *derecho* from the Infantes (i.e., will grant the plaintiff the "satisfaction" of avenging wounded honor in a heroic context). The king in justice has little choice but to affirm the right of the Cid to pursue this course of action, to acknowledge his own role in the marriage that has been impugned, and to call such a court of justice.

Therefore, King Alfonso responded to the Cid's request in laisse 134 by summoning the concerned parties to Toledo within seven weeks; anyone who refused to attend the court there would cease to be Alfonso's vassal. Fearing to face the wrath of the Cid in person, the Infantes begged leave of their king to forgo the assembly, to which the king's answer was curt and unequivocal: *No lo fere*, "absolutely not," the king proclaimed, for he knew of the complaint that the Cid had concerning the brothers and he made it clear that he intended to provide the Campeador with the opportunity for *derecho*, "honorable justice." Fernando and Diego therefore came to wait upon King Alfonso's pleaser, although they did so in the company of a grand bando, "large retinue," of the Cid's enemies in the hopes of attacking their erstwhile father-in-law before the court had the opportunity to hear the case against them. Toward the end of the allotted period the Campeador arrived, and he and the king exchanged affectionate greetings outside of the town. However, when the king returned into Toledo in laisse 136, the Cid begged leave to stay the night in a holy place and stand vigil, promising his lord that he would join him the next day in the company of his own vassals.

The Cid prayed that night in the shrine at San Servando; laisse 137 informs us that after mass in the morning he gathered together his men and instructed them to prepare for their entrance to the royal court. Designating 100 followers to accompany him to the court, he commands these warriors to wear their armor and to carry their swords beneath their garments in case of treachery on the part of the Infantes. During the proceedings proper, the Cid cleverly ups the ante several times, first reclaiming his swords; then demanding the dowry money; and finally, in laisse 138, issuing a challenge to combat. The Infantes are lulled into a false sense of security by a legal precedent that suggests that the Cid's first claim will be his final appeal to the court, but they soon find themselves giving up more and more to judges who clearly have sympathy with the Cid's position. Reaching the climax of his appeal, the Campeador concludes that the Infantes have *desondraron*, "dishonored," him so terribly that it would not be proper to allow them to escape without *rriebtos*, appropriate "challenges" to judicial combat through which the Judgment of God may be manifested for the court and all the world to see.

The Cid then delivers in laisse 139 an impassioned speech directly to the Infantes rather than to the court. Many find this passage, which concludes with the harsh assessment that—through these infamous actions—*menos valedes vos*, "you have rendered yourselves worthless," amongst the most moving in the entire poem. It incites intemperate, unapologetic, and ill-advised responses in laisses 140 and 141 from Garcia Ordonez and Fernando Gonzalez, respectively, which further alienate the Infantes from the court. Moreover, Fernando's closing comment that in this course of action the Infantes were *derecho*, "right," or in this context "honorable," sets up the scene for a challenge proper in laisse 143, allowing Pedro Bermudez to contradict his opponent directly: *Mientes, Ferrando, de quanto dicho has*; "You lie, Fernando, in everything you have said!" Pedro then offers a rebuttal of Fernando on his primary point of the value of the match between the Infantes and the daughters of the Cid, listing the many examples of Fernando's cowardice and concluding laisse 144 with the prediction that God will, through combat, make known that Fernando is a *malo* and a *traidor*, an "evil-doer" and a "traitor"; further, Pedro vows that, through force of arms, *de quanto he dicho verdadero sere yo*, "I shall prove the truth of all I have said."

This sequence of events and formulaic issuing of challenges is replicated in laisses 145 and 146, in the first of which Diego Gonzalez asserts that the superiority of his family over that of the Cid was ample justification for the actions of the Infantes, a claim he offers to defend against *el mas ardido*, "the greatest champion." Martin Antolinez leaps to his feet to accept this challenge, taking the opportunity to recount Diego's past cowardice and concluding with the vow that *[a]l partir de la lid, po rtu boca diras que eres traidor e mintist de quanto dicho has*, "at the end of the battle you will confess with your own mouth that you are a traitor and that you have lied in all that you have said." Again, as in the *Chanson de Roland*, the judicial duel is depicted as a way in which evidence of God's Will may be entered into court proceedings through victory or defeat in sanctified combat.

In laisses 147 and 148, and in the very opening of laisse 149, a third duel is arranged that speaks to the central issue—from the perspective of the Infantes—of the Cid's base origins. Ansur Gonzalez disrupts the proceedings to question the very premise of the Cid's right to conduct himself as a nobleman of any rank by telling the Campeador to be off to mind his millstones and to collect his fees for milling—what could seem on the surface to be a tangential and rather off-hand slur in fact speaks to the Cid's legal right to evoke the tradition of the judicial duel in the first place. However, Ansur goes too far when he concludes with the question of *[q]uil darie*, "who gave the right," for the Cid to pretend to a union with the House of Carrion; the answer, of course, is King Alfonso himself, who did so reluctantly and only at the request of the Infantes themselves. Muno Gustioz takes the opportunity to challenge Ansur, calling him a liar *a todos e mas al Criador*, "to everyone, and more so to the Creator," and he promises, through strength of arm and keenness of blade, *[f]azer te lo dezir*, "to force you to confess," to the truth of these charges.

At this point early in a very long laisse 149, King Alfonso calls a halt to the challenge portion of the proceedings, commanding that those who have committed themselves to combat to ready themselves to prove or disprove the charges in each case. However, as he finished speaking, two messengers, the representatives of the Princes of Navarre and Aragon, came forward to ask for the hands of the daughters of the Cid for their lords, who wished to make Dona Sol and Dona Elvira the queens of those realms. After this arrangement had been compacted through the agency of

King Alfonso, Minaya Alvar Fanez rose to challenge the Infantes, adding to his litany of their misdeeds his pleasure at the fact that the wives Diego and Fernando had abandoned because of low birth had now risen through their new unions to heights above the Infantes of Carrion.

The king now cut off such challenges for the second time, ordering the combatants to join battle the next day at sunrise. At this the Infantes protested, claiming that they had given over all of their arms and armor to the Cid in repayment of the dowry they owed him. The king therefore allowed the parties the space of three weeks during which to prepare themselves, admonishing all present that he who failed to appear at the appointed time at the designated field in Carrion would be considered *vencido*, "defeated," and thus according to the legal procedures of the judicial duel his case would be declared lost. Furthermore, any party who lost his case in this way would suffer the additional penalty of being formally declared a *traidor*, a "traitor," and as such would lose the legal protections of his status, which generally would mean he would forfeit his property and his right to remain within the domain of King Alfonso. Thus the penalty for cowardice in the face of this ritual combat would be to suffer an exile analogous to that the Cid himself underwent at the opening of the poem.

Although the Infantes delayed as long as they might, the parties were finally assembled for the combat. We learn in laisse 150 that the allies of Carrion conspired to murder the champions of the Cid for the *desondra*, "dishonor," of the Campeador, but their fear of the king was such that they failed to carry out their plot. Before battle was joined, the Infantes begged Alfonso to disallow the use of Colada and Tizon against them, for they greatly regretted having given up those swords. However, the king denied this request, and soon the duels began. Pedro Bermudez and Fernando Gonzalez were the first to clash: The Cid's champion succeeded in unhorsing the Infante, who blanched at the very sight of Tizon; indeed, as Pedro cast aside his spear and drew his sword, Fernando quailed and shouted *[v]encudo so*, "I am vanquished."

In laisse 151, the second pair of duelists, Martin Antolinez and Diego Gonzalez, charged each other with such force that each shivered his lance upon the other's shield. However, when Martin drew Colada, the blade was so *linpia e clara*, "brilliant and clear," that it illuminated *tod' el campo*, "the entire field." Like his brother, Diego was unable to stand firm in the face of the Cid's sword, and after receiving a glancing blow that sheared mail and hair alike from the skin of his skull, he fled the field of battle like the coward he was, crying out to God himself to protect him *d'este espada*, "from this sword." Left without an opponent on the field of battle, Martin was declared the victor. Meanwhile, the third duel was decided when Muno Gustioz threw Ansur Gonzalez from his horse with a mighty thrust of his lance; when Ansur's family requested quarter, the ritual battle was completed, and the champions of the Cid had proven the case against the Infantes through force of arms: *[V]encieron esta lid, grado al Criador,* "they won the battle, through the Grace of the Creator." In other words, the victories of Pedro, Martin, and Muno were earthly evidence of God's Divine Justice.

Very much like the *Chanson de Roland,* the *Cantar de Mio Cid* concludes with a trial-by-combat sequence that touches upon the honor of the wronged protagonist of the epic in question and does so in a way that explicitly evokes the Judgment of God. It is noteworthy that in both texts the trope of holy war against an external, diabolical enemy—although certainly thematically related to the concept of Divine Justice, especially as that justice might be writ large upon the bodies of the participants in a judicial duel—is ultimately subordinated to an internal struggle for justice in the face of co-religionist enemies who hate the protagonist because of personal pride and cowardice.

In other words, although both of these texts are at least ostensibly concerned with the exploits of a great Christian champion who carried the holy banner of God into battle against the enemies of the True Faith, in the end each text is concerned with enacting justice upon those Christians who have wronged that great champion. Although the themes of holy war and trial by combat are undeniably similar, the fact that the *Chanson de Roland* and the *Cantar de Mio Cid* both end with such sequences in which God's justice must be wrought upon the bodies of internal Christian adversaries might well be read as an injunction for unity amongst those forces that rightfully should be unified in the struggle of holy war.

Notes

1. For critical commentary on and analysis of elements of the historical *Reconquista* and in particular its implications upon a study of the mythological theme of holy war as it is manifested in the *Cantar del Mio Cid,* see especially O'Callaghan 1–3, 7–14, 188–189, 193, 201–202, 207, 209–210; and Reilly 51–89, 90–128.

2. For critical commentary on and analysis of the sources, manuscript, and structure of the *Cantar del Mio Cid,* see especially Deyermond *Epic Poetry* 1, 7, 162–163, 199, 202; Hamilton and Perry 13–16; Lindahl 57–58; and Smith 49–72.

3. For critical commentary on and analysis of elements of the historical Rodrigo Diaz de Vivar and in particular its implications upon a study of the

mythological theme of holy war as it is manifested in the *Cantar del Mio Cid*, see especially O'Callaghan 17, 23, 30–31, 133, 140–141, 168; Hamilton and Perry 1–4, 219; Lindahl 57–58; and Reilly 98, 105–107, 126.

4. For critical commentary on and analysis of the mythic content of the *Cantar del Mio Cid*, see especially O'Callaghan 190; Hamilton and Perry 4–5; Lindahl 57–58; and Montgomery vii–viii, 3–11, 41–55.

5. For critical commentary on and analysis of the multivalent approach of the treatment of the Moors in the *Cantar del Mio Cid* and in particular the implications of such ambiguity upon a study of the mythological theme of holy war, see especially O'Callaghan 17.

6. For critical commentary on and analysis of the mythic function of the *Infantes* in the *Cantar del Mio Cid*, see especially Lindahl 57–58; and Montgomery vii–viii, 3–11, 41–55.

Sources and Further Reading

Burke, James F. *Desire against the Law: The Juxtaposition of Contraries in Early Medieval Spanish Literature.* Stanford, CA: Stanford University Press, 1998.

Constable, Olivia Remie. *Medieval Iberia: Readings from Christian, Muslim, and Jewish Sources.* The Middle Ages series. Philadelphia: University of Pennsylvania Press, 1997.

Constable, Olivia Remie. *Trade and Traders in Muslim Spain: The Commercial Realignment of the Iberian Peninsula, 900–1500.* Cambridge studies in medieval life and thought, 4th series, Vol. 24. Cambridge, United Kingdom: Cambridge University Press, 1994.

Deyermond, A. D. *Epic Poetry and the Clergy: Studies on the Mocedades De Rodrigo.* London: Támesis, distributed by Grant & Cutler, 1968.

Deyermond, A. D. *A Literary History of Spain: the Middle Ages*, Vol.1. London: Ernest Benn, 1971.

Hamilton, Rita, Janet H. Perry, and Ian Michael. *The Poem of the Cid.* Harmondsworth, United Kingdom: Penguin, 1984.

Lindahl, Carl, John McNamara, and John Lindow. *Medieval Folklore: A Guide to Myths, Legends, Tales, Beliefs, and Customs.* Oxford, United Kingdom: Oxford University Press, 2002.

Montgomery, Thomas. *Medieval Spanish Epic: Mythic Roots and Ritual Language.* Penn State studies in Romance literatures. University Park: Pennsylvania State University Press, 1998.

O'Callaghan, Joseph F. *Reconquest and Crusade in Medieval Spain.* The Middle Ages series. Philadelphia: University of Pennsylvania Press, 2003.

Reilly, Bernard F. *The Medieval Spains.* Cambridge medieval textbooks. Cambridge, United Kingdom: Cambridge University Press, 1993.

Smith, Colin. *The Making of the Poema De Mio Cid.* Cambridge, United Kingdom: Cambridge University Press, 1983.

PART III

HEROES OF THE ISLAMIC WORLD

The Persian Elephant-Bodied Hero

The Historical Context of Medieval Persia[1]

Who Were the Persians?

What we identify as present day Iran was known to classical commentators as the central region of Persia, a reality that is complicated by the fact that the Persian Empire waxed and waned to various sizes encompassing numerous regions ruled by several successive dynasties. Modern readers perhaps best remember the Persian Empire as the oppressive enemy of the ancient Greeks. What we today refer to as "Iran" is at the very heart of this empire of old, and the culture of Iran today draws upon a deep well-spring of Persian art, literature, history, mythology, legend, and folklore. To be sure, the course of this cultural flow was modified greatly by the conquest of Persia by Moslem Arabs nearly 1400 years ago, but in the depths of the channels the currents of old still flow. Although properly known as Iran in modern times—and indeed, regularly called such in most translations of the *Shahname*, the great Persian epic—the traditional Western name for this country, "Persia," stems from *Persis*, an ancient Greek version of the name of a single province of the vast Persian Empire properly known as *Parsa*. Persia and Iran may be used, but the latter is to be preferred.

What Is Zoroastrianism?

Before the Arab conquest, the predominant religion of Iran was Zoroastrianism, founded by the prophet Zoroaster approximately one thousand years before the birth of Christ. For nearly a millennium before the advent of Islam, Zoroastrianism was in fact the dominant religion throughout much of Western Asia. *Zoroaster* is a hellenization of the Persian *Zarathustra*. Briefly put, Zoroastrianism posited a dualist view of the universe, in which the forces of good, embodied by Ahura Mazda, are constantly in conflict and more or less evenly matched with those of evil, incarnated by Ahriman. Flame was seen as the ultimate vehicle of purification, and thus fire plays a crucial role in Zoroastrian ritual, although it is incorrect to view these ceremonies as inherently fire-worshipping. Zoroastrianism—unlike polytheistic pagan religions, which were eradicated by the sword—was treated as a religion "of the book" by the conquering Moslems and was thus tolerated rather like Christianity and Judaism. However, although Zoroastrianism is still practiced in Iran today, as well as in the Parsee community of India, and although there are pockets of believers throughout the world, most Iranians converted to Islam within the first few centuries under Moslem rule.

How Did Islam Transform Persian Language and Mythology?

Ancient Persian, Sassanian or Middle Persian (also called Pahlavi—the New Persian of the Middle Ages) and the descendant tongue modern Farsi are all clearly Indo-European languages and are therefore more closely related to Greek or to English than they are to Arabic. However, this fact is somewhat obscured because after the conquest of Persia by the Moslem Caliphate in the seventh century, Persian language texts began to be written in an Arabic script, albeit with several extra characters to represent Persian sounds not found in Arabic. Therefore, although through Western eyes—modern or medieval—Persia seems deep in the core of the Islamic world, such an assumption is a bit misleading. Although Iran is—and has long been—staunchly Islamic, its ancient roots are in fact Indo-European; ergo, the mythology of the Persia of antiquity had much in common with that of, for example, ancient Greece or India.

The Indo-European mythology thus transformed through an Arabic and Islamic lens therefore provides a particularly compelling counterpoint to similar mythic themes in—to cite two great examples—Germanic and Celtic analogues. Indeed, the episode of Rostam and Sohrab, a story of a superhuman warrior's slaying of his own heroic son, which is drawn from the great medieval Persian epic, has some clear resonance with parallel stories throughout medieval European literature. This storyline as it is developed in the *Shahname* echoes a recurring Indo-European theme most commonly associated with the Old High German episode concerning Hildebrand and Hadubrand. Another notable example survives in the Russian byliny tradition. However, of the other texts using similar motifs, one of the best known and most fully developed is the Old Irish tale of Cuchulainn and Connla.

The Literary Context of Medieval Persia: The Iranian Homer, Abol-Qasem Ferdowsi, Compiler of the *Shahname*[2]

The cultural importance of an epic concerned with the history, majesty, and kings of the Persians necessarily diminished after the subjugation of that nation to an alien people speaking a different language and following an entirely new religion. Indeed, an often-quoted passage from the end of the *Shahname*—issuing from the mouth of the commander of the defeated Iranian army—alludes directly to the necessity of such a phenomenon. However, some two centuries after the conquest of the Persian Empire, the rise of the Samanid dynasty to power caused a shift of focus that resulted in the resurgence of the importance of the *Shahname*: Although Islamic and heavily influenced by Arabic customs and language, the Samanids were in fact ethnically Iranian, and they identified with this culture and fostered this identification through patronage, most notably in the commission of a verse rendering of the *Book of Kings* by the poet Daqiqi, who died around 980, and who never completed the monumental task. The mantle of enshrining the cultural legacy of the *Shahname* thus fell to Abol-Qasem Ferdowsi, who has been revered ever since for his stunning success in this endeavor.

At points in the *Shahname*, Ferdowsi quite self-consciously alludes to his role as a poet breathing new life into the shell of an Iranian epic shunted to one side for centuries. Moreover, the bitter conclusion of the *Shahname* reflects not only the distant subjugation of the ancient Iranian monarchy; indeed, in the battle between the Iranians and the Turanians of the poem one might also capture glimpses of the struggle between the pro-Iranian Samanids and the Turkic Ghaznavids who displaced them in 999. This slave army based in Ghazna in Afghanistan replaced existing aristocratic structures with administrators drawn from its own ranks, and although they continued to support artistic efforts however grudgingly, they must have seemed proper Philistines to a cultured minor aristocrat such as Ferdowsi. Moreover, this perception might well have been emphasized in the mind of the poet, given the ongoing theme of the border wars between the Iranians and the Turanians throughout the *Shahname*. Indeed, the irony that—in the end—he was compelled to dedicate his masterwork of Iranian culture to what he might well have viewed as usurping descendants of the Turanians he vilified seems unlikely to have been lost upon a poet of Ferdowsi's stature and sensitivity.

A scion of the *dihqan* class (i.e., a member of the minor landed nobility), Ferdowsi embodied in his work the noble impulses and the growing resentment of that stratum of society, which had for some time been gradually losing its real power and wealth while retaining its traditional pride and sense of entitlement. Indeed, the eventual decline of this class was so complete that the term *dihqan* in modern Farsi denotes a "peasant." The dihqan class traditionally performed the crucial administrative task of tax collection, and in this role they continued to be useful to subsequent dynasties long after the advent of Islamic rule. Still, this layer of what we might term the Persian country gentry may have found increasing reason for discontent, a possibility that some scholars have construed as a basis for a certain cynicism on the part of Ferdowsi.

The compilation of his life's work took some 35 years, a fact that is emphasized by the poet's mention upon occasion of his age as he completed a particular section. Moreover, because we know that Ferdowsi died around 1025, we can date the period in which he completed his version of the *Shahname* fairly precisely within the last quarter of the 10th century and the first quarter of the 11th century. Ferdowsi approached his task with the skills of an accomplished scholar and a disciplined editor as well as those of an inspired poet, and the choices he made to include or exclude various episodes or particular versions thereof—although not universally popular in every case—established the canon from which subsequent editors of the vast compendium of Iranian heritage would choose. Ferdowsi seems to have tackled his project in an episodic and nonlinear fashion, selecting and completing a particular section as it appealed to him. Sometime after Ferdowsi's attempt was completed it was organized into chronological order, either by the hand of the author himself or by that of a later editor.

The Medieval Persian *Book of Kings:* Sources, Manuscripts, And Structure of the *Shahname* [3]

The sources of the *Shahname*, the Iranian "*Book of Kings*," stretch back into extreme antiquity; indeed, classical Greek historians record the existence of compilations of the history of the Persian kings at least as far back as Darius. Such texts, which were often panegyric, were distributed far and wide in several tongues and traditions; in addition, several Persian kings are known to have sponsored revisions. The ancient sources for the extant text of the *Shahname* that we may identify with any certainty include myths antedating the prophet Zoroaster and yet preserved within the *Avesta*, the sacred text of the pre-Islamic Persian religion that bears that figure's name. Although in its roots it dates back some 2,500 years, the *Avesta* reached its final form only in the Sassanid period in the three or four centuries just previous to the Islamic conquest of Persia in the mid-seventh century; still, exactitude is crucial to Zoroastrian priests, and thus the text has suffered little change in the meantime. However, only one quarter or so of the holy book of that faith remains, and this is the portion most concerned with religious ritual.

Several sections of the *Avesta* contain much incidental mythic material; for example, the twenty-four *Yashts* are sacred hymns that evoke various gods, including Mithras, whereas the seventeen *Gathas*, or hymns of Zoroaster, make up part of the *Yasna*, a ritual that includes a range of chants and prayers, some of which seem undoubtedly to predate the Zoroastrian faith. A clear example would be an invocation to *Haoma*, a vegetative-deity known in Indian texts as *Soma*. This figure is at once a warrior against evil, a celestial priest who sacrifices himself for the faithful, and a sacred plant that manifests the Divine presence in the mortal sphere. The parallels between the Avestan and Vedic figures make it clear that this god is a very ancient one that has been preserved in the sacred texts of India and Iran.

As primary sources, Ferdowsi is thought to have drawn upon now lost prose histories of the Persian kings that stretched from the beginning of time to the Islamic conquest; these texts place historical figures such as Darius III and his nemesis Alexander the Great—known in the *Shahname* as Dara and Iskandar, respectively—with mythic and folkloric heroes and fantastic monsters such as the White Div, a mighty demon, and the Simorgh, a giant, magical bird. Indeed, Ferdowsi's sources seem to have treated mythic and legendary material as historical, and—although excluding or reworking that material most likely to offend Islamic sensibilities—Ferdowsi extended the euhemerization of ancient gods and heroic demi-gods. Although he is thought likely to have drawn primarily upon an Arabic translation or translations of a Sassanian prose redaction of the ancient tale of the Persian sovereigns, it is quite probable that he would have been familiar with alternate versions in oral and literate forms; he would almost undoubtedly have had access to contemporary Persian-language sources and might well have also consulted earlier Middle Persian texts.

In any case, the poet seems to have taken care to retain some of the ancient themes and flavor of his sources, and the resulting text clearly may be read in terms of the universal conflict between good and evil, an approach that resonates closely with the primary tenets of Zoroastrianism. This tension is manifested in the *Shahname* largely as such a struggle may be understood in the terms of kingship and in the qualities that distinguish a divinely anointed just ruler from an infernal tyrant. It traditionally was argued that the Iranian monarchial view of rightful succession and anointed leadership preserved in Ferdowsi's version of the *Shahname* can be linked to the Iranian adoption of Shi'ism, a minority position in an almost overwhelmingly Sunni Islamic world: One of the fundamental divisions between these sects concerns the proper line of succession following the Prophet Mohammed, with the Shiites favoring direct lineal descendants whenever possible. This view is difficult to substantiate with hard evidence, but it certainly is true that a fundamental lesson of the *Shahname* seems to be that the right to rule passes to legitimate descendants of an anointed sovereign, and that it is a sin of monumental proportions to attempt to disrupt such succession, however good the reasons. Such divine anointment in general is regularly referred to as *farr*.

An Ancient Iranian God in the Guise of a Medieval Persian Dragon-Slayer Hero: Faridun of the Shahname⁴

Almost the first thing we learn about Faridun is that he radiated *farr*—a term that comes from the Old Persian *farnah*, which in turn appears to derive from *xvar*, the Avestan word for "sun," which would be cognate with its Latin cousin *sol*—a sort of effulgent sign of royal blood that also seems to have comprised marvelous powers. *Farr* is generally translated as "halo" or "nimbus" and is a clear sign of the favor of the gods manifested by the rightful ruler of Iran. In an earlier section of the *Shahname* concerning the reign of Jamshid, it is related that farr may be lost through hubris, and when those who had suffered under the tyranny of the dragon-king Zohak sought refuge with Faridun, they spoke of seeking protection under his farr. It seems clear that this radiant, protective power, which signifies the right to rule, is derived ultimately from vestiges of the mythic godhead that still adheres in general to the early shahs in the Shahname and specifically to the figure of Faridun.

Faridun was destined to do battle with Zohak, a man transformed into a monster by the treachery and cunning of the devil Eblis. In the guise of a cook, Eblis gained the confidence of Zohak and so arranged it that black serpents sprouted from the shoulders of his unsuspecting victim. Although Zohak tried everything to remove these heads, nothing worked, and if they were cut off they would regrow. The only way that Zohak could control his misery was to feed human brains to the snakes each night. This horrible monster ruled the land of the Arabs for some time and eventually supplanted Jamshid upon the Iranian throne, where for one thousand years he continued the grisly ritual of a nightly dish of brains.

Zohak had a dream that foretold that his reign would be cut short by a hero named Faridun who would slay him and take his throne; the dragon-king accordingly hunted high and low for this usurper. Although Faridun's father, Abtin, perished at the hands of Zohak, Faranak, the hero's mother, was able to avoid the wiles of the dragon and sought refuge in the Alborz Mountains. Of course the flight of the infant Faridun and his mother bears some resemblance to the Holy Family's flight into Egypt, especially when one considers the nightly slaughter of the innocent boys to sate the appetite of the dragon-king Zohak.

Terrified by the prospect of being supplanted by Feridun, Zohak called together a council at which he announced his intention to raise an army of demons, peris, and men; in addition, Zohak called upon the conclave before him to ratify a proclamation testifying to the righteousness of his rule. Amongst the notable figures gathered around the Court of Zohak that day was a humble supplicant named Kava. The sorrow of Kava the blacksmith was due in large measure to the monstrous nature of the king himself, because each of the tradesman's 18 sons had been chosen in turn to satisfy the dragon's appetite for human brains. Calling upon his sovereign for justice, Kava pleaded that his last son, condemned to be sacrificed that very night, be released from this horrible fate. The blacksmith's petition was swiftly granted, and the king went so far as to deign to offer this humble subject the opportunity to sign the proclamation of the royal beneficence. Kava indeed did read the document; however, when he had finished he was so enraged that the wisest and most powerful men of the realm would countenance such an atrocious falsehood in the face of the excesses of their monstrous tyrant that he cursed them all, ripping the proclamation and treading it underfoot as he fled the great hall of the king. Kava then proceeded through the marketplace, waving his leathern blacksmith's apron at the end of a spear and rallying the people to desert the dragon-king Zohak and seek protection under the beneficent *farr* of Feridun. Kava then led a mighty throng determined to do just that; as they approached, Feridun could see from a distance the humble banner of the blacksmith's apron, which he and his descendants ever after carried before them, embroidered and emblazoned with generations of finery. This pennant came to be known as the Kaviani banner.

It is indicative of his own demonic nature that Zohak specifically mentions his intent to use supernatural creatures and humans in his army. *Peris* are the epic and folkloric descendants of the *pairaka* of Avestan literature, which were clearly evil creatures of ill intent. Witchy female entities whose power and activity seems to have waxed in the dark of night, these creatures—although they might take on semblances of great beauty and allure to seduce the unwary—might also appear as rats or other nocturnal creatures or phenomena, such as shooting stars. The most powerful of the demonic female spirits of malice was Nausch, who took the form of a fly and was said to hail from the North, the home of evil in the Persian tradition. Nausch is generally classified as one of the *drug*, the "deceivers," a category of devil-like creatures whose name is reflected in the modern Farsi *durugh*, which means "lie." The peris developed in later Persian literature into creatures of great beauty and often unspecified supernatural powers; indeed, in this combination of attributes the peris are to be compared to the *fairies* of British tradition, whose name stems from a common Indo-European ancestor. In both cases, mythic supernatural creatures of great and frightening potency seem to have been sublimated into folkloric forms that often shroud and obscure their origins and latent powers. Indeed, beauty is the signature characteristic of the peris of the *Shahname*, and any individual of great personal allure might well be described as "peri-like."

Feridun's ancient provenance in the Indo-European pantheon of gods is emphasized by his possession of Gurz, the great ox-headed cudgel, and his use of this mighty weapon to subdue the great demonic dragon-king. Indeed, in Indo-European mythology, the sky god—patron and defender of his human followers—commonly enters a struggle to the death with the great monster that seeks to destroy life. Indra famously battles a dragon in Indian myth, and the theme of the hero's battle with the monster-serpent is of course central to Germanic mythology generally and to the Norse tradition in particular, in which Sigurd's victory over Fafnir is the paramount example. Moreover, the fact that Thor uses an ox head to battle his enemy the World Serpent also recalls Gurz. Moreover, Feridun is linked through his signature weapon to figures throughout Indo-European mythology; such gods and demi-gods include the classical Hercules and the Dagda of the Irish tradition.

Faridun marched upon Zohak's palace and took up residence in the monarch's personal apartments in the dragon-king's absence. Zohak had a regent who ruled when he was away, a man named *Kondrow*, "Slack

Pace," so called because of the snail-like rate of movement he adopted in the presence of his monstrous master, whom he attempted to appease in all things. Kondrow waited upon Faridun according to his wishes in the evening, but in the early light of dawn he sought out Zohak, who at first appeared disinclined to challenge the usurper. However, Kondrow soon inflamed his master's jealousy with sordid tales of Faridun's amorous activities with the favored beauties within the royal apartments. When Zohak, clad in iron armor from head to toe, charged one of his faithless lovers with the intent of venting his jealousy upon her with his dagger, Faridun intervened with Gurz, with which he shattered his foe's helmet, grievously wounding the dragon-king. However, when Faridun raised his hand to finish his enemy, an angel appeared unto him and counseled a different course: Binding the evil Zohak with a lion-skin rope, Faridun took the dragon-king deep into the mountains, where he chained Zohak beneath Mount Damavand, wherein a cataract of blood flowed continually from the wound of the humiliated king. The imprisonment of such a demonic figure within a mountain derives from an ancient Indo-European mythic theme that evokes such disparate traditions as the classical and the Scandinavian, as when the Norse gods bound the evil Trickster Loki in a subterranean cavern with a serpent dripping poison into his face.

Medieval Persian Heroic Heritage: The Remarkable Lineage of Rostam and Sohrab [5]

The mighty hero Sam, the son of Nariman, was the progenitor of the line of Rostam and his son Sohrab, the great, tragic father-son heroic duo of the Persian tradition. Although clearly superhuman, this line was not derived directly from the gods of old; rather, the service of this family of heroes under sovereigns depicted as mortal but clearly derived from ancient divine figures served simultaneously to preserve and to sublimate pre-Islamic Iranian mythology within the legendary history of the *Shahname*. Sam was the mighty champion of the court of Manuchehr, who was bequeathed the Iranian throne by his great-grandfather Faridun, a euhemerized form of the ancient Persian thunder god. This mighty weapon and the hero's destruction of the dragon-king Zohak recall Faridun's pedigree as an ancient god of the Indo-European tradition, most generally compared with the Greek Zeus.

However, in a misstep often compared to that of King Lear, Faridun divided his earthly domain into three, bequeathing these to his sons Salm, Tur, and Iraj. In a twist of the Cain and Abel story, when the first two conspired in the death of the third, Faridun bided his time until Manuchehr, the son of Iraj's daughter, came of age. Faridun then supported his great-grandson in his successful attempt to supplant Salm and Tur and thus to avenge Iraj. Sam was the great warrior of the court of Manuchehr; Sam begot Zal, who in turn fathered Rostam. Thus, the narrative thread of the Rostam and Sohrab story helps to tie the medieval Persian epic to its ancient Indo-European mythic roots.

The Unusual Parentage, Fantastic Conception and Birth, and Remarkable Nursemaid of a Great Medieval Persian Hero: The Genesis of Rostam in the Shahname[6]

Rostam is marked as special in several ways before he is born—indeed, even before he is conceived. When Zal paid a nocturnal visit to the tower that held the beautiful Rudaba, the future mother of Rostam who is often described as "peri-faced," she undid her tresses and allowed them to cascade all the way to the ground, calling upon the pining lover to climb the citadel upon this fragrant and fine rope. Although the hero declined to avail himself of his beloved's offer, determining instead to cast his own loop to the top of the tower to manage the climb, the Rapunzel-like nature of this episode clearly evokes a supernatural theme that resonates with the conception of a hero.

The prophecy of the Simorgh is another sign that Rostam's birth is different from that of ordinary mortals and that he is destined for great things. The Simorgh was a magical bird that lived in the inaccessible peaks of Mount Alborz. The Simorgh had many fabulous powers, including gifts of speech, foresight, and magical instantaneous communication and transportation across mighty expanses. The Simorgh was also a formidable opponent in battle and fed herself and her young from the flesh and blood of great prey. Zal himself had been raised in the eyrie of the Simorgh, taken there by the great bird when he had been left on the slopes of Alborz to die of exposure. When Zal was born, he was unique in that his hero's body and handsome visage were capped with a shock of white hair, an anomaly entirely unknown in that region, which caused his father Sam to suspect that he was the progeny of a demon or a peri. Shamed by his son's bizarre appearance, Sam abandoned Zal in the dominion of the Simorgh, which adopted the infant, whom she called *Dastan*, "Duplicity," due to his father's treachery. Zal grew to be a great hero under the tutelage of his feathered foster-mother; when the young man left the Simorgh's care to be reunited with his penitent father, she gifted him with one of her feathers, which she commanded him to burn if ever he found himself in distress. Noting that she would be alerted in an instant of his extremity through such a ritual, the Simorgh promised to deliver her young charge from any danger.

When Rudaba conceived Rostam, it became clear that it was to be a problematic pregnancy. Zal hastened to his beloved's side and dampened her with his tears; however, his spirits were buoyed by the memory of the Simorgh's pledge to him, and so he hastened to burn a barb of the bird's feather. His plumed foster-mother then appeared, as if in a shower of tiny pearls; moreover, her words and wisdom brought joy to Zal's heart: Rudaba's child was to be a mighty warrior, tall as the clouds and graceful as the cypress in form, strong as an elephant and terrible as a lion in combat, but wise and just as his grandfather Sam in judgment. However, concerning the safe birth of the hero, the Simorgh gave explicit instructions: Certain potions must be prepared for the mother's ingestion, and specific spells must be incanted over her drugged body; most importantly, the babe must be removed from the mother's womb at the point of a knife. The wound must then be stitched and treated with a special herbal poultice and then blessed with a feather drawn from the Simorgh herself; thus would mother and son survive and thrive. This all was done, and thus was Rostam the elephant-bodied hero delivered into the world. The Simorgh's prophecy concerning the destiny and birth of this hero, the caesarian nature of his delivery, and the magical healing of his mother Rudaba are all indicators of Rostam's identity as a hero of more than ordinary proportions.

The Prodigious Growth and Remarkable Childhood Deeds of a Great Medieval Persian Hero: The Coming-of-Age of Rostam in the Shahname[7]

The newborn Rostam displayed a gargantuan appetite from earliest infancy. Ten wet-nurses took turns around the clock feeding him a veritable river of mother's milk. After he had been weaned from such pap, each day the growing lad ate the equivalent of five men's portions of bread and meat, and it took a great deal of energy to keep Rostam satisfied. Nor was this sustenance wasted: Soon it became apparent that the son of Zal would prove to be a veritable giant amongst more ordinary men, and Rostam sprouted to the stature of a mighty cypress, towering eight times the height of his companions. Indeed, he seemed very much like a shining star in the firmament of the Persian sky. Because of his enormous size, Rostam was often referred to as *Tahamtan*, the "Giant-Bodied"—sometimes rendered the "Elephant-Bodied"—one. Meanwhile, in his perspicuity and his visage, as in his courtesy and his judgment, he seemed the image of his grandfather Sam.

One evening, after the young Rostam had spent the day imbibing wine with his comrades, Tahamtan awoke from a befuddled slumber to hear that his father's pet white elephant had escaped and was running amok, injuring several warriors who had attempted to capture or to corral it. Leaping from his bed, Rostam gripped the mighty club that was the heirloom of his family and rushed to confront the creature. The wardens of his chamber attempted to dissuade the youth from such a rash course of action, emphasizing how angry Zal would be with them if they opened his doors on such an occasion. Rostam responded curtly with his club, knocking one guard's head cleanly from his shoulders. The other porters quickly withdrew, and the hero smashed the bar and chains securing the door with one blow from his mace.

Rushing out into the maelstrom surrounding the stampeding elephant, Rostam noted that a great many warriors raced before it, attempting to flee its wrath and thus to escape the pain that others had suffered before them; Rostam thought these timid sorts were like sheep fleeing the slavering jaws of the wolf. Tahamtan himself attacked like a lion, shattering the head of the elephant with a single blow of his mace. Rostam's prodigious thirst for the grape, alluded to in this episode, simply underscores his outsized appetite in all things. His heroic spirit at such an early age, manifested by his violent refusal to be sidelined during such a crisis—in conjunction with his martial prowess—and clarified by his quick and easy destruction of a beast that terrified and threw off the best of his father's warriors—serve to highlight Rostam's role as an epic hero, a larger-than-life warrior with superhuman abilities.

The Herculean Testing of a Great Medieval Persian Hero: The Heroic Labors of Rostam in the Shahname[8]

Rostam long sought and finally found and mastered a horse worthy of him, none other than the mighty steed *Rakhsh*, "Lightning," a mount as strong as an elephant and as fast as a racing camel with hooves of steel and a dappled coat like rose petals upon saffron. Having accomplished this feat, Rostam longed to prove himself in the seemingly endless Iranian wars against the Turanians. The chance to do so unfolded most notably in a series of seven labors Rostam undertook during his rescue of King Kavus, who had fallen into the clutches of the Great White Div, a demon who inhabited the realm of the wizard king of Mazandaran, a rebellious vassal of Kavus.

In the course of his quest to free King Kavus, Rostam encountered and overcame a series of obstacles representing the forces of nature, the trials of combat, and the supernatural powers of the otherworld. The son of Zal proved himself against the forces of nature when he faced the harsh conditions of the pitiless desert, traversing burning sands and surviving toxic air to find a well of sweet water and survive. The hero also overcame a fierce lion and a horrific dragon in battles in which he tested his mettle against the greatest of natural and supernatural beasts. In addition, Rostam overpowered Awlad, captured him, and forced him to act as a guide to the lair of the Great White Div, where he might rescue King Kavus.

The great hero also defeated a powerful sorceress and the Great White Div himself, thereby proving his valor and power against the forces of evil embodied in witchcraft and in the otherworldly potency of demonic nature. Like the Greek mythological figure Herakles, or indeed any number of other heroes, Rostam fully came of age and established his identity as a larger-than-life cultural champion through his successful negotiation of this series of challenges, which comprised the full array of perils and powers pitted against humanity in the medieval Persian tradition. Thus, the heroic imagination of this people might be said to have created the figure of a hero capable of overcoming the dangers and destructive forces that people perceived to surround it. Further, the culmination of this arduous process was the successful rescue of the king, the divinely mandated ruler of his people.

King Kavus himself is depicted as something of a sorcerer-king, at some points as a reasonably wise ruler, and at others as a rather ash and foolhardy one with dealings—of various degrees of success—with demons. As his very name indicates, Kavus represents a class of wizard with deep Indo-European roots; it has been argued that the Persian *kavi* is analogous with the classical Indian *kavi*, which might be rendered something like "wizard priest" or "court magician," and that seems to have no immediate relationship to kingship or any office of political power. Indeed, King Kavus of the *Shahname* seems to echo Kavi Usan of the ancient Avestan tradition of Persian literature and Kavya Usanas, the wily wizard of the early episodes of the Indian *Mahabharata* who plies his trade in league with demons. As if to illustrate the ambiguity suggested by the etymology of his name, King Kavus is often overtly depicted and even described by his most powerful followers as a weak leader with poor judgment. More evocative still are his dealings with the divs, which bargains seem at times to border on the Faustian. Indeed, the ongoing conflict between Kavus and the subject King of Mazandaran underscores the volatility of this relationship between the Iranian sorcerer-king and his unwilling, otherworldly minions.

For example, it is through his subjugation of the infernal powers of the divs of Manzandaran that Kavus is able to construct a mystical capital deep within the Alborz Mountains, a charmed abode where cold, illness, decay, and death are banished and where the buildings themselves sparkle with gold and jewels. However, the same demons that did the bidding of Kavus were quick to conspire in his downfall with Eblis, the Devil himself, who was ever seeking the damnation of the soul of Kavus. Although the text makes clear that it is the king's prostrate repentance before the One True God that saves Kavus from perdition again and again, it is just as clear that it is the strong arm of Rostam, the elephant-bodied champion of Iran, which pulls his king from scrape after scrape of his own devising.

For example, Rostam defeated *Juya*, "Seeker," the great warrior of the army of *divs*, "demons," and *pahlavans*, "champions," assembled by the Manzandarani shah, known as the king of magicians. Then, at the culmination of a great seven-day battle, it was Rostam who broke through the enemy lines and challenged the king of magicians at spear point. When that wizard transformed himself into a mighty boulder, all of the forces of the Iranians were perplexed and unable to shift the great stone even a mite. However, Rostam, flexing his great muscles, lifted the rock with no discernable effort and cast it before the tent of Kavus. Threatening to shatter the boulder into a million shards, none but Rostam could have forced the rebellious vassal king to reappear before Kavus, who ordered his rival executed.

The term *div* in Persian may be rendered something along the lines of "demon" and appears to be descended from the Avestan *daeva*, usually taken as "false deity"; this term seems to have undergone a process of pejoration because it clearly is related to the Latin *deus*, a less judgmental term meaning, generically, "god." Moreover, the name of the *div* of Russian lore (i.e., of the mythical bird who laments the fall of Prince Igor) may also be a related term. Evil beings in general might be classified in ancient Persian texts as *yatu*, which survives in modern Farsi as *jadu*; wizards in particular might be grouped in this category, although this is not always a term of condemnation and may in fact refer to a mortal who has harnessed supernatural forces to combat the powers of darkness. The modern Persian term for a wizard, *jadugar*, reflects this derivation.

The Tragedy of a Great Medieval Persian Hero: The Battle Between Rostam and His Son Sohrab in the Shahname [9]

It came to pass that the theft of Rakhsh, his mighty steed, threw Rostam into the embraces of Tahmina, the daughter of the King of Samangan.

This occurred because after a day's sport hunting onagers, Rostam sated his hunger by spitting and broiling one of the wild jackasses whole; he then ate up the beast entirely, flesh and marrow, and dropped into a deep sleep. During the night a small party of raiding Turanians came across Rakhsh's trail and managed to capture him, although the warlike stallion managed to kill several of his kidnappers in the attempt. When Rostam awoke he was distraught to discover the absence of Rakhsh; indeed, his lament likened such a loss to his own death, as he imagined the glee of the Turks to report how the mighty Rostam had perished. Searching high and low with a heavy heart, Rostam made his way on foot to Samangan, where he received a cordial welcome and the assurance of the king that a horse so noble as Rakhsh would not remain hidden for long.

Having suffered through the feast his host offered him out of courtesy, Rostam retired to his bedchamber to drown his sorrow in the elixir of sleep. However, in the middle of the night, the hero was awakened by the light of a candle held by a slave preceding her mistress Tahmina, the daughter of the king, who entered the hero's presence in secret. Giving voice to her longing to wed Rostam, the lovely maiden told of her own noble lineage, and she prophesied that their union might produce a hero worthy of the elephant-bodied one himself. Finally, Tahmina promised to restore Rakhsh to Rostam. At these words the hero's decision was made, and he quickly sought to receive the king's blessing and to sanctify this union. After a night of bliss, Rostam removed a bejeweled amulet from his arm and gave it into Tahmina's keeping for their child: If the baby were a daughter, she was to plait the trinket into her hair and thus ensure good fortune; if a son, he was to wear the medallion upon his arm even as his father had. Rostam foresaw a hero of the stature of Sam, for whom the eagle in the clouds would be obedient and the Sun in the sky would be mild. Although he shared Tahmina's grief at their parting, Rostam was overjoyed to be reunited with Rakhsh, and the hero mounted his beloved horse with many a caress and then departed from Samangan.

The loss of his steed is the perfect plot device for bringing Rostam together with a woman worthy enough to be Sohrab's mother; indeed, several passages are dedicated to the poet's description of the maiden's beauty and virtue and Tahmina's own recitation of her noble lineage and unsullied character. Moreover, Tahmina extols at length her desire to give herself to Rostam, as well as a prophecy concerning the heroic nature of their offspring. However, it is of particular significance that it is only after this breathless beauty assures the unhorsed hero that she will return his steed to him that he immediately capitulates to her offer and sends for her father's blessing of their union. The figure of Rakhsh serves in this episode as a totemic symbol of the virility of Rostam that will reach its utmost manifestation in the person of the hero Sohrab, who will himself represent the fruit of the consummation offered by Tahmina; indeed, it seems more than a coincidence that it is through the agency of this princess of Samangan that Rostam's mount is returned to him almost at the same moment that his son is conceived. It also does not require a particularly sensitive reader to note that Rostam's joy at his reunion with Rakhsh seems a bit more heartfelt than the lip service paid to his sorrow at parting from Tahmina.

Nine moons waxed and waned, and then Tahmina was delivered of a son whose magnificent physique would put one in mind of Rostam, Sam, or Niram. At a mere month of age the babe had achieved the stature of a toddler of a year, and his chest was as massive as that of his father. At the tender age of three Sohrab began to study the arts of war, and by five he had displayed a leonine ferocity few heroes could match. Indeed, by the time the boy-warrior was 10 years old, no warrior in all of that land could face down Sohrab on the field of battle. Soon thereafter, the lad approached his mother and questioned her concerning the identity of his father; he felt that he had need of a firm answer when he was asked about his lineage and the names of his sires.

Tahmina was prepared for this interview and instructed her son to rejoice because he was no less than Sohrab, son of Rostam of the line of Dastan, Sam, and Niram. That his own head seemed to scrape the very firmament of the sky was evidence of his noble birth, she continued, because his fathers before him were likewise too great to be confined within the orbit that constrains ordinary men. Tahmina then produced the tokens of patrimony Rostam had given into her keeping against the day of their son's maturity: A letter confirming the boy's lineage, three beautiful rubies, and three purses of gold. However, his mother then begged Sohrab to keep his identity a secret because they lived under the sway of the Turanian king Afrasiyab, the sworn enemy of Rostam who would joy in the destruction of the son of his nemesis. Tahmina also felt sure that Rostam himself, should he learn of Sohrab's existence, would cause her a different kind of grief: The elephant-bodied one would be unable to restrain his pride at the knowledge of such a marvelous son, she asserted, and he would immediately summon Sohrab to him, thus bringing anguish to Tahmina. The hero's mother therefore begged her son to continue to abide in obscurity. Overjoyed to learn that he was descended from the greatest of heroes, Sohrab rejected his mother's plea out of hand and indeed formulated a plan to raise an army in Turan to place Rostam upon the throne of Iran.

Having accomplished this heady goal, the young champion thought to turn back upon his own country and cast down its ruler so that his family might command both mighty kingdoms. The stars of Kavus and Afrasiyab, he declared to Tahmina, would by rights be eclipsed by the sun and moon of Rostam and Sohrab.

The episode detailing the revelation of Sohrab's lineage includes several vital elements. The token left with the mother of the unborn son is a recurring theme in various traditions, as is the young hero's need—or, as in this case, the mother's vain plea to her son—to keep his identity a secret. In tandem, these two motifs generally doom the young warrior to death at the hands of his father while ensuring that the older hero will discover that his opponent is his son a little too late. In this episode several ensuing circumstances conspire to keep Rostam's identity veiled from Sohrab until it is too late: A captured Iranian who seeks to protect the champion of his people by denying his presence on the field of battle; Rostam's own denial of his identity when he first encounters his son; and the duplicitous words of Human, the Turkish warrior who assures Sohrab that the great warrior he is to encounter is not his father, although the lying Turanian allows that the unknown warrior's horse is somewhat similar to Rakhsh.

Having determined to seek Rostam, Sohrab prepared for his journey. Like his father before him, the young hero sought a mount worthy of him: His mother sent far and wide throughout the domain of her father until a suitable steed was found for the young hero. With the scent of his mother's milk still upon his breath, the fledgling champion approached his grandfather, the King of the City of Samangan, and stated his desire to journey to Iran to visit his mighty father Rostam, the elephant-bodied one. Overjoyed to grant such a request, Sohrab's grandfather was liberal in dispensing lavish and suitable gifts from his treasury and his armory. Moreover, when news came to his ears of the young hero's preparations for war against Iran, Afrasiyab was quick to lend support to Sohrab's campaign: He sent his greatest champions to add their strong arms and heavy maces. However, from the duplicitous words of the king it was clear that he himself had divined the secret of Sohrab's birth and hoped to use the son to topple the father, his enemy, with the desire of sending them both eventually into an abyss of despair and death.

Thus amply equipped and accompanied by a great force, the son of Rostam began his journey from the home of his mother to the empire of Persia in search of his father. On his march to meet the army of the Iranians, Sohrab had several adventures that paralleled his own father's journey to manhood through a Herculean series of challenges and obstacles.

Notable amongst Sohrab's adventures was his encounter with Gordafarid, an Amazon shield-maiden; this conflict reflects a common thread in the adventures of heroes in Indo-European mythology and legend generally and in the tales of the Near East specifically. Indeed, Basil's battles with Amazons are a central theme of the Byzantine epic. Clearly Sohrab's precocious growth, prodigious size, and ability evoke the age-old theme of the hero's remarkable childhood, whereas his efforts to seek Rostam manifest the questing theme of the young hero of mysterious origins who searches for his father.

Word of a great army on his borders soon reached the ears of Kavus, who in his panic sent a message of alarm to Rostam concerning a huge Turanian force led by a mighty champion who might prove the equal of Tahamtan himself. Scoffing at the mere thought that such a hero might spring from Turanian loins, Rostam dismissed the report. He knew indeed that he had a son by the daughter of the King of Samangan, but it was far too soon and the boy far too young, the hero felt sure, for this lad to have become such a great warrior as Kavus feared. Satisfied that Kavus was once again playing the fool, Rostam dedicated himself to a drinking competition. The king for his part was outraged at Rostam's light-hearted response to his warning and ordered the immediate execution of the hero and any warrior who stood with him. At this Rostam threatened to leave Iran to its fate and seek his fortune elsewhere; it was only through the intercession of cooler heads that the champion realized that it would be the land itself and not its headstrong ruler who would be the true victim of such an act. Rostam and the king were thus reconciled, and they sought to prepare for the advance of the Turanians. However, before they could complete their preparations, their enemies were upon them.

Before battle was joined, the Turanians captured an Iranian warrior and Sohrab asked him to point out Rostam; loathe to betray the great champion of his people and perhaps to spur on the Turanians should the elephant-bodied Tahamtan fall before the might of the great young hero before him, the Iranian soldier lied to Sohrab and claimed that Rostam was not amongst the Persian host. When Rostam himself rode out upon Rakhsh to survey the field of battle, he encountered a mighty champion, tender of years, who was unknown to him. The young warrior challenged Rostam to single combat, noting that a lone warrior from each host could settle the conflict between Iran and Turan. However, the lad expressed dismay at the injustice of the match because Rostam's broad shoulders and great stature were weighed down by the tides of time. Incensed by Sohrab's words, Rostam countered with an account of his many victories over man and div and assured his youthful rival that—should he survive an encounter with his aged opponent—he would thenceforth have no need to fear a dragon. Never having suffered a loss upon the field of battle, the elder warrior promised an Iranian rout of the Turanians, although he expressed a hesitancy to dispatch such a wondrous warrior as the youth before him, whose mighty stature, noble mien, and warlike prowess seemed not derived from any Turanian line.

While Rostam was speaking Sohrab was watching him closely, and he became convinced that this hoary giant was none other than his father himself; however, when the young lad questioned the old warrior Rostam denied his identity, and Sohrab's hopes were dashed and his visage darkened. Grasping a spear, Sohrab rode to do battle with his unknown antagonist, and the fury of their conflict was such that soon the heads were shivered from their spears. The champions then drew their flashing blades, which were reduced to shards through the tumult of their duel, which was so violent and full of crashes and flying sparks that it seemed a veritable preview of Judgment Day. When their blades fell in pieces from their hands, the duelists next seized heavy clubs with which thcy poundcd onc another to bloody pulps until father and son were reduced to quivering exhaustion, as were their mounts. Then Rostam thought back upon his many great battles against divs and dragons alike, and it seemed to him that such struggles had been mere child's play compared to the cataclysmic battle with his young rival.

Having given their horses a slight respite, the heroes then drew their bows and released volley after volley of arrows against one another; however, this rain of death fell harmless against their mail-shirts and shields. Rostam attempted to bring his opponent to grips in his powerful hands, hoping to squeeze the life from Sohrab since that mighty champion could reduce a great boulder to gravel through the strength of his grasp. However, the young Sohrab proved too elusive in his movements and canny in the ways of combat to be caught. The youthful champion then turned the tables on his elder rival with a stunning blow to the shoulder, laughing at the power of youth over age when the opportunity presents itself. Utterly spent in the battle against one another, each champion raced to the lines of his enemy's army and spent his exhausted fury destroying lesser warriors than his rival. Finally, fearing for Kavus his king, Rostam returned to the Iranian host and confronted Sohrab, whom he convinced to enter into a truce until dawn.

Having paused in their battle until daybreak, at first light the champions girded their loins and prepared to meet once again on the field of combat.

Surveying his own massive body, Sohrab expressed unease to Human, a Turkish warrior: He had noted that his opponent was of a similar stature, and recalling his mother's description of Rostam, the young hero still feared that he was in conflict with his own father. However, Human, anxious to see Sohrab destroy the strong arm of Iran, purposefully deceived the lad, assuring him that he had himself encountered Rostam many times, and that—although the mount of his opponent bore some resemblance to Rakhsh—this man was not Rostam, nor his steed the great horse of the elephant-bodied one. Satisfied by this craven counsel, Sohrab sought his opponent.

However, when he came upon Rostam, Sohrab was still uneasy and attempted to engage the Iranian champion in conversation, acknowledging that he felt a bond between them and asking once more if the other great warrior were not in fact Rostam himself. Confident that his own son was far too young to be the mighty warrior before him, and fearing some sort of trick, Rostam rebuffed all such attempts to forge an alliance with the Turanian champion; Rostam once again denied his identity and provoked his opponent to combat. The two warriors dismounted and circled each other like wary lions, finally springing upon each other and struggling for an advantage. Finally Sohrab gained the upper hand, drew his sharp knife, and moved to behead his opponent; however, at this point, just as Rostam seemed about to lose his life at the hand of his son, the wisdom and wiles of age found purchase against the callow credulity and foolishness of youth.

At this crucial juncture, Rostam called out to Sohrab to stay his hand to adhere to the ancient custom of the Iranians: When a champion engaged in a wrestling bout with an opponent—the clever old hero falsely claimed—he might not take the head of his opponent when first he pinned his victim's back to the ground. Only upon the second pin, having earned the reputation of a lion amongst warriors was it acceptable for such a combatant to claim his rival's head as a trophy. Moved by the duplicitous words of his father, the youthful Sohrab acceded to his request, although it did not please him to do so; his nobility and natural generosity forced him to act in this way, behavior that was fated. Leaping upon his noble steed without a backward glance, the young hero forsook his battle with Rostam and immediately raced off in pursuit of antelope he perceived frolicking far away down on the steppe below him. Sohrab continued in this endeavor until Human encountered him and inquired as to the outcome of his great conflict with Rostam; however, when the Turk heard of the young warrior's generosity, he lamented Sohrab's great nobility and foresaw that the hero would suffer for it.

Meanwhile, Rostam made his way in exhaustion and desperation to a stream, where he drank deeply of the water, performed his ritual ablutions, and prayed to God for his deliverance from Sohrab. The superhuman stature of the great Persian hero's farr had been so great that he had to request that it be reduced simply so that he might be able to function among mortals: Indeed, from his earliest youth, Rostam's elephantine body had been endowed with such massive power and might that his very feet sank down into the stone of the earth, even as he walked upon the roads. The man-mountain had prayed to the Lord above to reduce his great vitality by such a degree as to make it possible to live amongst ordinary men. Now—in the extremity of his intimidation by his own son—Rostam supplicated the Creator to return unto him that portion of mass and force that he had lost. God granted this request, and thus the great Tahamtan who faced Sohrab shortly thereafter was fully rejuvenated to his original heroic stature and indeed manifested such a wondrously increased farr that even the confident young champion who beheld him noted the change, although he still inquired as to why one who had by chance escaped the lion's jaws would return so soon to the lair of the ravenous beast.

The two champions threw themselves upon one another, each grasping the other about the waist and attempting to throw him. Now exuding his superhuman power, Rostam extended his mighty arm around Sohrab's shoulders and head, pinning him until his strength ebbed. Then the father drew his knife and slit open his son's chest. Aware that his lifeblood was ebbing quickly from him, Sohrab lamented not death itself but the fact that he should die before completing his quest to find Rostam and setting his eyes upon the visage of his father. Mentioning that his mother had granted him tokens by which he might be known by Rostam, the dying champion of the Turanians promised that his father would avenge him upon his slayer and that someone among the host of warriors would inform Tahamtan of the death of his only son.

When he heard these words, Tahamtan was chilled to his very core; his eyes saw only darkness, and he lost consciousness of his surroundings for a time. When he had recovered enough to speak, Rostam begged his dying opponent to tell him by what tokens the boy's mother had promised his father might know him. When Sohrab revealed the sign of his arm ring, Rostam knew at last for certain the truth of his deadly encounter with his son. Wandering dazed from the scene, Rostam was at first presumed dead by the Iranians. When at last they found him, the elephant-bodied hero tried to make an end to his grief by slaying himself. Restrained from this rash action, Rostam attempted to cheat fate by sending Goudarz to King Kavus to seek some of that sovereign's all-healing magical potion. Jealous and afraid of the might and farr of Rostam combined with that of a son cast from the same mold, Kavus refused, and Sohrab died before his father could attempt to secure a healing elixir from his king in person. Thus died Rostam's son Sohrab, a mighty scion of the greatest line of Persian heroes felled even before his prime by his own pride, his father's obstinacy, and the king's malicious envy.

An interesting twist on the concept of royal farr is manifested by the fact that Rostam sent to his king to request a magical healing potion in the extremity of his son's distress; this action underscores how the character of Kavus in the medieval Persian epic was still strongly associated with the powers of sorcery manifested by the ancient Indian and Iranian figures of the same name. Meanwhile, the king's rejection of his stalwart vassal's request—on the selfish and rather pathetic grounds that his own farr would be eclipsed by that of such a mighty warrior with a son of Sohrab's stature—underscores not only the weakness of Kavus as a king in the *Shahname*, but also how fundamentally unsuitable such a sorcerer-priest figure of the mythic age is in a position of political and military leadership in the epic world that supplanted that in which such an icon originally developed.

Thus, King Kavus, through spiteful inaction, provided a crucial counterpoint to the action of Rostam and Sohrab; his absence, as it were, was as significant as his presence might have been. This point is telling because kings provide the essential structural framework for the entire *Shahname*. Heroes, battles, and monsters abound in the great medieval Persian epic, but its organization around the kings of Iran—a structure that lends the text ample legendary material and at times even a quasi-historical feel—reflects notions of kingship that weave together the many threads that make up the tapestry of what is, after all, commonly known as the *Book of Kings*. Indeed, the Divine Right of the Shahs of Iran, the trials and tribulations inherent in ensuring dynastic succession, and the necessity of unstinting loyalty to the anointed rulers of Persia are central thematic concerns of the *Shahname*. Therefore, it is perhaps of particular interest that the importance of kingship looms large in the text and subtext of the episode of Sohrab and Rostam, the best-known and most commonly referenced portion of the entire vast narrative juggernaut compiled by Ferdowsi and a section that takes as its protagonists two great heroes who are not, in fact, kings themselves.

Issues of kingship, loyalty to the king, and ambitions to rule nevertheless are recurring tropes in the Sohrab and Rostam episode; moreover, reading this episode with an understanding of the centrality of sovereignty to the larger text as a whole helps to clarify what might otherwise seem an avoidable and unnecessary tragedy. It is made clear in the text that Kavus is hardly an ideal ruler; indeed, Ferdowsi has been compared with Shakespeare in his clear-sighted and even cynical portrayal of kings who are considerably less than one might hope. Still, Kavus is the anointed ruler of Iran, and as long as he is endowed with the farr of rulership it is not for Rostam to criticize or be slow in his obedience to his sovereign; nor is it for Sohrab to plot the overthrow of the rightful king. Of course it is these precise sins that require the blood of Sohrab to be spilt, and to be spilt by none other than Rostam himself. The tragedy of the warrior son's demise at the hands of his heroic father is replicated elsewhere, to be sure, and clearly seems drawn in this case from ancient Indo-European roots. However, in the hands of Ferdowsi this commonplace is reconceived and recast to emphasize the most crucial thematic tenets of the entire *Shahname*.

Notes

1. For more information concerning the historical context of the *Shahname,* see especially Clinton xiii–xv; Curtis 6–10; Hinnells 11–20; Levy xv; Morgan 1–16; and Puhvel 94–97.

2. For critical commentary concerning the figure credited with the medieval compilation of the *Shahname,* see especially Clinton xiv–xviii; Curtis 29; Hinnells 20–21; Lapidus 141, 155; Levy xv–xvi; Morgan 8, 12, 16, 19, 22; Puhvel 117–118 (see *Firdausi* in index, page 294).

3. For critical commentary on and analysis of the sources, manuscripts, and structure of the *Shahname,* see especially Clinton xiii–xxii; Curtis 29–52; Hinnells 20–21, 38; Levy xv–xxvi; Morgan 16; and Puhvel 117–125.

4. For critical commentary on and analysis of the great euhemerized hero of the *Shahname,* see especially Curtis 24, 28, 34–36, 77; Hinnells 43, 117–119; Levy 17–34; and Puhvel 30–31, 102, 106, 111, 118, 120–121, 181, 201.

5. For critical commentary on and analysis of the heroic genealogy of the great champions of the *Shahname,* see especially Curtis 36–38; Levy 17–34; and Puhvel 120–121.

6. For critical commentary on and analysis of the parentage, conception, birth, and fosterage of Rostam in the *Shahname,* see especially Curtis 38–39; Levy 35–39, 45–48; and Puhvel 112, 122.

7. For critical commentary on and analysis of the childhood growth and feats of Rostam in the *Shahname,* see especially Curtis 38–41; Levy 48–52; and Puhvel 112.

8. For critical commentary on and analysis of the great heroic labors of Rostam in the *Shahname*, see especially Curtis 21, 43–52; Hinnells 65; Levy 52–61; and Puhvel 122–123, 231–232.

9. For critical commentary on and analysis of the great tragedy of Rostam and Sohrab in the *Shahname*, see especially Clinton xiv–xv; Curtis 41–42; Levy 64–80; and Puhvel 118, 123, 186, 187, 238.

Sources and Further Reading

Clinton, Jerome W. *The Tragedy of Sohráb and Rostám: From the Persian National Epic, the Shahname of Abol-Qasem Ferdowsi*. Publications on the Near East, University of Washington, No. 3. Seattle: University of Washington Press, 1996.

Curtis, Vesta Sarkhosh. *Persian Myths*. Austin: University of Texas Press, 1993.

Ferdowsi, A. *The Legend of Seyavash*. Washington, DC: Mage Publishers, 2004.

Ferdowsi, A., and D. Davis. *The Lion and the Throne: Stories from the Shahnameh of Ferdowsi*, Vol. 1. Washington, DC: Mage Publishers, 1998.

Ferdowsi, A., and D. Davis. *Fathers and Sons: Stories from the Shahnameh of Ferdowsi*, Vol. 2. Washington, DC: Mage Publishers, 2000.

Ferdowsi, A., and D. Davis. *Sunset of Empire: Stories from the Shahnameh of Ferdowsi*, Vol. 3. Washington, DC: Mage Publishers, 2004.

Ganjavi, Nizami, and Julie Scott Meisami. *The Haft Paykar: A Medieval Persian Romance*. Oxford, United Kingdom: Oxford University Press, 1995.

Hinnells, John R. *Persian Mythology*. London: Hamyln Publishers, 1975.

Lapidus, Ira M. *A History of Islamic Societies*. Cambridge, United Kingdom: Cambridge University Press, 2002.

Levy, Reuben. *The Epic of the Kings: Shah-Nama, the National Epic of Persia*. London: Routledge & K. Paul, 1985.

Meisami, Julie S. *Medieval Persian Court Poetry*. Princeton, NJ: Princeton University Press, 1987.

Meisami, Julie S. *A Sea of Virtues: Bahr Al-Favaid: A Medieval Islamic Mirror for Princes*. Salt Lake City: University of Utah Press, 1991.

Meisami, Julie S. *Persian Historiography*. Edinburgh, United Kingdom: Edinburgh University Press, 1999.

Morgan, David. *Medieval Persia 1040–1797*. London: Longman, 1997.

Puhvel, Jaan. *Comparative Mythology*. Baltimore: Johns Hopkins University Press, 1987.

Robinson, B. *The Persian Book of Kings: An Epitome of the Shahnama of Firdawsi*. New York: Curzon Press, 2002.

Ross, Denison. *The Hafez Poems of Gertrude Bell*. New York: Penguin, 1981.

Rypka, Jan. *History of Iranian Literature*. Dordrecht: D. Reidel Publishing Co., 1968.

Yarshater, Ehsan. *Cambridge History of Iran, Volume 3: The Seleucid, Parthian, and Sassanian Periods*. Cambridge, United Kingdom: Cambridge University Press, 1968.

The Turkish Steppe-Raider Hero

The Historical Context of the *Book of Dede Korkut* [1]

Who Were the Oghuz Turks?

First sweeping onto the stage of history as another in a seemingly endless wave of nomadic raiders whose tide covered the steppes with a sea of horse warriors, by the end of the 10th century the nomadic Oghuz Turks had been converted to Islam. With the Saljuq family as their khans, it was a mighty Oghuz army that forged a new Turkic empire in the course of the 11th century, extending across Iraq and Iran, into Georgia and Armenia, and across the Anatolian Peninsula. Indeed, it was none other than a massive Saljuq force made up of Oghuz Turks that defeated the Byzantine army at the Battle of Manzikert in 1071, at which the Byzantine emperor himself was captured and held for ransom. All of what we now know as Turkey lay open for conquest. The Oghuz traveled in warbands known as *ghazis*, each led by its *bey*, "chief," or *baba*, "shaman." Driven by the desire for glory, booty, and pasturelands for their herds, these raiders destroyed the infrastructure of civilization, razing agricultural areas, slaying and enslaving their captives, and cutting off isolated urban centers that could withstand isolated forays. In this manner the Oghuz rather quickly decimated the Christian population of Byzantine Anatolia.

Who was Dede Korkut?

Dede Korkut, or "Grandpa Korkut," himself is, as his name implies, a sort of universal village elder figure for the Oghuz: He is a wiseman and a counselor, to be sure, but he is also an *ozan*, a "bard" not unlike the Scandinavian *skald* or the Anglo-Saxon *scop*; indeed, the fundamental narrative function of this figure is to represent the storehouse of wisdom, knowledge, and entertainment contained in the Turkish tradition: Time and again, the tales in this collection end with formulaic phrases that attribute each story to this primal storyteller, to whom credit is given for the shaping of each episode and the crafting of the themes and techniques in each telling. Within the stories themselves, Dede Korkut acts as a *bilici*, a "seer," a prophet of sorts who has access to hidden and perhaps even forbidden knowledge. Dede Korkut also functions as the traditional name-giver, the master of folk tradition who presides over the ritual that acknowledges that a boy has crossed the threshold into manhood. Less overtly but perhaps equally vitally, Dede Korkut performs a significant mythic function as a shaman-figure who provides guidance for the heroes of this epic cycle through his great wisdom and otherworldly insight. In this role he provides a distant Turkic echo to such a one as the Merlin of Arthur's court, or—perhaps more aptly—the druid Cathbad of the Irish tradition.

The Literary Context of the Medieval Turkish Heroic Cycle: Sources, Manuscripts, and Structure of the *Book of Dede Korkut* [2]

The *Kitab-i Dede Qorqut*, or the *Book of Dede Korkut*, is generally accepted to be a courtly literary compilation of much older oral heroic lays and elegiac odes hearkening back to the days when Turkish nomadic raiders roamed the steppes on fiery steeds, lived in their felt tents wherever best pleased them, and sought above all things honor and glory upon the field of battle. It is, in short, a collection of short episodic adventures and gnomic sayings that purport to manifest generations of traditional wisdom of the Oghuz tribesmen who were to prove a driving force in forging the first substantial Turkish states; as such, the *Book of Dede Korkut* seems to offer a cornucopia of mythic, legendary, and folkloric material preserved from earlier times. However, as in all such cases of what we reasonably take to be oral traditions preserved in a literate context, we must proceed with care, and it is safest to keep a tight rein on the desire to take this information at face value. Therefore, a good place to begin is with a brief overview of the ongoing tension between just such a heroic horse culture and the civilized life that quickly supplanted and then later valorized nomadic ways.

Not unlike *Digenes Akritis*—the epic tale of the mighty border-warrior and raider from the very marches of Rum itself, that great hero of the enemies of Dede Korkut and his men—the *Book of Dede Korkut* seems an idealized account of the great deeds of the heroes of a past that already seemed distant. Chronicling a life of free Oghuz raiders roaming the endless steppe in search of adventure and glory, the narratives are deeply steeped in legend, myth, and folklore. Not surprisingly given its likely provenance in oral tradition, the precise dating and sources of the *Book of Dede Korkut* are disputed. Probably beginning as oral tales of a bardic nature some centuries before, some scholars have suggested that these works had most likely achieved something approaching their present form sometime in the 13th century.

Moreover, it has been asserted that textual evidence suggests a compilation date not later than the end of the 14th century. If these hypotheses are correct, we are left with a period of nearly two hundred years during which the tales may have been rendered into their current literary form. We are on somewhat firmer ground concerning the written records: Preserved in two manuscripts dated to the 16th century, one of which contains only half of the tales, the *Book of Dede Korkut* in any case provides a telling glimpse into the culture that produced the narrative. In other words, although some details of a lost Oghuz life on the steppe might in fact be preserved in the text, it also offers an evocative perspective on the later, more sedentary court culture of the Turks who looked back to their Oghuz forebears for heroes and tales of adventure. Thus, the *Book of Dede Korkut* offers what we might term a "halcyon days of yore" heroic ethos: Honor, truth, valor, are the primary currencies of this text, which provides an idyllic vision of a past that was everything its audience might have wished.

The Sacrificed Son Saves His Father: How Dirse Khan Betrayed His Son Boghach but Was Later Saved by Him[3]

Bayindir Khan called the Oghuz nobles together annually to a great feast. One year he ordered that the flesh of stallions, male camels, and rams be prepared, and that three great pavilions be set up for the feasting of the Oghuz nobles. A white tent was erected for those with sons, a red tent for those with daughters, and a black tent for those luckless men with no children at all. The childless were thought to have lost the favor of the Almighty. Dirse Khan was amongst the Oghuz nobles seated in the black pavilion. However, when he discovered the reason for his humiliation, he called his forty favored retainers to him and left without eating. Dirse Khan and his two score chosen companions then rode home to his encampment, where the humiliated chieftain cajoled and berated his wife, seeking to know the reason for his shame, which surely, he felt, lay in the fault of one of the two of them.

Meeting her husband's anguish and anger with a grief that was manifested in crimson tears of blood flowing down her cheeks, the wife of Dirse Khan implored her husband to make them worthy of the favor of the Almighty so that he might give them a healthy child: Dirse Khan should, she said, sacrifice a great herd of stallions, many a male camel, and a mighty flock of rams; he should brew kumis until it pooled in mighty lakes; he should give alms to the beggar, clothe the naked, and feed the hungry; and he should make a great feast for the Oghuz nobles of the meat and kumis he had prepared, and then he should implore his guests to pray to Almighty God that he and his wife be granted a healthy child. All this Dirse Khan did according to his wife's instruction, and in the end she conceived and was delivered of a fine baby boy, who would later become known as Boghach. The story of the humiliation of Dirse Khan and his subsequently successful attempt to win the favor of the Almighty provides the context of the miraculous conception of the protagonist so common in heroic narratives.

When the son of Dirse Khan was but fifteen years of age, he was casting knucklebones with three other lads in the huge arena of Bayindir Khan. Now it so happened that once a year that great khan baited his fighting camel upon his mighty bull, a monstrous beast that could pulverize stone with a mere twist of its horn. Unfortunately, the bull was released into the ring while the four youths amused themselves there, and the horrified onlookers shouted for the lads to run from the beast to save their lives. The other three youths fled the arena in panic, but not the only son of Dirse Khan: The boy stood his ground as the mighty beast charged, and when it was upon him he gave it such a blow of his fist upon its head that the animal tumbled back all of the way across the arena. Angered all the more, the monster charged the boy once again; once more the lad let fly another great blow, but this time he kept his hand upon the bull so that they pushed and struggled across the open space until the son of Dirse Khan was covered with the foam of his opponent. Finally, the boy realized that he himself was keeping the bull on its feet rather like a pole in its center keeps a tent from collapsing. Suddenly changing his tactics, the youth pulled his arm away from the bull's head and simultaneously stepped to one side so that the great beast fell headlong onto the ground; seizing his opportunity, the boy drew his knife and took the head of the bull.

Witnessing this feat, the Oghuz nobles were overjoyed to discover such a youthful hero amongst them. They exclaimed that he should receive name, title, and possessions immediately. Dede Korkut was called to sing the praises of the boy and to grant him his name, which was *Boghach*, the "Bull Warrior." Dirse Khan was so proud of his son, who so early in life entered into manhood and earned a name, that he immediately granted young Boghach title and throne, flocks, herds, and dominions. Moreover, Dirse Khan was so pleased with his son, and he bestowed so much favor upon Boghach—now made a khan himself—that his bodyguard of forty hand-picked warriors—formerly those upon whom his gifts and honors were bestowed—were forgotten and ignored, and thus their enmity for their khan's successor festered and grew.

In addition to providing a tale of a heroic conflict of a lone youth against a monstrous beast, the story of how Boghach earned his name comprises a tale of the archetypal childhood feats of a heroic figure and manifests the common theme of the rite of manhood through which a boy becomes recognized by his people as a fully mature member of the warband. Indeed, the Turkish motif of the concept of the earning of an adult name underscores the cultural importance of such rites. Moreover, the function of the wise man and bard Dede Korkut in this ritual naming ceremony also evokes the archetype of the shaman-guide, the wizened oracular mentor who gifts his young protégé with hard-won wisdom and poetic insight gleaned from his otherworldly experiences and knowledge.

The forty warriors of the retinue of Dirse Khan, formerly his most beloved comrades, gathered together in their envy and hatred of Boghach Khan. They determined that they would slander the lad so foully to his father that Dirse Khan would have no choice but to slay his son. The first score of these scheming cowards went therefore to their khan and told him monstrous lies about his son. They claimed that Boghach Khan rode roughshod across the land, rampaging the nation of the Oghuz at the head of his band of forty. Where he found the beauty of a lovely maiden, these scoundrels claimed, Boghach Khan sullied it; where he found the snowy beard of an elder, so they said, he plucked it; where he found the white head of a matron, they lied, he battered it. Indeed, some have gone so much further as to claim that these slanderers actually accused the young warrior of milking old women like beasts. The 20 rascals finished their fabric of lies with the fearful threat of what Bayindir Khan would say when word of such atrocities reached his ears.

As Dirse Khan pronounced his ill-advised judgment of such crimes—which were of course the twisted inventions of his jealous retainers—the second score of his chosen warriors arrived with still more disturbing false-hoods of almost unspeakable proportions: Boghach Khan, these villains claimed, had entered his mother's tent after hunting, drunk deeply from his father's vats of wine, and unlawfully caressed his mother, fondling her in sinful ways that were sure to bring judgment crashing down upon the family of Dirse Khan. Overcome with rage, Dirse Khan commanded his retainers to bring his son to him; craftily they replied that Boghach Khan would not come upon their word alone. However, if Dirse Khan went to the hunt with his son, he might take the opportunity to slay him with his own hand.

When dawn broke, Dirse Khan rode forth to the hunt and his son accompanied him. When the party had reached the mountain slopes where game was plentiful, the forty treacherous scoundrels told the young khan that his father wished to see his son disport before him so that he might be proud of Boghach's prowess. Unsuspecting, the boy therefore drove deer before his father in veritable herds, displaying his skill with horse and bow. However, the villainous deceivers whispered in Dirse Khan's ear that his son would use this opportunity to slay his khan while he feigned a shot at a stag, and so they counseled their lord to kill the boy quickly as he passed back and forth in front of his father. Accordingly, Dirse Khan drew back on his bow and loosed a mighty shot that struck the innocent Boghach right in the midst of his back. The boy sank from his mount as his lifeblood poured forth, and although his father—appalled and distraught at his own act of treachery—attempted to come to him, the forty retainers corralled their khan back to their encampment.

Meanwhile Boghach Khan's mother had prepared a great feast in celebration of her son's first hunt. However, when Dirse Khan returned without the boy, the lady lamented her son loudly, beseeching her husband to inform her of Boghach's fate. Dirse Khan could not find words to answer his lady, and the forty curs took him off to his bed, claiming that he was befuddled by drink, and that Boghach, still hot in pursuit of game, would return in a day or two. However, the lady knew better than to believe such falsehood, and calling her forty reed-like maidens to her, she mounted her horse and went in search of her son in the direction from whence Dirse Khan had ridden.

As Boghach lay upon the slopes of the mountain with his lifeblood pouring out, suddenly an ancient wanderer mounted upon a gray horse appeared and comforted him. This pilgrim was none other than Hzir, the eternal traveler who ever gives aid to those in need. Thrice Hzir laid his hand upon the wound of Boghach, and he assured the lad that he would not die of this grievous injury: The blossoms of the high escarpments and the milk of his mother's breast would provide the healing poultice that would save the young hero. With these words Hzir vanished. At that moment Boghach's mother galloped upon the scene, saw her bruised and bloodied son seemingly in his death throes upon the ground, and in her grief she cursed the mountain, its rushing streams, its billowing grasses, and its graceful harts; moreover, she begged her son to whisper with his last breaths, if he could, whether a lion or a tiger had thus laid him low.

Turning his head to her and opening his eyes as he heard her words, Boghach told his mother not to curse the mountain, nor its streams, grasses, and leaping harts; further, he told her that his wound was the work not of a lion, nor of a tiger, but rather was the handiwork of his own father, upon whom any curse should be laid. The boy then offered glad tidings to follow such a dire proclamation: Hzir had visited him and assured him that he would survive if treated with a poultice comprised of mountain flowers mingled with his mother's milk. Quickly the forty willowy maidens of the lady's retinue gathered the blossoms while Boghach's mother drew pap from her breast. She struck herself hard upon the chest thrice, and at the third blow milk mixed with blood flowed forth. Helping the wounded warrior to mount his horse, his mother led Boghach back to his camp, where his physicians took him into their care. In forty days the young khan was fully recovered, although Dirse Khan knew nothing of this and thought his son dead.

Although Dirse Khan heard no word of his son's recovery, this news was received with fear and loathing by the forty villains, who understood that doom would fall upon them quickly should their lord discover that his son lived and consequently take the trouble to ascertain his innocence in the face of their slanders. They therefore determined to betray their master and to seize Dirse Khan and bind him and deliver him into captivity in the land of the infidels. However, the wife of the humiliated khan discovered what had occurred, and she quickly sought her son and begged him to show mercy to the father who had betrayed him. Boghach Khan immediately agreed to his mother's request, and he and his forty chosen warriors had soon picked up the trail of poor Dirse Khan and his forty merciless betrayers.

Setting his own forty warriors in ambush, Boghach Khan approached the encampment of the forty scoundrels alone. Deep in their cups, these heartless fiends determined to seize this unsuspecting stranger and to sell him into slavery along with Dirse Khan. Beseeching his forty captors to allow him to turn back the stranger, Dirse Khan took his lute and sang a lay in which he offered the young man the choicest of his possessions without a struggle if only the lad would go back. The old man exclaimed that he had brought his own fate upon himself when he killed his own son, and thus deserved no pity, but he added that he wished to save this innocent young visitor from sharing his fate.

Boghach Khan responded to this lay by declaring that his horse, camel, sheep, tent, and beloved all abided within the domain of Dirse Khan, and that he would not abandon them to the forty villains who held that khan in bondage. Further, the young hero acknowledged that he did, in fact, have a hoary-headed father amongst the elders of Dirse Khan's clan, and although that father had lost his wits and his way, he would not abandon the poor man. With these words, Boghach Khan signaled to his own hidden retainers, and the slaughter of the scoundrels commenced. Some he decapitated and some he enslaved, but all of the guilty forty were punished, and their master was freed. Father and son then embraced, and the wife of Dirse Khan gave thanks to God. Dede Korkut himself composed and recited this account of the boy's valorous deeds.

As is made evident time and again in this tale, forty is a number of great significance in the folklore and literature of medieval Turkey: The forty evil villains of the bodyguard of Dirse Khan are counterbalanced by the forty virtuous handmaids who gather the mountain blossoms for the magic poultice that heals the wounded Boghach in forty days. Indeed, it is a commonplace in Turkish texts of this sort to note the forty retainers of a khan or the forty maids-in-waiting of his lady, and wedding celebrations are often said to last for forty days. This tradition is linked to belief in "the forty," the conclave of Islamic saints thought to hold sway over the world.

Several themes that cross cultural boundaries act as catalysts and provide central themes throughout this tale. For example, the jealousy of the forty retainers toward Boghach Khan evokes the familiar theme of a sort of "sibling" rivalry in general terms, whereas the fact that Dirse Khan is later bound and beaten and on the road to bondage in a foreign land in provides something like an inversion of the Joseph story from the Old Testament. Meanwhile, the fear of supplantation upon his throne and in his own bed that the forty villains evoke and stoke in Dirse Khan to alienate him from his steadfast and heroic son elucidates an Oedipal theme. Moreover, the theme of the resurrection of the hero is a popular one in epics across Central Asia, appearing in similar or related traditions ranging as far afield as Mongolia; of course, in this text the hero is only nearly dead. Meanwhile, the healing powers of the mother's milk recalls Kirghiz and Altaian episodes.

Several elements of this tale link it to commonplace Turkish folk beliefs and customs. For example, the color black has long had negative connotations in the folklore of the Turks, and the belief that black was an unlucky color and that wearing black betokened ominous tidings is thought to hearken back to the days of the Oghuz. The fact that the young son of Dirse Khan was playing *ashik*—or "casting knucklebones"—in the arena before the attack of the bull weaves this story into a fabric of Turkic pastimes that dates back at least fifteen hundred years or so and that continues to the present day. Played with sheep bones, these games have taken many forms and may, in fact, have played a role in some ritual fortune-telling practices, a function that may serve to underscore the propitious circumstances that allow Boghach Khan to rise to manhood, to earn his name, and to achieve his status as a hero.

The fertility theme of this tale is underscored by the sacrifice of male animals, which is said to have been an ancient folkloric practice amongst Turkic peoples. According to this belief, males were considered more worthy of sacrifice, and thus a man who wished his wife to conceive a child would sacrifice as many male animals as possible. This theme is fore-shadowed by the preparation of Bayindir Khan's feast and the erection of the three pavilions; is emphasized by the barrenness of Dirse Khan's wife; and is reinforced by the appearance of Hizr, a wandering Islamic saint with possible roots in an ancient fertility god.

Like the Biblical story of Abraham and Sarah, Dirse Khan and his wife have long been denied the offspring that they desire. In addition, the Turkish tradition places special emphasis on the miraculous conception of the hero who springs from the loins of the barren couple. Through prayer, sacrifice, and good deeds, Dirse Khan, like Abraham before him, is able to propitiate God so that he is granted the son he desires, who, like Isaac, becomes the apple of his eye. However, the willingness of Dirse Khan to believe evil of his son and his attempted murder of him offers something of an inversion of the sacrifice of Isaac. Indeed, letting loose his arrow into his son's back upon the slopes of the mountain under the influence of evil counsel seems almost a parody of Abraham's resolute willingness to offer his beloved son at his own hand at the command of the Almighty.

Hzir is a wandering, immortal servant of God who is cited as a companion to Moses in Sura 18 of the Koran and is, through his peregrinations, closely associated with the Hebrew Elijah, or Ilyas, as he is commonly known in Anatolia. In Turkish, in fact, the names of the two figures have been com-bined in the term *Hidrellez*, which is used to denote the festival that marks the traditional start of spring in early May, the date upon which these two prophets are thought to have met on Earth. Hzir is said to have imbibed the draught of ever-lasting life and to roam the Earth in search of those in need. Indeed, Turkish folklore suggests that whatever one wishes on the night of Hidrellez will come true. Moreover, the fact that Hzir is so closely entwined with the figure of Ilyas provides an interesting if tenuous connection with the Russian tradition in which Saint Ilya represents an amalgamation of the Hebrew prophet Elijah and the ancient Slavic thunder god Perun. Hzir is sometimes linked to Saint George, especially through the suggestion of "Green Man" festivals long associated with George; it has been suggested that this relationship may be based on the literal interpretation of an Arabic derivation of *Hzir*, which might suggest his origin in an ancient pagan fertility figure.

The Everyman Hero of the Oghuz: How the Abode of Salur Kazan was Pillaged, and How a Superhuman Shepherd Saved the Son of the Khan[4]

Salur Kazan was a great khan, and he feasted his Oghuz followers lavishly in his encampment of ninety pavilions topped with gold. They sat upon ninety red silk carpets and were served by nine beautiful infidel slave girls. These lovely serving maidens brought forth vast quantities of rich wine from the bountiful storerooms filled with brimming clay pots and shining golden vessels. The chieftains of the Oghuz drank deeply, and Salur Khan began to become light-headed from the powerful wine. He called out to his followers to rise from their couches to ride forth and hunt upon the mountainsides. The Oghuz heroes clamored to join their khan, and when Salur Kazan's mother's brother Uruz Koja pointed out the danger of the infidels—who might at any moment raid across the border from Georgia—the khan agreed to leave his son Uruz and three hundred Oghuz warriors to protect their encampment.

However, as soon as his spies informed him that the Oghuz tents were nearly unguarded, Shokli Melik—the damnable infidel king—saw the opportunity to chasten his proud rival Salur Kazan. Storming into the Oghuz camp in the middle of the night, the godless Shokli led seven thousand short-haired, black-coated infidel warriors against Uruz and his three hundred warriors, whom they captured and shackled. Saru Kulmash fell attempting in vain to defend the home of his khan, although Salur Kazan knew nothing of this tragedy. The infidel raiders rode off with many a fine charger, troops of camels, and fine treasures plundered from the storehouses of their enemy. They led Uruz and his warriors into bondage, but—moreover—they likewise took captive Lady Burla Hatun the Tall, the wife of Salur Kazan, along with her forty reed-like maids in waiting.

The mother of the khan they trussed and threw over the back of a black camel. The followers of King Shokli left the great pavilion of Salur Kazan in tatters and ashes, bereft of its former beauty and glory, its golden crown fallen.

Intoxicated with their easy success, the infidels thought to add further misery and humiliation to that they had wrought in one night upon the unsuspecting khan: Having pillaged his home, stolen his horses and camels, and imprisoned his family and their retainers, they sought to add insult to injury by rustling the great flock of ten thousand sheep that Salur Kazan left in pasturage in the shadow of the pass of the Black Gate. Pleased at this suggestion, King Shokli dispatched six hundred infidel raiders to carry off the flocks of Salur Kazan, which were in the care of the shepherd Karajuk.

Awakened from his slumber by an ominous nightmare, the shepherd called to his brothers to help him build up the sheepfold. Having reinforced the walls in several places, Karajuk took up his sling just as the infidels arrived. Boasting of their triumph over the hapless Salur Kazan, the warriors of King Shokli offered to make the shepherd a prince if only he would give to them the sheep in his care. However, the brave shepherd laughed disdainfully at such an offer and told the infidel dogs that they might better ask his hounds to share their filthy dish to sup from than dare aspire to the sheep in his care. Karajuk would not trade his humble shepherd's cap or his crook for their helmets and spears, he assured them, and he would rather have his own goat and sling rather than their steeds or bows. Infuriated by the shepherd's insulting refusal, the six hundred warriors attacked, showering the sheepfold with their shafts.

Karajuk's brothers fell in the hail of missiles, and the shepherd himself was wounded in a spot or two; however, these losses were nothing at all in comparison to the death and destruction the keeper of Salur Kazan's sheep rained upon the enemies of his khan: His first stone felled two or three of the enemy, whereas his second laid low three or four. Soon the infidels were scattered in terror and wished nothing more than to escape from the Hell on Earth in which they found themselves. When he ran out of stones, Karajuk used what came to hand: Sheep and goats fell amongst the foul invaders, and with each shot four or five met death until three hundred infidels had met their fates and the rest had fled. The shepherd then raised a mound over his fallen enemies and buried his brothers with proper rites. He then burned a piece of his garment and staunched his wounds with the ashes. Only then did Karajuk have leisure to lament the fate that had befallen his khan. He did not know whether Salur Kazan knew anything of the infidel incursion, or even if the chieftain still lived.

That same night Salur Kazan awoke in terror from a horrible nightmare in which he saw several dark visions: His falcon fell dying from his hand, thunderbolts pelted his many gold-topped tents from the lowering clouds of heaven, wolves rent these pavilions to shreds, and a great fog engulfed his entire encampment. Meanwhile he himself was attacked in his nightmare by a black camel that bit him on the throat, and his hair grew in inky waves into long unkempt tresses like waving weeds. His hands dripped blood from the wrists to the tips of his fingers in this vision. Utterly scared witless, Salur Kazan asked his brother Kara Gone what such a vision might portend, but his brother answered only in part: The dark clouds, Kara Gone said, might be the power of Salur Kazan, whereas the wild elements represented his warriors, the hair was his woes and cares, and the bloody fingers were coming calamity. Unnerved still further by this reading of his dream, Salur Kazan commanded his brother and followers to continue the hunt while he returned as swiftly as the wind to his encampment, covering the three-day journey in one morning. If all were well he would return to the hunt by sunset; if not, Kara Gone and the rest should seek their own protection because the fate of Salur Kazan would follow in the wake of that of his home.

Riding hard to the place his pavilion had stood only hours before, Salur Kazan found nothing but scraps and refuse, a desolate ghost of his encampment populated by crows and wild dogs. The distraught Khan addressed himself to his former home, but his words went unanswered. Following the path taken by the infidel raiders, Salur Kazan came to a stream that he likewise asked for tidings, but the rushing water gave no answer. Wandering on, he came upon brother wolf and finally a shepherd's hound, but neither answered his questions with more than a growl. Finally, Salur Kazan came upon the dog's master, Karajuk the shepherd.

Questioning the keeper of his sheep, Salur Kazan learned of the fate of his loved ones, carried away by the infidels after their unexpected raid. Hearing these terrible words, the Khan called down a great curse upon his shepherd, asking God to parch the mouth that spoke these harsh tidings and to rot that tongue. Karajuk responded indignantly, telling his master of the battle that followed the raid, of his part in it, and of the death of his brothers. The shepherd then cried out to be given his master's arms and mount so that he might put the infidel raiders to the sword. Considering such an offer from a shepherd an insult to his own honor, Salur Kazan continued on; however, the shepherd followed him, insisting that he be allowed to fight by his khan's side. Finally—determined to protect his honor, which he felt would be besmirched if a mere shepherd were to serve as his champion—Salur Kazan tricked the young boy into allowing himself to be tied to a tree. However, the shepherd was undeterred and uprooted the tree and ran after his lord with the great burden still strapped to him. When Salur Kazan saw his shepherd approaching with the tree upon his back, he asked Karajuk why he was hurrying along with such a burden; the shepherd's reply—that he was toting firewood to roast his khan a snack—so lifted the spirits of the khan that he embraced the lad, kissed his forehead, and declared that, should they succeed in their quest, none but Karajuk should be the keeper of the khan's horse.

Meanwhile, King Shokli was well pleased with his dastardly work and sought to improve the sport and shame his enemy still further by making Lady Burla, the wife of Salur Kazan and the mother of Prince Uruz, his cup-bearer. However, the lady overheard this plot and instructed all of her attendants to answer when Shokli's men called for Lady Burla; this was done, and so King Shokli's servants returned to their master without the lady. The infidel king, enraged to be thus denied his desire, commanded that Uruz be roasted until his white flesh was nicely browned; when this foul feast was offered to the ladies, Shokli surmised, the mother of the boy would be she who refused to eat.

Suspecting this evil intention, Lady Burla rushed to her son's side and warned him of his impending doom, telling him that in this way the infidel king thought to identify her and take her as the server of his table and the concubine of his bed. Horrified by his mother's display of affection and concern, which might betray her, Uruz threatened to strike her down then and there rather than to see his father humiliated as his enemy intended. Further, he scoffed at his doom and commanded his mother to gorge herself upon his flesh so that Shokli and his men would never guess who the true wife of Salur Kazan might be.

The followers of King Shokli rejoiced as they took the son of Salur Kazan to hang him upon the gibbet-hook affixed to the mighty gallows tree, the site of execution. Addressing the towering tree upon which he was to be slain, Uruz noted the life-protecting role of wood: It is the wood of trees that comprises the gates of the holy cities of Mecca and Medina, the staff of Moses, the saddle upon the mule given to Ali by Mohammed, the scabbard encasing the sword likewise carried by the great Islamic hero, the cradle of Hassan and Hussein, and the bridges and boats that carry men safely across dangerous waters. Calling out upon the tree likewise to keep him safe by bending down under his weight, Uruz called down a curse upon his gallows if it held him. Despairing of all of the joys about to be taken from him, the prince then addressed himself to his heavenly lord.

At the very moment that Uruz raised his face to the heavens and invoked the intercession of the Almighty in the name of his prophet, Salur Kazan and the shepherd Karajuk arrived on the scene.

Flinging two hundred pounds of stone with every shot, the shepherd's sling had the power to loose missiles that could fly like dust on the wind and burn the ground like cinders; indeed, if a stone from that sling hit the earth, no grass would grow in that place for three full years. The wolves of the mountains had learned to fear that sling so greatly that they left alone even unattended sheep. When Karajuk saw the infidels before him, his fury was such that he could not stay his hand but unleashed his sling. The terror of his enemies was great as the sky seemed to darken with the flight of the shepherd's stones.

However, Salur Khan called out for the shepherd to abide a bit; the khan wished to rescue his mother from the clutches of his enemies so she might not be trampled under the hooves of their horses. Calling out to King Shokli, Salur Kazan offered to vouchsafe to his infidel enemy all of the flocks, herds, and treasures he had stolen, and to abandon to Shokli's enslavement his wife Lady Burla, his son Prince Uruz, and all their attendants; all of this Salur Kazan offered to do without a struggle, if only Shokli would release to him his aged mother. Scoffing at these terms, the infidel king responded that he would keep all he had gained; moreover, he promised to increase his enemy's shame by giving Salur Kazan's mother to Yahyan the priest so that she might bear him a son who would grow to be an enemy of the Oguz. Outraged, Karajuk answered this insult in kind, noting that, although his lord's mother was past child-bearing, the same effect might be gained by taking one of Shokli's daughters to Salur Kazan's bed; such a young concubine might indeed produce a bastard son whom Shokli could attempt to turn against his Oghuz father. Meanwhile, the heroes of the Oghuz, hearing of the plight of Salur Kazan, hurried to his side.

After making their ablutions and offering prayers to the almighty, the Oghuz nobles rushed into battle with the infidel, and the carnage was great: Twelve thousand infidels were sent screaming into the abyss, and five hundred Oghuz warriors fell. Salur Kazan himself charged the center of the enemy ranks, taking King Shokli's head with his own hands. Those who fled the battlefield were allowed to escape with their lives, whereas those who begged quarter were given it. Salur Kazan released his family from their bondage and freed forty male slaves and forty female slaves to celebrate his reunion with Prince Uruz. Meanwhile, the shepherd Karajuk was raised to the position of the master of the Khan's horse. Dede Korkut himself then composed this tale of Salur Kazan and Karajuk his faithful shepherd, which he declaimed for the benefit of the Oghuz nobles.

The detail that crows flocked over and wild dogs wandered through the scene of desolation that was once Salur Kazan's encampment brings to mind the commonplace of wolves and ravens lurking upon battlefields in the Northern European epic tradition. Incidentally, insulting references to dogs are particularly demeaning within an Islamic framework in which such creatures are considered unclean. In any case, although roving scavengers may or may not impart or accrue mythic or folkloric significance in various traditions, it is clear in the present case that the presence of carrion eaters is used to good effect to intensify the pathos of the passage and to underscore the *ubi sunt* theme: Where is the home of Salur Kazan, once so happy and prosperous? It has been transformed into a wasteland, the domain of scavengers. Where are the loved ones once so cherished? Literally they are in the hands of the infidel, of course, but metaphorically they abide in the belly of the wolf.

The *bozkurt*, or "gray wolf," on the other hand, was a sacred animal to the early Oghuz, who often venerated him as an ancestor; Oghuz Khan himself was said in at least one 14th-century source to have followed a visionary wolf to enact his victories. Near Eastern Christian records of the Seljuk expansion in the 11th century mention Oghuz forces proceeding under the banner of a dog or wolf, and as early as the 6th century the Gokturk armies carried before them a golden wolf's head. Although the Oghuz clearly revered the wolf, they also had reason to fear it as an opportunistic raider of their livestock.

Given the central importance of the horse to the nomadic lifestyle and warrior culture of these peoples, it is no surprise that the horsetail—in addition to the wolf's head—was a symbol of rank and totemic power from the time of the Goturks in the sixth century to that of the Ottoman Empire one thousand years later. The *tugh*, or "horsetail banner," evoked the power and importance of the horse in the form of a ubiquitous totem that was explicitly linked to rank in a way that suggests that military power, individual virility, and political influence might be understood symbolically through an ancient emblem linking imperial officials and the military leaders with the central image of their nomadic past. Although amongst the Goturks the number of *tughs* varied according to one's status, in the course of the 10th and 11th centuries Oghuz khans often displayed nine. By the time of the Ottomans, the Sultan himself boasted six, whereas the governor of a province might unfurl two. The Ottoman appropriation of the ancient horsetail banner is especially noteworthy in the present context, because one might go so far as to suggest that the *tugh*—like the literary echo of a lost horse culture that comprises the *Book of Dede Korkut* itself—represents a self-conscious attempt on the part of later Ottomans to appropriate the heroic ethos of their Oghuz past.

It seems no coincidence that this tale features a tree upon the back of Karajuk and a gallows tree upon which Uruz is to be executed. The pagan Turks revered trees as the givers of life in myths that resonate with the Norse Yggdrasil and that northern tradition's vision of the rebirth of mankind after the Doom of the Gods. In pre-Islamic Turkish belief, mankind was spawned by the union of Father Beech and Mother Hazelnut, a life-giving association Uruz evokes in an Islamicized manner in his invocation to the protective nature of wood. The inversion of the Tree of Life theme in this passage also begs comparison to Crucifixion imagery: Clearly an ancient Turkic motif is inverted through the Gibbet Tree, and the sacrifice of the young hero, the princely son of the great khan Salur Kazan—who arrives in a *deus ex machina* fashion just as the condemned's prayer for deliverance leaves his lips—seems more than a little like a allusion to the Crucifixion of Christ; the Cross is often likewise portrayed as an inversion of the Tree of Life motif, and it seems startlingly coincidental that this theme is evoked directly after a reference to cannibalism that one might well read as an ironic Moslem appropriation of the concept of the Christian Eucharist as the body of Christ.

The Turkic Epic Hero Recast in a Classical Mold of a Giant-Slayer: How Basat Son of Uruz Defeated the Turkish Cyclops [5]

Once when the enemies of the Oghuz raided their encampment, Basat, the son of Uruz Koja, was lost as his people scattered in the darkness. A lioness found the abandoned infant and took him to her den, where she suckled him as one of her own. When time had passed and the Oghuz had returned to their encampment, the keeper of Uruz Koja's horses came before his khan and reported that a man-shaped lion was raiding the herds and sucking the blood of those he attacked. Grasping at once that this feral lion-boy might be his own long-lost son, Uruz sought out and brought back this wild-boy. However, The boy only remained in the camp of his father once Dede Korkut had granted him his name, *Basat*, "Attack-Horse," which emphasized his leonine nature and his preternatural heroism and abilities.

Sometime after the naming of Basat, the Oghuz moved to their summer pasturage. Uruz Koja had a shepherd named Konur Koja Saru Choban, who always went first with the herds. This year, as he came to the spring known as Uzan Pinar, he noticed that some of the animals had become distressed. He soon discovered that peris had taken over the spring, and when he saw them flying away he became inflamed with lust. Throwing his cloak over one before she could escape, he pinned her to the ground and had his way with her. However, when he realized that his herd was scattering, he leapt up, giving the peri a chance to spread her wings and fly away. As she disappeared she shouted to the shepherd that he had left in her care something he should retrieve in a year, and that he had brought ruination upon the Oghuz.

The next season the Oghuz returned to their pasturage, and again the shepherd Konur Koja preceded them with his herds. Again the sheep became agitated at the same spring. When the shepherd moved forward to investigate this disturbance, he saw a large glittering shape stuck in the ground. At his moment the peri reappeared, telling Konur Koja to claim what was his, but reminding the shepherd that he had brought doom down upon the heads of the Oghuz. Terrified by her words and horrified at the sight of the mysterious lump in the mud, the shepherd let fly a hail of stones from his sling, but as each shot found its mark the lumpy mass grew larger. Finally Konur Koja fled the scene, with his sheep at his heels.

It so chanced that Bayindir Khan happened by soon thereafter, surrounded by the Oghuz nobles; they saw in the mud of the spring a giant, formless mass, of which they could not tell the head from the tail. A warrior leapt from his mount and kicked the misshapen lump, but it simply grew in response; he kicked it again and again, and the lump grew and grew. Several other warriors joined in the kicking, and the mass grew all the more as a result. Finally, Uruz Koja himself dismounted and kicked the now towering mud-egg, and his spur split the mass down the middle, revealing a giant child, man-like in form except for one monstrous feature: It had a single eye in the middle of its forehead. Uruz Koja took up the baby in the folds of his garments and asked Bayindir Khan for the right to raise it as his own in the company of his son Basat. This request Bayindir Khan granted.

Uruz Koja took the child home and arranged for a wet-nurse to suckle it; the woman came and offered the infant her breast. With the first suck, the monstrous baby emptied her breast of milk; with the second, he emptied her body of blood; with the third, he took the soul from her corpse. Several other nurses died in the same way, until finally his fosterers attempted to feed him milk drawn from an animal, but a great vat-full proved insufficient to fill the monster. The child grew and grew, and began to walk and to play with other children; eventually it grew to massive size, with one great eye in the midst of its forehead, from which it took its name *Tepe Goz*, maturing eventually into the monocular giant known as "Pinnacle-Eye." However, even in its childhood Tepe Goz was vicious with others, chewing the nose from one playmate and eating the ear off another. Finally the uproar was such that Uruz Koja drove the boy from his tent.

When Tepe Goz was banished, his peri mother gave him a magic ring that would protect him from the swords and arrows of men. The One-Eyed Giant then left the domain of the Oghuz for a lofty peak, and from then on he spent his time raiding the roads and environs thereabout, slaying and eating those poor men unlucky enough to cross his path. Many men were sent to dispatch this man-eating monster, but to no avail: Their swords, arrows, and spears left him unscathed. Soon no shepherds nor herdsmen were left alive because Tepe Goz had gorged upon them all. Next he turned his insatiable appetite upon the Oghuz themselves.

The heroes of the Oghuz were therefore marshaled and marched in force against the great One-Eyed Giant; but Tepe Goz was too great for them, and soon they had cause to lament the rash decision to attack a man-eating monster. Pinnacle-Eye uprooted a mighty tree as his enemies came upon him, and, as the cream of Oghuz manhood advanced, he hurled the mighty missile, ripping a great gap in the ranks of the heroes and felling fifty or sixty warriors with this one blow. The One-Eyed Giant then slew many of the greatest men of arms from amongst the Oghuz. Seven times the Oghuz broke like a wave against a stone and ran back, and seven times Tepe Goz trapped the fleeing Oghuz and channeled them back to the place from whence they had come.

Finally the Oghuz acknowledged that they were completely within the giant's power, like lambs for the slaughter that he could herd as he pleased. They determined therefore to send Dede Korkut to come to terms with Tepe Goz. At first he of the Pinnacle-Eye demanded the flesh of 60 warriors a day to fill his greedy belly; however, Dede Korkut pointed out that at such a rate the Oghuz would soon be without warriors, and Tepe Goz without meat. However, the giant and the shaman came to craven cannibalistic terms soon enough: Dede Korkut promised two men and 500 sheep a day to sate the blood-thirsty monster's appetite, as well as two men to prepare the foul feast. The Oghuz arranged a lottery. Each family gave a son, until finally those who had given already were called upon to give again. A man named Kapak Kan had but two sons, and shortly after the first was taken, the second one was called to take his place in the giant's larder. The lad's mother, crazed with grief, sought a way to save her only remaining boy.

It so happened that Basat, son of Uruz, had recently been raiding in the lands of the infidels, and the doomed man's mother sought the tent of Basat, thinking that perhaps the hero had brought home a prisoner who might take her son's place. Having heard the woman recount the woes of the Oghuz and her own loss, Basat wept for his brother's death and offered the woman a captive to send in her second son's stead to provide fodder for the giant. Basat then went to his parents and announced his intention to avenge his brother upon one-eyed Tepe Goz. Although the princes of the Oghuz attempted to dissuade him from sacrificing himself upon such a hopeless quest, Basat was resolute, girded his loins, and set off for the giant's cave with a bunch of arrows in one hand, his bow in the other, and his sword thrust into his belt.

Drawing near to Salakhana, the peak where Tepe Goz made his abode, Basat saw the ogre sunning himself and quickly fitted an arrow on his string; although he let two missiles fly in rapid succession, both broke upon the monster's impenetrable hide and fell away in pieces, causing no harm at all to Tepe Goz, although he did call out to his cooks that the flies were biting viciously that day. The third arrow Basat let loose bounced off its target and fell to the ground before the giant, who looked up and spied his assailant. Roaring with mirth at such a pathetic attempt to wound him, Tepe Goz quickly snatched up the young hero, crying out to his servants that he had found another yearling lamb courtesy of the Oghuz, and commanded them to spit and roast his catch. Thrusting Basat into a boot for safekeeping, Tepe Goz took his afternoon nap.

Taking out his dagger, Basat quickly extricated himself from the giant's boot. Approaching the cooks, the hero asked how Tepe Goz best be attacked. It appeared, they informed him, that the giant was utterly invulnerable; no part of his body was made of flesh, they said, with the exception of his monocular orb. Hearing this, Basat crept to the side of the ogre, gently lifting up the eyelid; the single eye of the sleeping giant was, indeed, vulnerably fleshy. Seeing this, the hero commanded the cooks to heat the tip of the roasting spit; when the spit was fiery hot, Basat took it to the head of Tepe Goz, lifted the giant's eyelid, and—saying a quick prayer to glorify the name of the Prophet—thrust the point of the hot spit deep into the depths of the monster's lone eye, destroying it utterly. Tepe Goz woke with a cry of pain and despair that shook the very roots of the mountains; meanwhile, Basat leapt lightly into the cave of the giant, hiding himself amongst the ogre's sheep.

Knowing that his antagonist was hiding within the cavern, Tepe Goz straddled the entrance and called to his flock to come out to pasture.

As each beast passed through his legs, the giant ran his hands over its head. When the blinded ogre called out to his favorite ram—that with the white-starred forehead—Basat leapt upon the beast and slew it as it rose. Quickly flaying it—although leaving head and tail intact—the hero cast the bloody skin over himself and strode between the giant's legs. Suspecting treachery, Tepe Goz grabbed the ram's head by the snout, while Basat slipped between the giant's legs and escaped. Casting down the bloody skin, the giant called out to his nemesis, asking if he had escaped; Basat responded that the One God had been merciful.

The giant then cast his magical ring to the hero, assuring him that no weapon could hurt the wearer; as if to prove this point, Tepe Goz flailed at Basat with his knife but was unable to wound him. However, the ring rolled from Basat's finger and came to rest under the blinded monster's foot. The giant then requested his assailant to seal up against thieves the treasure chest that the blind giant was unable to see. Entering the room-sized chest, Basat stood agog at the riches before him. Meanwhile, when he was sure that his enemy had entered the vault, the giant took it up and made to shake it, thinking to dash Basat's brains out upon the walls of the chest. However, saying a prayer to the Almighty, Basat was able to invoke the Creator to cause the chest to open miraculously in seven places, and thus the hero escaped the prison of the giant's treasure chest just before Tepe Goz ground the vault to dust between his fingers.

Enraged that Basat had survived another attempt on his life, Tepe Goz sent the young hero into the cave to fetch the magical blade that might behead the giant. However, when Basat found this sword, he discovered that it was suspended by a chain from the middle of the ceiling of the cavern, that it never ceased sweeping back and forth, and that it could slice anything clean in two. The giant had been truthful when he stated that this was the only blade that might behead him, but he had clearly hoped that Basat would be cut to shreds in his attempt to gain the sword for this purpose. However, in this vain hope Tepe Goz was soon to be disappointed: Although the swinging sword sliced in twain Basat's own weapon—as well as a tree he brought to test its edge upon—the hero was able to claim the blade by loosing an arrow into the chain from which the sword was hanging, causing it to bury itself into the floor of the cave. Extracting the still moving sword from the stone, thrusting it into his own now empty scabbard, and holding it within by main force, Basat returned to face the now downhearted Tepe Goz.

Forcing Tepe Goz to kneel on the cave floor in front of him, Basat beheaded the giant with the monster's own sword. Then the hero took his enemy's head, made a hole in it, and ran his bowstring through it so that he might drag this gruesome trophy to the threshold of Tepe Goz's cave. The young hero then sent the cooks of the slain monster to gather the Oghuz nobles to come and see how their oppressor had been slain at the hand of Basat. When the rejoicing Oghuz arrived, they brought out the head of the One-Eyed Giant for all to see. Dede Korkut himself then sang a lay recounting the exploits of Basat, son of Uruz, who heroically avenged his brother's death and the humiliation and suffering of his people by slaying Pinnacle-Eye, the giant Tepe Goz, the single-orbed bastard son of a peri.

In its evocation of traditions as disparate as the Persian and the classical Greek, this tale amply illustrates the cultural influences of neighboring cultures—and, not incidentally, episodes and figures drawn from differing branches of Indo-European mythology—upon the epic cycle of the Turks. For example, the peris of this tale show the obvious influence of Persian mythology and folklore upon the Turkish tradition. The peris in Turkish tales tend toward the demonic and their name is generally used pejoratively, as evidenced by the fact that the term *perili* is still used in modern Turkish to denote possession or haunting by a devilish spirit. On the other hand, Basat's fosterage at the teat of the lioness exemplifies a folkloric motif that is common throughout the world, but that is best known from the Roman story of Romulus and Remus. Most compelling of all, given the obvious resonance between Basat's encounter with Tepe Goz and Odysseus's adventure in the cavern of Polyphemus—especially considering the fact that the world that produced the *Book of Dede Korkut* was heavily influenced by contact with Greek culture—it has long been suggested that the cave episode in the Turkish story was influenced by that in the classical Greek account. Considering that the Turkish conquest of Constantinople encompassed the absorption of the culture of late Byzantine *Rum* as much as its environs, it is hard to believe that the similarity between the lioness foster-mother and the wolf-mother of the founders of ancient Rome was lost upon the courtly audience of the *Book of Dede Korkut*, whether or not these particular episodes spring from related sources.

The misshapen misanthropic monster's life on the periphery of the world of men described in this tale is something of a commonplace across cultures, and might be thought to resonate somewhat with the description, to cite but one obvious example, of Grendel's life in the opening passages of *Beowulf.* Both monsters occupy a luminal space on the edges of civilization, both have a voracious appetite for human-flesh, both seem able to master great numbers of heroes with little effort, both are protected through enchantments, and both are closely associated with their mothers.

Violence begets violence in the Turkish tale of the One-Eyed Giant. Conceived through an act of violent rape, the otherworldly mud-egg containing the half-peri offspring of the guilty shepherd grows with each sling-stone and buffet it receives. As the peri herself told her attacker, his wanton act would rain destruction down upon the Oghuz. This abstract threat is rendered concrete in the person of Tepe Goz, and the means of his growth is an evocative testament to how the thoughtless, random violence of the Oghuz is to be returned to them 10-fold. The sins of the Oghuz in general, and of the shepherd Konur Koja in particular come back to haunt them in the form of this monster sprung from Oghuz loins who literally sucks the life out of his nursemaids and who maims his playmates through cannibalistic attacks upon their ears and noses. Interestingly, the foundling Tepe Goz's vampiric slaying of his nurses, whom he sucks dry of milk and then blood, may also serve as an inversion of the feral Basat's attack upon the horse herds, which were the most precious possessions of the nomadic Oghuz. In any case, there are several points of contact between the accounts of monster and hero in this tale.

The unusual origin and remarkable childhood feats of the hero clearly are manifested in the loss of the infant Basat, his adoption by the lioness, and his feral childhood, culminating in his bestial prowess in stalking, catching, and feeding from the stallions of the Oghuz herds. Moreover, the "wild-child" origin of this hero is counterbalanced by the conception and birth of his nemesis Tepe Goz. If the main thrust of the confrontation between this one-eyed giant and an Oghuz hero finds its parallel in one of the best-known episodes of classical mythology, the genesis of the monstrous Tepe Goz draws upon a folkloric theme widely known throughout world folklore. Commonly known as the Swan Maiden Tale, this motif involves a mortal man who gains an otherworldly wife by stealing her magical feather-coat while she bathes; thus unable to take her animal form and flee, the Swan Maiden is at the mercy of her captor. The man and maiden generally marry, sometimes producing offspring, before the husband breaks one of the conditions of their marriage, thus losing his wife. In most versions of the folktale the distraught man seeks and often wins back his lost spouse. Although this version of the story omits the reunion of the husband and wife, and indeed fails to detail the specific reason for her departure, the otherworldly wife theme offers an evocative explanation for Tepe Goz's supernatural attributes, and his monstrosity may suggest the taboo that resulted in the Swan Wife's departure. Certainly this folkloric origin offers a compelling lens through which we may understand the malformed mass from which Tepe Goz is hatched. This rocky lump seems literally and metaphorically to represent an egg.

The magic ring motif is common in world folklore, although here it might be seen to have resonance with what is sometimes called the Valkyrie reflex, a thematic descendant of narrative aspects associated with ancient Indo-European battle-goddesses that may survive in attributes of the peri of this tale. Many readers might associate aspects of the Valkyrie reflex concerning a magical ring most closely with the Sigurd and Brunhild of Scandinavian lore. However, the function of the ring and the nature of its protection is somewhat unclear in this text. When Basat consulted with the giant's captive cooks, they suggested that his only point of vulnerability was his eye, stating that this gristly orb was in fact the only flesh on the body of Tepe Goz; the implication may be that the ring provided magical protection for all of the body with the exception of the eye. Given the detail that the eye was Tepe Goz's only fleshy organ, it is perhaps logical to assume that the ring did not simply project some sort of abstract magical shield, but that the giant may have developed a protective horny hide as a result of possessing his mother's ring. Presumably such an armored covering would fail to protect the eye.

The episode of Basat within Tepe Goz's cave bears a striking resemblance to that in the *Odyssey* in which the eponymous hero blinds and then escapes from the Cyclops Polyphemus. The blinding of the One-Eyed Giant, the hero's sojourn in his enemy's lair, the daring escape of the protagonist in the guise of a sheep, and the giant's loving words toward his ram all offer direct parallels between the classical tale and its Turkish variation. In any case, some have suggested that the ring episode is a conflation from an entirely different source that makes little sense in the context of the Polyphemus plotline. Certainly the giant would have no reason to share his magical protection with the enemy who blinded him, and he most certainly would not expect to be able to wound anyone wearing his ring. It is possible that an earlier form of the narrative included a sequence wherein the hero stole the magic ring from the slumbering giant, which could also explicate his ability to blind the monster. It has been suggested that in such a storyline, the Basat might have been cuffed by the Tepe Goz and the force of the blow—although unable to penetrate the magical protection imparted by the ring, and thus to hurt the hero—might have caused the ring, which was surely far too large for a human finger, to fly off of Basat's hand and roll beneath Tepe Goz's foot.

It is worth noting the repetitive ritual invocation of the Almighty and his prophet throughout this tale, most notably in Basat's miraculous escape from the blinded giant's treasure chest. This act of divine intervention is explicitly triggered by the hero's ritual recitation of the foundational precepts of Islam; that is, that there is no God but Allah, and that Muhammad is his messenger. This particular scene distills and crystallizes the essence of the layering of mythologies in the tale of Basat and Tepe Goz: An Islamic prayer breaks the strongbox and foretells the doom of the classical cyclops that has been translated into a heroic Turkic context.

Basat's claiming of the magical sword by which the giant may be decapitated resonates with the story of many a hero who comes of age by claiming a marvelous blade. In his pulling of the wriggling sword from the solid rock of the cavern floor in which it had embedded itself, Basat might be compared to the young Arthur who marks himself as king by pulling the sword from the stone. The ritual exorcism through decapitation of the bloodthirsty otherworldly demon evokes similar tales such as that of Beowulf and Grendel or that of Grettir and Glamr. Moreover, the phallic significance of the young hero who enters into manhood by claiming a sword must not be overlooked, especially in the context of ritual decapitation. Such episodes are sometimes overtly imbued with fertility imagery and sexual subtext, as in the story of Sir Gawain's encounter with the Greene Knight or Culhwch's with Chief Giant Ysbaddaden.

Notes

1. For more information concerning the historical context of the *Book of Dede Korkut*, see especially Cahen 1–3, 7–15; Kennedy 343–345; Lapidus 142, 144–145, 303–322; Lewis 9–12; and Reichl 43–55.

2. For critical commentary on and analysis of the sources, manuscripts, and structure of the *Book of Dede Korkut*, see especially Cahen 1–3, 7–15; Kennedy 343–345; Lapidus 303–322; Lewis 10–23; Reichl 43–44, 54–55; and Sumer, Uysal, & Walker ix–xxiii, 177–180.

3. For critical commentary on and analysis of the story of Boghach Khan, see especially Lewis 27–41, 195–196; Reichl 44–53, 164; Silay 128, 144; and Sumer, Uysal, & Walker 9–22, 182–185.

4. For critical commentary on and analysis of the story of Salur Kazan, see especially Lewis 42–58, 196–199; and Sumer, Uysal, & Walker 23–39, 185–189.

5. For critical commentary on and analysis of the story of Basat and Tepe Goz, see especially Lewis 140–150, 205–206; Reichl 53; and Sumer, Uysal, & Walker 122–133, 199–201.

Sources and Further Reading

Andrews, Walter G., and James Stewart-Robinson. *Intersections in Turkish Literature: Essays in Honor of James Stewart-Robinson.* Ann Arbor: University of Michigan Press, 2001.

Cahen, Claude, and P. M. Holt. *The Formation of Turkey: The Seljukid Sultanate of Rüm: Eleventh to Fourteenth Century.* A history of the Near East. Harlow, United Kingdom: Longman, 2001.

Chadwick, Nora K., and Viktor Maksimovich Zhirmunskĭ. *Oral Epics of Central Asia.* London: Cambridge University Press, 1969.

Clauson, Gerard. *An Etymological Dictionary of Pre-Thirteenth-Century Turkish.* Oxford: Clarendon Press, 1972.

Findley, Carter V. *The Turks in World History.* New York: Oxford University Press, 2005.

Kennedy, Hugh. *The Prophet and the Age of the Caliphates: The Islamic Near East from the Sixth to the Eleventh Century.* Harlow, United Kingdom: Pearson/Longman, 2004.

Lapidus, Ira M. *A History of Islamic Societies.* Cambridge, United Kingdom: Cambridge University Press, 2002.

Lewis, Geoffrey. *The Book of Dede Korkut.* Harmondsworth, United Kingdom: Penguin, 1974.

Nerimanoğlu, Kamil Veli. *The Poetics of "The Book of Dede Korkut."* Maltepe, Ankara, Turkey: Atatürk Culture Center Publications, 1998.

Reichl, Karl. *Turkic Oral Epic Poetry: Tradition, Forms, Poetic Structure.* New York: Garland, 1992.

Sılay, Kemal. *Nedim and the Poetics of the Ottoman Court: Medieval Inheritance and the Need for Change.* Bloomington: Indiana University, 1994.

Sümer, Faruk, Ahmet Edip Uysal, and Warren S. Walker. *The Book of Dede Korkut: A Turkish Epic.* Austin: University of Texas Press, 1991.

The Arabian Every-Man Hero

The Historical Context of Medieval Arabia[1]

Who Was the Prophet Muhammad?

In the early seventh century a voice from the hinterlands of the Arabian Peninsula issued a clarion call for humility before a single, Almighty God, a spiritual invitation demanding the reformation of the individual soul, the larger society, and the world itself. This call issued from the town of Mecca, in the person of Muhammad. Muhammad was born around 570 AD into a minor house of the Quraysh tribe, traders who had relationships extending throughout the pale of Mecca, south along the coast of the Arabian Peninsula, and north as far as Syria. This group also seems to have had some responsibility for the shrine known as the Ka'ba, the site where the pre-Islamic Meccan gods were housed and venerated. This particular aspect of his family's historical duties was to loom large after the advent of Islam.

Muhammad married a widow and managed her business affairs for her, becoming around the age of forty something of a recluse who sought the will of God in the wilderness. After a time, Muhammad received direction from God in the form of an angelic messenger. On what was to become known as the Night of Destiny, Muhammad was granted a vision of the path he was to follow: As the anointed Prophet of the Almighty, Muhammad was to teach a faith based on total submission to the will of God, a submission rooted in ritual acts, prayers, observances, and abstinence as well as in spiritual humility. Muhammad preached the worship of one omnipotent God, whom he called Allah, borrowing a name from an ancient local pagan deity. This new religion was known as Islam, meaning "surrender" or the "complete submission" before the will of Allah; adherents were known as Moslems, a term from the same root that basically denotes those who submit to God. Moslems date the beginning of the Islamic era from the *Hijra*; that is, from the time that Muhammad moved from Mecca to Medina—his "flight," or, more properly, his "emigration," which is to say in the year 622 of the Christian era.

The Literary Context of Medieval Arabia[2]

Medieval Arabic literature combined elements of traditional Arabic narratives and motifs, paeans to the glorious submission of the detractors of the Prophet and the enemies of Islam, and external textual and thematic influences, notably from Persian and Hellenic literatures. Although the court cultivated and embraced a vibrant literary culture—especially insofar as such a culture extended the agenda of the Caliphate—Arabic literature of the medieval period certainly had popular as well as erudite sources and audiences. Much of Arabic literary culture, especially in the early period of Islam, was essentially an outgrowth of Koranic studies, the branch of knowledge concerned with the Word of God. The *Qu'ran*, often known as the Koran in Western sources, is the scriptural testament to God's revelations to his Prophet Muhammad.

As numerous external linguistic and sophisticated literary movements and influences threatened to establish new norms in the Arabic language, Koranic scholars based in Basra in the eighth century attempted to fix and stabilize a form of classical Arabic that would remain faithful to the Meccan dialect of Muhammad and thus would ground the meaning of the Qu'ran in an immutable language through which the will of Allah might be faithfully discerned. As part of this attempt to quantify and codify a static Arabic language of the period of the Prophet, scholars recorded in written form a great deal of oral Bedouin poetry, aphoristic lore, and popular stories, thus to a certain extent enshrining pre-Islamic oral Arabic culture in the process.

The Enchanted Lamp of Medieval Arabian Myth, Legend, and Folklore: Sources, Manuscripts, and Structure of the *Alf-Layla Wa-Layla (The Thousand and One Nights)* [3]

The earliest narrative well-springs that would one day produce the *Thousand and One Nights* we know today entered the Arabic world some thirteen hundred years ago. It is of particular note in the context of a study that concerns, in great part, Indo-European sources of myth, legend, and folklore that the two great *ur*-sources of the massive compilation of medieval Arabic tales of the fantastic came from India and Persia, homes of the best-developed early Indo-European mythic traditions. The Persian *Hazar Afsaneh* was translated into Arabic in the early eighth century and became known as the *Alf Layla*; both titles mean "A Thousand Nights," although we are assured by the 10th century book-cataloguer Ibn al-Nadim that the Persian original only had approximately two hundred stories, the content of which the bookseller did not find compelling. During the 9th and 10th centuries, Arabic threads began to be woven into the tapestry of the *Alf Layla*, first in the form of shorter stories but eventually including longer cycles.

The earliest extant manuscript fragment of a text entitled *Kitab Hadith Alf Layla*, or "The Book of the Tale of the Thousand Nights," is from ninth century Egypt. Only a portion of this narrative survives, but it includes the title and the basic premise that a character named Dinazad asks one by the name of Shirazad to tell her a story pertaining to the virtues and vices of men. This clearly is a narrative seed that will over time blossom into the form familiar to modern readers. Moreover, this earliest example hardly existed in a vacuum because we have records from as early as the 12th century indicating that a book known as *The Thousand and One Nights* was circulating widely. Additional tales—often concerning sex, magic, and the shenanigans of the lower classes—found their way into the collection from Syrian and Egyptian sources in the course of the 1200s and afterwards.

The narrative development of *The Thousand and One Nights* might thus be examined in layers. A Persian fabric, some of which was Indian in ultimate origin, was embroidered with Arabic threads. The first Arabic version of the Persian collection comprises what is known as the "Baghdad" material and was augmented with the frame tale technique. The later layer includes what is called the "Cairo" material, resulting ultimately in a Syrian tradition that provided the manuscript that offered the foundation for the first European edition of the tales. Unfortunately, the complex and somewhat speculative story of the origins and development of the *Nights* has not been clarified overmuch by its transmission by Western hands, nor did such treatment emphasize the most sophisticated literary elements of the collection.

Although it is clear that some versions of certain component tales had been transmitted into Western texts during the Middle Ages and the

Renaissance, the first European edition of a version of *The Thousand and One Nights* proper was produced by Antoine Galland in the opening years of the 18th century on the basis of his translation of a 14th or 15th century manuscript. Like the Medieval and Renaissance audiences that preceded them, early readers of the Galland version of the tales seem to have been imbued with a desire for exotic entertainment, and thus these stories were seen as little more than fairy tales set in a faraway land. This perception reflects in some measure a fundamental reason for some of the scholarly Arab disdain for these tales, a contempt that was in no way alleviated by popular European sentiments concerning the charm and quaintness of this collection. Indeed, it was only a century or so Galland's edition, with the advent of Orientalism as a scholarly discipline, that the tales in this collection began to be analyzed with any sort of academic rigor by Europeans.

Arab dislike for the *Nights*, at least in scholarly circles, seems to have had developed fairly early in the history of the compilation of the text. Critics have identified several possible reasons for this trend. These were popular, oral tales, some of which clearly had origins in the lower strata of the society that gave birth to them. In addition, the morals offered by these tales might not always have been in synch with those of the dominant elites, just as the protagonists and narrative voices of the tales were drawn from the lower and the upper echelons of society. In short, the tone, compositional methods, and heroes of the *Nights* might simply have provided a discordant note in the rich symphony of medieval Arabic literature, a supposition that suggests another reason why the *Nights* is often perceived as one of a kind.

Moreover, some scholars have suggested that the fact that the voices that indicate that this text circulated early and widely for the most part exist in an environment of deafening silence suggests that this compendium of folklore, myth, and magic enjoyed popular acclaim and critical disdain. In other words, the evidence of the existence and transmission of various versions of the tales we know as *The Thousand and One Nights* is indisputable. Developing versions of these tales were known in the Arab world from at least the eighth century on, and it is attested by contemporary sources that they were well known throughout the Middle Ages. That said, Ibn al-Nadim's 10th-century critique of the Persian source text might well speak to scholarly reception of the tales throughout the medieval period.

What Is a "Frame Tale"?

The "frame tale" comprises, as its name suggests, a narrative structure that encloses a selection of other stories; the characters within the frame tale recount and comment upon those interior narratives. The frame tale itself, although following a plot of its own, is structured around and relies upon the stories its characters tell, and its fundamental purpose is the presentation of those inner tales. Moreover, these fictional narrators provide an interior mechanism through which the text can comment upon some components of itself, therefore allowing the frame tale to provide context for and even criticism of the various stories included in the larger work. Frame tales can gather unto themselves all manner of stories and indeed often contain a large proportion of traditional oral narratives. Thus, frame tales could act as the means of preserving and transmitting oral storytelling modes, methods, and material, including not insubstantial quantities of folklore, legend, and even myth.

The frame tale is at least three thousand years old, originating in Asia, most probably in India. By the 10th century after Christ frame tales were known in the Middle East, and the earliest European examples date from about two centuries later. The frame tale reached the high point of its popularity in Europe about 200 years after that, culminating in the *Decameron* of Boccaccio and the *Canterbury Tales* of Chaucer, the two best-known examples of medieval European frame tales. However, *The Thousand and One Nights* is perhaps the very model of the frame tale, using at times as many as five layers of narrators to lead the reader through stories within stories. The basic structure of the frame of the *Nights* is simple.

Shahriyar, a tyrannical ruler and despotic husband, takes a new virgin to wife each day, consummates the marriage that evening, and has his new bride executed in the morning, all to salve his anxiety that all women are inherently deceitful by thus nipping in the bud any possibility of marital infidelity. This brutal reign of terror is a pestilence that threatens to destroy every marriageable maiden in the kingdom, thus leaving it barren. However, Shahriyar finally marries Sheherazade, who is an epitome of wifely virtue and a fascinating and indefatigable storyteller, a seemingly boundless source of wit and wisdom. Each night Sheherazade tells Shahriyar another entertaining and engaging story, keeping him in suspense so that he spares her life night after night in his desire to learn what will happen next in the marvelous tapestry of tales woven by his wife.

Sheherazade is at one and the same time a paragon of virtue and an emblem of fertility in terms of womanhood and those of narrative. Indeed, through her apparently endless stream of stories she keeps herself alive for several years, during which time she gives birth to three sons. She also proves loyal and steadfast to her bloodthirsty husband, illustrating for him once and for all that women are worthy of love and respect. Sheherazade thus effectively ensures the reproductive vitality of a kingdom on the brink of sterility, all of the while instilling in Shahriyar a passion for well-told tales. Her modes of telling tales and her numerous narrative devices offer a primer of storytelling technique in addition to the captivating content of the stories themselves. Indeed, while saving herself and the virgins of her kingdom, Sheherazade concurrently conceives and gives birth to the best-loved and most widely-known stories from the medieval Middle East, and although many of these tales may abound with crude and immoral material, they often impart important moral lessons and keep popular wisdom from a range of ages and cultures alive and fresh.

The Everyman Arabian Hero Descends Into The Underworld: Aladdin Finds the Magic Lamp That Illuminates Medieval Arabian Myth[4]

Aladdin's descent into the treasure vault where he obtains the magic lamp is the most well known of the tales in the *Nights*; it is also an obvious example of the archetype of the hero's descent into the otherworld. In this context this episode also performs the function of the hero's coming-of-age adventure. Aladdin has, up until the time of the appearance of a North African sorcerer, been something of a ne'er-do-well. The appearance of the sorcerer, an evil Moorish dervish who wishes to use Aladdin to his own selfish ends, marks the beginning of a transformation that eventually results in a heroic, confident, and responsible Aladdin who is fit, not just to run his own humble father's shop, but to rule upon his royal father-in-law's throne.

The dervish in question masqueraded as Aladdin's long-lost uncle and treated the boy and his mother liberally to allay any possible suspicion. However, unbeknownst to them, the wizard had secretly ascertained that Aladdin was in fact the only person who could safely retrieve from its underground vault a certain treasure after which the dervish lusted. Having gained the confidence of his intended victim, the sorcerer invited the boy to wander with him, eventually arriving at a high mountain well outside of the city gates where he had divined that the hidden treasure he sought lay in a hidden cavern.

Bidding Aladdin be seated and rest himself, the wizard began his incantations: The sky grew dark and the earth quaked, and a mighty crevasse open up right at the feet of Aladdin and the wizard. At the base of the opening was a large trapdoor of marble topped with a giant copper ring. The dervish sought to send Aladdin into these depths because he understood the boy to be the only being who might brave the dangers therein and survive, but the lad himself was terrified and desired nothing so much as to flee the spot. Enraged, the sorcerer cuffed the boy with such a blow that Aladdin was knocked completely senseless.

When the lad regained consciousness, the deceitful wizard revealed to the boy that Aladdin alone of the entire world could enter the cavern beneath them and bring back a fabulous treasure, which the sorcerer claimed he intended to share equally with Aladdin. All Aladdin need do to see his fondest wishes come true, claimed the dervish, was descend into the depths, follow the wizard's instructions to the letter, and bring back the treasure below. Aladdin immediately agreed to do as he was bid.

Although he feared the marble slab would prove far too heavy for him, Aladdin followed the wizard's instructions, speaking his name and his mother's and his father's. He then found that he was able to lift the door single-handedly almost without effort, and he peered into the cavern below. The wizard gave the boy careful instructions to pass down the steps, through four chambers overflowing with treasure, and through another doorway that would open into a fragrant and beautiful garden. However, the dervish warned Aladdin in the sternest terms that he must under no circumstances touch—or even so much as allow his robes to touch—any of the treasure within the subterranean chambers, or even the walls thereof: To do so would result in instant petrification. Once on the threshold of the garden, Aladdin was once again to speak the names that had granted him entry into the cavern.

Once inside of the garden, the boy was to make his way up several steps and across a wide veranda to a lamp hanging from a chain. The lad was to empty the oil from the lamp and secret this treasure within his robes. Only then was Aladdin to make his way back to the entry into the cavern. The dervish then informed the boy that he might help himself to the fruit of the trees as these pleased him. The sorcerer also gave to the lad a ring that he claimed would keep the boy safe from any hazards he might face, emphasizing that Aladdin stood not only on the threshold of a mystical cavern and at the frontier of magic and riches, but also on the very verge of manhood itself, and he admonished his "nephew" to act accordingly and to be a heroic man rather than a callow youth.

Aladdin followed the wizard's instructions to the letter, finding his way through the cavern and the chambers and the garden, procuring the lamp, and returning through the garden, wherein he stuffed his pockets full to bursting of the fruit of the trees. However, the growth of this garden was not edible but rather it was gems and jewels and colored stones of the most precious kinds—rubies, emeralds, diamonds, and the like. However, Aladdin was so naïve and unsophisticated that he took these priceless treasures to be mere baubles of sparkling and colored glass, and he gathered them as a child or a senseless animal might, because they caught his eye and tickled his fancy, not because he thought them valuable.

When he could carry no more, Aladdin retraced his steps back to the staircase into the cavern. However, when he reached the topmost step, he found that it was a bit steeper than the rest, and that he could not quite manage to surmount it. Calling out to the man he took to be his uncle, Aladdin asked for a hand up out of the cavern. The wizard replied that it was the lamp that overly burdened the boy, and that Aladdin should pass that treasure up and he would find himself able to climb the step. However, the boy replied truthfully that laden as he was he could not reach into his robes to grasp the lamp and thereby hand it to his uncle.

Believing himself thwarted and betrayed by the boy he had come so far to dupe and to use as his tool, the sorcerer spoke a spell more fearsome and fell than the last; the great stone slab slammed shut in accordance with this incantation, and Aladdin found himself imprisoned in the inky blackness of the cavern that had suddenly become his crypt. Lamenting his fate and realizing that no brother of his father would ever have imprisoned and abandoned him, Aladdin came to the conclusion that he had been the stooge of a wizard who was no kin to him. The sorcerer, for his part, seeing his life's labor wasted in the vain pursuit of a great treasure that he would rather forsake to the depths than risk falling into the possession of a rival, thought nothing of entombing Aladdin with the lamp. Unable to fulfill his quest, the wizard spent his rage upon the hapless boy and then returned to his own country.

Trapped beneath the ground and unable to see, Aladdin attempted to grope his way back to the magical gardens, only to find that the cavern had been sealed on both ends. Giving himself up into the grip of despair, Aladdin spent three days and nights without food or drink in the darkness of the cave. Finally, clasping his hands in utter hopelessness, the lad chanced to rub the ring the wizard had given to him, thus unwittingly summoning the potent spirit that dwelt therein, who brought him once more to the surface of the Earth. Aladdin subsequently made his way home; discovered the secret of the lamp; and gained power, riches, and the daughter of the sultan only to lose them all to the cunning of the Moorish wizard, who discovered through his arts of divination that Aladdin had escaped his cavernous tomb. However, in the end Aladdin proved more than a match for his enemy in a battle of wits, and he regained the lamp and decapitated the Moor, thus completing a journey to full maturity begun under that selfsame wizard's tutelage deep in the bowels of the magic cavern. Aladdin emerged from this journey no longer an immature boy but a grown man and a fully developed hero capable of ascending from the depths of the Underworld to the heights of the sultan's throne, to which he was raised upon the death of his father-in-law.

In addition to the clear resonance between Aladdin's descent into the magic cavern and the hero's archetypal plunge into the Underworld, any journey through a forbidden and treacherous garden bears some passing resonance with the Garden of Eden, especially with reference to the fruits of the trees, precious gems that Aladdin in his innocence does not understand for what they are but he is attracted to them merely for their beauty. Given his demonic powers and evil intent, it is not difficult to see aspects of the satanic in the Moorish dervish, an association that is subtly emphasized by the encouragement he offers to Aladdin to partake of the fruits of the trees of the garden. Moreover, the servant spirits abiding in the magic ring and the enchanted lamp provide the most well-known introduction to Western readers of medieval Arabic spiritual beings such as the *jinn* and the *ifrit*, which merit a dedicated discussion in a section of their own.

Although the dervish attempts to manipulate Aladdin solely to further his own ends and has no scruples about sacrificing the boy on the altar of his own inexorable greed, it is noteworthy that time and again early in the tale the wizard plays on the lad's feelings of inadequacy to spur him on. However, what is most intriguing about this subtext is that—in the end—Aladdin's journey into the Underworld becomes in fact a rite of passage through which the selfish and foolhardy boy begins to travel the road to self-actualization that ultimately leads to maturity, wisdom, and self-confidence. Thus, the dervish's words are truer than he knows, and in the end Aladdin profits immeasurably through the wizard's self-centered ploy that sends him into the depths of the Earth.

Sibling Rivalry and the Everyman Arabian Hero: Judar and the Treasures of Al-Shamardal[5]

Like Aladdin, Judar undertakes a journey to the Underworld. Moreover, the tale of Judar, although sharing several significant elements and motifs with that of Aladdin, extends more fully and more clearly the archetypes of the young hero coming of age through his subterranean journey. However, Judar is more of a protohero right from the onset. In contrast to the vain and self-centered Aladdin, who was a parasitic youth whose long-suffering mother was forced to support him despite his lazy ways, Judar is the exact opposite and turns to fishing specifically so that he may take care of his mother. In addition, whereas Aladdin is a spoiled and unworthy only child, Judar is the wronged younger brother of lesser siblings. However, the hidden value of each is soon manifested by the fact that both young men are sought out by sorcerers. It quickly becomes clear in each story that the protagonist is destined for great things because the wizards in each case have divined that the given seemingly nondescript young man is in his particular case the only individual who may gain a great treasure.

Whereas a single sorcerer who posed as Aladdin's uncle sought the boy across a vast distance and found him loitering in the streets not far from his home, Judar seems to have been lured to the location where he came across the first of four magician brothers who were seeking the elusive treasure of the mighty enchanter al-Shamardal. The young fisherman, who had for some time been able to pull up his family's daily needs in his nets without excessive effort, suffered a week without a catch before he determined to travel a bit further afield and ply his trade along the shores of Lake Karun, outside of Cairo. However, as he approached the edge of the water he was greeted by name by a stranger, a richly garbed Moor astride a mule encumbered with an ornately adorned saddle and saddlebag. The traveler presented Judar with an unusual request: After ritually chanting the first chapter of the Koran, Judar was to bind the Moor's arms tightly at the elbows and cast the stranger into the lake. If the traveler's arms were to rise above the level of the water, Judar was to cast his net immediately to the man and thus to save him; however, if the Moor's feet were to bob to the surface, Judar would know his new acquaintance to be dead and was then to seek a certain trader in the markets of Cairo, a merchant who would take charge of the Moor's mule and give Judar one hundred dinars for his trouble with the provision that Judar keep these events a secret. Judar did as he was asked, and when the Moor's feet broke the surface of the lake he knew the traveler was dead and thus took the mule to the market, where he received his one hundred dinars.

The next day Judar returned to Lake Karun, where he encountered another richly-robed Moor mounted upon a mule with a fine saddle and a saddlebag containing two elegant boxes. The stranger asked Judar if he had met another man dressed as he was the day before. At first the fisherman denied having met such a man, but he relented when it became clear that the second stranger knew the whole story. This second Moor then revealed himself to be the brother of the first and asked Judar to do for him what he had done for the first brother. The fisherman agreed, and soon a second drowned Moor bobbed amongst the waves of the lake and Judar found himself receiving another hundred dinars for the mule in the marketplace. The third day the fisherman returned to Lake Karun ready and willing to provide the same service to as many Moors as might avail themselves of it. A third stranger, robed in even more costly garments than the first two, did indeed appear and he greeted Judar. At first the story seemed destined to repeat itself once more; however, this time the fisherman was amazed to see hands reach out of the water instead of feet, and he quickly fulfilled his end of the bargain by casting his net out and hauling in the soaking wet Moor, who grasped in each hand a bright red fish. As the Moor's feet touched the shore he called out for Judar to bring to him the two elegantly worked boxes from the richly embroidered saddlebag upon the mule's back, and this the fisherman did. Into each casket the Moor thrust one of the fish and then quickly locked each lid back in place.

The Moor then revealed that he was one of four brothers who were the sons of a great enchanter. When their father died they divided his possessions equally, but they argued over a great tome of magic that offered all of the secrets of the universe. Their dispute reach such a level of contention that finally their father's venerable master—under whose tutelage their father had grasped the subtle niceties of sorcery—intervened and decreed that only he who opened the cavern of al-Shamardal and gained the magical treasures of that enchanter might gain the tome, which the old lore-master would only offer in exchange for the sword, ring, vial, and crystal ball of al-Shamardal. Each of these treasures had marvelous qualities: The flaming sword ensured victory for its possessor, whereas Crackling Thunder, the Jinn of the ring, was powerful enough to grant his master control over all the earth. The kohl in the vial, when applied beneath the eyes, opened up every subterranean treasure for examination, whereas the crystal ball offered vision across the entire world and the ability to focus the rays of the Sun upon one's enemies and thus to destroy them in a holocaust of flame. These great treasures of al-Shamardal, which the master demanded in exchange for the Tome of All Knowledge, was under the protection of the sons of the Red King, powerful spirits who had transformed themselves into red fish in Lake Karun. The old master foresaw that it was only with the help of the fisherman Judar that one of the sons would be successful, and it would be clear which was the son fated to succeed when each matched wits in turn against the sons of the Red King. He who stepped back ashore alive after that encounter would gain, with the help of Judar, the treasures of al-Shamardal, and he would thus gain the tome he desired.

Having been provided with a quantity of gold for the maintenance of his mother in his absence, Judar agreed to go with the Moor in pursuit of the treasures of al-Shamardal, which would only be revealed in the presence of the humble fisherman. Judar soon had reason to wonder at the powers of his companion, who took them across vast distances in short spans of time with the help of a jinn in the form of a mule, and who provided endless, mother-watering banquets out of his saddlebag, which was also possessed by a jinn. Having rested some time at the house of the Moor, upon the appointed day Judar and his companion went to a particular spot on the banks of a river where the enchanter was to open the way for Judar to reach the treasures of al-Shamardal. Bringing forth the two sons of the Red King, the Moor caused them to reveal their true forms and forced them to promise to open the gates to the hidden treasures. Then the conjurer began reciting the spells needful to allow Judar access to the resting place of the treasures, but not before carefully instructing the fisherman concerning the challenges and obstacles he was to face and exactly how to navigate each successfully. He described seven doors behind which lay seven phantoms, figures of fear but not substance, so long as Judar followed his instructions carefully. Beyond these seven perils he would find a hall full of treasure, which he should ignore, and within it a small tabernacle that contained the sleeping form of al-Shamardal, reclined upon a couch of gold, surrounded by the four treasures that the Moor sought and which Judar was to win for him; these the fisherman was to claim and to bring to the sorcerer.

When the enchanter had completed his spell, the river immediately disappeared and across its parched bed Judar discerned a great golden door with two door-rings that were like that unto the gate in a city wall. Following the instructions of the Moor, the fisherman approached the door and gave a stipulated series of knocks. Finally, after Judar had been asked his name and had given it, the door was opened by the figure of a man brandishing a sword who demanded that the fisherman offer his neck to the blade. Doing as the Moor had bade him, Judar lowered his head and accepted the blow without flinching, which caused the phantom to dissipate; had he quailed under the blow, the sorcerer had assured him, Judar would have been slain. In a similar manner Judar was challenged at a series of doors in turn by a warrior with a spear, another with bow and arrow, a lion, a huge African eunuch who demanded once more that Judar identify himself, and two mighty serpents who might only be reached by an invocation to Jesus and Moses. However, at the seventh door Judar had his most perilous encounter: In this chamber, Judar encountered a spirit in the shape of his mother, whom he was required to force to disrobe entirely by brandishing the sword he found mounted upon the wall.

This final challenge proved too much for the poor fisherman, and when he had forced the figure of his mother to remove all but her undergarments he relented rather than see his mother's naked form, and this modesty was his undoing. Calling to all of the other spirits to help, the shape of Judar's mother thrashed the boy to within an inch of his life and cast him out into the river, which rushed to fill its bed once more.

Totally humiliated and badly beaten, Judar had to face the wrath of the Moor and his own shame for a full year until he could attempt to reenter the treasure-trove on the appointed day. This time he made no mistake, and having defeated all seven phantoms, Judar entered the tabernacle of al-Shamardal. The fisherman then claimed the sword, the orb, and the vial of the enchanter and departed from the underground vault to the strains of a triumphant march and the voices of the guardians of the treasure singing the praises of Judar the son of Omar, he who gained the fabled treasure of al-Shamardal. In exchange for the magical talismans he had so long sought, and as a reward for Judar's faithfulness and courage, the Moorish sorcerer sent Judar home with the jinn-possessed bag of plenty, along with another bag brimming with gold and jewels. He then mounted the fisherman upon a mule and sent a slave to guide him to his native land. Although his brothers attempted to steal his wealth and magic bag by selling him into bondage in another land, Judar eventually escaped and was reunited with his friend the Moorish enchanter, who repaid his loyalty once more, this time with the magic ring wherein abided Crackling Thunder the Jinn. Returning home thus empowered, Judar eventually rose to such a high station that he was able to marry none other than the sultan's daughter, and after the death of her father Judar himself became the lord of that domain. Judar continued to love and forgive his faithless brothers who had always cheated him and robbed their mother until one day they betrayed and murdered him. However, Judar's loving wife avenged him, faithful always to the memory of Judar the son of Omar, the humble fisherman who descended into the treasure house of the great enchanter al-Shamardal and emerged with the most powerful magical objects in the world.

Several elements in this tale seem to evoke rites and rituals of initiation; in addition, the ritual recitation of Koranic passages as part of the sorcerer's descent into the depths of Lake Karun seems to evoke a folkloric practice of incantation. Whereas on the one hand the magic ring, the magic bag, and the spirits that possess them are classic manifestations of lore associated with the Arabic figure of the jinn, the jinn-inhabited saddle bag also evokes the ancient cornucopia fertility theme that is well known in

Western European traditions (e.g., through the Cauldron of Plenty). The tale of Judar clearly evokes the archetype of the young hero who descends to the Underworld, conquers the monsters there, and ascends a mature and courageous man bearing a great treasure. The universal coming-of-age motif in this story is representative of the struggle of a young man to face the fears and uncertainties of adulthood. At the same time, this episode bears some resemblance to initiation rites that promise manhood for that postulant courageous enough to risk death itself and willing along the way to face down childhood fears and to sacrifice family ties. The final challenge, which seems to require heartlessly debasing the young man's mother, is especially evocative of such an initiation by trial. Like the biblical Joseph, Judar is a worthy youngest son whose older siblings hate him for supplanting them in their father's affection. Judar is also sold into slavery by his jealous siblings, and like Joseph he escapes this bondage through natural abilities and the workings of inscrutable powers, eventually rising to high station and great esteem in the eyes of the King of Egypt.

However, the setting of this tale is significant above and beyond the resonance it provides with the Biblical account of Joseph; indeed, this story is indicative of an entire subclass of tales in the *Nights*, a category not coincidentally largely of Egyptian origin that dealt with the practices, perils, and potential rewards of the *mutalib*, or the professional treasure hunter. Egypt, of course, as the Land of the Pharaohs, had spawned treasure hunters—factual and fictional—for thousands of years before the composition of the *Nights*. Mutalibun were those individuals who sought to make their fortunes by finding the treasure commonly believed to be buried underground in Egypt; it is not incidental that this pervasive belief was bolstered by actual discoveries of hoards of treasure from time to time. However, such a trade was taxing and demanded extensive knowledge of ancient stories and folk-beliefs, as well as an array of practical grave-robbing skills, physical strength and stamina, and more than a little courage. The survival of how-to guidebooks for aspiring mutalibun are not insignificant in this context, although it is clear that sharps and con-men could be every bit as dangerous as the perils of the pit themselves, as some tales in the *Nights* also make clear. In any case, narrative manifestations of professional treasure hunters often cast them as heroes who braved subterranean terrors and curses to emerge with unimaginable hoards of priceless riches and seemingly limitless magical powers. Jinns, enchanters, and others who evoked otherworldly powers inhabited these realms, of course, but these stories are often particularly rich in magical objects, notably concerning tricks, traps, and dangers in the form of what we would recognize as elaborate mechanical constructions. In point of fact, it is clear that the Arabs inherited a great deal of classical knowledge of Greek machines; however, in the context of the genre of the mutalib tale, such mechanical function is regularly attributed to magic, often in the form of a resident spirit (e.g., a jinn charged with the task of protecting the treasures of a long-dead king or sorcerer).

Sorcery, Spirits, and Power: The Arabian Hero as Master of the Jinn[6]

The *jinn*, commonly called the "*genie*" in Western appropriations of Arabic narratives, are powerful denizens of the spirit world. Although commonly invisible, the jinn can make themselves seen when it pleases them to do so or when they are forced to through magic or the terms of their enslavement. Generally thought of as creatures with bodies of flame, they are shape-shifters who most often appear in human form, although they sometimes are described as hideous monsters, occasionally with body parts drawn from various animals. The jinn are generally distinguished from angels in that the former are beings of fire, whereas the latter are beings of light. Iblis, or the Devil himself, is at some times associated with the jinn and at other times defined as a type of fallen angel. Jinn are often described as using whirlwinds as a form of transport and as being imprisoned in stones, pillars, bottles, or lamps. It seems to have been generally accepted that jinn could be controlled through specific magical objects such as rings.

Medieval Arabic compendia of magic and spells treat the subject of jinn seriously, offering instructions for summoning, controlling, and even mating with jinn, evidence that suggests that popular interest in such spirits may not have been limited to the suspension of disbelief for the duration of a tale. Some legal judgments also seem to have been rendered concerning the standing of jinn under human law, suggesting that the belief in the interaction between people and jinn was somewhat commonplace. Indeed, no lesser source than the Koran itself makes reference to the jinn, which makes it clear that these spirits—although extremely powerful—could be controlled and certainly were not to be confused with Allah nor venerated as they had been in pagan times.

The world of the jinn was thought to mirror that of humans, rather like the fairies of Celtic tradition. Thus, jinn are described as having kings and courts and warriors and the like. Moreover, jinn are divided into good and evil bands; that is, into groups comprised of "believing" jinn—who are good Moslems and who venerate the One True God—and "unbelieving" jinn—infidels of the spirit world who are often termed *shaytans*, or "devils."

Some sources suggest that the unbelieving jinn are the children of devils, whereas the believing jinn are descended from angels. A particularly potent form of jinn was known as a *marid*, whereas the most powerful of all were denoted as the *ifrit*, a name that seems to imply that these fearful evil spirits forced their enemies to "twist in the dirt." Some specific jinn were associated with particular powers or functions and were often invoked by name. For example, Kabikaj was commonly held to hold sway over the universe of insects, and thus medieval Arabic copyists would sometimes use his name as a protective charm on their manuscripts, hoping thereby to protect their work from the ravages of destruction wrought by tiny worms and mites.

A subset of the jinn were said to haunt cemeteries, to rob graves, and to feast on human flesh; the *ghul*, which became known in English as "ghoul," took its name from an Arabic verb meaning "to seize" and became synonymous with "cannibal." A particularly noisome form of ghul was the *udar*, which would waylay solitary travelers in the desert, sodomizing unsuspecting men so that their rectums exploded with disgusting worms. The *atra* was a form of devil not unlike an unbelieving jinn: The peculiar function of the atra was to obstruct the path to faith by causing those at prayer to fall asleep by urinating in the ears of its victims.

The influence of Persian traditions upon *The Thousand and One Nights* is well established, and thus it is no surprise that the *divs* and *peris*, the "demons" and "fairies," respectively, of Iranian mythology and folklore make notable appearances in the great Arabian compendium of such motifs. However, in the *Nights* these beings are hardly distinguishable from the jinn, which is perhaps understandable in that the jinn by themselves provide a broad category of supernatural creatures. Other monsters and magical beings that are more clearly distinct from the jinn include the qutrub and the nasnas. The *qutrub*, or Arabian "werewolf," fed upon the corpses of the dead. The *nasnas* was a humanoid creature split down the middle: It had half a head, half a torso, one arm, and one leg, and its means of locomotion was hopping. The *rukh* is an example of a fanciful creature perfectly suited to the popular medieval tradition of travel literature. The rukh makes its most famous appearance in the story of Sinbad the Sailor, the great voyager-hero of the *Nights*, the Odysseus of the Arabian tradition.

The Ancient Voyager-Hero Boards an Arabian Vessel: Sinbad Sails the Seas of Legend, Myth, and Folklore[7]

Egyptian sources and antecedents for material to be found in the *Nights* is not by any means limited to those in the tale of Judar; indeed, an ancient papyrus of the 12th Egyptian dynasty contains a narrative of a ship-wrecked hero whose exploits clearly resonate with the adventures of Sinbad, albeit in a more rudimentary form. Travel literature and tales of the marvels of the world beyond the horizon were so popular in the Arab world of the Middle Ages that such fantastical narratives comprised their own genre, known as that of *aja'ib*, or the "marvelous." The aja'ib were meant to be entertaining, to be sure, but ultimately they were narratives thought or at least purported to be based in fact. Moreover, there is a spiritual element to the aja'ib that is derived from the transformation wrought to the individual soul through the astonishment engendered through encountering a marvel. The *ajab*, or reaction of "astonishment" caused by exposure to the marvelous, is a state referenced by the Koran that suggests that the signs of the Almighty cause such wonder to blossom in the souls of those faithful who witness them. Thus, Arabic aja'ib were akin to the *mirabilia* (i.e., the "wonders") of medieval European literature. Although not all such wonders trigger spiritual insight, and certainly many are recounted for their entertainment value alone, medieval Arabic commentators make it clear that ajab was often the cause for a transformation of the *nafs*, or "soul," through its exposure to the inexplicable. Moreover, this foundational spiritual subtext in Arabic thought is not entirely different from medieval Christian concepts concerning the change undergone by those with personal experience of the miraculous. For example, to witness a miracle is generally, in medieval saints' lives, the trigger for spiritual conversion, and those who ignore the evidence of this experience are usually the foolish and the damned whose spiritual blindness provides a fitting counterpoint to the acuity of the faithful, who rightly interpret the marvels they witness.

The stories of Sinbad's adventures represent the examples of the genre of the aja'ib best known to Western audiences, and elements of the Sinbad Cycle certainly were drawn from Old Salts' tales. Moreover, it has long been argued that this collection of travelers' tales and marvels has been organized around the principles of the guidebook and the Romance in addition to any latent subtext of spiritual transformation. The first point is driven home by several descriptions of navigational techniques and the like, some of which resonate closely with a ninth-century guidebook of travel to China and India. That the cycle contains some elements of the Romance is suggested both by the marvelous adventures and by the cycle of development undergone by its eponymous hero. It is through this material that the Sinbad Cycle embraces a great deal of mythic and legendary material in terms of the adventures and obstacles thrown in the path of the protagonist as well as in several archetypes manifested by the hero and his expeditions, to say nothing of the obvious borrowing from established mythic traditions, perhaps most notably in the form of the cyclops episode borrowed from the saga of Odysseus. On the other hand, other aspects of the Sinbad tradition may have been developed out of whole cloth. The Sinbad episodes first surface in rather late versions of the *Nights*, although they appear to have reached their familiar form by the Abbasid Dynasty; moreover, they may have influenced some European stories. Travel narratives and related tales of marvels were also extremely popular in Europe, and some scholars have noted that the Sinbad Cycle may bear some points of resemblance, to cite one example, with the Middle High German *Herzog Ernst*, an epic that dates from the 11th century.

The Second Voyage of Sinbad: The Arabian Voyager-Hero Flies on the Wings of Indo-European Myth

Numerous elements of the Sinbad story have obvious classical parallels, and some of these—upon further examination—extend back into a mythic past even older than classical antiquity. For example, at one point the sailor-hero comes upon a rukh, a giant bird the likes of which was described at least as early as the writer Lucian in the second century after Christ. Having returned from his first voyage a wealthy man, Sinbad established the pattern for his cycle of tales when—forgetting the hardship and perils of his first voyage—the voyager-hero determined to take ship yet again. The first portion of his journey was uneventful, and Sinbad and the other merchants aboard his ship did a brisk trade in port after port. However, one day, having unexpectedly fallen asleep on a lovely but deserted island, Sinbad woke to find himself marooned.

After venting his spleen and lamenting his fate for some time, the castaway took stock of his surroundings. From the top of a tall tree he saw a marvelous dome in the distance and made his way thence. Upon arriving at the smooth white wall of the dome, Sinbad sought an entrance to this refuge. Although he walked half a hundred paces around its perimeter, the castaway could not find so much as a crack or pit in the smooth surface of the wall, let alone a door or window. Suddenly, the light of the sun dimmed and Sinbad wondered at the rapid nightfall on this island. However, looking to the sky, the sailor discovered that the solar rays were obscured not by the curtain of falling dusk, nor even by the passing of a mighty cloud, but rather by the wings of a gigantic bird of a size he could scarcely believe to be true. Surmising that this gargantuan avian was none other than the legendary rukh—said to rear its offspring on the flesh of entire elephants—Sinbad suddenly realized that the massive dome that towered over him was no structure raised by human hands but rather an egg laid by the tremendous bird that was even at that moment soaring down from the heavens toward the lair in which he all at once realized himself to be.

The sailor hid himself while the great bird arranged itself on its egg and subsequently went to sleep. Seizing his opportunity, Sinbad untied his turban and used it to bind himself to the claw of the rukh. After the great bird awoke, it flew off to find food, unwittingly carrying the stowaway Sinbad dangling from beneath its talons. When the rukh alighted, Sinbad released himself and ran away from the bird, which paid him no heed but instead began immediately to hunt the great serpents that lived in the rocky vale in which the sailor now found himself. Sinbad at first berated himself for leaping from the frying pan of the rukh's island home to the fire of the Valley of the Giant Serpents. Although he passed one night cowering in the lair of a huge reptilian mother watching over her eggs, Sinbad soon turned his misadventure to profit when he realized that the entire valley was encrusted with precious gems that were gathered from the cliff walls by merchants who cast down flayed sheep to gather what would stick to their bloody flesh. Filling his pockets with the choicest gems available, Sinbad mounted one of these carcasses and ascended with it out of the Valley of the Giant Serpents and back into the world of men. The voyager-hero then made his way back home, once more a wealthy man.

The rukh of the *Nights* was envisioned as a giant, magical fowl reminiscent of the Simorgh of Persian myth and folklore; it is noteworthy that the rukh appears also in Turkic contexts, sometimes as a creature wholly of spirit, with no fleshly body. In this manifestation it bears some resemblance to the Russian spirit of omen known as the div. On the other hand, in Arabic tradition it is the very corporeal form of the great bird that grants the creature its significance: Its very size is the signature attribute of this manifestation of the creature. For instance, in the tale of Abd al-Rahman and the rukh, the giant bird's egg is described as an alabaster dome of some one hundred cubits. The rukh ultimately may be descended from the *garuda*, a giant creature that is half man and half bird and is generally described as Vishnu's mount; such an origin would suggest an interesting mythic influence that might have extremely ancient Indo-European roots.

The Third Voyage of Sinbad: The Arabian Odysseus Meets His Polyphemus

Since Sinbad's earliest appearance in a European version of the *Nights*, careful readers have taken note of the resonance between Sinbad's encounter with a giant upon his third voyage and the adventure of Odysseus in the cave of Polyphemus. Having once again forgotten the lessons of his earlier adventures, Sinbad again succumbed to wanderlust and to the desire for material profit and embarked once more upon the perils of the seas. All went well until his ship was beset by the ape-men of Ape Mountain, who swarmed the vessel like flies and cut the anchor ropes and rigging with their teeth, setting it adrift until it beached itself upon the shore of their island. Making off then with the ship and its cargo, the ape-men left Sinbad and his comrades to their fates.

Having spent some time upon the island, the companions eventually spied in the distance a great fortress to which they made their way in haste. When they arrived they marveled at the size of the structure, but they found no one at home. Weary from their efforts the men fell asleep and drowsed away the day from before noon until nightfall. However, they awoke to great horror when the lord of that demesne returned to his stronghold: Black as pitch and tall as a tree, the monster was man-like in shape but with oversized, tusk-like fangs, sharp, claw-like nails, and blazing, torch-like eyes. The giant's mouth hung open like the gaping maw of a whale, with loose lips like those of a camel, and his ears flapped upon his shoulders. The ravenous creature chose the captain, the plumpest of the lot, as his first victim, breaking the man's neck against his foot and splitting him from mouth to anus. After roasting the poor man over a fire, the giant sated his hunger until nothing remained but a few bones. The beastly maneater then took his noisome rest. The same grisly scene repeated itself twice more before Sinbad and his comrades blinded the sleeping giant with two red-hot spits, escaping their captor and his great hag of a dam upon a raft cobbled together of fragments of wood. Sinbad lost most of his companions to the great missiles cast from shore by the giant and his hideous bride, and the remaining two to a great serpent haunting the island where they subsequently landed. Saving himself from a similar fate by building a primitive crate the snake could not swallow, Sinbad eventually signaled a passing ship—which contained his former companions and goods from his second voyage—and made his way home a wealthy man.

The Final Voyage of Sinbad: The Arabian Voyager-Hero Returns Home to True Wisdom

Sinbad's cyclical travels—adventures that at first delight and then terrify and imperil the voyager—provide a counterpart to the pleasures of the flesh in which the sailor delights when he returns to his home. This relationship is hardly coincidental, and Sinbad's thirst for adventure manifests an earthly appetite that reflects his spiritual immaturity. Each time the sailor returns from the sea his joyful homecoming soon pales, and after a period of dissipation he begins the process anew. This is a pattern that is only broken at the conclusion of the seventh journey, when the iterative lessons of the cycle finally take root and the former sailor forswears his wanderlust, vows to the Almighty never to travel again, and concomitantly eschews the appetites of the flesh that provided the spiritual counterpoint to the adventures upon the high seas that he has at long last rejected. This repudiation of the allure of travel and concurrent moderation of his personal habits mark the final maturity and latter-day coming of age of Sinbad. Proper, deliberate, and wise thanksgiving to God takes the place of foolish and immature activities, at home and abroad, until Death, the destroyer of all, finally comes to Sinbad, who is at long last spiritually prepared to meet his Maker.

It has been argued that the two faces of Sinbad—that of the courageous adventurer and that of the more cautious homebody—represent the id and the ego of the individual, respectively. However, even allowing for the rather tart truism that one's id is generally more interesting than one's ego, especially in regards to engaging and memorable stories, it is important to note that a significant criticism of this theory has been offered by those who note that Sinbad the Landsman is little more than a narrative foil for Sinbad the Sailor, and turning the lens of psychoanalysis upon this supposed duality may simply be trying too hard. In any case, it is clear that, in the context of his seventh journey, the story of Sinbad clearly organizes several adventures, travel tales, and marvels into a coherent coming-of-age journey of a hero who moves from immaturity to full and thoughtful responsibility. Rather like the challenges Aladdin and Judar faced in the depths of the Underworld, it is through his exposure to adventures and hardships—as well as the witnessing of wonders that attest to the powers of the Almighty—that this every-man hero, a man of common, humble origins who is representative of each of us, learns true wisdom, gains real discretion, and lives out the balance of his life properly prepared for eternity.

Notes

1. For more information concerning the historical context of medieval Arabian mythology, see especially Hourani 1–58; Hovannisian and Sabagh 14–28; Kennedy xi–xiv, 1–49; and Lapidus xix–xx, 3–80.

2. For more information concerning the literary context of medieval Arabian mythology, see especially Hourani 193–197; Hovannisian and Sabagh 14–28, 40–55, 78–105; Irwin 1–41; and Lapidus 89–97, 925.

3. For critical commentary on and analysis of the sources, manuscripts, and structure of the *Thousand and One Nights*, see especially Beaumont 15–31; Hourani 196, 300; Hovannisian and Sabagh 3–5, 6–13, 106–113, 78–105; Irwin 42–62; and Lindahl 156–157, 406–407.

4. For critical commentary on and analysis of the major mythic archetypes and key folkloric elements manifested in the story of Aladdin in the *Thousand and One Nights*, see especially Beaumont 23–24, 88, 129; Hovannisian and Sabagh 4; Irwin 185; and Lindahl 407. Aladdin is included in this study because it is so well-known and manifests the given archetypes so well. Further, this story exemplifies the permeable nature of the Frame Tale: It may represent an Arabian oral tradition with medieval roots and ancient elements which was preserved by European compilers and thus reentered Arabic literature through translations of Western versions of the *Thousand and One Nights*.

5. For critical commentary on and analysis of the major mythic archetypes and key folkloric elements manifested in the story of Judar in the *Thousand and One Nights*, see especially Beaumont 24, 158; and Irwin 185–190.

6. For critical commentary on and analysis of the nature and function of the jinn in the *Thousand and One Nights*, see especially Beaumont 30, 69, 72, 96, 151, 152, 160, 180; Hovannisian and Sabagh 64; Irwin 202–207; and Lindahl 3, 407.

7. For critical commentary on and analysis of the major mythic archetypes and key folkloric elements manifested in the story of Sinbad in the *Thousand and One Nights*, see especially Beaumont 16, 23–24, 169; Haddawy 311–315, 316–323, 343–349; Hovannisian and Sabagh 4, 10–12, 29–39; and Irwin 71–75, 96, 122, 182, 207, 210, 232, 236.

Sources and Further Reading

Beaumont, Daniel E. *Slave of Desire: Sex, Love, and Death in the 1001 Nights.* Madison, NJ: Fairleigh Dickinson University Press, 2002.

Dawood, N. J., and William Harvey. *Tales from the Thousand and One Nights.* London: Penguin, 2003.

Haddawy, Husain, Muhsin Mahdi, and Daniel Heller-Roazen. *The Arabian Nights.* New York: W. W. Norton & Company, 2010.

Hamori, Andras. *On the Art of Medieval Arabic Literature.* Princeton essays in literature. Princeton, NJ: Princeton University Press, 1974.

Hourani, Albert. *A History of the Arab Peoples.* Cambridge, MA: Belknap Press of Harvard University Press, 2002.

Hovannisian, Richard G., and Georges Sabagh. *The Thousand and One Nights in Arabic Literature and Society*. Giorgio Levi Della Vida conferences, 12th conference. Cambridge, United Kingdom: Cambridge University Press, 1997.

Irwin, Robert. *The Arabian Nights: A Companion*. London: Allen Lane, 1994.

Kennedy, Hugh. *The Prophet and the Age of the Caliphates: The Islamic Near East from the Sixth to the Eleventh Century*. Harlow, United Kingdom: Pearson/ Longman, 2004.

Lapidus, Ira M. *A History of Islamic Societies*. Cambridge, United Kingdom: Cambridge University Press, 2002.

Lindahl, Carl, John McNamara, and John Lindow. *Medieval Folklore: A Guide to Myths, Legends, Tales, Beliefs, and Customs*. Oxford, United Kingdom: Oxford University Press, 2002.

Lyons, M. C. *The Arabian Epic: Heroic and Oral Story-Telling*. Cambridge, United Kingdom: Cambridge University Press, 1995.

Meisami, Julie Scott, and Paul Starkey. *Encyclopedia of Arabic Literature*. London: Routledge, 1998.

Stetkevych, Jaroslav. *Muḥammad and the Golden Bough: Reconstructing Arabian Myth*. Bloomington: Indiana University Press, 1996.

Epilogue: Transmuting Heroic Fragments

Sinbad the Sailor provides a fitting figure with which to conclude our exploration of medieval mythology. The journeys of Sinbad emphasize how the adventures of the hero may represent on a grand scale the challenges that face more ordinary mortals. The odyssey of a hero is the journey through life writ large, and in simplest terms the monsters and perils of a heroic quest are epic reflections of the stumbling blocks and obstacles that obstruct the path to even the humblest of objectives. More evocatively, the rich amalgamation of classical mythology, Persian and Indian literatures, and Arabic folklore that characterize *The Thousand and One Nights* in general and the voyages of Sinbad in particular illustrate amply how composite portraits of medieval heroes were wrought from fragments of far older myths, legends, and folktales. The mythology of the Middle Ages is populated by epic heroes, and each such hero reflects in some measure how a particular tradition drew together ancient heroic aspects to sketch a portrait of a protagonist that well served the needs of that culture.

Thus, in the faces of the champions of the pagan frontier we glimpse reflections of ancient gods, protector-figures who courageously stare down monsters bequeathed from days of yore. On the other hand, warriors for the Christian faith to varying degrees comprise heroes recast as types of Christ, holy warriors ostensibly in mortal combat with demonic foes. Meanwhile, heroes of the Islamic world often gild ancient pagan elements with the merest veneer of Islam, and quick wit is as celebrated as martial prowess. In all of the cases, we have examined how the great monotheistic religions of the Middle Ages assert themselves, although seldom to the detriment of a good story. Rather, the pressure applied by medieval Christianity and Islam to the myths, folktales, and legends of old serve, rather like the crucible of alchemical lore, as a means of almost magical transformation, through which disparate ancient heroic fragments emerge transmuted into unified, powerful new forms.

General Bibliography

Alcock, Leslie. *Arthur's Britain: History and Archaeology* AD *367–634*. London: Penguin, 1971.

Alexiou, Stylianos. *"Digenes Akrites: Escorial or Grottaferrata? An Overview." Digenes Akrites: New Approaches to Byzantine Heroic Poetry*. Roderick Beaton and David Ricks, Eds. Aldershot, Hampshire: Ashgate, 1993, 15–25.

Andersson, Theodore Murdock. *A Preface to the Nibelungenlied*. Stanford, CA: Stanford University Press, 1987.

Andrews, Walter G., and James Stewart-Robinson. *Intersections in Turkish Literature: Essays in Honor of James Stewart-Robinson*. Ann Arbor: University of Michigan Press, 2001.

Baldick, Chris. *The Oxford Dictionary of Literary Terms*. Oxford, United Kingdom: Oxford University Press, 2008.

Baldwin, Barry. *An Anthology of Byzantine Poetry*. Amsterdam: J. C. Gieben, 1985.

Baldwin, Barry. *Studies on Late Roman and Byzantine History, Literature, and Language*. Amsterdam: J. C. Gieben, 1984.

Balzer, Marjorie Mandelstam. *Russian Traditional Culture: Religion, Gender, and Customary Law*. Armonk, NY: M. E. Sharpe, 1992.

Barbero, Alessandro. *Charlemagne: Father of a Continent*. Berkeley: University of California Press, 2004.

Barron, W. R. J., ed. *The Arthur of the English: The Arthurian Legend in Medieval English Life and Literature*. Cardiff: University of Wales Press, 2001.

Beaton, Roderick. "An Epic in the Making? The Early Versions of *Digenes Akrites*." *Digenes Akrites: New Approaches to Byzantine Heroic Poetry*. Roderick Beaton and David Ricks, Eds. Aldershot, Hampshire: Ashgate, 1993, 55–72.

Beaton, Roderick, and David Ricks. *Digenes Akrites: New Approaches to Byzantine Heroic Poetry*. Brookfield, VT: Variorum, 1993.

Beaumont, Daniel E. *Slave of Desire: Sex, Love, and Death in The 1001 Nights*. Madison, NJ: Fairleigh Dickinson University Press, 2002.

Becher, Matthias. *Charlemagne*. New Haven, CT: Yale University Press, 2003.

Birnbaum, Henrik, Michael S. Flier, and Daniel B. Rowland. *Medieval Russian Culture*. Berkeley: University of California Press, 1984.

Borroff, Marie, trans. *Sir Gawain and the Green Knight, Patience, Pearl: Verse Translations*. New York: W. W. Norton, 2000.

Branston, Brian. *Gods of the North*. New York: Thames and London, 1980.

Brault, Gerard J. *La Chanson de Roland: Oxford Text and English Translation*. University Park: Pennsylvania State University Press, 1984.

Bryer, Anthony. "The Historian's *Digenes Akrites*." *Digenes Akrites: New Approaches to Byzantine Heroic Poetry*. Roderick Beaton and David Ricks, Eds. Aldershot, Hampshire: Ashgate, 1993. 93–102.

Bulliet, Richard W. *The Case for Islamo-Christian Civilization*. New York: Columbia University Press, 2004.

Burgess, Glyn, trans. *Chanson de Roland*. New York: Penguin Books, 1990.

Burke, James F. *Desire against the Law: The Juxtaposition of Contraries in Early Medieval Spanish Literature*. Stanford, CA: Stanford University Press, 1998.

Butt, John J. *Daily Life in the Age of Charlemagne*. Westport, CT: Greenwood Press, 2002.

Byock, Jesse. *The Saga of the Volsungs: The Norse Epic of Sigurd the Dragon Slayer*. New York: Penguin Classics, 1999.

Byock, Jesse, ed. *Viking Age Iceland*. New York: Penguin, 2001.

Cahen, Claude, and P. M. Holt. *The Formation of Turkey: The Seljukid Sultanate of Rūm: Eleventh to Fourteenth Century. A History of the Near East*. Harlow, United Kingdom: Longman, 2001.

Carr, A. D. *Medieval Wales. British History in Perspective*. Houndmills, Basingstroke, Hampshire: Macmillan Press, 1995.

Castleden, Rodney. *King Arthur: The Truth Behind the Legend*. New York: Routledge, 2000.

Chadwick, Nora K., and Viktor Maksimovich Zhirmunskiï. *Oral Epics of Central Asia*. London: Cambridge University Press, 1969.

Cheynet, Jean-Claude. *The Byzantine Aristocracy and its Military Function*. Aldershot, Hampshire: Ashgate, 2006.

Clauson, Gerard. *An Etymological Dictionary of Pre-Thirteenth-Century Turkish*. Oxford, United Kingdom: Clarendon Press, 1972.

Clinton, Jerome W. *The Tragedy of Sohráb and Rostám: from the Persian National Epic, the Shahname of Abol-Qasem Ferdowsi*. Publications on the Near East, University of Washington, no. 3. Seattle: University of Washington Press, 1996.

Coghlan, Ronan. *The Encyclopedia of Arthurian Legends*. Rockport, MA: Element Books, 1991.

Collins, Roger. *Charlemagne*. Toronto: University of Toronto Press, 1998.

Constable, Olivia Remie. *Medieval Iberia: Readings from Christian, Muslim, and Jewish Sources*. The Middle Ages series. Philadelphia: University of Pennsylvania Press, 1997.

Constable, Olivia Remie. *Trade and Traders in Muslim Spain: The Commercial Realignment of the Iberian Peninsula, 900–1500*. Cambridge studies in medieval life and thought, 4th series, 24. Cambridge: Cambridge University Press, 1994.

Cook, Robert Francis. *The Sense of the Song of Roland*. Ithaca, NY: Cornell University Press, 1987.

Cotterell, Arthur. *A Dictionary of World Mythology*. Oxford, United Kingdom: Oxford University Press, 1991.

Crossley-Holland, Kevin. *The Norse Myths*. New York: Pantheon, 1981.

Curtis, Vesta Sarkhosh. *Persian Myths*. Austin: University of Texas Press, 1993.

Davidson, H. R. Ellis. *Norse Mythology: Gods and Myths of Northern Europe*. New York: Penguin, 1965.

Davies, Wendy. *Wales in the Early Middle Ages*. Studies in the early history of Britain. Leicester, United Kingdom: Leicester University Press, 1982.

Dawood, N. J., and William Harvey. *Tales from the Thousand and One Nights*. London: Penguin, 2003.

Deyermond, A. D. *Epic Poetry and the Clergy: Studies on the Mocedades de Rodrigo*. London: Grant & Cutler, 1968.

Deyermond, A. D. *A Literary History of Spain: The Middle Ages*. New York: Barnes & Noble, 1971.

DuBois, Thomas A. *Nordic Religions in the Viking Age*. Philadelphia: University of Pennsylvania Press, 1999.

Duggan, Joseph J. *The Song of Roland: Formulaic Style and Poetic Craft*. Berkeley: University of California Press, 1973.

Ellis, Peter Berresford. *Dictionary of Celtic Mythology*. New York: Oxford University Press, 1994.

Ellis, Peter Berresford. *A Dictionary of Irish Mythology*. New York: Oxford University Press, 1991.

Faulkes, Anthony. *Edda*. Rutland, VT: Charles E. Tuttle, 1995.

Fee, Christopher R., with David A. Leeming. *Gods, Heroes, & Kings: The Battle for Mythic Britain*. New York: Oxford University Press, 2004.

Fee, Christopher R., and James Rutkowski. *The Medieval North Atlantic*. December 31, 1999. http://public.gettysburg.edu/~cfee/MedievalNorthAtlantic.

Ferdowsi, A. *The Legend of Seyavash*. Washington, DC: Mage Publishers, 2004.

Ferdowsi, A., and D. Davis. *The Lion and the Throne: Stories from the Shahnameh of Ferdowsi, Volume 1*. Washington, DC: Mage Publishers, 1998.

Ferdowsi, A., and D. Davis. *Fathers and Sons: Stories from the Shahnameh of Ferdowsi, Volume 2*. Washington, DC: Mage Publishers, 2000.

Ferdowsi, A., and D. Davis. *Sunset of Empire: Stories from the Shahnameh of Ferdowsi, Volume 3*. Washington, DC: Mage Publishers, 2004.

Findley, Carter V. *The Turks in World History*. New York: Oxford University Press, 2005.

Finke, Laurie A., and Martin B. Shichtman. *King Arthur and the Myth of History*. Gainesville: University Press of Florida, 2004.

Galatariotou, Catia. "The Primacy of the Escorial *Digenes Akrites:* An Open and Shut Case?" *Digenes Akrites: New Approaches to Byzantine Heroic Poetry*. Roderick Beaton and David Ricks, Eds. Aldershot, Hampshire: Ashgate, 1993, 38–54.

Ganjavi, Nizami, and Julie Scott Meisami. *The Haft Paykar: A Medieval Persian Romance*. Oxford, United Kingdom: Oxford University Press, 1995.

Gantz, Jeffrey. *The Mabinogion*. New York: Penguin, 1976.

Gaunt, Simon. *Retelling the Tale: An Introduction to French Medieval Literature*. London: Duckworth, 2001.

Geanakoplos, Deno. *Byzantium: Church, Society, and Civilization Seen through Contemporary Eyes*. Chicago: University of Chicago Press, 1984.

Geanakoplos, Deno. *Medieval Western Civilization and the Byzantine and Islamic Worlds*. Lexington, MA: D. C. Heath, 1979.

Gentry, Francis G. *The Nibelungen Tradition: An Encyclopedia*. New York: Routledge, 2002.

Goodrich, Norma Lorre. *King Arthur*. New York: F. Watts, 1986.

Green, Miranda J. *The Celtic World*. New York: Routledge, 1995.

Green, Miranda J. *The Gods of the Celts*. Gloucester: Barnes & Noble, 1986.

Green, Miranda J. *Celtic Myths*. Austin: University of Texas Press, 1993.

Haddawy, Husain, Muhsin Mahdi, and Daniel Heller-Roazen. *The Arabian Nights*. New York: W. W. Norton & Company, 2010.

Hamilton, Rita, Janet H. Perry, and Ian Michael. *The Poem of the Cid*. London, Penguin Classics, 1984.

Hamori, Andras. *On the Art of Medieval Arabic Literature*. Princeton essays in literature. Princeton, NJ: Princeton University Press, 1974.

Hanning, Robert and Joan Ferrante, trans. *The Lais of Marie de France*. Durham, NC: Labyrinth Press, 1982.

Hatto, A. T. *The Nibelungenlied*. London: Penguin Books, 1965.

Haymes, Edward, and Susann T. Samples. *Heroic Legends of the North: An Introduction to the Nibelung and Dietrich Cycles*. Garland reference library of the humanities, Vol. 1403. New York: Garland Publishers, 1996.

Higham, N.J. *King Arthur: Myth-Making and History*. New York: Routledge, 2002.

Hinnells, John R. *Persian Mythology*. London: Hamyln Publishers, 1975.

Hodges, Richard. *Mohammed, Charlemagne & the Origins of Europe: Archaeology and the Pirenne Thesis*. Ithaca, NY: Cornell University Press, 1983.

Hook, David. "*Digenes Akrites* and the Old Spanish Epics." *Digenes Akrites: New Approaches to Byzantine Heroic Poetry*. Roderick Beaton and David Ricks, Eds. Aldershot, Hampshire: Ashgate, 1993, 73–85.

Hourani, Albert. *A History of the Arab Peoples*. Cambridge, MA: Belknap Press of Harvard University Press, 2002.

Hovannisian, Richard G., and Georges Sabagh. *The Thousand and One Nights in Arabic Literature and Society*. Giorgio Levi Della Vida conferences, 12th conference. Cambridge, United Kingdom: Cambridge University Press, 1997.

Hreinsson, Viðar. *The Complete Sagas of Icelanders, including 49 Tales*. Reykjavík, Iceland: Leifur Eiríksson Press, 1997.

Hubbs, Joanna. *Mother Russia: The Feminine Myth in Russian Culture*. Bloomington: Indiana University Press, 1993.

Hull, Denison B. *Digenis Akritas, The Two-Blood Border Lord: The Grottaferrata Version*. Athens: Ohio University Press, 1972.

Hussey, J. M. *The Orthodox Church in the Byzantine Empire*. Oxford, United Kingdom: Oxford University Press, 1986.

Irwin, Robert. *The Arabian Nights: A Companion*. London: Allen Lane, 1994.

Jack, R.I. *Medieval Wales*. London: Hodder and Stoughton for the Sources of History, Ltd., 1972.

Jackson, Kenneth. *Celt and Saxon; Studies in the Early British Border*. Cambridge, United Kingdom: Cambridge University Press, 1963.

Jeffreys, Elizabeth. *Digenis Akritis: The Grottaferrata and Escorial Versions*. Cambridge, United Kingdom: Cambridge University Press, 1998.

Jeffreys, Elizabeth. "The Grottaferrata Version of *Digenes Akrites:* A Reassessment." *Digenes Akrites: New Approaches to Byzantine Heroic Poetry*. Roderick Beaton and David Ricks, Eds. Aldershot, Hampshire: Ashgate, 1993, 26–37.

Jones, Gwyn. *A History of the Vikings*. Oxford, United Kingdom: Oxford University Press, 1984.

Jones, Gwyn, and Thomas Jones. *The Mabinogion*. New York: Knopf, 2001.

Kellogg, Robert. *The Sagas of Icelanders: A Selection*. New York: Viking, 2000.

Kelly, Douglas. *The Art of Medieval French Romance*. Madison: University of Wisconsin Press, 1992.

Kennedy, Hugh. *The Prophet and the Age of the Caliphates: The Islamic Near East from the Sixth to the Eleventh Century*. Harlow, United Kingdom: Pearson/Longman, 2004.

Kinsella, Thomas, ed. *The Táin*. New York: Oxford University Press, 2002.

Lacy, Norris J., Geoffrey Ashe, and Debra N. Mancoff. *The Arthurian Handbook*. Garland reference library of humanities, Vol. 1920. New York: Garland Publishing, 1997.

Lapidus, Ira M. *A History of Islamic Societies*. Cambridge: Cambridge University Press, 2002.

Larrington, Carolyne. *The Poetic Edda*. Oxford World's Classics. New York: Oxford University Press, 1999.

Leeming, David Adams. *Mythology: The Voyage of the Hero*. Oxford, United Kingdom: Oxford University Press, 1998.

Leeming, David Adams. *The Oxford Companion to World Mythology.* Oxford, United Kingdom: Oxford University Press, 2005.

Levin, Eve. *Sex and Society in the World of the Orthodox Slavs, 900-1700.* Ithaca, NY: Cornell University Press, 1995.

Levy, Reuben. *The Epic of the Kings: Shah-Nama, the National Epic of Persia.* London: Routledge & K. Paul, 1985.

Lewis, Geoffrey. *The Book of Dede Korkut.* Harmondsworth, United Kingdom: Penguin, 1974.

Lindahl, Carl. *Medieval Folklore: An Encyclopedia of Myths, Legends, Tales, Beliefs, and Customs.* Santa Barbara, CA: ABC-CLIO, 2000.

Lindahl, Carl, John McNamara, and John Lindow. *Medieval Folklore: A Guide to Myths, Legends, Tales, Beliefs, and Customs.* Oxford, United Kingdom: Oxford University Press, 2002.

Lindow, John. *Norse Mythology: A Guide to the Gods, Heroes, Rituals, and Beliefs.* New York: Oxford University Press, 2001.

Littlewood, A. R. *Originality in Byzantine Literature, Art, and Music: A Collection of Essays.* Oxford, United Kingdom: Oxbow Books, 1995.

Lupack, Alan. *The Oxford Guide to Arthurian Literature and Legend.* New York: Oxford University Press, 2005.

Lyons, M. C. *The Arabian Epic: Heroic and Oral Story-Telling.* Cambridge, United Kingdom: Cambridge University Press, 1995.

MacKillop, James. *Dictionary of Celtic Mythology.* New York: Oxford University Press, 1998.

Mackridge, Peter. "'None but the Brave Deserve the Fair': Abduction, Elopement, Seduction and Marriage in the Escorial *Digenes Akrites* and Modern Greek Heroic Songs." *Digenes Akrites: New Approaches to Byzantine Heroic Poetry.* Roderick Beaton and David Ricks, Eds. Aldershot, Hampshire: Ashgate, 1993, 150–160.

Maddox, Donald. *Fictions of Identity in Medieval France.* New York: Cambridge University Press, 2000.

Magdalino, Paul. "*Digenes Akrites* and Byzantine Literature: The Twelfth-Century Background to the Grottaferrata Version." *Digenes Akrites: New Approaches to Byzantine Heroic Poetry.* Roderick Beaton and David Ricks, Eds. Aldershot, Hampshire: Ashgate, 1993, 1–14.

Maier, Bernhard. *Dictionary of Celtic Religion and Culture.* Rochester, NY: Boydell Press, 1997.

Malory, Thomas, and Helen Cooper. *Le Morte Darthur: The Winchester Manuscript.* Oxford, United Kingdom: Oxford University Press, 1998.

Mango, Cyril. *The Oxford History of Byzantium.* Oxford, United Kingdom: Oxford University Press, 2002.

Martin, Janet. *Medieval Russia: 980–1584.* New York: Cambridge University Press, 2007.

Mavrogordato, John. *Digenes Akrites.* Oxford, United Kingdom: Clarendon Press, 1999.

Mavrogordato, John. *Digenes Akrites: Edited with Introduction, Translation, and Commentary.* Oxford, United Kingdom: Oxford University Press, 1956.

McConnell, Winder. *A Companion to the Nibelungenlied.* Columbia, SC: Camden House, 1998.

McCrum, Robert, Robert MacNeil, and William Cran. *The Story of English.* New York: Penguin, 2002.

Meisami, Julie Scott. *A Sea of Virtues: Bahr Al-Favaid: A Medieval Islamic Mirror for Princes.* Salt Lake City: University of Utah Press, 1991.

Meisami, Julie Scott. *Medieval Persian Court Poetry.* Princeton, NJ: Princeton University Press, 1987.

Meisami, Julie Scott. *Persian Historiography.* Edinburgh, United Kingdom: Edinburgh University Press, 1999.

Meisami, Julie Scott, and Paul Starkey. *Encyclopedia of Arabic Literature.* London: Routledge, 1998.

Merwin, W. S. *The Song of Roland.* New York: Modern Library, 2001.

Millward, C. M. *A Biography of the English Language.* Fort Worth, TX: Harcourt Brace, 1996.

Milner-Gulland, R. R., and Nikolai J. Dejevsky. *Cultural Atlas of Russia and the Former Soviet Union.* New York: Checkmark Books, 1998.

Mitchell, Stephen. *Anatolia: Land, Men, and Gods in Asia Minor, Volume I: The Celts in Anatolia and the Impact of Roman Rule.* Oxford, United Kingdom: Oxford University Press, 1995.

Mitchell, Stephen. *Anatolia: Land, Men, and Gods in Asia Minor, Volume II: The Rise of the Church.* Oxford, United Kingdom: Oxford University Press, 1995.

Moll, Richard J. *Before Malory: Reading Arthur in Later Medieval England.* Buffalo, NY: University of Toronto Press, 2003.

Montgomery, Thomas. *Medieval Spanish Epic: Mythic Roots and Ritual Language.* University Park: Pennsylvania State University Press, 1998.

Morgan, David. *Medieval Persia 1040–1797.* London: Longman, 1997.

Morrissey, Robert John. *Charlemagne & France: A Thousand Years of Mythology.* Notre Dame, IN: University of Notre Dame Press, 2003.

Nerimanoğlu, Kamil Veli. *The Poetics of "The Book of Dede Korkut."* Maltepe, Ankara: Atatürk Culture Center Publications, 1998.

O'Callaghan, Joseph. *Reconquest and Crusade in Medieval Spain.* Philadelphia: University of Pennsylvania Press, 2003.

Page, R.I. *Norse Myths.* Austin: University of Texas Press, 1990.

Papadopoullos, Theodore. "The Akritic Hero: Socio-Cultural Status in the Light of Comparative Data." *Digenes Akrites: New Approaches to Byzantine Heroic Poetry.* Roderick Beaton and David Ricks, Eds. Aldershot, Hampshire: Ashgate, 1993, 131–138.

Partner, Peter. *God of Battles: Holy Wars of Christianity and Islam.* Princeton, NJ: Princeton University Press, 1998.

Puhvel, Jaan. *Comparative Mythology*. Baltimore: Johns Hopkins University Press, 1987.

Rautman, Marcus. *Daily Life in the Byzantine Empire*. Westport, CT: Greenwood Press, 2006.

Reichl, Karl. *Turkic Oral Epic Poetry: Tradition, Forms, Poetic Structure*. New York: Garland, 1992.

Reilly, Bernard F. *The Medieval Spains*. New York: Cambridge University Press, 1993.

Ricks, David. *Byzantine Heroic Poetry*. Bristol, United Kingdom: Bristol Classical Press, 1990.

Ricks, David. *"Digenes Akrites* as Literature." *Digenes Akrites: New Approaches to Byzantine Heroic Poetry*. Roderick Beaton and David Ricks, Eds. Aldershot, Hampshire: Ashgate, 1993, 161–170.

Robinson, B. *The Persian Book of Kings: An Epitome of the Shahnama of Firdawsi*. New York: Curzon Press, 2002.

Ross, Denison. *The Hafez Poems of Gertrude Bell*. New York: Penguin, 1981.

Rypka, Jan. *History of Iranian Literature*. Dordrecht: D. Reidel Publishing Co., 1968.

Sılay, Kemal. *Nedim and the Poetics of the Ottoman Court: Medieval Inheritance and the Need for Change*. Bloomington: Indiana University, 1994.

Simek, Rudolf. *Dictionary of Northern Mythology*. Translated by Angela Hall. Rochester, NY: Boydell and Brewer, 1993.

Smith, Colin. *The Making of the Poema de Mio Cid*. New York: Cambridge University Press, 1983.

Smyth, Daragh. *A Guide to Irish Mythology*. Dublin, Ireland: Irish Academic Press, 1996.

Snyder, Christopher A. *The Britons*. Malden, MA: Blackwell Publishers, 2003.

Snyder, Christopher A. *The World of King Arthur*. London: Thames & Hudson, 2000.

Stetkevych, Jaroslav. *Muḥammad and the Golden Bough: Reconstructing Arabian Myth*. Bloomington: Indiana University Press, 1996.

Sümer, Faruk, Ahmet Edip Uysal, and Warren S. Walker. *The Book of Dede Korkut: A Turkish Epic*. Austin: University of Texas Press, 1991.

Thury, Eva M., and Margaret K. Devinney. *Introduction to Mythology: Contemporary Approaches to Classical and World Myths*. Oxford, United Kingdom: Oxford University Press, 2009.

Trapp, J. B., Douglas Gray, and Julia Boffey. *Medieval English Literature*. The Oxford Anthology of English Literature. Oxford, United Kingdom: Oxford University Press, 2002.

Uitti, Karl D. *Story, Myth, and Celebration in Old French Narrative Poetry, 1050–1200*. Princeton, NJ: Princeton University Press, 1973.

Váňa, Zdeněk, Pavel Vácha, and Pavel Major. *The World of the Ancient Slavs*. Detroit: Wayne State University Press, 1983.

Vance, Eugene. *Reading the Song of Roland*. Englewood Cliffs, NJ: Prentice-Hall, 1970.

Warner, Elizabeth. *Russian Myths*. The legendary past. Austin: University of Texas Press, 2002.

White, Richard, ed. *King Arthur in Legend and History*. New York: Routledge, 1998.

Yarshater, Ehsan. *Cambridge History of Iran, Vol. 3: The Seleucid, Parthian, and Sassanian Periods*. Cambridge, United Kingdom: Cambridge University Press, 1968.

Zenkovsky, Serge A, trans. *Medieval Russia's Epics, Chronicles, and Tales*. New York: Penguin, 1974.

Index

About the Author

CHRISTOPHER R. FEE is the Johnson Distinguished Teaching Professor in the Humanities at Gettysburg College in Gettysburg, Pennsylvania. Fee earned his doctorate in English language at the University of Glasgow and is the author of *Gods, Heroes, and Kings: The Battle for Mythic Britain*.

Praeger Series on the Middle Ages

Jews and Judaism in the Middle Ages
Theodore L. Steinberg

Materials, Methods, and Masterpieces of Medieval Art
Janetta Rebold Benton

Islam in the Middle Ages: The Origins and Shaping of Classical Islamic Civilization
Jacob Lassner and Michael Bonner